CONTEMPORARY STRATEGY ANALYSIS

Concepts, Techniques, Applications

Second Edition

by
Robert M. Grant
Georgetown University

BLACKWELL
Business

First published 1995
Reprinted 1995, 1996

Blackwell Publishers Inc.
238 Main Street
Cambridge, Massachusetts 02142
USA

Blackwell Publishers Ltd
108 Cowley Road
Oxford OX4 1JF
UK

Library of Congress Cataloging-in-Publication Dat

Grant, Robert M.
   Contemporary strategy analysis: concepts, techniques, applications / Robert M. Grant. — 2nd ed.
     p. cm.
   Includes index.
   ISBN 1-55786-513-2
   1. Strategic planning.   I. Title.
HD30.28.G72   1995
658.4'012—dc20   94-48102
                                                                                    CIP

British Library Cataloguing in Publication Data

A CIP catalogue record for this book is available from the British Library.

Typeset by AM Marketing

Printed in the USA by Quebecor Printing / Book Press

This book is printed on acid-free paper

CONTEMPORARY STRATEGY ANALYSIS

Contents

IV   Corporate Strategy   313

Preface

My objective in writing the first edition of this book was to produce an introduction to business strategy that combined rigor with relevance. The origins of the book lay in my dissatisfactions with the available strategic management texts. These thousand-page monsters were analytically flabby, provided inadequate coverage of the latest thinking by academics and practitioners, lacked penetrating insight into the fundamental issues of business success, and failed to communicate the excitement of the subject matter.

The guiding principle of the book is to focus upon the fundamental determinants of business success. This emphasis on fundamentals is the basis of the book's practicality. Rather than provide the compendium of checklists and buzzwords so prevalent among many "practitioner-oriented" strategy books, I have tried to develop "deep knowledge" of the fundamental characteristics of companies, markets, and the competitive process. This focus upon the determinants of business success has meant that *competitive advantage* forms the central theme of the book.

The book is determinedly up to date. At the same time, I have not attempted to survey all recent developments in the field of strategic management. In selecting concepts, theories, and frameworks for inclusion I have been guided by two principles: first, the desire to provide an integrated framework for strategic decision making rather than a smorgasbord of ideas and techniques; second, the criterion of *relevance* – I have included only those concepts and theories that show potential for assisting managers in making their companies more successful.

Emphasis upon the analysis of competition and competitive advantage inevitably means that the book draws heavily upon the concepts and theoretical insights of industrial economics. At the same time, I have been careful to avoid being seduced by the theoretical elegance of modern economics. Thus, although game theory lies at the intellectual core of strategy analysis, its limited practical usefulness in guiding management decisions has resulted in a limited coverage of the concepts and tools of game theory in this book.

The need to choose between the different disciplinary foundations of strategic management has been partly alleviated by increasing integration of the field. For example, the analysis of the role of resources and capabilities in competitive advantage draws upon the economic theory of rent, the psychology of knowledge and learning, and the sociology of group behavior and team integration.

This book attempts to avoid the conventional (and mistaken) dichotomy between strategy formulation and strategy implementation. A strategy that cannot be implemented is worthless. Hence, strategy formulation must take account of implementation. Similarly, strategy is formulated through its implementation. However, I recognize that a book that deals with the principles of strategic management cannot deal comprehensively with strategy implementation without covering every aspect of firm management, from finance to human resources.

In this second edition of *Contemporary Strategy Analysis,* I have attempted to update the contents of the book to take account of the accelerating development of the field and to respond to the suggestions of students and instructors in leading business schools in Europe and North America. The principal changes in the book are the following:

- a more extensive treatment of the "process view" of strategy and the role of mission and strategic intent (chapter 1);
- greater emphasis on the "resource-based" view of the firm and the nature and determinants of organizational capability (chapter 5);
- greater consideration of dynamic aspects of competition and competitive advantage (chapters 3, 6, 9 and 10);
- extending the strategic management of innovation and technology to explore in greater depth the role of standards, the determinants of first-mover advantage, and the imitation of innovations (chapter 10);
- a fuller examination of corporate strategy within a more integrated analysis of the scope of the firm, including a new chapter on vertical integration (chapter 12);
- the integration of contemporary management practice such as outsourcing, horizontal and team-based structures, total quality management, time-based management, strategic alliances, business process reengineering, and firm networks within a structured approach to cost and differentiation advantage, organizational flexibility, strategic innovation, and organizational capability;
- increased emphasis on the international dimension of strategic management. This has meant not only extending the material in chapter 13 to take fuller account of the evolution of global strategies and the organizational structures and management systems of multinational companies, but also a more determined attempt to include the experiences of Asian and European companies throughout the book.

A further feature of the second edition is a more extensive instructors' manual that includes specimen course outlines, advice on cases and other accompanying teaching materials, lecture outlines, and transparency masters. The instructors' manual is available from the publisher.

I have relied heavily upon the ideas and insights of other people. I should like to thank all those who have taken the time and trouble to share their experiences, thoughts, and opinions with me. This book has benefited greatly from what I have learned over the last 15 years in discussions with Charles Baden Fuller, Dean Berry, Tony Boardman,

Sebastian Green, Peter Grinyer, Gary Hamel, Anne Huff, John Kay, Ram Krishman, John McGee, Shiv Mathur, Steve Postrel, Elaine Romanelli, Dick Rumelt, Rami Shani, J.-C. Spender, John Stopford, Howard Thomas, Margarethe Wiersema, George Yip, and many other comrades-in-arms. Thanks too to my students at British Columbia, Cal Poly, University of California, and Georgetown. I've had fun and learned a lot.

Robert M. Grant

To Sue

Robert M. Grant is Professor of Management at Georgetown University, Washington, D.C. he has also taught at California Polytechnic, UCLA, University of British Columbia, London Business School, City University, and St Andrews University. He was formerly economic adviser to the British Monopolies and Mergers Commission.

I

Fundamentals of Strategic Management

ONE

The Concept of Strategy

Strategy is the great Work of the organization. In Situations of life or death, it is the Tao of survival or extinction. Its study cannot be neglected.
– Sun Tzu, from R. L. Wing, *The Art of Strategy: A New Translation of Sun Tzu's Classic "The Art of War"*

Outline

Introduction and Objectives

Strategy is about winning. This chapter investigates the role of strategy in organizational and personal success – not only in its business context but also in relation to other fields of human endeavor, including warfare, entertainment, and sport. We will examine the nature of strategy, and we will distinguish strategy from detailed planning: strategy is not a rule book, a blueprint, or a set of programmed instructions. Strategy is the unifying theme that gives coherence and direction to the individual decisions of an organization or a person.

We will go on to examine the role of analysis in strategy formulation. If strategy is purely a matter of intuition and experience, then there is little point in studying this book – the only way to learn is to go and do it. The key premise that underlies this book is that there are concepts, frameworks, and techniques that are immensely useful in formulating and implementing effective strategies. By the end of this chapter you will understand the contribution that strategy can make to successful performance – both for organizations and individuals. You will learn how business strategy initially grew out of military strategy and how its concerns and its approach have evolved over the last three decades. You will appreciate that strategy has multiple roles within an organization. Its primary purpose is to confer success through guiding management decisions toward establishing and sustaining competitive advantage for the firm. In addition, you will understand how strategy is a vehicle for communication and coordination within an organization. Finally, you will be equipped with a framework and set of ideas that will give you insight into the fundamentals of business success and will provide the foundations for further learning in how to formulate winning strategies.

Because the purpose of strategy is to help us to win, let us start by looking at the role of strategy in success.

The Role of Strategy in Success

In the accompanying cases (exhibits 1.1 and 1.2), I outline two examples of success in quite different fields of endeavor: Madonna in popular entertainment and the North Vietnamese military in warfare. The issue that I wish to explore here is whether, behind these examples of achievement, there is any common explanation of why each of the examples was so successful.

In neither case can success be attributed to overwhelmingly superior resources:

- Madonna possesses vitality, intelligence, and a tremendous capacity for work, but in terms of the attributes normally associated with outstandingly successful popular entertainers, she is notably lacking. Her dancing is competent, her acting weak, and her singing was likened, by one recording executive, to "Minnie Mouse on helium." She doesn't write songs and is not proficient on any musical instrument;
- the military, human, and economic resources of the Vietnamese communists were dwarfed by those of the United States and South Vietnam. The final evacuation of U.S. military and diplomatic personnel from Saigon in 1975 marked the humiliation of the world's greatest power by one of the world's poorest countries.

Nor can success be attributed either exclusively or primarily to luck. In both stories, lucky breaks provided opportunities at critical junctures. But none of the two were subject to a consistent run of good fortune. More important was their ability to recognize opportunities when they presented themselves and to have the clarity of direction and the flexibility necessary to exploit these opportunities.

It is my contention that the key common ingredient in the two success stories is the presence of a soundly formulated and effectively implemented strategy. For neither did strategy exist as a plan, and in neither

Exhibit 1.1 Madonna

Madonna Louise Ciccone was born on August 16, 1958, in Michigan, one of eight children. In 1978, she traveled to New York to find work as a dancer. A succession of small-time dancing and singing jobs eventually led to a recording contract, and her first album, *Madonna,* released in 1984, eventually sold close to 10 million copies worldwide. Her second album, *Like a Virgin,* released in 1985, sold over 12 million copies. During the next eight years Madonna achieved a remarkable feat. She succeeded in a building an image for herself that transcended any single field of entertainment. She became not only a pop singer but also an actor and an author. She became the world's highest-paid female entertainer with earnings of $80 million between 1985 and 1991 and $20 million of earnings in 1991 alone.

How do we account for this phenomenal popular and financial success? It is difficult to attribute Madonna's success to outstanding talent. Although she has sought comparison with female stars of the past – Monroe, Garbo, and Mae West – the most noticeable feature of her performances has been competence rather than brilliance. Her singing voice is undistinguished, her dancing competent, and her acting mediocre. Under any conventional criteria, it is difficult to regard her as outstandingly beautiful.

So what factors can account for her success?

A first observation is that, unlike so many bands and singers, she is not the product of any media organization or protégé of any entertainment entrepreneur. Madonna's success is the result of her own efforts. She fought her way into the pop music business, and since her initial success has directed her own career. It was at her own initiative that she flew to Los Angeles in 1982 to persuade Freddie De Mann, Michael Jackson's manager, to take her on and eventually to drop Jackson in favor of managing herself. The relationship has continued. Madonna is chairman of her group of companies; De Mann is president. By 1992, her staff had grown to 150, all of whom were personally picked by Madonna.

Madonna's drive and directedness suggest clear and consistent goals. Her chameleon-like transformations in appearance and image and her shifting between live performances, music videos, recorded music, movies, and publishing belie a remarkable dedication to a single goal: the quest for superstar status. For over ten years, Madonna has worked relentlessly to market herself and to maintain her public image by establishing, adapting, and renewing her appeal. She is widely regarded as a workaholic who survives on little sleep and, apart from short breaks, has had no holiday since her honeymoon with Sean Penn in 1985: "I am a very disciplined person. I sleep a certain number of hours each night, then I like to get up and get on with it. All that means that I am in charge of everything that comes out." Her career motivation has been largely undeflected by other goals. Most of her social relationships appear to be work related. After arriving in New York, she formed a relationship with a rock musician and later with a disc jockey named John Benitex. Following her successful entry into pop music, she was briefly married to an actor, Sean Penn, and later had an affair with Warren Beatty. These relationships helped to pave her way into movies. As Jeff Katzenberg, head of Disney studios, observed: "She has always had a vision of exactly who she is, whether performer or businesswoman, and she has been strong enough to balance it all. Every time she comes up with a new look it is successful. When it happens once, OK, maybe its luck; but twice is a coincidence, and three times it's got to be a remarkable talent. And Madonna's on her fifth or sixth time."

Central to Madonna's success has been careful recognition and exploitation of the keys to success in the world of "show biz." In terms of gaining access to the music and movie businesses, she clearly recognized the importance of the "gatekeepers" to the channels of distribution in her choice of manager, her cultivation of friendships with the famous, and her relationships with record and film producers. In terms of generating customer awareness and appeal, she has walked a fine line between the acceptable and the outrageous. Common to all the media in which she has performed has been a blatant exploitation of sexuality, capitalizing in particular on nudity, sexual deviance, and pornographic images (sometimes under the banner of "art"). The evolution of her market offerings has followed a "product life cycle" approach. As her recorded music sales have waned (her sales peak occurred with her *True Blue* album), she has capitalized upon her star status and recognizability to develop other media. Every time her career appears to be in decline she has shown a remarkable ability to stage publicity coups and somehow renew her image and appeal – the launch of her 1992 book *Erotica* is a notable example. In common with the tradition set by Frank Sinatra, the Grateful Dead, and the Rolling Stones, she has recognized that falling record sales are no barrier to increasingly popular live performances. The nine shows of her "Blond Ambition" tour grossed $40 million in 1991. Her ability to recognize trends and opportunities in the fast-moving world of youth entertainment is critical to her ability to tailor her product offerings to market trends. In terms of technology, she has effectively exploited the appeal of music videos and multimedia technology in live performances. In terms of broader cultural trends, she has exploited increased openness and acceptance of sexual deviation and ambiguity with regard to male/female, hetero-/homosexual distinctions.

Her success has also involved a very careful exploitation of her own talents and endowments. Her foremost ability is designing and projecting images that combine music, dance, theater, and her physical presence. To be effective, such images need to supplement her weaknesses as an entertainer. She lacks the voice of Whitney Houston or Tracy Chapman, the dancing ability of Michael Jackson, and the musical talent of Elton John. Hence, her recordings rely heavily upon good songs, capable musicians, and recording technology while her live shows depend upon her theatricality and force of personality. Her limited resources of natural beauty are compensated by a heavy reliance upon sexual suggestion and innovative use of dress, coiffure, and cosmetics.

Above all, like all other successful purveyors of fantasy (Walt Disney Company, for example), Madonna's success depends upon her obsessive attention to detail. Her insistence on control is reflected in the organization of her business interests. Most of her entertainment ventures have been owned and operated by her own companies, which have included Boy Toy Inc. (publishing), Siren Films, and Slutco Inc. (video). In 1992, she formed Maverick Inc., a joint venture with Time Warner. In addition to her share in Maverick's profits, she is paid $8 million a year in salary until 1997. Her desire for commercial and artistic control has resulted in her refusal to endorse or advertise products. The one exception was PepsiCo, which, in exchange for her making three advertisements, paid her $3 million and sponsored her concert tour.

The Maverick venture represents yet another stage in Madonna's strategic evolution. Now that Madonna's career approaches some form of maturity, Maverick will provide a vehicle for using her creative and promotional intuition and experience and the wealth of talented specialists that she has gathered around her to develop new entertainers and enterprises. As Madonna noted: "I've met these people along the way in my career and I want to take them everywhere I go. I want to incorporate them into my little factory of ideas. I also come into contact with a lot of young talent that I feel entrepreneurial about." Although Madonna's driving force is popular appeal and visibility rather than profit and several of her projects have lost significant sums of money (notably the *Erotica* book), the overall financial returns to Madonna's business empire have been impressive. Her personal net worth is around $80 million. As Harry Scolinos, a Los Angeles attorney, observes: "I would take her street-smart business sense over someone with a Harvard MBA any day."

Source: "Madonna Is America's Smartest Business Woman," *Business Age*, June 1992, 66–9.

Exhibit 1.2 General Giap and the Vietnam Wars, 1948–75

"As far as logistics and tactics were concerned we succeeded in everything we set out to do. At the height of the war the army was able to move almost a million soldiers a year in and out of Vietnam, feed them, clothe them, house them, supply them with arms and ammunition and generally sustain them better than any army had ever been sustained in the field. . . . On the battlefield itself, the army was unbeatable. In engagement after engagement the forces of the Vietcong and the North Vietnamese Army were thrown back with terrible losses. Yet, in the end, it was North Vietnam, not the United States that emerged victorious. How could we have succeeded so well yet failed so miserably?"

Despite having the largest army in Southeast Asia, North Vietnam was no match for South Vietnam so long as it was backed by the world's most powerful military and industrial nation. South Vietnam and its U.S. ally were defeated not by superior resources but by a superior strategy. North Vietnam achieved what Sun Tzu claimed was the highest form of victory: the enemy gave up.

The prime mover in the formulation of North Vietnam's military strategy was General Vo Nguyen Giap.

In 1944, Giap became head of the Vietminh guerrilla forces and remained commander-in-chief of the North Vietnamese Army until 1974 and minister of defense until 1980. Giap's strategy was based upon Mao Tse-tung's three-phase theory of revolutionary war: first, passive resistance during which political support is mobilized; second, guerrilla warfare aimed at weakening the enemy and building military strength; and, finally, general counteroffensive. In 1954, Giap felt strong enough to begin the final stage in the war against the French, and the brilliant victory at Dien Bien Phu fully vindicated the strategy. Against South Vietnam and its U.S. ally, the approach was similar. Giap explained his strategy as follows:

"Our strategy was . . . to wage a long-lasting battle. . . . Only a long-term war could enable us to utilize to the maximum our political trump cards, to overcome our material handicap, and to transform our weakness into strength. To maintain and increase our forces was the principle to which we adhered, contenting ourselves with attacking when success was certain, refusing to give battle likely to incur losses. . . ."

The strategy built upon the one resource where the communists had overwhelming superiority: their will to fight. As Clausewitz, the nineteenth-century military theorist, observed: war requires unity of purpose between the government, the military, and the people. Such unity was never achieved in the United States. The North Vietnamese, on the other hand, were united in a "people's war." Capitalizing upon this strength necessitated "The Long War." As Prime Minister Pham Van Dong explained: "The U.S. is the most powerful nation on earth. But Americans do not like long, inconclusive wars. . . . We can outlast them and we can win in the end." Limited military engagement and the charade of the Paris peace talks helped the North Vietnamese prolong the conflict, while diplomatic efforts to isolate the United States from its Western allies and to sustain the U.S. peace movement accelerated the crumbling of American will to win.

The effectiveness of the U.S. military response was limited by two key uncertainties: what were the objectives and who was the enemy? Was the role of the U.S. to support the South Vietnamese regime, fight Vietcong terrorism, inflict a military defeat on North Vietnam, or combat world communism? Lack of unanimity over goals translated into confusion over whether America was fighting the Vietcong, the North Vietnamese, the communists of Southeast Asia, or whether the war was military or political in scope. Diversity of opinions and a shifting balance of political and public opinion over time was fatal to the establishment of a consistent long-term strategy.

The consistency and strength of North Vietnam's strategy allowed it to survive errors in implementation. In particular, Giap was undoubtedly premature in launching his general offensive. The heavy infiltration and mounting guerrilla actions by North Vietnamese regulars during 1965–7 was followed in 1968 by the Tet Offensive and in 1972 by the Easter Offensive. Both these offensives on South Vietnamese and U.S. positions were beaten back and huge losses sustained. General Giap was replaced as commander-in-chief by General Van Tien Dung, who recognized that the Watergate scandal had so weakened the U.S. presidency that an effective American response to a new communist offensive was unlikely. On April 29, Operation Frequent Wind began to evacuate all remaining Americans from South Vietnam, and the next morning North Vietnamese troops entered the Presidential Palace in Saigon.

Sources: Colonel Harry G. Summers Jr., *On Strategy* (Novato, CA: Presidio Press, 1982); G. K. Tanham, *Communist Revolutionary Warfare* (New York: Praeger, 1961), 9–32; Vo Nguyen Giap, *Selected Writings* (Hanoi: Foreign Languages Publishing House, 1977); and J. Cameron, *Here Is Your Enemy* (New York: Holt, Rinehart, Winston, 1966).

was the strategy explicit. Yet in both we can observe a consistency of direction based upon a clear view of the "game" being played and guidelines for competing in order to achieve a position of advantage:

- Madonna's preeminence as a "superstar" and her earnings over the ten-year period 1984–93 have reflected a multimedia scope of operation that has spanned recorded music, live performances, music videos, films, and books. Within these markets her positioning has been at the far extreme of public acceptability, based heavily upon exploitation of sexuality and sexual imagery and a continual "repackaging" of her offerings to take account of current trends in technology, fashion, and society;

- the victory of the Vietnamese communist forces over the French and then the Americans is a classic example of how a sound strategy pursued with total commitment over a long period can achieve final victory despite inferior resources. Fundamental to the ultimate success of North Vietnam was General Giap's strategy of a protracted war of limited engagement. So long as the American forces were constrained by domestic and international opinion from using their full military might, the strategy was unbeatable once it began to sap the willingness of the American government to persevere with a costly, unpopular foreign war.

Yet, while a strategy can help achieve success, it does not guarantee it. What are the features of a strategy that contribute to success? In our two examples, four critical elements stand out:

- *Goals that were simple, consistent, and long term.* Both enterprises were associated with a notable single-mindedness of goals. Madonna's career features a relentless drive for stardom. Almost all other dimensions of her life were subordinated to her career as an entertainer. Most of her social relationships and romantic attachments appear to be ancillary to and supportive of her career objectives. The critical difference between the North Vietnamese and the American forces during the Vietnam War was over clarity of goals. North Vietnam never questioned its ultimate goal: to reunite Vietnam under communist rule and to remove a foreign army from Vietnamese soil. U.S. efforts in Vietnam, by contrast, were bedeviled by confusion over objectives. Was the United States supporting an ally, stabilizing Southeast Asia, engaging in a proxy war against the Soviet Union, or fighting a global, ideological war against communism?
- *Profound understanding of the competitive environment.* Both examples designed their strategies around a deep and insightful appreciation of the arena in which they were competing. Fundamental to Madonna's continuing success has been a shrewd understanding of what it takes to be a star and how to maintain and renew popular appeal. This understanding extends from simple recognition of the enduring power of sexual attraction to insight into the key ingredients of a successful live performance and recognition of the need to manage the critical channels of distribution. Giap understood his enemy and the battlefield conditions where he would engage them. In addition, the Vietnamese high command possessed a sound appreciation of American political pressures and cultural biases, which assisted North Vietnam in a key element of its strategy – undermining the will of the American people to support the Vietnam War;
- *Objective appraisal of resources.* Common to both strategies was an emphasis upon exploiting internal strengths to the fullest, while

protecting areas of weakness. As we have observed, Madonna's critical resources lie in her ability to synthesize image, her aptitude for self-publicity, and her capacity for appealing to and exploiting contemporary trends. By positioning herself as a "personality" and a "star" she exploits these strengths highly effectively, while avoiding being judged simply as a singer, a rock musician, or an actor. Giap's strategy was carefully designed to protect against his army's deficiencies in arms and equipment, while exploiting the commitment and loyalty of his troops. Both examples sought to acquire critical resources in order to bolster their competitive positions. Madonna has built a team of some 150 creative, technical, and managerial professionals. Giap sought to moderate his material weaknesses with support from the Soviet Union and captured weaponry from the South Vietnamese;

- *Effective implementation.* Not only were the strategies sound, but their implementation was effective. Madonna and Giap were both highly effective leaders: eager to make decisions, to implement them, and to demand loyalty and commitment from subordinates. Both individuals established organizations that were structured to implement the strategies effectively. Critical to such organizations were structures and systems that permitted the effective exploitation of the specialized skills of individual organization members with the coordination and communication needed to integrate these individual efforts and focus them upon achieving the underlying strategic goals.

These observations about the role of strategy in success can be made in relation to most fields of human endeavor. Whether we look at warfare, chess, politics, sport, or business, the successful individuals and organizations are seldom the outcome of some random process. Nor is superiority in initial endowments of skills and resources typically the determining factor. Strategies that build upon the four elements outlined above almost always play an influential role. Look at the "high achievers" in any competitive area. Look especially among your own circles of friends and acquaintances. My own observations support the view that successful individuals in terms of recognition, power, and material rewards are not, most commonly, those with the greatest innate abilities. Central to the success of individuals within each of their highly competitive spheres is the pursuit of strategies that share the same elements identified above:

- *They have clear, long-term career objectives.* Equally importantly, these career goals take primacy over the multitude of life's other goals – friendship, love, leisure, knowledge, spiritual fulfillment – which the majority of us spend most of our lives contemplating, juggling, and reassessing. The biographies of leading figures in business, politics, entertainment, and the creative arts often show that remarkable career success is matched by dismal failure in other aspects of living such as friendships, family relations, and spiritual development;
- *They know their environment.* They are adept at selecting the careers that offer the best opportunities, and once in they tend to be fast

learners in terms of understanding "the game" – what needs to be done to secure advancement in a particular career or organization;

- *They know themselves well.* In particular, they appreciate their strengths and weaknesses in terms of those activities they can perform well and those they cannot;
- *They pursue their careers with commitment, consistency and determination.*

These same ingredients of successful strategies – clear objectives, understanding the environment, resource appraisal, and effective implementation – will form the key components of our analysis of business strategy. These principles are not new; over 2,000 years ago Sun Tzu wrote:

Know the other and know yourself:
Triumph without peril.
Know Nature and know the Situation:
Triumph completely.[1]

As a preliminary to developing our analysis of business strategy, let us trace the historical development of strategy.

The Development of Business Strategy

Origins and military antecedents

Business strategy is a comparatively young field of study – even within the management sciences. In order to clarify its meaning, table 1.1 offers some different definitions of strategy, both within its generic and business contexts.

Although business strategy is fairly new, many of its concepts and theories have their antecedents in military strategy, which extends back to principles enunciated by Julius Caesar and Alexander the Great[2] and further still to Sun Tzu's classic treatise written at about 360 B.C.[3] The word "strategy" comes from the Greek word *strategos*, which is formed from *stratos*, meaning *army*, and *-ag*, meaning *to lead*.[4]

The applicability of the principles of military strategy to business is a subject of continuing controversy. What is agreed, however, is that military strategy can yield important insights into business management, the most basic being the military distinction between strategy and tactics. *Strategy is the overall plan for deploying resources to establish a favorable position. A tactic is a scheme for a specific action.* While tactics are concerned with the maneuvers necessary to win battles, strategy is concerned with winning the war. Strategic decisions, whether in the military or the business sphere, share three common characteristics:

THE CONCEPT OF STRATEGY

- STRATEGY. The art of war, especially the planning of movements of troops and ships etc., into favorable positions; plan of action or policy in business or politics etc.

  Oxford Pocket Dictionary

- The determination of the long run goals and objectives of an enterprise, and the adoption of courses of action and the allocation of resources necessary for carrying out these goals.

  Alfred D. Chandler Jr., *Strategy and Structure:
  Chapters in the History of the Industrial Enterprise*

- A strategy is the pattern or plan that integrates an organization's major goals, policies, and action sequences into a cohesive whole. A well-formulated strategy helps to marshal and allocate an organization's resources into a unique and viable posture based upon its relative internal competences and shortcomings, anticipated changes in the environment, and contingent moves by intelligent opponents.

  James Brian Quinn, *Strategies for Change: Logical Incrementalism*

- Strategy is the pattern of objectives, purposes or goals and the major policies and plans for achieving these goals, stated in such a way as to define what business the company is in or is to be in and the kind of company it is or is to be.

  Kenneth Andrews, *The Concept of Corporate Strategy*

- What business strategy is all about is, in a word, *competitive advantage*. . . . The sole purpose of strategic planning is to enable a company to gain, as efficiently as possible, a sustainable edge over its competitors. Corporate strategy thus implies an attempt to alter a company's strength relative to that of its competitors in the most efficient way.

  Kenichi Ohmae, *The Mind of the Strategist*

- Lost Boy: "Injuns! Let's go get 'em!"
  John Darling: "Hold on a minute. First we must have a strategy."
  Lost Boy: "Uhh? What's a strategy?"
  John Darling: "It's er . . . It's a plan of attack."

  Walt Disney's *Peter Pan*.

Table 1.1 Some Definitions of Strategy

- They are important
- They involve a significant commitment of resources
- They are not easily reversible

Armies and business enterprises have similar needs for strategy. Both possess objectives: for the army these are established by the government, for the enterprise they established by its board of directors. For both, the competitive situation arises from the incompatibility between the objectives of different organizations: in 1990-1, Iraq wanted control of Kuwait and the United Nations wanted the restoration of Kuwaiti sovereignty; Coca-Cola and PepsiCo each aim for leadership in the world soft drink market. Both armies and companies possess resources that include people, capital equipment, and technical skills. Both face external environments determined partly by exogenous factors (the terrain in military conflict, the market in business competition) and partly by the strategies pursued by the rivals.[5]

At the more detailed level, specific principles of military strategy have been applied to business situations. Such principles include the relative strengths of offensive and defensive strategies, the merits of outflanking as opposed to frontal assault, the roles of flexible and graduated responses to aggressive initiatives, and the potential for deception, envelopment, escalation, and attrition.[6] Arithmetical theories of numerical superiority, such as Lanchester's theories of battle outcomes as functions of troops, firepower, and rates of reinforcement have been applied (by Japanese companies in particular) to predict critical levels of market share.[7]

At the same time, there are some clear differences in the nature of competition between warfare and business rivalry. The objective of war is (usually) to defeat the enemy. The purpose of business rivalry is seldom so aggressive: most business enterprises limit their competitive ambitions, seeking coexistence rather than the destruction of competitors. Hence, a closer analogy may be between diplomacy and business strategy. Diplomacy is concerned primarily with the management of peaceful relations; only when diplomacy breaks down do nations normally resort to war. Similarly, business relations typically comprise a duality between cooperation and competition. Competition at times may be intense, but seldom between established rivals does it become destructive.[8]

Toward a general theory of strategy?

The attempt to transfer theories of military strategy to business management depends upon the existence of some underlying principles of strategy that are common to both and may even be common to all competitive situations. In 1944, such a theory became available with the publication by Von Neumann and Morgenstern of their *Theory of Games*.[9] During the last 30 years, game theory has had a huge impact upon the analysis of competition; in particular, it has revolutionized microeconomic analysis and has been applied widely in military and political analysis. Although game theory developed out of mathematics, its basic principles have intuitive appeal and are applicable without mathematical formality. Thomas Schelling's classic study *The Strategy of Conflict* formulates the major elements of a theory of strategy common to most competitive situations, drawing heavily upon the insights offered by game theory.[10] The theory of *The Strategy of Conflict* deals with the principles of bargaining, threats, mutual distrust, and the balance between cooperation and conflict.

While game theory offers penetrating insights into particular categories of competitive situation (the most famous being that of the "prisoners' dilemma"), in terms of its applications to strategic management, overall progress has been disappointing. Rather than providing a general theory of strategic behavior, game theory has developed a large number of highly specific equilibrium models whose outcomes depend heavily upon the assumptions made and most of which lack applicability to real-world situations. Some of the most valuable applications of game theory concepts are in providing insights into situations that involve competition, bargaining, and collaboration.[11] In chapter 3, we will explore further the uses of game theory in analyzing competition.

The development of business strategy analysis

Explicit interest in business strategy emerged in the United States during the late 1950s and early 1960s in response to the problems of managing large, complex corporations. The primary problem for such enterprises was coordinating individual decisions and maintaining top management's overall control. The development of annual financial budgeting procedures provided a vital vehicle for such coordination and control, but coordinating capital investment decisions required a longer planning horizon. The emphasis on longer-term planning during the 1960s reflected concern for achieving coordination and consistency of purpose during an expansionary period. The postwar period was one of unprecedented stability and growth, which was conducive to the expansion of large enterprises. As companies sought efficiency and control of risk through scale-efficient production, mass marketing, vertical integration, and large long-term investments in technology, so long-term planning based upon medium-term economic and market forecasts became popular. The typical format was a five-year corporate planning document that set goals and objectives, forecast key economic trends (including market demand, the company's market share, and revenue and net income), established priorities for different products and business areas of the firm, and allocated resources. In 1963, SRI found that the majority of the largest U.S. companies had set up corporate planning departments.[12] Exhibit 1.3 provides an example of such formalized corporate planning.

A key element of corporate planning was the planning and management of growth. For this reason, diversification played a central role in many companies' corporate plans during the 1960s and 1970s. Indeed, Igor Ansoff defined strategy in terms of the firm's choices of products and markets: "Strategic decisions are primarily concerned with external rather than internal problems of the firm and specifically with selection of the product-mix which the firm will produce and the markets to which it will sell."[13] During the 1970s, portfolio planning matrices (see chapter 15) came into vogue as frameworks for selecting strategies and allocating resources within the diversified corporation. The enthusiasm for corporate planning during the 1960s and early 1970s paralleled the infatuation of governments and public authorities with economic,

Exhibit 1.3 Corporate Planning in a Large U.S Steel Company, 1965

The first step in developing long-range plans was to forecast the product demand for future years. After calculating the tonnage needed in each sales district to provide the "target" fraction of the total forecasted demand, the optimal production level for each area was determined. A computer program which incorporated the projected demand, existing production capacity, freight costs and so on, was used for this purpose.

Whenever the optimum production rate in each area was found, the additional facilities needed to produce the desired tonnage were specified. Then the capital costs for the necessary equipment, buildings, and lay-out were estimated by the Chief Engineer of the corporation and various district engineers. Alternative plans for achieving company goals were also developed for some areas, and investment proposals were formulated after considering the amount of available capital and the company debt policy. The Vice President who was responsible for long-range planning recommended certain plans to the President, and after the top executives and the Board of Directors reviewed alternative plans, they made the necessary decisions about future activities.

Source: Quoted from Harold W. Henry, *Long Range Planning Processes in 45 Industrial Companies* (Englewood Cliffs, NJ: Prentice-Hall, 1967), 65.

social, and investment planning. In both private and public sectors this interest in planning reflected the development of new "scientific" techniques of decision making and policy formulation: cost-benefit analysis, discounted cash flow techniques, linear programming, econometric forecasting, and Keynesian macroeconomic management. The transition of Western business from entrepreneurial capitalism to managerial "technocracy" was analyzed by J. K. Galbraith.[14] In Galbraith's view, the size, risks, and timescale of new investments implied the superiority of planning by firms over the haphazard workings of markets.

By the mid-1970s, however, circumstances had changed. Accumulating evidence on the failure of diversification to yield anticipated synergy slowed the drive toward conglomeration. Even more important was increased macroeconomic instability (associated in particular with the first oil shock of 1974), which discredited the elaborate planning systems installed by many leading corporations during the previous decade. As the world entered a period of intense turbulence, firms were forced to abandon their medium-term corporate plans in favor of more flexible approaches to strategic management. Increased international competition further threatened stability and survival. As U.S. firms' preeminence across a wide range of world industries – from steel to banking – was increasingly challenged, so interest shifted away from issues of diversification and planning new capacity and new products toward the need for *competitiveness*. The consequence was that top management began to perceive its role in terms of *strategic management* rather than *corporate planning*.

Henry Mintzberg's examination of the rise and fall of strategic planning in his book of the same name identifies three "fallacies of strategic planning":[15]

- *The fallacy of prediction.* The external environment cannot be predicted with any degree of accuracy. Indeed, to the extent that a key element of the external environment is the behavior of competitors, the environment is inherently unpredictable;

- *The fallacy of detachment.* Strategy formulation cannot be detached from the broader process of managing. The data needed for strategy formulation cannot be delivered to the corporate planning department: some of the most critical data are those that managers gather in the process of managing. Strategy formulation is not about a formalized design process in which the outcome is a strategy document. Strategy is continuously evolving; it must combine both deliberate strategy formulation and elements that *emerge* through the process of management;
- *The fallacy of formalization.* Formal procedures for strategy formulation have advantages of systematization but are inferior to informal systems with respect to the flexibility required to cope with discontinuities and promote organizational learning through the close linkage of thought and action.

The decline of corporate planning and the emergence of strategic management was associated with the following themes:

- a central concern with building competitive advantage by combining monitoring and analysis of the industry environment with appraisal and development of internal resources;
- a rejection of the rigidity of detailed corporate plans and an embracing of flexibility;
- a disillusion with corporate planning departments as the primary source of strategy formulation and a relocation of strategy formulation in the hands of the same managers who are responsible for its implementation.

During the late 1970s and early 1980s, increased awareness of the external environment meant that the principal focus of strategic management was the analysis of industry and competition. Michael Porter of Harvard Business School pioneered the application of industrial organization (IO) economics for analyzing the determinants of firm profitability.[16] Influential studies of the role of industry structure and competitive positioning on profitability were undertaken by the Strategic Planning Institute within its PIMS (Profit Impact of Market Strategy) project. Analysis of the role of market share in determining competitive advantage and profitability was also undertaken by the Boston Consulting Group.

During the late 1980s and early 1990s, the focus of interest in the analysis of competitive advantage shifted increasingly toward internal aspects of the firm. Competitive advantage was seen as depending less upon a firm's choices over market positioning and more upon the exploitation of unique internal resources and capabilities. Work on the *"resource-based view of the firm"* and *organizational competences and capabilities* helped shift the focus of attention of strategic management toward dynamic aspects of competitive advantage, the importance of innovation, and the central role of internal processes within the firm.[17]

Table 1.2 summarizes the development of strategic management over time.

The Role of Competition and the Quest for Competitive Advantage

Competition provides the rationale for strategy. Without competition, strategy is of limited importance or interest – it is concerned primarily with establishing objectives, forecasting the external environment, and planning resource deployments. The essence of strategy is the *interdependence* of competitors: because actions by one player affect outcomes for other participants, each player's decisions must take account of other players' expected reactions. Games of strategy (poker, chess) are thus radically different from games of chance (bingo) and games of skill (archery).[18]

Competition occurs whenever resources are finite and competitors' objectives are mutually inconsistent. What separates competition in human society from competition among other species is strategy. The evolutionary process is driven by *natural competition,* which involves no strategy. Genetic mutation results in variety, and those varieties that are best adapted to the prevailing environment multiply their numbers. Varieties that are less adapted to their environment die out.

In human society, competition is different. Unlike other living organisms, human beings have the capacity to anticipate competitors' actions and, on the basis of their expectations, to adjust their behavior and characteristics. In contrast to natural competition, which is governed by an environmentally determined selection process, the capacity for strategic behavior results in *strategic* or *rational* competition. The essential requirements for strategic competition have been specified by Bruce Henderson, founder of the Boston Consulting Group:

- a critical mass of knowledge concerning the competitive process;
- the ability to integrate the knowledge and understand cause and effect;
- imagination to foresee alternative actions and logic to analyze their consequences;
- availability of resources beyond current needs in order to invest in future potential.[19]

Although such strategic competition dominates the world of business, it is only with the "game theory revolution" of the last 20 years that economics has focused its efforts around analyzing conscious rivalry rather than trying to assume it away. The contribution of game theory to the analysis of strategic competition will be explored in subsequent

Table 1.2. The evolution of Strategic Management

Period	1950s	1960s	1970s	Late 1970s & early 1980s	Late 1980s & early 1990s
Dominant theme	Budgetary planning & control	Corporate planning	Corporate strategy	Analysis of industry & competition	The quest for competitive advantage
Main focus	Financial control through operating budgets	Planning growth	Portfolio planning	Choice of industries, markets, & segments and positioning within them.	Sources of competitive advantage within the firm. Dynamic aspects of strategy.
Principal concepts & techniques	Financial budgeting Investment planning Project appraisal	Market forecasting. Diversification & analysis of synergy	SBU as unit of analysis Portfolio planning matrices Analysis of experience curves and returns to market share	Analysis of industry structure. Competitor analysis PIMS analysis.	Resource analysis. Analysis of organizational competence & capability. Dynamic analysis: analysis of speed, responsiveness, & first-mover advantage.
Organizational implications	Financial management as key corporate function	Development of corporate planning depts. Rise of conglomerates. Diffusion of M-form.	Integration of financial & strategic control. Strategic planning as a dialogue between corporate HQ and the divisions.	Divestment of unattractive business units. Active asset management	Corporate restructuring and business process reengineering. Building capabilities through MIS, HRM, strategic alliances, and new organizational forms.

chapters. Suffice it to say at this stage that attempts to develop game theory into a general theory of strategic behavior have been overwhelmed by the sheer complexity of the competitive interactions between firms and the near infinite number of outcomes that can be generated by different assumptions about preferences, distribution of information, and order of play.[20]

The observation that competition in industries comprising closely matched competitors is difficult to analyze and has the potential to generate many different outcomes has an important implication for the emphasis on strategy analysis in this book. Our priority in strategy formulation will be less on "playing competitive games" through anticipating competitors' moves and engaging in bluff and counterbluff, threat and deterrence, and much more on seeking insulation from the uncertainties of competitive interaction by establishing a position of *sustainable advantage* over rivals. The notion that the primary goal for strategy is the establishment of unique advantages over competitors is consistent with an ecological approach to business strategy. Bruce Henderson argues that the implication of Gause's Principle that competitors that make their living in the same way cannot coexist implies that each business must differentiate itself:

Strategy is a deliberate search for a plan of action that will develop a business's competitive advantage and compound it. For any company, the search is an iterative process that begins with a recognition of where you are now and what you have now. Your most dangerous competitors are those that are most like you. The differences between you and your competitors are the basis of your advantage. If you are in business and are self-supporting, you already have some kind of advantage, no matter how small or subtle. . . . The objective is to enlarge the scope of your advantage, which can only happen at someone else's expense.[21]

If the content of this book could be distilled into a single theme, it is this: how to go about *identifying, establishing, and sustaining competitive advantage.*

The Strategy-Making Process: Criticisms of the "Rationalist" Approach

As indicated by its title, the concern of this book is with analysis. The implicit belief is that the senior management of the organization is able to objectively appraise the enterprise and its environment, to formulate an optimal strategy, and to implement that strategy. The primary concern of this book is the formulation of strategy, although as we shall see formulation and implementation cannot be dichotomized: a well-formulated strategy must take account of the process through which it will be implemented. In reformulating IBM's strategy, Lou Gerstner and his management team must take account of IBM's organizational structure, management systems, personnel, and the corporate culture that influences the way employees behave and perceive their roles.

This "rationalist" approach to business strategy makes implicit assumptions about the strategy-making process. First, strategy formulation is the preserve of top management – it is the CEO and the senior management team who analyze the current situation then determine the appropriate direction for the organization. Once formulated, the desired strategy is then passed down for implementation by the lower level of managers.

For most organizations, such a picture is a fiction: the process is less structured, more diffused, and the dichotomization of formulation and implementation is less apparent. Empirical research by Henry Mintzberg and his colleagues at McGill University of the long-term development of strategy in a number of organizations has identified a number of features of the strategy-making process.[22]

The rational, top-down strategy formulation of the type I have envisaged in this chapter is what Mintzberg terms *deliberate strategy*. Even here, however, the strategy is unlikely to be the result of decisions by a single person or group and is likely to reflect a complex political process of negotiation, bargaining, compromise, and window dressing. However, the strategy that we observe in the pattern of decisions of the organization, what Mintzberg terms *emergent strategy,* is likely to deviate substantially from deliberate strategy. Deviation occurs for several reasons. To begin with, no CEO has sufficient information to make his intended strategy fully explicit: implementation necessitates formulation of the details. Second, no CEO has full control over the organization: inevitably, the decisions and activities of subordinates deviate from the edicts from above. Third, even in the most rigidly hierarchical organizations, strategy formulation is never the exclusive preserve of top management. Top management has no monopoly over good ideas or decisions; discoveries of better ways of doing things occur at all levels of the organization and will be reflected in the organization's strategy.

An example of the process by which strategy emerges is Richard Pascale's account of Honda's successful invasion of the U.S. motorcycle market during the 1960s. According to the Boston Consulting Group, Honda exemplified the analytic approach to strategy formation based upon the exploitation of the experience curve to attain an unassailable position of cost leadership in the world motorcycle industry.[23] However, Pascale's research revealed otherwise.[24] The initial decision to enter the U.S. market was based upon little analysis and comprised no clear plan of how Honda would build a market position. The outstanding success of the Honda 50 was a surprise to the company – Honda had believed that its main opportunities lay with its larger bikes. As Mintzberg observes: "Brilliant as its strategy may have looked after the fact, Honda's managers made almost every conceivable mistake until the market finally hit them over the head with the right formula."[25]

The "process school" of strategy research focuses upon the realities of *how strategies emerge*. The central issues are how strategic decisions are made and the determinants of organizational change. Both areas draw upon a wide range of social science. Eisenhardt and Zbaracki identify three broad approaches: cognitive approaches that focus on the rationality of decision makers, political approaches that focus upon power in organizations, and "garbage can" approaches that view organizational process as random or anarchic.[26] Studies of strategic change have involved longitudinal studies of a single enterprise (e.g., Pettigrew's study of ICI)[27] and groups of companies (e.g., Romanelli and Tushman's study of computer companies).[28]

Strategy making as "crafting"

Henry Mintzberg, one of the most prominent advocates of the "process school," argues that not only is rationalism an inaccurate method for accounting for how strategies are actually formulated – it is also a poor way of making strategy. "The notion that strategy is something that should happen way up there, far removed from the details of running an organization on a daily basis, is one of the great fallacies of conventional strategic management."[29] The problem is that a divide between formulation and implementation precludes learning. In practice, the two must go hand in hand, with strategy constantly being adjusted and revised in the light of experience.

Mintzberg uses the images of *crafting* to contrast his conception of strategy formulation with the conventional planning approach:

Imagine someone planning strategy. What likely springs to mind is an image of orderly thinking: a senior manager, or a group of them, sitting in an office formulating courses of action that everyone else will implement on schedule. The keynote is reason – rational control, the systematic analysis of competitors and markets, or company strengths and weaknesses, the combination of these analyses producing clear, explicit, full-blown strategies.

Now imagine someone *crafting* strategy. A wholly different image likely results, as different from planning as craft is from mechanization. Craft invokes traditional skill, dedication, perfection through the mastery of detail. What springs to mind is not so much thinking and reason as involvement, a feeling of intimacy and harmony with the materials at hand, developed through long experience and commitment. Formulation and implementation merge into a fluid process of learning through which creative strategies emerge.[30]

The approach of this book is to follow a rationalist, analytical approach to strategy formulation in preference to the "crafting" approach advocated by Mintzberg. This is not because I regard planning as necessarily superior to crafting – planning in any detailed sense is not what strategy is about. Nor is it because I wish to downplay the role of skill, dedication, involvement, harmony, or creativity. These qualities are essential ingredients of successful strategies and successful enterprises. Strategy development is a multidimensional process that must involve both rational analysis and intuition, experience, and emotion. However, whether strategy formulation is formal or informal, whether strategies are deliberate or emergent, there can be little doubt as to the importance of systematic analysis as a vital input in the strategy process. Without analysis, the process of strategy formulation, particularly at the senior management level, is likely to be chaotic, with no basis for the comparing and evaluating of alternatives. Moreover, critical decisions become susceptible to the whims and preferences of individual managers, to contemporary fads, and to wishful thinking. The concepts, theories, and analytic frameworks are not alternatives or substitutes for experience, commitment, and creativity. But they do provide useful frames for organizing and assessing the vast amount of information available on the firm and its environment and for guiding decisions and may even act to stimulate rather than repress creativity and innovation.

Central to the rational approach to strategy analysis is the idea that we can systematically analyze the reasons for business success and failure and apply the lessons of our learning to formulating business strategies. The problem with the rationalist approach, as emphasized in Mintzberg's attacks on strategic planning, is that the analysis is too narrow – it has tended to be overformalized and has emphasized quantitative over qualitative data.[31] The danger of the Mintzberg approach is that by downplaying the role of systematic analysis and emphasizing the role of intuition and vision, we move into a Shirley MacLaine world of New Age mysticism in which rationality is devalued.

The goal of this book is to promote analysis that is sound, relevant, and applicable. If strategy analysis does not take account of experiential learning and the practicalities of implementation, it is poor analysis. Similarly, the process of strategy formulation must involve intuition, reflection, and the interaction between thought and action. Good analysis should encourage the development of intuition and promote creativity. Analysis can also greatly facilitate the process of strategy formulation. Analysis provides a conceptual framework for rational discussion of alternative ideas and a vocabulary for communicating the strategy throughout the organization.

Strategy in multiple roles

What emerges from this discussion of the "process" view of strategy is the ability to see strategic management within a wider context and as fulfilling a broader role. We can view strategy as fulfilling three key managerial purposes:

(1) *Strategy as a support for decision making* At the outset of this chapter, I identified strategy as a key element in success. But why is this so? Strategy is a pattern or theme that gives coherence to the

decisions of an individual or organization. But why cannot individuals or organizations make decisions that are optimal in the absence of such a unifying theme? Consider the game of chess. If a chess player were able to identify every possible move available and the full set of consequences of each move – to envisage, in short, a huge decision tree that covered the whole game – then a strategy would not be necessary. For every move by the opponent, the player would be able to identify the optimal move to play. However, chess players, even grand masters, are subject to the same cognitive limitations of all human beings: "*bounded rationality*" means that the human brain is incapable of assimilating and analyzing all the available information necessary for fully rational choices. In a world of bounded rationality, a strategy is a second-best solution – it establishes a set of guidelines, rules, and criteria for the way in which the player will make individual decisions. In the case of chess, such strategies often take the form of simple maxims: "Control the center of the board," "Be defensive when playing black," and so on.

In the case of business enterprises, strategy may be viewed similarly as a consequence of bounded rationality. Even in the smallest enterprise, many hundreds of decisions are likely to be made every day, ranging from whether to offer a discount to a particular customer to the choice of sending mail by express or regular delivery. It is not possible or desirable to optimize every single decision by considering the full implications of every permutation of decision choices. In these circumstances, strategies such as "We will seek technological leadership in military applications of wireless communication" or "We shall provide the lowest-cost car rental in Cincinnati" simplify decision making by imposing a constraint upon the range of decision alternatives considered and by acting as a heuristic – a rule-of-thumb that reduces the search required to find an acceptable solution to a decision problem.

(2) *Strategy as a vehicle for coordination and communication*   Not only can a strategy help to achieve consistency in decisions over time, in complex organizations a strategy can serve as a useful vehicle for achieving consistency of decision making across different departments and individuals. As noted earlier, the development of corporate planning was partly a response to the increasing size and complexity of companies. One of the important organizational roles of strategy is to provide a common direction for the enterprise.

For strategy to provide coordination requires that the strategy process act as a communication mechanism within the firm. One of the most important changes in strategy making in large enterprises over the last two decades has been the shift in the responsibility for strategy formulation from corporate planning departments to line managers. One of the benefits of this transition is that the strategic planning process provides a highly effective mechanism for dialogue between corporate and divisional managers and between general managers and functional specialists.

A more controversial aspect of strategy as a means of communication are company *mission statements*. A mission statement is a fundamental statement of a company's strategy. Andrew Campbell and Laura Nash of the Ashridge Strategic Management Center identify four elements of mission:

- *Purpose* – why the company exists
- *Strategy* – competitive position and distinctive competence
- *Values* – what the company believes in
- *Standards and behaviors* – the policies and behaviors that underpin values and distinctive competence.[32]

As Campbell and Nash recognize, company missions serve many purposes – they are mechanisms for aligning the goals and values of employees with those of the company and for developing an emotional commitment by employees to the company. Most importantly, however, the mission statement is a means of communicating the fundamental and enduring themes of a company's strategy both internally and externally. In the words of British Airways CEO Colin Marshall: "A corporate mission is more than good intentions and fine ideas. It represents the framework for the entire business, the values which drive the company and the belief that the company has in itself and what it can achieve."[33]

Other executives are less enthusiastic. Some regard mission statements as a 1980s fad or as a constraint upon the managerial freedom of senior executives. A few months after taking over as CEO of IBM, Lou Gerstner commented, "The last thing that IBM needs is a mission statement."

(3) *Strategy as target*   Where the concept of strategy merges with that of *mission* and *vision* is in defining where the firm wants to be in the future. The purpose of such goal setting is not just to establish a direction to guide the formulation of strategy but also to set aspirations for the company. Hence, a further role for strategy is as a target for the organization. Hamel and Prahalad argue that a critical ingredient in the strategies of outstandingly successful companies is what they term "strategic intent" – an obsession with achieving global leadership.[34] Table 1.3 presents examples of strategic intent as articulated by top management.

Hamel and Prahalad extend their argument further. In a dynamic environment, the conventional approach to strategy formulation, which emphasizes the fit between internal resources and external opportunities, is not conducive to long-run competitiveness. Critical to the success of upstart companies such as CNN in television, Apple in computers, Yamaha in pianos, and Richard Branson's Virgin group in music, retailing, and air travel was a mismatch between resources and aspirations in which unreasonable ambition became the driving force for innovation, risk taking, and continuous improvement. In place of *strategic fit* and *resource allocation,* Hamel and Prahalad emphasize *stretch* and *resource leverage.*[35]

Table 1.3 Examples of
Strategic Intent

COMPANY	STRATEGIC INTENT
NASA Apollo Program	To put a man on the moon before the Soviets
Komatsu	To "Encircle Caterpillar"
Canon	To "Beat Xerox"
Toyota	To become a second Ford – a leader in automotive innovation
NEC	To achieve the convergence of "Computing and Communication"
Coca-Cola	To put a Coke within "arm's reach" of every consumer in the world

Source: Gary Hamel and C. K. Prahalad, "Strategic Intent," *Harvard Business Review* (May-June 1989).

The Role of Analysis in Strategy Formulation

Recognition of the multiplicity of purposes that a company's strategy fulfills – and, in particular, strategy's role in disseminating values, communicating purpose, and setting aspirations – raises further questions about the analytical approach to strategy. Ever since Abernathy and Hayes identified "modern management techniques" as instrumental in the American firm's declining international competitiveness in many sectors, approaches to management have been castigated for being static, conservative, risk-averse, inflexible, short term, and detrimental to innovation.[36]

My purpose in this book is not to defend conventional approaches to business strategy analysis but to do better. Management's approach to strategy must be dynamic, flexible, and innovatory. It must recognize the powerful role that values and goals play in organizations and the importance of the strategy process in facilitating communication and coordination. It must recognize the importance of intuition, tacit knowledge, and learning-by-doing in complementing more "scientific" analysis.

It is vital that we recognize the limitations of analysis in guiding strategic management. Unlike mathematics, chemistry, or even economics, strategic management lacks an agreed-upon, internally consistent, empirically validated body of theory. Although it employs theory and theoretical concepts, these are drawn mainly from longer established social and administrative sciences – mainly from economics, psychology, and organization theory – and principally on an ad hoc basis. Even as applied science, strategic management differs substantially from engineering and more technically oriented managerial disciplines such as finance and production management. The main feature of analytic techniques based upon scientific theory is their ability, once the appropriate data has been entered, to generate solutions to complex problems and to choose between alternatives on the basis of preselected criteria. For instance, linear programming can determine optimal production scheduling, discounted cash flow analysis can select between alternative investment projects, and sampling theory can determine the appropriate size and structure of a market research activity.

A major feature of the techniques that I will introduce in this book is that they do not provide solutions. Just as strategic decisions in our personal lives are not amenable to quantitative decision techniques (Should I get married? have children? change my career? move to a new location?), the same is true in business. There are simply too many variables to reduce strategy analysis to a programmed algorithm.

The purpose of strategy analysis is not to provide answers but to help us to understand the issues. Many of the analytic techniques introduced in the book are simply frameworks to assist us in identifying, classifying, and understanding the principal factors that impinge upon strategy decisions. Such frameworks are invaluable in coming to grips with the complexities of strategy decisions: the infinite complexity of the firm's environment and the tangle of people, resources, structures, and traditions that make up the business enterprise. In some instances, the most useful contribution may be in assisting us to make a start on the problem: by guiding us in the questions we need to answer and by providing a framework into which the information gathered can be fitted, we are in a superior position to a manager who relies exclusively upon experience and tacit knowledge. Finally, analytic frameworks and techniques can assist our flexibility as managers. The analysis in this book is general in its applicability; it is not specific to particular industries, companies, or situations. Hence, it can help increase our confidence and effectiveness in understanding and responding to new situations and new circumstances. By encouraging depth of understanding in fundamental issues concerning competitive advantage, customer needs, organizational capabilities, and the basis of competition, the concepts, frameworks, and techniques in this book will encourage rather than constrain innovation, flexibility, and opportunism.

Summary and Prospect

This chapter has covered a lot of ground. I have introduced the concept of strategy, explained its role in success, traced its development over time, and examined a number of ideas concerning its purposes and limitations.

The fundamental premise of this chapter is that strategy is an important determinant of success in most areas of human activity. In military conflict, sport, business, and in our individual careers, a good strategy can create success out of initial weakness. Successful strategies typically consist of four key ingredients:

- they are directed toward unambiguous long-term goals;
- they are based on insightful understanding of the external environment;
- they are based on intimate self-knowledge by the organization or individual of internal capabilities;
- they are implemented with resolution, coordination, and effective harnessing of the capabilities and commitment of all members of the organization.

This book is concerned with the use of systematic analysis in the formulation of winning strategies. In the next chapter, I will outline the basis for the analysis of strategy that will form the framework for the remainder of the book.

Notes

1 Sun Tzu, in *The Art of Strategy: A New Translation of Sun Tzu's Classic "The Art of War,"* trans. R. L. Wing (New York: Doubleday, 1988).

2 V. J. Varner and J. I. Alger, eds, *History of the Military Art: Notes for the Course* (West Point, NY: U.S. Military Academy, 1978); Sun Tzu, in Wing, *The Art of Strategy.*

3 Sun Tzu, *The Art of Strategy.*

4 Roger Evered, "So What Is Strategy?" *Long Range Planning* 16, no. 3 (June 1983): 57–72.

5 For a review of the concepts and principles of military strategy, see B. H. Liddell Hart, *Strategy* (New York: Praeger, 1968).

6 For an interesting and informed survey, see Barrie G. James, *Business Wargames* (Harmondsworth, U.K.: Penguin, 1985).

7 "Lanchester Market Structures: A Japanese Approach to the Analysis of Business Competition," *Strategic Management Journal* 7(1986): 189–200.

8 For an informative discussion of the links between military and business strategy, see Evered, "What Is Strategy?" 57–72.

9 J. Von Neumann and O. Morgenstern, *Theory of Games and Economic Behavior* (Princeton, NJ: Princeton University Press, 1944).

10 Thomas C. Schelling, *The Strategy of Conflict,* 2d ed. (Cambridge: Harvard University Press, 1980).

11 For a highly practical and accessible introduction to game theory, see A. K. Dixit and B. J. Nalebuff, *Thinking Strategically: The Competitive Edge in Business, Politics, and Everyday Life* (New York: W. W. Norton, 1991).

12 Frank F. Gilmore, *Formulation and Advocacy of Business Policy,* rev. ed. (Ithaca, NY: Cornell University Press, 1970), 16.

13 Igor Ansoff, *Corporate Strategy* (London: Penguin, 1985), 18.

14 John K. Galbraith, *The New Industrial State* (Harmondsworth, U.K.: Penguin, 1968).

15 Henry Mintzberg, *The Rise and Fall of Strategic Planning* (New York: Free Press, 1994). See also his *Harvard Business Review* article of the same title (January–February 1994): 107–14.

16 See, for example, Michael E. Porter, *Competitive Strategy* (New York: Free Press, 1980).

17 For an account of the conceptual and intellectual development of strategic management, see J.-C. Spender, "Business Policy and Strategy: A View of the Field, with Comments on Rumelt, Schendel and Teece (1991)," discussion paper, Graduate School of Management, Rutgers University, 1992.

18 Although game theory deals with "games against nature" involving strategy choices when the external environment comprises stochastic elements, such games and the strategies associated with them lack the appeal or importance of competitive games.

19 Bruce D. Henderson, *The Logic of Business Strategy* (Cambridge, MA: Ballinger, 1984), 31-6.

20 On the contribution of game theory to business strategy analysis, see Franklin M. Fisher, "Games Economists Play: A Noncooperative View," *RAND Journal of Economics* 20 (spring 1989): 113-24; and Colin F. Camerer, "Does Strategy Research Need Game Theory?" *Strategic Management Journal*, special issue (winter 1991): 137-52.

21 Bruce D. Henderson, "The Origin of Strategy," *Harvard Business Review* (November–December 1989): 139–43.

22 See Henry Mintzberg, "Of Strategies: Deliberate and Emergent," *Strategic Management Journal* 6 (1985): 257–72; and Mintzberg, *Mintzberg on Management: Inside Our Strange World of Organizations* (New York: Free Press, 1988).

23 Boston Consulting Group, *Strategy Alternatives for the British Motorcycle Industry* (London: Her Majesty's Stationery Office, 1975).

24 Richard T. Pascale, "Perspective on Strategy: The Real Story behind Honda's Success," *California Management Review* 26, no. 3 (spring 1984): 47–72.

25 H. Mintzberg, "Crafting Strategy," *Harvard Business Review* 65 (July–August 1987): 70.

26 Kathleen Eisenhardt and Mark Zbaracki, "Strategic Decision Making," *Strategic Management Journal*, special issue, 13 (winter 1992): 17–37.

27 Andrew M. Pettigrew, *The Awakening Giant: Continuity and Change at ICI* (Oxford: Basil Blackwell, 1985).

28 Elaine Romanelli and Michael Tushman, "Organizational Transformation as Punctuated Equilibrium," *Academy of Management Journal* 37 (1994): 1141–66.

29 Mintzberg, "Crafting Strategy," 64.

30 *Ibid*, 66.

31 Henry Mintzberg, "Rise and Fall," *Harvard Business Review*, 107–14.

32 Andrew Campbell and Laura L. Nash, *A Sense of Mission: Defining Direction for the Large Corporation* (Reading, MA: Addison-Wesley, 1992).

33 Colin Marshall, talk to Strategic Management Society, London, September 1992.

34 Gary Hamel and C. K. Prahalad, "Strategic Intent," *Harvard Business Review* (May–June 1989).

35 Gary Hamel and C. K. Prahalad, "Strategy as Stretch and Leverage," *Harvard Business Review* (March–April 1993): 75–84.

36 W.J. Abernathy and R.H. Hays, "Managing Our Way to Economic Decline," *Harvard Business Review* (July/August 1980): 67–77.

TWO

A Framework for Strategy Analysis

The strategic aim of a business is to earn a return on capital, and if in any particular case the return in the long run is not satisfactory, then the deficiency should be corrected or the activity abandoned for a more favorable one.

Alfred P. Sloan Jr., *My Years with General Motors*

Introduction and Objectives

The first chapter established what strategy is and what it can do for a company. In this chapter, I outline a framework for the analysis of strategy in which strategy is viewed as linking the firm to its external environment. In developing this framework, I make a critical assumption: that the primary goal of the firm is profit maximization – or, equivalently, maximizing shareholder value. An important part of this chapter will be concerned with the definition and measurement of profit.

Once strategy is defined as a quest for profitability our ability to formulate strategy on an analytical basis is greatly enhanced: strategy analysis depends critically upon the ability to diagnose the sources of profit (or *rent*) available to the firm.

By the time you have completed this chapter you will:

- possess a view of strategy as a linkage between the firm and its environment (this will form the fundamental framework for the subsequent analysis in this book);

- be familiar with different measures of profit including accounting profit, pure economic profit, and cash flow;
- be capable of applying the principles of shareholder value maximization to the valuation of companies, business units, and strategies;
- recognize the distinction between corporate strategy and business strategy.

A Framework for Business Strategy Analysis

In the introductory discussion of organizational success, I identified four ingredients of successful strategies:

- Clear goals
- Understanding of the external environment
- Appreciation of internal strengths and weaknesses
- Effective implementation

Within the context of the firm, we can examine these ingredients of a successful strategy by viewing business strategy as forming a link between the firm and its external environment (see figure 2.1).

The firm is a complex institution, but for analytic purposes it is useful to distinguish just three key characteristics:

- Its goals and values
- Its resources
- Its organizational structure and systems

The external environment of the firm is also complex: it comprises all external influences on the firm's decisions and performance including the economic, social, political, and technological factors. However, for most strategy decisions, the core of the firm's external environment is its *industry*, which is defined by the firm's relationships with customers, competitors, and suppliers.

The task of business strategy, then, is to determine how the firm will deploy its resources within its environment and so satisfy its long-term goals and how it will organize itself to implement that strategy.

Figure 2.1 Strategy: The Link between the Firm and Its Environment

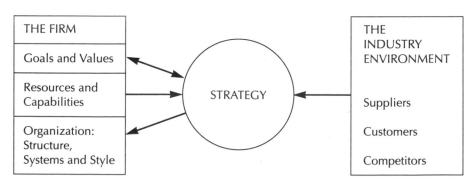

Strategic fit

Figure 2.1 illustrates the concept of strategic fit. For a strategy to be successful, it must be consistent with the firm's goals and values, with its external environment, with its resources and capabilities, and with its organization and systems. Let us examine these four aspects of strategic fit in a little more detail.

Consistency with goals and values   In developing strategy analysis, my primary assumption will be that the firm's principal responsibility is profitability. At the same time, all companies possess broader organizational goals and values that are integral to these companies' sense of identity and purpose and that augment, even transcend, the fundamental requirement of profitability. Such goals and values are reflected in companies' strategies, and, as we observed in the previous chapter, an important role of strategy is communicating goals in order to establish strategic intent and challenge the organization to stretch its performance. Linking profit objectives to the broader pursuit of organizational purpose may facilitate long-run profit performance. Establishing goals such as technological leadership within a particular industry, unmatched product quality, and the creation of a safe and satisfying working environment in which employees are offered unparalleled opportunities for skill enhancement and self-development can help operationalize profit goals by defining strategic intent and can inspire much greater commitment and effort from employees. If individual human beings are ultimately concerned more with the pursuit of meaning in their lives than with material rewards, then organizations that can help instill a sense of purpose within their employees will be at an advantage over those that do not. An important role of a *mission statement* is to articulate the linkage between a company's strategy and its underlying values.

For the U.S. discount retailer Wal-Mart and the British retailer Marks & Spencer, a clear sense of values has provided not only a raison d'être for the companies that employees can identify with but also a consistency of strategy over the long term. During Apple Computer's early development, Steve Jobs's vision of "one person – one computer" provided a similarly unifying theme. At Body Shop, Inc., the enthusiasm and loyalty of customers and the zeal of employees and franchisees is intimately dependent upon a strategy built upon the principles of environmental and social responsibility espoused by the founder, Anita Roddick. McDonald's ability to sell 60 billion hamburgers in 86 countries and in doing so make huge profits both for itself and its franchisees cannot be explained by reference just to low costs, quality control, or advertising. The organization is driven not by profit alone nor by the desire only to sell hamburgers but by a philosophy that transcends social class and national culture and is enshrined in the values of "quality, consistency, cleanliness, and value."

Consistency with the industry environment   Industries differ according to the nature of customer requirements, the characteristics of the product, and competitive structure. These factors determine the sources of competitive advantage in an industry. For a strategy to lead to success, it must exploit some opportunity for competitive advantage that exists within the industry. Tailoring strategy to industry conditions requires an intimate knowledge and understanding of that industry. Philip Morris's divestment of Seven-Up in 1987 followed several years during which business strategies that had proven so successful in cigarettes and beer failed to enhance the competitive position of Seven-Up – largely because the competitive structure of the market was so different from that of cigarettes and beer. American Express's difficulties in managing Shearson Lehman stemmed in part from a failure to understand the conditions for success in investment banking. Very different strategies may be appropriate to different segments within the same industry. The market for apparel is highly segmented, with a wide diversity of customer requirements and competitive conditions. In knitted goods, Fruit of the Loom exploits the cost efficiencies of the highly mechanized production of long runs of fairly standard T-shirts and sweatshirts; Benetton achieves highly flexible, fast-response production of a wide range of fashion-oriented knitwear products; and the British knitwear manufacturer Dawson International produces traditionally styled, high-quality knitwear for the world market.

Fit between strategy and the business environment also requires that strategy be adjusted in response to (or, preferably, in anticipation of) external change. The painful restructuring by most of the world's major oil companies during 1986-88 was a delayed response to changes in the industry environment that had occurred over the previous ten years or more. IBM's woes of the early 1990s reflect a strategy that was slow to adjust to the changing competitive conditions of the world's computer market.

Consistency with resources and capabilities   Strategy decisions are investment decisions involving the long-term commitment of resources. The resource demands of a strategy must be consistent with the resource availability of the firm in terms of the *amount* and the *types* of resources and capabilities. Some of the most spectacular corporate failures are the result of a mismatch between the requirements of strategy and the availability of resources and capabilities within the firm. At the most basic level, the firm's financial resources must be capable of meeting the investment requirements of the strategy. Some of the most spectacular failures of diversification strategy, such as Exxon's move into computers and office automation, have been due to the diversifying firm not having the right blend of capabilities to develop its new venture. Different stages of a firm's development are likely to require different strategies with different balances of resources and capabilities. Intel began with a strong core of capabilities in electronic technology and semiconductor design. As the company has grown, it has become increasingly dependent upon manufacturing and marketing capabilities.

Consistency with organization and systems   Successful implementation of a strategy also requires that organization and systems are appropriate to the strategy being pursued. In the early 1920s, General Motors adopted a multidivisional structure in order to support its strategy of a number of different model ranges, each targeted at a different segment of the car market. During the 1980s, a shift in strategy toward quality, cost efficiency, technological progressiveness, and responsiveness to market demand resulted in the amalgamation of most of these divisions, the elimination of many layers of corporate hierarchy, and the creation of multifunctional teams to promote quality and accelerate new product development.

In general, different management systems are appropriate to different types of business strategy. Companies that seek efficiency in the production of standardized products, such as railroad companies, hamburger chains, or delivery companies, are likely to favor mechanistic structures with relatively bureaucratic management systems. Alternatively, companies pursuing technological leadership and rapid response to change are likely to favor organic structures with less formality and a lack of rigid control mechanisms.

Internal consistency   Finally, a strategy must be internally consistent. Functional strategies must be consistent with business strategy and the business strategies of the individual business units must be consistent with the corporate strategy of the enterprise as a whole. Achieving such consistency is no easy matter. Consistency between functional strategies requires overcoming the propensity for functional specialists to optimize locally. Bruce Henderson, the founder of the Boston Consulting Group, has observed that "Every production man's dream is a factory that always runs at capacity making a single product that requires no change. . . . every salesman would like to give every customer whatever he wants immediately."[1]

Attaining consistency of objectives and decisions between the various departments, units, and members of the corporation may be an important function of strategy. While the emphasis of this book is on the *external* role of strategy through the creation of competitive advantage in the firm's industry, strategy may also fulfill an important *internal* role in so far as strategy formulation provides a mechanism for reconciling divergent goals and plans within the organization.

Strategy as a Quest for Profit

Profitability as the underlying goal of the firm

The goals of the firm will reflect the values and interests of the individuals who make up the firm and who play a role in its decisions. The "stakeholder" view of the firm sees firms as a coalition of interest groups including shareholders (whose goal is profit), top management (whose goals include salary, perks, prestige, and power), and employees (who are interested in their pay, working conditions, and job security). External stakeholders such as customers, suppliers, and government may also play a role. Even within each stakeholder group, diversity of goals is likely. For instance, managers tend to identify with the interests of their particular division or functional department. Cyert and March view the firm as a coalition in which different operational goals are associated with different functional interests (sales and marketing would seek increases in sales revenue and market share, production would pursue goals related to the level and stability of output).[2]

While strategies can be formulated by taking explicit account of multiple goals, the need to establish priorities and trade-offs results in excessive complication.[3] To avoid this complexity, I make the simplifying, yet realistic, assumption that business enterprises pursue a single dominant objective – *profit*. The case for the pursuit of profit as the primary goal for firms is supported by three observations:

1   The primary motivation for the owners of companies is profit because profit forms the income of these individuals. Although shareholders do not formulate the strategies of public corporations and their control over managers is limited, in Britain, Canada, the United States, and several other countries, the directors of public corporations are legally obliged to operate in the interests of their shareholders.

2   While different stakeholders within the firm are likely to favor different goals, increasing pressure of competition – international competition in particular – has caused divergent interests to coverage. The underlying common interest of all stakeholders is in the firm's survival. Survival requires that, over the long term, the firm earns a rate of profit that covers its cost of capital. During the 1980s, decreasing numbers of business firms have had the luxury of being able to diverge substantially from the goal of long-run profit maximization imposed by the need for survival. During 1991 and 1992, almost half of the top 50 members of the Fortune 500 failed to earn a return on equity that exceeded their cost of equity.

3   Developments in financial markets and the "market for corporate control" over the last decade and a half have limited top management's freedom to pursue goals that conflict with profit maximization. Leveraged buyouts (LBOs), more active institutional investors, and the trend toward divestment and "back to basics" have all resulted in the top management of public corporations becoming more vulnerable. The effect of such vulnerability is to make them more attentive to the stock market price of their shares and to the earnings that determine share prices.

The assumption that the purpose of strategy is to pursue profit over the long term greatly simplifies strategy analysis. At the same time, it does not succeed in eliminating ambiguity. What is the firm to maximize: total profit, margin on sales, return on equity, or return on invested capital? Over what time period? With what kind of adjustment for risk? And what is profit anyway: are we concerned with accounting profit, cash flow, or economic rent?

Problems of defining and measuring profit

The ambiguity of profit maximization is apparent once we consider the actual profit performance of companies. Table 2.1 considers the performance of companies drawn from the Fortune 500.

Several observations can be drawn from the table 2.1:

1 Does profit maximization mean maximizing *total profit* or *rate of profit*? If the latter, are we concerned with profit as a ratio to sales (return on sales), total assets (return on assets), or shareholders' equity (return on equity)? As an objective, each will lead to perverse results. The instruction to "maximize total profit" is likely to encourage investment in activities that are profitable but where the return falls below the cost of capital. Maximizing the rate of profit will encourage the firm to divest assets to the point where it is reduced to a residue of a few exceptionally profitable activities.

2 Whatever measure of profitability is chosen, the specification of time period is critical. The instruction to "maximize next year's profit" will lead to a very different strategy than the instruction to "maximize profit over the next ten years."

3 The measurement of profit. Accounting profit is defined by the accounting principles under which a company's financial statements are drawn up. When Daimler-Benz obtained a listing on the New York Stock Exchange in September 1993, the recalculation of its net income on the basis of U.S. accounting principles resulted in a sizable profit (under German accounting conventions) becoming a loss. Different rules with regard to the treatment of inflation, taxation, investment, capital gains and losses, exchange rate changes, and unusual items, produce wide variations in net profit. They also introduce discretion over the profits that a firm reports.[4]

	Return on sales		Return on assets		Return on equity		Return to stockholders	
	%	Rank	%	Rank	%	Rank	%	Rank
General Motors	1.8	296	1.3	326	44.1	9	73.2	27
Ford	2.3	272	1.3	330	16.2	114	55.0	48
Exxon	5.4	152	6.3	145	15.0	140	7.9	239
IBM	(12.9)	461	(10.0)	451	(41.0)	434	15.6	183
General Electric	7.1	87	1.7	314	16.7	107	26.0	131
Mobil	3.7	204	5.1	187	12.7	181	31.0	118
Philip Morris	6.1	114	6.0	152	26.6	30	(24.2)	400
Chrysler	(5.9)	431	(5.8)	427	(37.3)	429	68.7	35

Table 2.1 Profitability of the leading members of the *Fortune 500*, 1993

Identifying economic profit

Accounting profits do not correspond to economists' notions of profit as a pure surplus. To distinguish "pure" or "economic" profit from conventional accounting notions of profit, economists and business strategists use the term *"rent"* or *"economic rent"* to refer to income that is a surplus over and above the costs of all the inputs required for production. The principal difference between economic profit (or rent) and accounting profit is that accounting profit (or net income) comprises both economic profit and the cost of the equity capital employed by the firm.

The simplest approach to measuring the economic profit generated by a business is to take operating profit net of tax and to deduct the cost of all the capital used in the business – not only the interest paid on debt but also the cost of equity. This measure of profit is called *added value* by John Kay and *economic value added* by the New York consulting company Stern Stewart & Company.[5] Kay defines *added value* as "the difference between the (comprehensively accounted) value of a firm's output and the (comprehensively accounted) cost of the firm's inputs. In this specific sense, adding value is both the proper motivation of corporate activity and the measure of its achievement."[6]

A number of companies – among them AT&T, CSX, Briggs & Stratton, Quaker Oats, and Coca-Cola – report that, by adopting economic profit as a performance guide, they have greatly increased the efficiency with which they deploy capital within their businesses, with substantial gains in stock market performance. Exhibit 2.1 offers some examples.

Maximizing shareholder value

The DCF approach to shareholder value   While the notion of economic profit avoids many of the problems inherent in accounting profit, it does not address the problem of the time period over which profits are to be maximized. Resolution of this problem requires that future profits are capitalized and that the firm maximizes its present value. The principles of discounted cash flow (DCF) analysis that firms apply to their individual investment projects can also be applied to the firm as a whole. Strategies can then be selected that maximize the net present value of the firm.

The appeal of maximizing the net present value of the firm's cash flows is that such maximization corresponds to the firm's maximization of its stock market valuation and hence maximizes the wealth of its shareholders. By maximizing profits, the firm can thereby simultaneously *maximize shareholder value*. Maximization of shareholder value has received wide support as the appropriate goal of the firm and the primary yardstick for measuring performance.

If strategy decisions are to be guided by the interests of shareholders, then firms should seek to maximize shareholders' wealth by maximizing

Exhibit 2.1   Applying Economic Value Added (EVA)

To show how EVA or pure profit is calculated, take the example of Anheuser-Busch:

		$ millions
	Operating profit	1,756
less	Taxes	617
less	Cost of capital	904*
	Economic Value Added	235

*Cost of equity 14.3 percent, cost of debt 5.2 percent, weighted average cost of capital 11.3 percent, total capital $8.0 billion.

The appropriate cost of capital is the *opportunity cost of capital* – the return that the capital could earn in an alternative use. In the case of equity, this would be the total return to a portfolio of stocks with a similar risk to that of the company under consideration.

Examples of the application of EVA include the following:

AT&T   To focus business managers on the need to add value, CEO Robert Allen encouraged the six groups within AT&T to establish each of its businesses as a profit center with its own balance sheet. For example, the long distance services group has 40 business units. According to James Meenan, chief financial officer of the group, "The effect is staggering. 'Good' is no longer a positive operating earnings. It's only when you beat the cost of capital." The approach had a particularly dramatic effect on those businesses that suddenly found that, under the new rules, they had been posting negative profitability for years.

Coca-Cola   CEO Roberto Goizueto introduced EVA to Coca-Cola in 1987. Its impact has been to encourage:

1   divestment of diversified businesses including pasta, wine, instant tea, plastic cutlery, and desalination equipment. All posted returns that failed to cover their cost of capital.
2   increased leverage. Recognition that the cost of equity far exceeded that of debt encouraged increased borrowing with the result that average cost of capital fell from 16 to 12 percent.
3   increased efficiency of capital utilization in 11 of Coca-Cola's businesses. For example, concentrate production was focused upon 40 plants compared with 52 in 1982.

Source: Shawn Tully, "The Real Key to Creating Wealth," *Fortune*, September 20, 1993, 38–50.

the *market value of their shares*. The market price of a company's shares is determined in the same way as any other financial asset: it is the discounted value of the returns. Although investment analysts have conventionally concentrated upon accounting profits ("earnings per share") as the appropriate return to shareholders for valuing shares, a more satisfactory measure of returns is net cash flow. Thus, the market value of a company's equity (*E*) is the sum of net cash flow (*C*) of the company in each year t, discounted at the company's cost of equity capital (k_E):

$$E = \sum_t \frac{C_t}{(1 + k_E)^t}$$

Thus, valuing a firm involves the same DCF analysis that is used to value an investment project. As with DCF analysis of investment projects, the appropriate measure of profitability is *net cash flow*. That is:

Net income + Depreciation & Other non-cash expenses – Increase in working capital – Capital expenditures = Net cash flow.

The use of DCF analysis to value a firm or an individual business is explained in the appendix to this chapter.

Alternative measures of cash flow   In the same way that there are numerous measures of profit, there are alternative approaches to measuring cash flow. Whether choosing a measure of profitability or cash flow, the basis of choice is the same: the measure chosen depends upon the type of analysis being used. Two commonly used measures of cash flow are the following:

1   *Operating Cash Flow* = Operating earnings before interest and tax + Depreciation. This measure is used for analyzing acquisitions and LBOs as an indicator of the maximum potential cash flow yield from a business. The assumption is that interest, tax, and investment expenditure can be adjusted by new management in order to maximize the net cash flow generated by a given operating cash flow.
2   *Free Cash Flow* is the cash flow available to the firm after dividends and capital expenditures necessary for the continued survival of the firm have been undertaken:

Free cash flow = Net income + Depreciation & Other non-cash expenses – Increase in working capital – Replacement capital expenditures – Dividends

Michael Jensen, a primary advocate of agency theory, views the conflict between management and corporate raiders and LBO specialists as a battle for the ownership of free cash flow. While management prefers to minimize dividends in order to finance growth and discretionary projects such as luxurious head office buildings, shareholders such as Carl Icahn, Laurence Tisch, and Warren Buffett and LBO partners such as Kohlberg Kravis Roberts & Company and Clayton and Dubilier have sought to divert free cash flow to shareholders.[7]

Valuing strategies   In companies such as PepsiCo, shareholder value analysis has been refined to a performance criterion that acts as both a target and a comprehensive guideline for corporate monitoring and control of strategies and investment proposals among business units.[8] A strength of the shareholder value approach is its consistency. The same methodology of DCF analysis and the same objective of shareholder value maximization is used to evaluate individual investment projects, to evaluate alternative business strategies, and to value the firm as whole. The main steps in applying shareholder value analysis to appraising business strategies involve:

- identifying strategy alternatives (the simplest approach is to compare the current strategy with the preferred alternative strategy);
- estimating the cash flows and cost of capital associated with each strategy;
- selecting the strategy that generates the highest net present value.

Compared to the appraisal of individual investment projects, special problems arise from DCF analysis of strategies. While individual investment projects have finite lives, the firm (or the business unit) is much longer living, and strategies must also be chosen for the long term. Hence, forecasting cash flows over long periods of time gives rise to particular difficulties. The appendix to this chapter discusses in more detail the forecasting of cash flows and the choice of discount rates.

Some of the most useful applications of shareholder value analysis are in relation to corporate strategy decisions involving acquisition, diversification, and divestment. The critical issue here is estimating whether individual business units add positive or negative value to the firm as a whole. We shall return to this issue in chapter 15.

Problems of shareholder value maximization

Strategies as options   Valuation of individual business units within a company is an easier task than the valuation of alternative business strategies. Valuation of business strategy alternatives in terms of net cash flows discounted at an appropriate cost of capital is difficult because most strategies involve a stream of resource-allocation decisions over time in which subsequent investment decisions are contingent upon the performance and information generated by initial investments. As we have already noted, in an increasingly turbulent environment, strategy is less a predetermined program of investment plans and more a positioning of the firm to permit it to take advantage of profitable investment opportunities as they arise. Within this view of strategy, investments in early stages of projects are essentially *options* – they offer the firm the option of further investments in later stages of the projects. For example, investments in research and development (R&D) typically do not offer direct returns; their value is in the option to invest in new products and processes that may arise from the R&D. DCF does not accurately value investments where there is a significant option value. Conversely, standard option pricing models are applicable only to the specifics of the option contracts offered on the world's major securities markets. In order to assess the value of strategic options it is necessary to specify the successive stages of the investment process, to identify the alternatives available at each stage, and to specify the possible outcomes together with their probabilities.[9]

Merck & Company has been at the forefront of applying option theory to analyze investments in R&D. Merck's CFO, Judy Lewent, observes that "When you make an initial investment in a research project you are paying an entry fee for a right, but you are not obligated to continue that research at a later stage."[10] Merck's analysis is based upon the formula used to value stock options.

Short-term bias A criticism of the shareholder value approach is that a focus on the market value of a company's shares is likely to divert management's attention away from the critical issues involved in managing for long-run competitiveness and more toward managing the stock market's perceptions of a company. To the extent that the stock market is myopic and subject to "herd" behavior, concern with maximizing stock market value leads to an emphasis on short-term profit to the detriment of long-term profit.[11] The MIT Commission on Industrial Productivity has argued that U.S. firms' preoccupation with short-term payoffs has resulted in a low level of capital investment, inadequate investment in R&D, and a willingness to cede markets to aggressive Asian competitors.[12] A recent study of U.S. corporate investment by Michael Porter and his colleagues at Harvard University also found evidence of short-termism in the form of comparatively low rates of overall investment and a bias against investment in intangible assets (such as knowledge and skills) and long-term projects.[13] However, the evidence is not all one way. A number of studies have found no bias by the stock market toward short-term profits or short-term investments by companies. The main conclusion to be drawn is that for management to operate in the interests of shareholders does not require management of the company's stock market price, but the creation of the cash flows will ultimately determine the price of the shares.

Some practical rules of thumb

Establishing profitability as the primary long-run goal for the firm is uncontroversial. The difficulties arise in specifying the appropriate measure of profit to be used as a performance guide and in operationalizing this measure within formal analysis. Fortunately, however, different measures of profit tend to be highly correlated, taking one year with another. Which measure of profit is used is less important than recognizing the limitations and biases inherent in the measure employed. While most academic debate has emphasized the dangers of practical profit measures that diverge from the theoretically optimum, John Kay has concentrated upon identifying the circumstances under which accounting measures of profit approximate economic profit.[14] The longer the time period over which profits are measured, the more different measures of return tend to converge. Over the life of the firm, the net present value of net cash flows from operation, economic profit based upon historic cost accounting profit, economic profit based upon replacement cost measures, and excess returns to shareholders are the same.[15]

For certain types of strategic decisions, most notably those concerned with acquiring and divesting businesses and assets, precise calculation of the impact of strategic alternatives on shareholder value is critical. However, most business strategy decisions are concerned with building positions of sustainable competitive advantage where future cash flows associated with these strategic initiatives are impossible to forecast with any accuracy. In such circumstances, precise and sophisticated financial analysis is likely to be infeasible and unnecessary. In these circumstances, a more useful approach is to establish two general criteria for guiding strategic decisions:

- on existing resources, the firm should seek to maximize the after-tax rate of return that it earns;
- on new investment, the firm should seek an after-tax rate of return that exceeds its cost of capital.

Sources of Profit and the Distinction Between Corporate and Business Strategy

If we accept that the fundamental goal of the firm is to earn a return on its capital that exceeds the cost of its capital, what determines the ability of the firm to earn such a rate of return? There are two routes. First, the firm may locate in an industry where favorable industry conditions result in the industry earning a rate of return above the competitive level. Second, the firm may attain a position of advantage vis-à-vis its competitors within an industry that allows it to earn a return in excess of the industry average.

These two sources of superior performance define the two basic levels of strategy within an enterprise: *corporate strategy* and *business strategy*. Corporate strategy defines the scope of the firm in terms of the industries and markets in which it competes. Corporate strategy decisions include investment in diversification, vertical integration, acquisitions, and new ventures; the allocation of resources between the different businesses of the firm; and divestments.

Business strategy is concerned with how the firm competes within a particular industry or market. If the firm is to win, or even to survive, within an industry, it must adopt a strategy that establishes a competitive advantage over its rivals. Hence, this area of strategy is also referred

Figure 2.2 The
Sources of Superior
Profitability

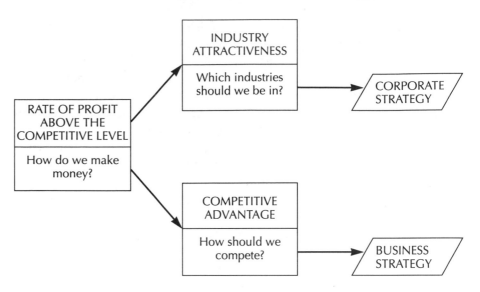

to as *competitive strategy*. Using slightly different terminology, Bourgeois has referred to corporate strategy as the task of *domain selection*
and business strategy as the task of *domain navigation*.[16]

The distinction between corporate and business strategy and their
linkage to the two basic sources of profitability may be expressed in
even simpler terms. The purpose and the content of a firm's strategy is
defined by the answer to a single question:

How can the firm make money?

This question can be elaborated into two further questions:

What business or businesses should we be in?

and, within each business,

How should we compete?

The answer to the first question describes the *corporate strategy* of the
company; the answer to the second describes the primary themes of
business strategy.

While business strategy defines the overall approach of the firm to
achieving a competitive advantage that is sustainable over time, the
detailed deployment of resources at the operational level is the concern
of *functional strategies*. This third level of strategy constitutes policies
toward production, R&D, marketing, personnel, and finance at the
industry or at the product level.

In the single-business firm, there is no distinction between corporate
and business strategy, and in the small, entrepreneurial firm there is
unlikely to be any organizational separation of business and functional

strategies or, for that matter, of strategic and operating decisions. In the larger corporation, the three levels of strategy are typically separated. Corporate strategy is formulated and implemented at the corporate head office. Business strategy is typically formulated jointly by corporate and business-unit management and is implemented at business-unit level. Functional strategies are, for the most part, dictated by business strategies, but their elaboration and implementation is primarily the responsibility of the functional departments. Figure 2.3 depicts the three levels of strategy and their location within the typical organizational structure of the large firm.

For the greater part of this book my emphasis will be on business rather than corporate strategy. This is justified by my conviction that the key to successful performance is establishing competitive advantage. A consequence of the increasing intensity of competition is that few industries exist where satisfactory profitability is assured for all participants, hence competitive advantage is a prerequisite for long-term profitability. A second reason is that in developing firms, issues of business strategy generally precede those of corporate strategy. Once the firm is established, its survival and success is dependent upon building competitive advantage in a single market. Only when it is successful in one product market can it contemplate diversification into other areas. Hence, issues of diversification and the allocation of resources between different business activities are typically the concern of mature organizations that have already achieved access as specialist enterprises. Even for the diversified corporation, business strategy must take primacy over corporate strategy: issues of resource allocation between different activities are redundant if the firm is unable to establish competitive advantage in any of its activities.

Summary and Conclusions

In developing our strategy analysis, our framework will be, for most purposes, even simpler than that shown in figure 2.1. The analysis that

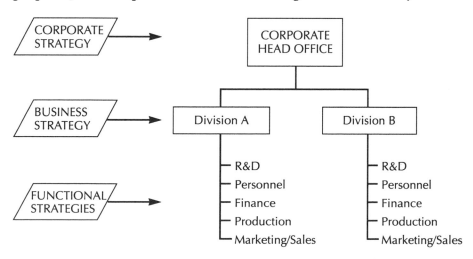

Figure 2.3 Levels of Strategy

I will be developing in this book is mainly concerned with the role of strategy in linking the firms' resources with its environment. Limited attention is given to the goals and values of the firm: these are matters for managers to identify rather than to analyze, and, in any event, I have already assumed the basic goal of the firm to be the pursuit of profit.

Consequently, we will concentrate upon two of the above ingredients of successful strategies: analysis of the external environment and analysis of internal capabilities. Note that this approach corresponds closely to the well-known "SWOT" analysis of strategy, where strategy is formulated in relation to four sets of considerations: Strengths, Weaknesses, Opportunities, and Threats. While strengths and weaknesses relate to the resources and capabilities of the firm, opportunities and threats relate to the external environment. The problem with SWOT analysis is that:

1   distinguishing between strengths and weaknesses is difficult. Is Michael Eisner a strength or weakness for Walt Disney Company? As the architect of Disney's turnaround between 1986 and 1992 he is a strength. As a long-serving CEO with serious health problems and having a new set of corporate challenges, he is a weakness.

2   distinguishing between opportunities and threats is similarly difficult. Is the advent of "information superhighways" a threat or an opportunity for established telephone companies? Obviously, it is both.

The analysis in this book hence concentrates upon just two sets of factors: the external environment of the firm and the internal environment of the firm (resources and capabilities). The purpose of strategy analysis is to *understand* the critical features of the internal and external environments of the firm, not to make dubious classifications between strengths and weaknesses and opportunities and threats.

Central to this book's analysis of strategy is the assumption that the underlying goal of the business enterprise is profit. Hence, my approach rests heavily upon identifying the sources of profitability available to the firm. The fundamental distinction between industry attractiveness and competitive advantage as sources of superior profitability available to the firm define the two main areas of strategy: corporate strategy and business strategy.

The two ingredients of our strategy analysis – environmental analysis and resource analysis – form the basis of both corporate and business strategy decisions. I will consider, first, the analysis of the industry environment and then the analysis of resources and capabilities. I will then bring these together to consider the nature and determinants of competitive advantage. Figure 2.4 sets out the framework of the book.

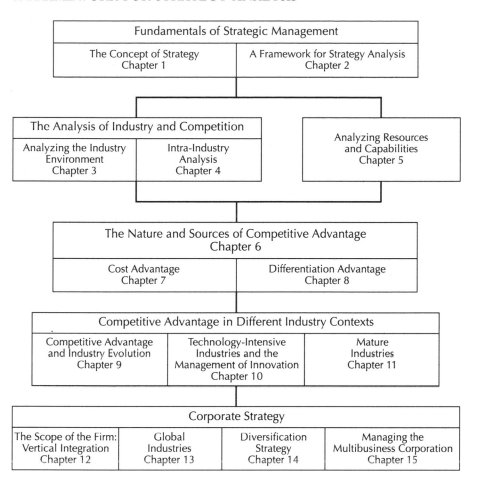

Figure 2.4 Strategy Analysis: The Framework of the Book

Appendix: Valuing Companies and Businesses

The net present value of a company or business unit (V) is the net cash flow before financing costs of capital employed (C) in each period t discounted at the cost of capital (k):

$$V = \sum_t \frac{C_t}{(1 + k)^t}$$

Using this basic formula involves two problems: first, forecasting cash flows in each period over the lifetime of the firm; second, estimating the appropriate cost of capital.

The problem of forecasting cash flows a long way into the future can be simplified in several ways. If the firm is in a static business situation and is expected to earn a constant cash flow into perpetuity, then:

$$V = \frac{C}{k}$$

In such a situation, the firm's invested capital is constant, hence depreciation is equal to capital investment, and it is possible to express our valuation formula in terms of accounting profits.

$$V = \frac{C}{k} = \frac{EBIT - Tax}{k} = \frac{I.r}{k}$$

Where $EBIT$ is earnings before interest and tax,
I is invested capital,

r is after-tax, preinterest return on invested capital $= \dfrac{EBIT - Tax}{I}$

If cash flows are growing at a constant rate g into infinity, then:

$$V = \frac{C}{k - g}$$

Since $C = EBIT - Tax + Depreciation - Replacement$ investment expenditure $-$ New investment expenditure
and, Replacement investment expenditure = Depreciation
and, New investment expenditure = $g.I$
then:

$$V = \frac{I(r - g)}{k - g}$$

In general, however, it is not possible to make any reliable forecast of cash flows beyond a certain valuation horizon. Hence, a more practical approach to valuing the firm may be to estimate the cash flows up to the valuation horizon (H), then to calculate the value of the firm at time H (V_H), which is called the "horizon value" or "continuing value":

$$V = C_0 + \frac{C_1}{1 + k} + \frac{C_2}{(1 + k)^2} + \quad \cdots \quad \frac{C_H}{(1 + k)^H} + \frac{V_H}{(1 + k)^H}$$

        Present value of cash   Present value of
        flows   horizon value

Horizon values can be calculated in different ways. Two simple alternatives are:

1 *Book value.* If the firm is to be wound up at the end of period H or if it is anticipated that returns will fall to a level that just covers the firm's cost of capital, then it is reasonable to assume that the book value of the firm's capital is a reasonable indicator of value at time H.
2 *Zero growth after period.* If cash flows become constant after period, then the present value of the horizon value is:

$$\frac{C_H}{k(1 + k)^H}$$

Even within a finite horizon period, estimating cash flow in each period can be difficult, and it may be simpler to apply a forecast growth rate g to current returns. Thus, if a firm at a constant rate g over H years at which time its value is equal to its book value, then:

$$V = \frac{I(r - g)}{k - g}\left[1 - \left(\frac{1 + g}{1 + k}\right)^H\right] + \frac{I(1 + g)^H}{(1 + k)^H}$$

The appropriate cost of capital to a firm or to a business unit is the opportunity cost of capital, which is the rate of return that the providers of capital could earn on alternative investments of similar risk. The cost of capital to the firm is the *weighted average cost of capital* (k), which is the weighted average of the cost of equity (k_E) and cost of debt (k_D):

$$k = (1 - T)\, L\, k_D + (1 - L)\, k_E$$

Where T is the tax rate on corporate profits and L is leverage:

$$L = \frac{D}{D + E}$$

The cost of debt financing is reduced relative to equity financing by the fact that interest on debt is tax deductible whereas dividends on stock are not. However, this does not imply that debt financing is always preferable to equity financing. As leverage increases, the cost of debt rises due to the increasing risk of bankruptcy, while the cost of equity also rises due to increasing cyclicality of return on equity.

The cost of equity is determined by two factors: the risk-free rate of interest (i) and the risk premium for the firm or for the individual business. The capital asset pricing model predicts that:

$$k_E = i + \beta(R_m - i)$$

Where β is the *beta coefficient* or *coefficient of systematic risk* for the firm or for the business unit, while R_m is the return on the stock market as a whole.[18]

Notes

1   Bruce D. Henderson, *The Logic of Business Strategy* (New York: Ballinger, 1984), 26–7.

2 R. Cyert and J. March, *A Behavioral Theory of the Firm* (Englewood Cliffs, NJ: Prentice-Hall, 1964).

3 See Kenneth R. MacCrimmon, "An Overview of Multiple Objective Decision Making," in *Multiple Criteria Decision Making*, ed. J. L. Cochrane and M. Zeleny (Columbia, SC: University of South Carolina Press, 1973).

4 For discussion of the problems of accounting-based measures of profitability see F. M. Fisher and J. J. McGowan, "On the Misuse of Accounting Rates of Return to Infer Monopoly Profit," *American Economic Review* 73 (1983): 82–7. For a more conciliatory view, see John Kay and Colin Meyer, "On the Application of Accounting Rates of Return," *Economic Journal* 96 (1986): 199–207.

5 John Kay, *Foundations of Corporate Success: How Corporate Strategies Add Value* (Oxford: Oxford University Press, 1993); Shawn Tully, "The Real Key to Creating Wealth," *Fortune*, September 20, 1993, 38–50.

6 Kay, Foundations of Corporate Success, 19.

7 Michael C. Jensen, *Organizational Change and the Market for Corporate Control* (Cambridge, MA: Basil Blackwell, 1990); Michael C. Jensen, "Eclipse of the Public Corporation," Harvard Business Review (September-October 1989): 61–84.

8 The development of the "shareholder value" approach to strategy analysis is closely associated with Alfred Rappaport. See Rappaport, *Creating Shareholder Value: The New Standard for Business Performance* (New York: Free Press, 1986); also Rappaport, "Selecting Strategies that Create Shareholder Value," *Harvard Business Review* (May-June 1981): 139–49; Rappaport, "Linking Competitive Strategy and Shareholder Value Analysis," Journal of Business Strategy (spring 1987): 58–67, Enrique R. Arzac, "Do Your Business Units Create Shareholder Value?" Harvard Business Review (January-February 1986): 121–6; and Rappaport, "CFO's and Strategists: Forging a Common Framework," *Harvard Business Review* (May-June 1992): 84–91.

9 Option pricing theory is outlined in R. A. Brealey and S. C. Myers, *Principles of Corporate Finance*, 3d ed. (New York: McGraw-Hill, 1988), chapters 20 and 21. For a discussion of option valuation approaches to strategic investments, see Stewart C. Myers, "Finance Theory and Financial Strategy," *Interfaces* 14 (January-February 1984) 134–6; and Tom Copeland, Tim Koller, and Jack Murrin, *Valuation: Measuring and Managing the Value of Companies* (New York: John Wiley, 1990), chapter 12. The application of option theory to strategic management is discussed by E. H. Bowman and D. Hurry, "Strategy through the Option Lens: An Integrated View of Resource Investments and the Incremental-Choice Process," *Academy of Management Review* 18, no. 4 (1993): 760–82.

10 Nancy Nichols, "Scientific Management at Merck: An Interview with CFO Judy Lewent," *Harvard Business Review* (January-February 1994): 89–105.

11 Michael T. Jacobs, *Short-Term America* (Boston: Harvard Business School Press, 1991).

12 The MIT Commission on Industrial Productivity, *Made in America* (Cambridge: MIT Press, 1989), chapter 4.

13 Michael E. Porter, "Capital Disadvantage: America's Failing Capital

Investment System," *Harvard Business Review* (September-October 1992): 65–82.

14 John A. Kay, "Accountants, Too, Could Be Happy in a Golden Age: The Accountant's Rate of Profit and the Internal Rate of Return," *Oxford Economic Papers* 28 (1976): 447–60; and John A. Kay and Colin Meyer, "On the Application of Accounting Rates of Return," *Economic Journal* 96 (1986): 199–207.

15 John Kay, *Foundations of Corporate Success: How Business Strategies Create Value* (Oxford: Oxford University Press, 1993), 207.

16 L. J. Bourgeois, "Strategy and the Environment: A Conceptual Integration," *Academy of Management Review* 5 (1980): 25–39.

17 Net cash flow was defined on p. 38, with the exception that interest payments on the firm's debt are included. The difference arises from the fact that in the appendix we are measuring the value of the firm in terms of the market value of all securities rather than only the market value of equity.

18 For a more detailed exposition of company valuation see R. A. Brealey and S. C. Myers, *Principles of Corporate Finance*, 3rd ed (McGraw-Hill, New York, 1988), especially pp. 59–66 and 173–99.

II.

The Analysis of Industry and Competition

THREE

Analyzing the Industry Environment

The reinsurance business has the defect of being too attractive-looking to new entrants for its own good and will therefore always tend to be the opposite of, say, the old business of gathering and rendering dead horses which always tended to contain few and prosperous participants.

— Charles T. Munger, Chairman, Wesco Financial
Corporation (extract from the 1986 *Annual Report*)

Outline
Introduction and Objectives
From Environmental Analysis to Industry Analysis
The Determinants of Industry Profit: Demand and Competition
The Analysis of Competition in an Industry
    Porter's "Five Forces of Competition" model
    Competition from substitutes
    Threat of entry
    Rivalry between established competitors
    Bargaining power of buyers
    Bargaining power of suppliers
Applying Industry Analysis
    Forecasting industry profitability
    Strategies to improve the balance of competitive forces
Opportunities for Competitive Advantage: Identifying key success factors
The Problem of Industry Definition
Dynamic Aspects of Competition
    Schumpeterian competition
    The contribution of game theory
    Chaos and catastrophe
Summary and Conclusion

Introduction and Objectives

Strategy, we have observed, forms a link between the firm and its environment. It follows that there are two major inputs into strategy analysis: the analysis of the industry environment of the firm and the analysis of resources and capabilities within the firm. In this chapter and the next, I present concepts and techniques to analyze the industry environment. Industry analysis is relevant to the formulation of both corporate strategy and business strategy.

Corporate strategy is concerned with deciding which industries the firm should be engaged in and allocating of corporate resources between them. To make such decisions, it is vital that the firm can evaluate the attractiveness of different industries in terms of their potential to yield profit in the future. The primary objective of this chapter is to analyze the determinants of industry profitability. Once the determinants of industry profitability are understood, it will then be possible to forecast the future profitability of an industry. Our analysis in this chapter concentrates upon the role of industry structure in determining competition within the industry, which in turn determines the level of profitability.

Understanding how industry structure drives competitive behavior, which in turn determines profitability, is also critical to the formulation of business strategy. First, understanding the determinants of industry profitability can indicate how strategy can be used to change industry structure and competitive behavior in order to enhance industry profitability. Second, understanding how firms compete in order to serve customer needs will help us to identify opportunities for competitive advantage within an industry (*"key success factors"*).

By the time you have completed this chapter you will be able to:

1   identify the main structural features of an industry that influence competitive behavior and profitability and analyze the relationships between industry structure, competition, and the level of profitability;
2   assess the attractiveness of an industry in terms of the industry's potential for generating above- or below-average returns;
3   use evidence on structural trends within industries to forecast changes in industry profitability in the future;
4   identify the opportunities available to a firm to influence industry structure in order to moderate the intensity of competition and improve industry profitability;
5   analyze competition and customer requirements in an industry in order to identify key success factors – opportunities for competitive advantage within an industry.

From Environmental Analysis to Industry Analysis

In this chapter, I restrict analysis of the firm's external environment to its immediate environment – the *industry*. Yet the environment of the firm constitutes all the external influences that impinge upon the firm's decisions and performance. The problem for managers is that, given the vast number and range of external influences, how can the firm hope to monitor, let alone analyze, environmental conditions? The starting point is some kind of system or framework for organizing information. For example, environmental influences can be classified by source into economic, technological, demographic, social, and governmental factors or by proximity: the "*microenvironment*" or "*task environment*" can be distinguished from the wider influences that form the "*macroenvironment*."

In principle, all firms should engage in systematic and continuous scanning of the whole range of external influences upon their performance and strategic decisions. In practice, such extensive environmental analysis is unlikely to be cost effective and creates information overload. The Royal Dutch/Shell Group is not only one of the world's largest enterprises – it probably invests more heavily in the systematic monitoring and analysis of its business environment than any other company. Its scenario-planning exercises are exceptionally farsighted and wideranging appraisals of its business environment. Nevertheless, the group's environmental scanning and analysis focuses upon factors that are directly relevant to its strategic planning: in particular, those factors that influence the demand and supply of oil and refined products.[1]

The prerequisite for effective environmental analysis is distinguishing the vital from the merely important. From the point of view of the firm, the core of its environment is its network of business relationships. These relationships constitute transactions with suppliers and customers and competitive interactions with rival producers. Hence, the core of the firm's environment is formed by competitors, suppliers, and customers. This arena is the firm's *industry environment*.

This is not to say that macrolevel factors such as general economic trends, changes in demographic structure, or social and political trends are unimportant to strategy analysis. These factors may be critical determinants of the threats and opportunities a company will face in the future. However, the key issue is that these more general environmental factors are important because of their effect on the firm's industry environment: they affect the firm's demand, its costs, and its competitive position relative to its rivals. By focusing on the industry environment, we can determine which of the general environmental influences are important for the firm and which are not.

The Determinants of Industry Profit: Demand and Competition

The approach of this book to strategy analysis is guided by the simple assumption that the purpose of strategy is to help the firm to survive and make money. Hence, the starting point for industry analysis is to ask: "What determines the level of profit in an industry?"

The basic source of profit is the creation of value for the customer. Production transforms inputs into goods and services for the customer. For production to be profitable, the first criterion is that the value of the product or service created (as measured by the price that the customer

Figure 3.1 The
Business Environment

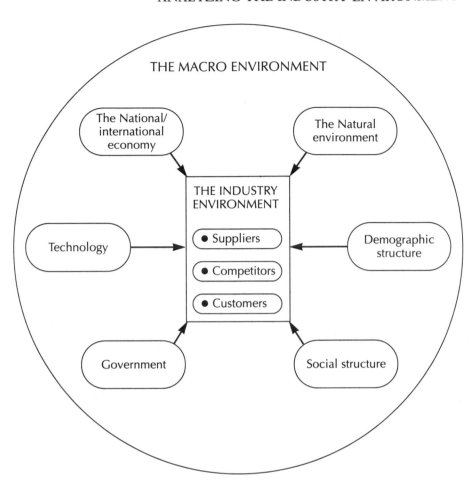

is willing to pay) exceeds the cost of the inputs used in its creation. The greater the surplus of value over cost, the greater the potential for profit in an industry. The value of a product or service to a customer is dependent upon the intensity of his or her need and the availability of substitutes.

But potential profit is not actual profit. The surplus of value over cost is distributed between customers and producers by the forces of competition. The stronger competition is between producers, the greater is the proportion of the surplus gained by customers ("*consumer surplus*") and the less producers earn ("*producer surplus*" or "*economic rent*"). If there is a single well at a desert oasis, its owner will be able to charge a price that fully exploits travelers' need for water. If there are many wells at the oasis, then, in the absence of collusion, competition between their individual owners will cause the price of water to fall toward the cost of supplying it.

The surplus earned by producers over and above the minimum costs of production is not entirely captured in profits. Where an industry has powerful suppliers – monopolistic suppliers of components or employees united by a strong labor union – then a substantial part of the surplus may be appropriated by these suppliers (the profits of suppliers' or high wages of union members).

Hence, the profits earned by the firms in an industry are determined by three factors:

- the *value of the product or service to customers*;
- the *intensity of competition*;
- the *relative bargaining power* at different levels in the production chain.

The analysis of industry competition that follows brings all three factors into a single analytic framework.

The Analysis of Competition in an Industry

Table 3.1 shows the average rate of profit earned in different U.S. industries. Some industries (such as tobacco and printing) appear to earn comparatively high rates of profit and others (such as textiles; primary metals; and stone, glass, and clay) earn consistently low rates of profit. The basic premise that underlies industry analysis is that the level of industry profitability is neither random nor the result of entirely industry-specific influences but is determined, in part at least, by the systematic influence of *industry structure*. These same industry structure variables determine competition and profitability across the whole range of manufacturing and service industries. As an example of how an attractively structured industry can support a firm's profitability, consider the case of the sausage-skin manufacturer Devro (see exhibit 3.1).

The underlying theory of the relationship between industry structure, competitive behavior, and industry profitability is provided by industrial organization economics. The two reference points are the theory of monopoly and the theory of perfect competition, which represent the two ends of a spectrum of industry structures. Where there is a single firm in an industry and new firms are unable to enter, *monopoly* exists: competition is absent and the monopolist can appropriate in profit the full surplus of value of output over the cost of inputs. Where there are many firms in an industry, all producing an identical product and with no restrictions upon entry, *perfect competition* exists: price competition causes profits to fall to "the competitive level" – over the long term, this is the level that just covers the firms' cost of capital. In the real world, industries fall between these two extremes. Table 3.2 identifies some key points on the spectrum. For any particular industry, it is possible to predict the type of competitive behavior likely to emerge as well as the resulting level of profitability by examining the principal structural features and their interactions.

Table 3.1 The
Profitability of U.S.
Manufacturing
Industries

(A) After-tax rate of return on invested capital, 1960–85.

	1960–85	1981–85
	%	%
Scientific instruments	9.1	4.2
Printing	8.6	7.3
Tobacco	8.1	9.5
Miscellaneous manufacture	6.1	5.6
Apparel	7.0	7.4
Electrical machinery	7.0	4.5
Chemicals	6.9	3.8
Transportation equipment	6.6	5.4
Paper	6.6	3.8
Leather	6.4	4.3
Nonelectrical machinery	6.1	2.1
Food	6.0	6.1
Fabricated metals	5.7	3.7
Rubber	5.4	2.1
Petroleum	5.3	2.8
Lumber	5.0	0.9
Furniture	4.3	4.3
Stone, glass, clay	4.3	1.1
Textiles	4.2	1.8
Primary metals	2.8	−2.2

Note: After-tax return on invested capital is measured as inflation-adjusted after-tax net income divided by the inflation-adjusted capital stock (net plant and equipment plus investments and intangibles).
Source: Lawrence F. Katz and Lawrence H. Summers, "Industry Rents: Evidence and Implications," *Brookings Papers: Microeconomics* 1989, no. 3: 214.

(B) FTC data on return on equity and assets by manufacturing sector, 1971–90

	ROE	ROA
	%	%
Drugs	21.4	11.8
Printing and publishing	15.5	7.1
Food and kindred products	15.2	6.6
Chemicals and allied products	15.1	7.5
Petroleum and coal products	13.1	6.5
Instruments and related products	12.9	7.2
Industrial chemicals and synthetics	12.9	6.2
Paper and allied products	12.5	6.0
Aircraft, guided missiles and parts	12.4	4.1
Fabricated metal products	12.3	5.7
Motor vehicles and equipment	11.6	5.6
Rubber and miscellaneous plastic products	11.6	5.1
Electric and electronic equipment	11.5	5.4
Machinery, expert electrical	11.1	5.8
Stone, clay, and glass products	10.4	4.8
Textile mill products	9.3	4.3
Nonferrous metals	8.3	3.9
Iron and steel	3.9	1.5

Source: U.S. Federal Trade Commission

Exhibit 3.1   Devro International PLC, the Sausage-Skin King

Devro International PLC is a Scottish company with headquarters in the village of Moodiesburn near Glasgow. With 930 employees and plants in Scotland, Australia, and the United States, Devro holds 56 percent of the world market for collagen sausage skins. The company obtained a floating on the London Stock Exchange in 1993, two years after a management buyout from its parent, Johnson & Johnson. During 1991 and 1992, operating profits averaged 25 percent of sales revenue. Devro holds 94 percent of the U.K. market, 83 percent of the Australian market, and 40 percent of the U.S. market. Although collagen casings are a substitute for natural gut sausage casings, collagen possesses some clear advantages, which have resulted in the steady displacement of natural gut. Scale economies, technology, and Devro's absolute cost advantages pose substantial barriers to would-be entrants. Because casings account for only a small proportion of the sausage manufacturer's total costs, they are relatively insensitive to the price of casing and do not exert substantial bargaining power.

Source: James Buxton, "A Leaner Business That Has More Bite," *Financial Times*, April 16, 1993, 33.

Table 3.2   The Spectrum of Industry Structures

Structural Features	Industry Type			
	Perfect Competition	Oligopoly	Duopoly	Monopoly
Number of producers	Many	Few	Two	One
Entry & exit barriers	None	Significant	High	High
Product differentiation	None	Extensive	Moderate	Low
Information	Perfect availability	Restricted	Restricted	Restricted

Porter's "Five Forces of Competition" Model

Table 3.2 identifies four structural variables influencing competition and profitability. In practice, there are many features of an industry that determine the intensity of competition and the level of profitability. A particularly useful framework for classifying and analyzing these factors was developed by Michael Porter of Harvard Business School.[2] Porter's "Five Forces of Competition" model views the profitability of an industry (as indicated by its rate of return on invested capital relative to its cost of capital) as determined by five sources of competitive pressure. These five forces of competition include three sources of "horizontal" competition – competition from the suppliers of substitutes, the threat of competition from entrants, and competition from established producers – and two sources of "vertical" competition – the bargaining power of suppliers and buyers (see figure 3.2).

The strength of each of these competitive forces is determined by a number of key structural variables, as shown in figure 3.3.

Competition from substitutes

We observed earlier that the potential for profit in an industry is determined by the maximum price that customers are willing to pay. This

Figure 3.2 Porter's
"Five Forces of
Competition"
Framework

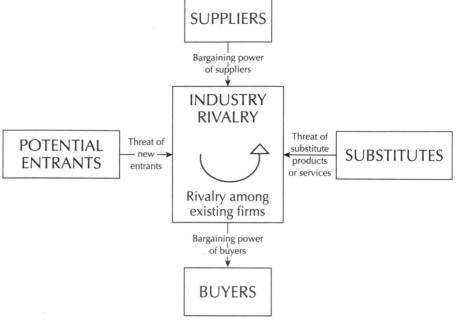

Source: Adapted from M. E. Porter, *Competitive Strategy* (New York: Free Press, 1980).

depends primarily on the availability of substitutes. If our desert oasis also sells Coca-Cola, this will limit the price that can be charged for water. Where there are few substitutes for a product, as in the case of gasoline or cigarettes, consumers are comparatively insensitive to price – that is, demand is *inelastic* with respect to price. If there are close substitutes for a product, then attempts by producers to raise prices causes customers to switch to substitutes – that is, demand is *elastic* with respect to price. An important constraint upon the pricing policies of the suppliers of frozen foods are the prices of canned and fresh produce.

The extent to which the threat of substitutes constrain industry pricing depends upon two factors:

1 *The propensity of buyers to substitute* Are there close substitutes for the product or service, and how willing are customers to shift their purchases on the basis of changes in relative prices? The critical issue is the willingness to substitute: even though substitutes exist, customers may be unresponsive to changes in relative prices. For example, efforts by city planners to relieve traffic congestion either by charging the motorist or by subsidizing public transport have been remarkably ineffective in encouraging motorists to forsake their cars for buses.

2 *The price-performance characteristics of substitutes* The willingness of customers to switch between substitutes in response to price changes depends upon their relative performance in relation to price. If city-center to city-center travel between Washington and New York is two hours quicker by air than by train and the average traveler values

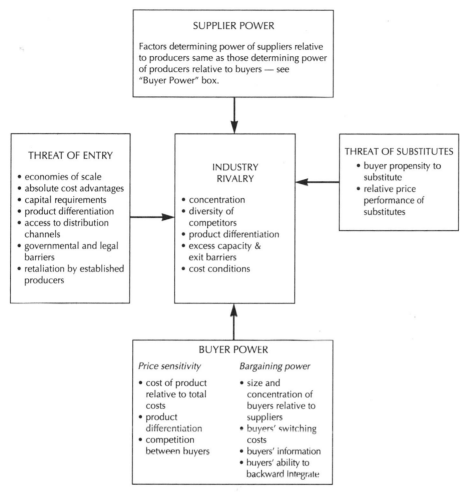

time at $25 an hour, the implication is that the train will be competitive with air travel at fares of $50 below those charged by the airlines. The more complex are the needs being fulfilled by the product and the more difficult it is to discern performance differences, the lower the extent of substitution by customers on the basis of price differences will be. The failure of low-priced imitations of leading perfumes to establish significant market share reflects, in part, consumers' difficulty in discerning the performance characteristics of different fragrances.

Threat of entry

If an industry earns a return on invested capital in excess of its cost of capital, that industry will act as a magnet to firms outside the industry. Unless the entry of new firms is barred, the rate of profit must fall to the competitive level. It may not even be necessary for entry to take place; the threat of entry may be sufficient to ensure that established firms constrain their prices to the competitive level. Only American Airlines offers a direct service between Dallas/Fort Worth and Santa

Barbara, California. American may be unwilling to exploit its monopoly position by charging higher fares if other airlines can easily extend their routes to cover the same two cities. An industry where no barriers to entry or exit exist is termed "contestable" – prices and profits will remain at the fully competitive level, irrespective of the number of firms within the industry.[3] Contestability depends critically upon the absence of "sunk costs." Sunk costs exist where entry requires investment in industry-specific assets whose value cannot be recovered on exit. Absence of sunk costs makes an industry vulnerable to "hit-and-run" entry whenever established firms raise their prices above the competitive level.

However, in most industries new entrants cannot enter on equal terms to those of established firms. The size of the advantage of established over entrant firms (in terms of unit costs) measures the height of *barriers to entry*, which determine the extent to which the industry can, in the long run, enjoy profit above the competitive level. The principal sources of barriers to entry are:

- Capital requirements
- Economies of scale
- Absolute cost advantages
- Product differentiation
- Access to channels of distribution
- Legal and regulatory barriers
- Retaliation

Capital requirements   The capital costs of getting established in an industry can be so large as to discourage all but the largest companies. During the last 30 years, there have been no new entrants into the commercial jet aircraft industry or into volume manufacture of passenger cars. In satellite television broadcasting to Britain, Rupert Murdoch's Sky TV incurred almost $1 billion in capital costs and operating losses and Robert Maxwell's British Satellite Broadcasting spent some $1.8 billion before the two were amalgamated in 1991. In other industries, entry costs can be modest. Start-up costs for franchised fast-food restaurant are around $260,000 for a Wendy's and $1 million to $1.5 million for a Carl's Jr.[4]

Economies of scale   In some industries, particularly those that are capital- or research-intensive, efficiency requires producing at a very large scale. In large jet engines, the importance of scale economies in R&D and manufacture has resulted in the survival of just three producers in the world: General Electric, Pratt & Whitney, and Rolls-Royce. Economies of scale in automobiles have caused the acquisition of smaller manufacturers (such as Jaguar, Saab, AMC/Jeep, Seat, and Rover) by larger producers. The problem of scale economies for new entrants is that they are faced with the choice of either entering on a small scale and accepting high unit costs or entering on a large scale and running the risk of drastic underutilization of capacity while they build up sales volume.

Absolute cost advantages Irrespective of scale economies, established firms may have a cost advantage over entrants across all levels of output. Such advantages are usually associated with *first-mover advantages*: by being early into the industry, the established firms may have been able to acquire low-cost sources of raw materials, and by being in the industry for longer they benefit from economies of learning. In the oil industry, the established oil majors' ownership of the world's main low-cost oil reserves poses a barrier to entry to would-be new entrants. In small gasoline engines, Honda and Briggs & Stratton are so far down their experience curves that it is doubtful whether any new entrant could compete on cost.

Product differentiation In an industry where products are differentiated, established firms possess an advantage over new entrants by virtue of brand recognition and customer loyalty. The percentage of U.S. consumers loyal to a single brand varies from under 30 percent in batteries, canned vegetables, and garbage bags up to 61 percent in toothpaste, 65 percent in mayonnaise, and 71 percent in cigarettes.[5] New entrants into highly differentiated markets must spend disproportionately large amounts on advertising and promotion to gain levels of brand awareness and brand goodwill similar to established suppliers. Alternatively, the new entrant can accept a niche position in the market or can seek to compete by cutting price. In producer goods too, bonds between suppliers and their customers based on loyalty and understanding of reciprocal needs are often strong. Establishing credibility and goodwill can be slow and costly for a new entrant. It took Apple between 1984 and 1987 to get its Macintosh computer accepted by corporate customers as a serious business computer. U.S. banks and securities companies including Citicorp, Bankers Trust, and Merrill Lynch took a considerable time to build strong positions in European underwriting.

Access to channels of distribution Product differentiation barriers relate to the preferences of final customers for established products. However, for consumer goods manufacturers, the biggest barrier may be *distributors'* preferences for established firms' products. Limited capacity within distribution channels (e.g., shelf space), risk aversion, and the fixed costs associated with carrying an additional product result in distributors' reluctance to carry a new manufacturer's product. In the United States and Britain, food and drink processors are increasingly required to make lump-sum payments to the leading supermarket chains in order to gain shelf space for a new product. One study found that, compared to early entrants, late entrants into consumer goods markets incurred additional advertising and promotional costs amounting to 2.12 percent of sales revenue.[6]

Governmental and legal barriers   Some economists have claimed that the only really effective barriers to entry are those created by government. In industries such as taxicab services, banking, telecommunications, and broadcasting, entry may require the granting of a license by a public authority. In knowledge-intensive industries, patents, copyrights, and trade secrets are frequently the most effective barriers to entry. Xerox Corporation's near monopoly position in the world plain-paper copier business until the mid-1970s was protected by a wall of over 2,000 patents relating to its xerography process. In industries subject to heavy government involvement through regulation, procurement, and environmental and safety standards, new entrants may be at a disadvantage to established firms because of discrimination against newcomers because of the costs of gaining "approved supplier" status or because the costs of compliance weigh more heavily on newcomers.

Retaliation   The effectiveness of the above barriers to entry in excluding potential entrants depends upon the entrants' expectations as to possible retaliation by established firms. Retaliation against a new entrant may take the form of aggressive price cutting, increased advertising, sales promotion, or litigation. British Airways's retaliation against competition from Virgin Atlantic on its North Atlantic routes included not only promotional price cuts and advertising but also a variety of "dirty tricks" such as accessing Virgin's computer system, poaching its customers, and attacking Virgin's reputation. Southwest and several other small, low-cost airlines alleged that American Airlines's price cuts during the summer of 1992 amounted to predatory pricing designed to drive them out of business. The likelihood of retaliation is influenced by the nature of the entry. Small-scale entry that does not directly threaten established firms is unlikely to provoke retaliation. In the U.S. car and consumer electronics markets, Japanese entrants initially introduced small products, targeting segments that had been dismissed by U.S. producers as inherently unprofitable. If retaliation is to be effective, it must be used as a threat that is credible enough to intimidate would-be entrants. It has been argued that threats of aggressive price competition against new entrants are only credible when backed by excess capacity.[7]

A number of empirical studies have measured the impact of entry barriers on industry profitability. Studies by Bain and Mann found return on equity to be, on average, five percentage points higher in industries with "very high entry barriers" than in those with "substantial" or "moderate to low" barriers.[8] Studies using capital intensity and advertising intensity as proxies for scale economy and differentiation barriers, respectively, show both variables to be positively related to profitability.[9]

The effectiveness of barriers to entry in deterring potential entrants depends upon the resources of the would-be entrants. Barriers that are effective in impeding the entry of new companies may be ineffective in deterring firms that are diversifying from other industries. A study by George Yip found no evidence that entry barriers deterred new entry.[10] Entrants were able to successfully overcome entry barriers for one of two reasons: either they possessed resources and capabilities (such as finance, technology, expertise, and transferable brands) that permitted them to surmount barriers and compete effectively with incumbent firms using the similar strategies or they successfully circumvented entry barriers by adopting different strategies from those of incumbent firms. Examples of firms that used their strong resource bases in existing markets to enter new markets include American Express's use of its brand name to enter a broad range of financial services, and Mars's ability to use its strong position in confectionery to enter the ice cream market.[11] Examples of different strategies circumventing entry barriers include:

- Southwest Airlines's use of a low-cost, "no-frills" strategy to challenge the major U.S. airlines;
- Dell Computer's use of direct-mail distribution and telephone-based customer service to establish itself as a leading supplier of microcomputers in the United States.

Rivalry between established competitors

For most industries, the major determinant of the overall state of competition and the general level of profitability is competition among the firms within the industry. In some industries, firms compete aggressively – sometimes to the extent that prices are pushed below the level of costs and industrywide losses are incurred. In others, price competition is muted, and rivalry focuses on advertising, innovation, and other non-price dimensions. Among the major factors determining the nature and intensity of competition between established firms are:

- Concentration
- Diversity of competitors
- Product differentiation
- Excess capacity and exit barriers
- Cost conditions

Concentration   Seller concentration refers to the number of competitors in an industry and their relative sizes. Seller concentration is most commonly measured by the *concentration ratio*, which is the combined market share of the leading producers. For example, the four-firm concentration ratio (conventionally denoted "CR4") measures the combined market share of the four largest producers in an industry. An industry dominated by a single firm, such as Xerox's dominance of plain-paper copiers during the early 1970s, displays little competition, and the dominant firm can exercise considerable discretion over the prices it charges. Where an industry is comprised of a small group of leading companies (an "oligopoly"), price competition may also be restrained, either by outright collusion or more commonly through "parallelism" of pricing decisions. In markets dominated by two suppliers – Duracell and Eveready in alkaline batteries, Kodak and Fuji in color film, Coke and Pepsi in soft drinks – prices tend to be set at similar levels, and competition focuses upon advertising, promotion, and product development. Even where there are several competitors, closely coordinated prices can moderate competition.[12] As the number of firms supplying a market increases, coordination of pricing behavior becomes more difficult and the the likelihood that one firm will initiate aggressive price competition increases. On the Los Angeles-San Francisco route, 11 airlines compete for business, including two low-cost newcomers, Southwest Airlines and Reno Air. During 1993, a full-fare, unrestricted seat could be bought for $69.

Diversity of competitors   The ability of the firms in an industry to avoid competition depends not only upon the number of firms but also on their similarities in terms of origins, objectives, costs, and strategies. The cozy atmosphere of the U.S. steel industry prior to the advent of overseas competition and the new minimills was possible because of the similarities of the companies and the outlooks of their senior managers. By contrast, the inability of OPEC to maintain oil prices during the 1980s and 1990s was due, in part, to differences between member countries in objectives, production costs, language, politics, and religion.

Product differentiation   The more similar the offerings of rival firms, the more willing are customers to substitute between them and the greater is the incentive for firms to cut prices in order to expand business. Where the products of rival firms are virtually indistinguishable, the product is a *commodity*, and the sole basis for competition is price. Commodities include both basic materials (crude oil, wheat, gold bullion) and finished products (256K DRAM chips, U.S. Treasury bills). It has been argued that Intel/DOS-based personal computers are now a commodity product because competition is concerned simply with price and specifications. By contrast, in industries where products are highly differentiated (perfumes, pharmaceuticals, restaurants, management consulting services), price competition is limited by customers' unwillingness to shift their purchases simply on the basis of small price differentials. Even though these industries may comprise many producers, lack of price competition can result in high margins.

Excess capacity and exit barriers   Over time, profitability in many industries is highly cyclical because of changes in the balance between demand and capacity. The presence of unused capacity encourages firms to offer price cuts when seeking additional business in order to spread fixed costs over a greater sales volume. Excess capacity is most commonly the result of declining market demand, which may be long term (e.g., steel) or cyclical (e.g., building materials). Overinvestment may also lead to periodic excess capacity (personal computers in 1984-5, U.S. automobiles during the late 1980s). In the case of long-term decline, how long will excess capacity overhang the market? This depends upon "barriers to exit": costs and other impediments to capacity leaving an industry. Where resources are durable and specialized and where employees are entitled to job protection, barriers to exit may be substantial.[13] The prolonged depression of profits in metals mining during the 1980s and early 1990s reflected excess capacity and the high costs of mine closure, which encouraged firms to continue operation despite heavy losses. Conversely, when demand exceeds available capacity, margins fatten. In the memory chips (DRAMs) industry, excess capacity during 1985-6 was quickly reversed during 1987-8 when capacity shortage pushed the price of 256K DRAMs from $2 to $11.50, providing a short-term profit bonanza for NEC, Toshiba, Micron Technology, and other manufacturers.[14]

Cost conditions: scale economies and the ratio of fixed to variable costs The aggressiveness with which rivals compete for market share is crucially dependent upon the cost conditions they face. In the short term, the ratio of fixed to variable costs determines how far companies will slash prices in order to utilize spare capacity. The willingness of airlines to offer heavily discounted tickets on flights with low bookings reflects the fact that the variable costs associated with filling empty seats on a scheduled flight are close to zero. The devastating impact of excess capacity on profitability in chemicals, tires, and steel reflects the high fixed costs in these businesses and the willingness of firms to accept additional business at any price that covers variable cost.

Empirical verification of the impact of these structural variables on profitability is not clear cut. The effect of seller concentration on profitability is especially contentious. Richard Schmalensee concludes that "The relation, if any, between seller concentration and profitability is weak statistically and the estimated concentration effect is usually small."[15] However, in the case of individual industries, the impact of concentration in raising prices and profits is clearer.[16] The effect of other variables on profitability is also more obvious. The balance between capacity and demand has a strong effect on profitability. Studies using the PIMS database show market growth is positively associated with profitability, although cash flow declines with higher growth reflecting the greater investment needs of growing businesses (see table 3.3).[17] The tendency for excess capacity to depress return on investment (ROI) and

Table 3.3 The
Relationship between
Real Market Growth
and Profitability

	Real annual rate of market growth				
	Less than −5%	−5% to 0	0 to 5%	5% to 10%	Over 10%
Gross margin on sales	23.5	25.6	26.9	25.7	29.7
Return on sales	7.8	8.3	9.1	8.3	9.4
Return on investment	20.6	23.0	23.2	22.2	26.6
Cash flow/Investment	6.0	4.9	3.5	2.4	−0.1

Source: Robert D. Buzzell and Bradley T. Gale, *The PIMS Principles: Linking Strategy to Performance* (New York: Free Press, 1987), 56–7.

return on sales (ROS) is particularly great in capital-intensive businesses.[18]

Bargaining power of buyers

The firms in an industry operate in two types of markets: in the markets for *inputs*, they purchase raw materials, components, finance, and labor services from the suppliers of these factors of production; in the markets for *outputs*, they sell their products and services to customers (who may be distributors, consumers, or other manufacturers). In both these markets, the relative profitability of the two parties to a transaction depends upon relative economic power. Dealing first with the sales to customers, two sets of factors are important in determining the strength of buying power:

- Buyers' price sensitivity
- Relative bargaining power

Buyers' price sensitivity depends on the following:

1 The greater the importance of an item as a proportion of total cost, the more sensitive buyers will be as to the price they pay. Beverage manufacturers are highly sensitive to the costs of metal cans because this is one of their largest single cost items. Conversely, most companies are not sensitive to the fee charged by their auditors because auditing costs are such a small proportion of overall corporate expenses.

2 The less differentiated are the products of the supplying industry, the more willing is the buyer to switch suppliers on the basis of price. The suppliers of commodity items such as steel, packaging materials, and paper are particularly vulnerable to buying power because of the ease with which their customers can switch.

3 The more intense is competition between buyers, the greater their eagerness for price reductions from their sellers. As international competition in the automobile industry has intensified, so component suppliers have experienced greater pressures for lower prices, higher quality, and faster delivery.

4 The greater the importance of the industry's product to the quality of the buyer's product or service, the less sensitive are buyers to the

prices they are charged. The buying power of personal computer manufacturers relative to the manufacturers of microprocessors (Intel, Motorola, Advanced Micro Devices) is limited by the critical importance of these components to their product.

Relative bargaining power Bargaining power rests, ultimately, upon refusal to deal with the other party. The balance of power between the two parties to a transaction depends upon the credibility and effectiveness with which each makes this threat. The key determinants are, first, the relative costs that each party sustains as a result of the transaction not being consummated and, second, the expertise of each party in leveraging its position through gamesmanship. Four factors are likely to be important in determining the bargaining power of buyers relative to that of sellers:

1 *Size and concentration of buyers relative to suppliers* The smaller the number of buyers, the less easy is it for a supplier to find alternative customers if one is lost. The bigger the purchases of the customer, the greater is the damage from losing that customer. The success of health maintenance organizations (HMOs) in lowering health care costs results from their bargaining power against hospitals and doctors being much greater than that of the individual patient.

2 *Buyers' information about suppliers' products, prices, and costs* The better informed buyers are about suppliers and their relative price, the better are they able to bargain. Doctors and lawyers do not normally display the prices they charge, nor do traders in the bazaars of Tangier and Istanbul. Keeping customers ignorant of relative prices is an effective constraint upon their buying power. But knowledge of price is of little value if the quality of the product is unknown. In the markets for haircuts, investment advice, and management consulting, the ability of buyers to bargain over price is limited by uncertainty over the precise attributes of the product they are buying.

3 *Buyers' switching costs* The lower the cost of switching between suppliers, the more effective is buyer power.

4 *Ability to vertical integrate* In refusing to deal with the other party, the alternative to finding another supplier or buyer is to do it yourself. Large food processors such as Heinz and Campbell Soup have reduced their dependence upon the oligopolistic suppliers of metal cans by manufacturing their own. The leading retail chains have increasingly displaced their suppliers' brands with their own brand products.

The tendency for buyer concentration to depress prices and profits in supplying industries has been well documented in the empirical literature.[19] PIMS data show that the larger the average size of customers' purchases and the larger the proportion of customers' total purchases that the item represents, the more price sensitive customers become, and the lower is the profitability of supplying firms (see table 3.4).

Table 3.4 The Impact
of Customers' Purchases
on Profitability

	ROI (%)	ROS (%)
Typical size of customers' purchase		
less than $1000	27	10
$1,000 to $10,000	22	7
over $10,000	21	6
Purchase importance: customers' purchases of the product or service as % of their total purchases		
Less than 1%	25	10
1% to 5%	23	9
Over 5%	20	8

Source: Robert D. Buzzell and Bradley T. Gale, *The PIMS Principles: Linking Strategy to Performance* (New York: Free Press, 1987), 64–5.

Bargaining power of suppliers

Analysis of the determinants of relative power between the producers in an industry and their suppliers is precisely analogous to the analysis of the relationship between producers and their buyers. Because the factors that determine the effectiveness of supplier power against the buying power of the industry are the same as those that determine the power of the industry against that of its customers, they do not require a separate analysis.

Because raw materials, semifinished products, and components tend to be commodities supplied by small companies to large manufacturing companies, their suppliers usually lack bargaining power. Hence, commodity suppliers often seek to boost their bargaining power through cartelization – for example, OPEC, the International Coffee Organization, and farmers' marketing cooperatives. A similar logic explains labor unions.

PIMS studies of the impact of supplier's bargaining power upon firms' profitability is complex. Increasing concentration of a firm's purchases is initially beneficial because it permits certain economies of purchasing. Thereafter, increasing concentration among purchasers results in profitability becoming depressed due to increased supplier power. Supplier power is significantly increased by forward integration into its customers' own industry. When a firm faces its suppliers as competitors within its own industry, its ROI is reduced by two percentage points. Unionization is unambiguously associated with decreasing profitability. Table 3.5 shows some of these findings.

Applying Industry Analysis

Forecasting industry profitability

Decisions to commit resources to a particular industry must be based upon anticipated returns five to ten years ahead. Over these periods,

	ROI (%)	ROS (%)
Supplier concentration: the percentage of total purchases from the three biggest suppliers		
Under 25%	21	8.9
25% to 50%	24	9.8
Over 50%	23	8.9
Percentage of employees unionized		
None	25	10.8
1% to 35%	24	9.0
35% to 60%	23	9.0
60% to 75%	18	7.9
Over 75%	19	7.9

Table 3.5 The Impact of Supplier Power on Profitability: PIMS Estimates

Source: Robert D. Buzzell and Bradley T. Gale, *The PIMS Principles: Linking Strategy to Performance* (New York: Free Press, 1987), 62, 67.

profitability cannot be accurately forecast by projecting current industry profitability. But, while we cannot directly forecast industry profitability, we can predict with some accuracy changes in the underlying structure of an industry. Structural changes will be driven by current changes in product and process technology, the current strategies of the leading players, the changes occurring in infrastructure and in related industries, and by government policies. If we understand how industry structure affects competition and profitability, then we can use our projections of structural change to forecast the likely changes in industry profitability.

Consider the world automobile industry (exhibit 3.2). During the early 1990s, profitability was depressed by a combination of long-term and short-term factors. What is the outlook for competition and profitability for the second half of the 1990s? Exhibit 3.2 identifies a number of structural trends that are likely to have a significant effect on competition and profitability. Although it is possible to predict with some confidence the qualitative impact of individual structural changes, there are difficulties, first, in predicting the *quantitative* impact of structural changes, and second, in predicting the *aggregate* effect of simultaneous structural changes that have conflicting effects on profitability. Then, unless all the changes are working in the same direction, the aggregate effect is difficult to predict. Thus, in the case of the world automobile industry, most of the structural changes are tending to increase competition and depress profitability. However, the potential for world economic recovery to reduce the overhang of excess capacity offers the potential for an improvement in margins – especially among the depressed Japanese and European manufacturers.

Where all the principal structural changes are influencing profitability in the same direction, predicting whether profitability in the future will be higher or lower than the current level is relatively easy. Consider,

Exhibit 3.2   Competition and Profitability in the World Automobile Industry

During the early 1990s, the overall profitability of the world automobile industry deteriorated sharply. Historically, the industry had earned above-average returns, reflecting the broadly attractive structure of the industry. Although at the global level, the industry was relatively unconcentrated, in practice, the effective concentration was higher. The companies were geographically differentiated with the result that, rather than a single global industry, there was a series of regional industries: the "Big Three" dominated North America, while the European market was divided between national champions – Fiat in Italy, Volkswagen in Germany, Renault and Citroen in France, British Leyland in the United Kingdom. During the 1960s and 1970s, demand was strong, with capacity short for most of the period. Two key trends have reduced differentiation and therefore increased competition. First, the products of the different companies have become increasingly similar. Volume cars are typically front-wheel drive, with four- or six-cylinder engines. In terms of technology and styling, competitors' models have become increasingly similar. American cars are no longer substantially bigger than those built in Europe and Japan, and significantly differentiated models such as the air-cooled, rear-engined VW "Beetle," have all but disappeared. Second, globalization has caused the leading companies to be less geographically differentiated. In particular, Japanese companies have made substantial incursions into the North American and European markets. In the United States, the share of the "Big Three" fell from 72 percent in 1980 to 63 percent in 1990.

Over the medium term, a critical factor increasing competitive pressure and reducing profitability has been the emergence of a substantial overhang of excess capacity in the industry. Despite a strong recovery of demand in the United States during 1992-3, European and Japanese sales fell sharply. Meanwhile, world automobile capacity had grown as a result of heavy Japanese

investment in "transplant" facilities in America and Europe and investments by U.S. and European carmakers in advanced-technology plants.

Looking ahead, the major hope for a moderation of competition and improvement in profitability lies in a better balance between capacity and output. If the world economy achieves modest growth over 1994-6 and the leading companies eliminate excess capacity through downsizing and plant closures, this is likely to improve margins. However, most of the longer-term structural trends in the industry point toward continued intense competitive pressure:

1   *Substitutes* Environmental and congestion considerations suggest increasing competition to automobile transport from two sources: first, electrically driven cars and, second, public transport.

2   *Supplier power* Increased outsourcing and increased dependence upon suppliers for new technology promises to increase the bargaining power of the leading suppliers of components and subassemblies such as TRW Inc., GKN PLC, Bosch, and Lucas PLC.

3   *New entry* Despite the huge capital costs of entry, there are considerable opportunities for small assembly companies in the newly industrializing countries to increase their presence in the industry. Proton in Malaysia demonstrates the potential for a small low-cost supplier to establish a viable market position.

4   *Rivalry between established suppliers* Although seller concentration is growing with multiplying mergers and joint ventures, rivalry is likely to increase as smaller manufacturers seek to expand their market shares in order to obtain the volume necessary for viability. Economies of scale are most important in new product development. The $6.5 billion development cost of the Ford Mondeo indicates the accelerating new product development costs. A shakeout seems likely both in Europe and Japan; in this battle for survival, profits are likely to be a primary casualty.

for example, the outlook for profitability in U.S. network broadcasting during the 1990s. Almost all the changes occurring during the early 1990s appear to be negative for the industry:

- increasing substitute competition in the form of cable and satellite TV, and viewers increasingly using their TVs for videos and games;

Exhibit 3.2   continued

The World's Top 26 Automakers, 1982

	Output (m)	Revenues ($ billions)	Nameplates
General Motors	7.1	132.8	Chevrolet, Buick, Opel
Ford Motor Company	5.8	100.8	Ford, Lincoln, Jaguar
Toyota Motor	4.2	79.1	Toyota, Lexus
Volkswagen	3.5	56.7	VW, Audi, Seat
Nissan Motor	3.0	50.2	Nissan, Infiniti
Chrysler	2.2	36.9	Plymouth, Dodge, Jeep
Peugeot	2.1	29.4	Peugeot, Citroen, Talbot
Renault	2.0	33.9	Renault
Honda Motor	1.9	33.4	Honda, Acura
Mitsubishi Motor	1.8	25.5	Mitsubishi
Fiat	1.8	47.9	Fiat, Lancia, Alfa-Romeo
Suzuki Motor	1.4	10.2	Suzuki
Mazda Motor	1.2	20.9	Mazda
Daihatsu	0.8	7.0	Daihatsu
Hyundai	0.7	8.6	Hyundai
VAZ (Volzhky)	0.7	n.a.	Lada, Zhiguli
Fuji Heavy Industries	0.6	8.5	Subaru
BMW	0.6	20.6	BMW
Daimler-Benz	0.5	63.3	Mercedes-Benz
Kia Motors	0.5	4.4	Kia
Isuzu Motors	0.5	12.5	Isuzu
British Aerospace	0.4	17.8	Rover, Land Rover
Volvo	0.3	14.9	Volvo
Daewoo	0.3	28.3	Daewoo
FSM	0.1	n.a.	Fiat

Note: m = millions of cars
$b = billions of U.S. dollars
n.a. = not available

Source: Fortune magazine.

- increased power of the production studios as suppliers of TV shows;
- increased rivalry among established networks (ABC, CBS, NBC, and Fox) in response to declining audiences;
- new entry by Paramount and Criss-Craft Industries to create new national networks.

A similar result occurred with the U.S. bank credit card industry during the 1990s. At the beginning of the 1990s it was apparent that (a) power in the industry lay with the franchisers, Visa International and MasterCard International, rather than with the issuers of the cards, (b) that entry barriers had fallen to the point where entrants included companies from outside the financial services industry – including AT&T and General Motors, (c) competition from other forms of payment and credit instruments was increasing – including bank ATM cards and company account cards such as those issued by oil companies and retailers. The implication of these changes was that banks' profits from credit cards during the 1990s were unlikely to match those of the 1980s.

Strategies to improve the balance of competitive forces

Understanding how the structural characteristics of an industry determine the intensity of competition and the level of profitability provides a basis for identifying opportunities for adjusting industry structure in order to increase the hospitality of the industry environment. The first issue is to identify the key structural features of an industry that are responsible for depressing profitability. The second is to consider which of these structural features are amenable to change through appropriate strategic initiatives. For example:

- in consumer electronics, suppliers of leading brands (such as Sony and Pioneer) have sought to limit the buying power of discount chains by refusing to supply those chains that advertise cut prices or that do not display their products within "an appropriate retailing environment";
- the key factor depressing profitability in European petrochemicals has been excess capacity, and during the late 1980s, exchanges of plants between producers facilitated capacity rationalization.[20] During 1993, ICI attempted to imitate a program of plant swapping with BASF, Bayer, and Dow in order to reduce excess capacity in European polyurethane production;[21]
- building entry barriers is a vital strategy for preserving high profitability into the long run. A primary goal of the American Medical Association has been to maintain the incomes of its members by exerting control over the numbers of doctors trained within the United States and imposing barriers to the entry of doctors from overseas.

Opportunities for Competitive Advantage: Identifying Key Success Factors

Usually, it is only large firms that occupy strong market positions that are able to make changes in the structure of their industries. For most firms the primary objective for business strategy is not improving overall industry conditions but establishing a competitive advantage over rivals. A comprehensive analysis of competitive advantage follows in chapters 6, 7, and 8. However, with the tools of industry analysis outlined in this chapter, we can undertake some basic groundwork. Specifically, by analyzing competition and demand, we can identify the potential for competitive advantage in a particular industry in terms of the factors that are important in determining a firm's ability to survive and prosper. I refer to these factors as "*key success factors*."[22] In exhibit 3.3, Kenichi

---

Exhibit 3.3 Probing for Key Success Factors

As a consultant faced with an unfamiliar business or industry, I make a point of first asking the specialists in the business, "What is the secret of success in this industry?" Needless to say, I seldom get an immediate answer, and so I pursue the inquiry by asking other questions from a variety of angles in order to establish as quickly as possible some reasonable hypotheses as to key factors for success. In the course of these interviews it usually becomes quite obvious what analyses will be required in order to prove or disprove these hypotheses. By first identifying the probable key factors for success and then screening them by proof or disproof, it is often possible for the strategist to penetrate very quickly to the core of a problem.

Traveling in the United States last year, I found myself on one occasion sitting in a plane next to a director of one of the biggest lumber companies in the country. Thinking I might learn something useful in the course of the five-hour flight, I asked him, "What are the key factors for success in the lumber industry?" To my surprise, his reply was immediate: "Owning large forests and maximizing the yield from them."

The first of those key factors is a relatively simple matter: purchase of forest land. But his second point required further explanation. Accordingly, my next question was: "What variable or variables do you control in order to maximize the yield from a given tract?"

He replied: "The rate of tree growth is the key variable. As a rule, two factors promote growth: the amount of sunshine and the amount of water. Our company doesn't have many forests with enough of both. In Arizona and Utah, for example, we get more than enough sunshine but too little water, and so tree growth is very low. Now, if we could give the trees in those states enough water, they'd be ready in less than fifteen years instead of the thirty it takes now. The most important project we have in hand at the moment is aimed at finding out how to do this."

Impressed that this director knew how to work out a key factor strategy for his business, I offered my own contribution: "Then under the opposite conditions, where there is plenty of water but too little sunshine – for example, around the lower reaches of the Columbia River – the key factors should be fertilizers to speed up the growth and the choice of tree varieties that don't need so much sunshine."

Having established in a few minutes the general framework of what we were going to talk about, I spent the rest of the long flight very profitably hearing from him in detail how each of these factors was being applied.

Source: Kenichi Ohmae, *The Mind of the Strategist* (Harmondsworth, U.K.: Penguin, 1982), 85.

Ohmae, the senior vice president of McKinsey & Company's Tokyo office, discusses key success factors in forestry and their link with strategy.

Like Ohmae, my approach to identifying key success factors is straightforward and commonsensical. To survive and prosper in an industry, a firm must meet two criteria: first, it must supply what customers want to buy; second, it must survive competition. Hence, my approach is to ask two questions:

- *what do our customers want?*, and
- *what does the firm need to do to survive competition?*

To answer the first question we need to look more closely at the customers of the industry and view them not so much as a source of bargaining power and hence as a threat to profitability but more as the basic rationale for the existence of the industry and as the underlying source of profit. This implies that the firm must identify who its customers are, identify their needs, and establish the basis on which they select the offerings of one supplier in preference to those of another.

The second question requires that the firm examine the basis of competition in the industry. How intense is competition, and what are the key dimensions of competition? If the industry supplies a commodity product where there is limited scope for differentiation, then the focus of competition is likely to be price. To survive and prosper in the face of price competition requires that the firm establish a low cost position. Examination of cost conditions in the industry – for example, the importance of scale economies, the extent of excess capacity, the ratio of fixed to variable costs – then indicates the major opportunities of a cost advantage.

A basic framework for identifying key success factors is presented in figure 3.4. Application of the framework to identifying key success factors in three industries is outlined in table 3.6.

At a more formal level, identifying key success factors can also be derived from efforts to model the determinants of firm profit within an industry. In building such a model of profitability, a starting point is likely to be a simple accounting identity that can then be progressively elaborated in order to identify the fundamental economic and strategic

Figure 3.4 Identifying Key Success Factors

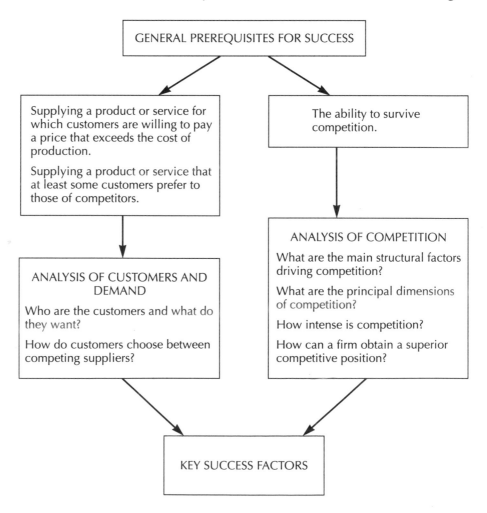

Table 3.6 Identifying Key Success Factors: Some Examples

	WHAT DO CUSTOMERS WANT? (Analysis of demand)	+ HOW DOES A FIRM SURVIVE COMPETITION (Analysis of Competition)	= KEY SUCCESS FACTORS
Steel	Customers include auto, engineering, & container industries. Customers acutely price sensitive. Also require product consistency & reliability of supply. Specific technical specifications required for special steels.	Competition primarily on price. Competition intense due to declining demand, high fixed costs and low-cost imports. Entry and exit barriers high. Strong union bargaining power. Transport costs high. Scale economies important.	Cost efficiency through scale-efficient plants, low cost location, rapid adjustment of capacity to output, low labor costs. In special steels and some special uses, scope for differentiation through quality.
Fashion clothing	Demand fragmented by garment, style, quality, color. Customers willing to pay price premium for fashion, exclusivity, and quality. Retailers seek reliability & speed of supply.	Low barriers to entry and exit. Low seller concentration. Few scale economies. International competition strong. Retail buying power strong. Price and nonprice competition strong.	Need to combine effective differentiation with low-cost operation. Key differentiation variables are speed of response to changing high fashions, style, reputation with retailers or consumers. Low labor & overhead costs important except in less price-sensitive segments.
Grocery Super-markets	Low prices. Convenient location. Wide range of products.	Markets localized & concentration normally high. But customer price sensitivity encourages vigorous price competition. Exercise of bargaining power an important influence on input costs. Scale economies in operations & advertising.	Low cost operation requires operational efficiency, scale-efficient stores, large aggregate purchases to maximize buying power, low wage costs. Differentiation requires large stores (to allow wide product range), convenient location, easy parking.

determinants of revenues and costs. For example, in considering key success factors in retailing, we might begin with the elementary notion that:

$$\text{Profit} = \text{Revenue} - \text{Costs}$$

We could then restate this accounting definition rather more fully:

Profit = (Sales per square foot x Selling area x Gross margin) – Costs of administration, selling, inventory, and so on.

Investigation of these factors is likely to indicate:

- the role of store location in determining sales per square foot;
- the importance of buying power in determining gross margins and in permitting competitive pricing that generates high sales per square foot;
- the influence of merchandise mix on sales and margins;
- the role of inventory management systems on inventory costs and sales (through rapid response to customer requirements).

Exhibit 3.4 applies this same approach, identifying key success factors in the airline industry.

Exhibit 3.4   Modeling Profitability and Identifying Key Success Factors in the Airline Industry

Profitability, as measured by operating income per available seat-mile (ASM), is determined by three factors: *Yield*, total operating revenues divided by the number of revenue passenger miles (RPM); *Load factor*, the ratio between RPMs and ASMs; and *Cost*, total operating expenses divided by ASMs. Where an ASM is one seat flown one mile with a passenger in it or not, RPM is one seat flown one mile with a passenger in it. Thus:

$$\frac{\text{Income}}{\text{ASMs}} = \left[\frac{\text{Revenue}}{\text{RPMs}} \times \frac{\text{RPMs}}{\text{ASMs}}\right] - \frac{\text{Expenses}}{\text{ASMs}}$$

Some of the primary determinants of each of these measures will be the following:

Revenue/RPMs	Intensity of competition on routes flown
	Ability to quickly adjust prices and price structures to changing market conditions
	Ability to attract business customers
	Offering superior customer service
Load factors	Competitiveness of prices
	Efficiency of route planning (e.g., through hub-and-spoke systems)
	Building customer loyalty through quality of service, frequent-flyer programs
	Achieving customer preference through control of computer reservations systems
Expenses/ASMs	Level of wages
	Fuel efficiency of aircraft
	Productivity of employees (determined partly by their job flexibility)
	Load factors
	Level of administrative cost

In their quest for survival and competitive advantage, the airlines have sought to manipulate as many of these levers as possible in order to improve their profitability. In terms of revenue enhancement, several airlines have withdrawn from the most intensely competitive routes, others have sought to achieve a fare premium over the cut-price airlines through punctuality, convenience, comfort, and services (e.g., in-flight telephones, personal video monitors with choice of movies). To improve load factors companies have sought flexibility in allocating plane capacity to routes and used their CRS to achieve more flexible pricing. Most notably, companies have sought cost economies through increasing employee productivity, reducing administrative overhead through outsourcing, investing in fuel-efficient aircraft, and reducing wages and benefits.

Some strategic management experts dispute the value of success factors in formulating strategy. For example, Pankaj Ghemawat observes that the "whole idea of identifying a success factor and then chasing it seems to have something in common with the ill-considered medieval hunt for the *philosopher's stone*, a substance which would transmute everything it touched into gold."[23] The objective of this section is less ambitious. I accept that there is no universal blueprint for a successful strategy and that, even in individual industries, there is no "generic strategy" that can guarantee superior profitability. However, within a specific market, there are specific performance dimensions that a firm much achieve if it is to attract customers and survive competition. This is not to imply that firms must adopt common strategies. Because every firm consists of a unique set of resources and capabilities, every firm must pursue a unique strategy in pursuing key success factors.

The Problem of Industry Definition

One of the most difficult problems in industry analysis is defining the industry. No industry has clear boundaries either in terms of products or geographical areas. In analyzing the industry environment of BMW, should we consider the "motor vehicles and equipment" industry (SIC 371), the automobile industry (SIC 3712), or the luxury car industry? Should we view the industry as global, regional (e.g., Western Europe, North America) or national? Economists define an industry as a group of firms that supply a market where a market is the defined in terms of *substitutability*, both on the demand side and the supply side.

From a demand perspective, if customers consider the products of two firms to be close substitutes for one another, then the two firms should be viewed as competing within the same market. If customers substitute between the cars of BMW, Honda, and Volvo on the basis of price differentials, then the firms should be regarded as competing within the same industry. If customers are unwilling to substitute Mercedes-Benz trucks for BMW cars, then we should regard cars and trucks as falling into separate industries.

On the supply side, if manufacturers find it easy to switch their production facilities to manufacture one another's products, then such supply-side substitutability would suggest classifying the two firms in the same industry. The automobile industry is usually defined to include the manufacture of vans and light trucks because these can be manufactured at the same plants as automobiles. "Major appliance" manufacturers tend to be classified in a single industry not because consumers are willing to substitute between refrigerators and dishwashers but because the manufacturers can easily substitute between different appliances.

Typically, defining industries and markets by demand-side substitutability results in a narrower definition than by supply-side substitutability. For this reason, it is helpful to distinguish between markets and industries: defining markets in terms of demand-side substitutability and industries in terms of supply-side substitutability. Thus, in terms of supply-side substitution, we can identify a single global automobile industry; in terms of demand-side substitution, this global industry is segmented into a number of distinct markets that are defined by national boundaries and product groups (luxury cars, sports cars, family sedans, passenger vans, etc.).

Ultimately, drawing boundaries around industries and markets is a matter of judgment, and judgment needs to take account of the purposes of the analysis. For some issues, we may need to define the industry broadly; for examining more specific matters, we may want to define the industry much more narrowly. Fortunately, the precise delineation of an industry's boundaries is seldom critical to the outcome of analysis so long as we remain wary of influences that are external to the industry. For example, if we choose to identify BMW's industry as the manufacture of luxury cars, then we need to remain cognizant of the competition from other cars as substitutes for luxury cars and view the manufacturers of nonluxury cars as potential entrants into the luxury car industry.

Dynamic Aspects of Competition

One of the chief criticisms leveled at the "Five Forces" approach to industry analysis, and the *structure-conduct-performance* paradigm that underlies it, is that it fails to take account of the *dynamic* nature of competition and industry structure. The analysis begins with an industry's structure, which determines the nature and intensity of competition, which in turn determines profitability. But industry structure is not exogenously determined. A key feature of the competitive process is that industry structure is continually being changed both consciously by firms' strategic decisions and as an outcome of the competitive interaction between firms.

Hence, one danger of the Porter framework is in failing to recognize the two-way interaction between strategy and industry structure. The essence of competition is that it is a dynamic process in which equilibrium is never reached and in the course of which industry structures are continually being reformed. For example, the U.S. airline industry of the early 1990s had developed a structure that few of the architects of deregulation had predicted. The economists of the Civil Aeronautics Board had predicted that, in the absence of government regulation of routes and fares, entry would be easy, concentration would fall, and fares would drop to their perfectly competitive level. In practice, the industry has been shaped by the strategies of the leading players: mergers and acquisitions have increased concentration, the hub-and-spoke system has given rise to local near monopolies, and barriers to entry have been recreated through computer reservations systems, frequent flyer programs, and control over gates and landing slots at individual airports.

Schumpeterian competition

Joseph Schumpeter's contribution to industry analysis was to recognize the dynamic interaction between competition and industry structure. Schumpeter focused upon innovation as the central component of competition and the driving force behind industry evolution. Innovation represents a "perennial gale of creative destruction" through which favorable industry structures, monopoly in particular, contain the seeds of their own destruction by providing incentives for firms to attack established positions through new approaches to competing.[24]

The key issue raised by Schumpeter for our analysis is whether we can use current industry structures as a reliable guide to the nature of competition and industry performance in the future. The relevant consideration is the speed of structural change in industry. If the pace of transformation is rapid, if entry rapidly undermines the market power of dominant firms, if innovation speedily transforms industry structure by changing process technology, creating new substitutes, and by shifting the basis on which firms compete, then there is little merit in using industry structure as a basis for analyzing competition and profit.

Most empirical studies of changes over time in industry structure and profitability show Schumpeter's process of "creative destruction" to be more of a breeze than a gale. Studies of U.S. and Canadian industry have found entry to occur so slowly that profits are undermined only gradually.[25] One survey commented: "the picture of the competitive process . . . is, to say the least, sluggish in the extreme."[26] Overall, the studies show a fairly consistent picture of the rate of change of profitability and structure. Both at the firm and the industry level, profits tend to be highly persistent in the long run.[27] Structural change, notably concentration, entry, and the identity of leading firms, also appears to be, on average, slow.[28]

However, some industries conform closely to Schumpeter's model. Jeffrey Williams identifies "Schumpeterian industries" as those subject to rapid product innovation with relatively steep experience curves. In these industries, structure tends to be unstable. The *Economist* titled its 1993 survey of the computer industry "Within the Whirlwind."[29] To forecast the future of competition and profitability in this industry, there is little advantage to be gained in predicting the evolution of industry structure. Competition, industry structure, and profitability are all driven by technology. The key to forecasting profitability is to forecast technological change and to analyze its implications and the appropriability of its benefits.

The contribution of game theory

Central to the criticisms of the Porter "Five Forces" framework is its failure to take account of the competitive interaction between firms. I noted in chapter 1 that the essence of strategic competition is that the players are involved in an interactive game such that the decisions made by any one player are dependent upon the actual and anticipated decisions of the other players. "Five Forces" analysis (and the structure-conduct-performance paradigm upon which it is based) fails to take account of explicit rivalry and, in particular, fails to take account of rival's choices to compete or not to compete, of sequential competitive moves, and of the role of threats and promises. Game theory has two especially valuable contributions to make to strategic management:

1   It permits the framing of strategic decisions. Apart from any theoretical value of the theory of games, the description of the game in terms of:
    • identifying the players,
    • specifying each player's options,
    • establishing the payoffs from every combination of options, and
    • defining sequences of decisions using game trees facilitates rational decision making.
2   It offers considerable insight into situations of competition and bargaining and is capable of considerable predictive power. The basic game theory models, most notably the "prisoners' dilemma," are fundamental to the analysis of coordination, while the analysis of reputation, endurance, information, and commitment – especially within the context of multiperiod games – provides penetrating insight into central issues of strategy that go well beyond pure intuition.[30] Particularly important for practicing managers, game theory can indicate strategies for improving the structure and outcome of the game through manipulating the payoffs to the different players.[31]

Despite an explosion of interest in game theory during the 1980s, its applications to strategic management remain limited. In terms of the modeling of strategic decisions as games, the power of the game theory approach is much more in relation to negotiations and specific decisions than long-term strategies. Thus, game theory has provided illuminating insights into President Reagan's 1981 tax cut, subsidies for Airbus Industrie, the problems of OPEC in agreeing to production cuts, choices in America's Cup yacht races, and bidding for wireless communication licenses.[32] Game theoretic modeling is readily applicable to decisions such as a price cut, a new product launch, or a joint venture formation; and it can provide valuable decision support during negotiations. However, the game theory provides only limited direct application to the main theme of this book – the long-term pursuit of superior profitability – partly because such strategies are less about "playing the game" and more about transforming the game by achieving a sustainable competitive advantage.[33]

While business strategy is concerned with competitive advantage, game theory is concerned with equilibrium. Game theory's preoccupation with equilibrium has resulted in its prediction of an enormous range of outcomes from a variety of highly stylized situations involving few exogenous variables and highly restrictive assumptions. The result is a mathematically sophisticated body of theory that in terms of application to strategic management suffers from unrealistic assumptions, lack of generality, and an analysis of dynamic situations through a sequence of static equilibriums.[34]

Chaos and catastrophe

During recent years, perceptions of the business environment have been influenced by scientific study of the behavior of dynamic systems. The most influential has been the development within mathematics of chaos theory and its diffusion throughout the natural and social sciences. Chaos theory studies complex, dynamic processes where nonlinear relationships give rise to erratic behavior that is nonrepeating but nonrandom. The principal applications of chaos theory within business have been in analyzing financial markets.[35]

A related area of theoretical analysis of the dynamic behavior of complex systems is *catastrophe theory*, which models the propensity for structurally stable systems to demonstrate *discontinuity* (sudden shifts in behavior or outcomes), *divergence* (the tendency for small divergences to become magnified), and *hysteresis* (reversals of behavior that typically do not restore the initial situation). The cusp catastrophe model may have interesting applications for analyzing competitive behavior (especially price wars and technological competition) and patterns of organizational change.[36]

Summary and Conclusions

Every industry is unique in terms of the competitive behavior that we observe during any period of time. At the same time, the different patterns of competition across industries can be explained and predicted within a common analytical framework. The underlying premise of this chapter is that the structural characteristics of an industry play a key role in determining the nature and intensity of competition within it. Competition, in turn, determines the overall rate of profit in an industry.

This premise is of crucial importance for managers and students of management. It means that to understand competition and profitability within an industry we do not need to acquire over a long period of time specific knowledge of the industry but that we can utilize a general framework of cause and effect to understand past patterns of competitive activity and to predict the course of competition and profitability in the future.

The principal framework used in this chapter is Porter's "Five Forces of Competition" model. The merit of this model is that it provides a simple, yet powerful, organizing framework for classifying the relevant information about an industry's structure and for predicting what the implications of these structural features are for competitive behavior.

By understanding the links between industry structure, competition, and profitability, it is possible to analyze three important strategic issues:

- *predicting industry profitability* – The key questions of corporate strategy, such as the appropriate level of investment in an industry and the choice of directions of diversification, require a forecast of the attractiveness of industry environments;
- *indicating how the firm can influence industry structure in order to moderate competition and improve profitability*;
- *identifying key success factors – the prerequisites for survival and success in a particular industry*. Their identification is an essential step in determining how the firm can establish a position of competitive advantage.

The framework suffers from some critical limitations. In particular, it fails to take account of the dynamic character of competition. Competition is not determined wholly by industry structure; it is a complex social process of action and reaction where the objectives, perceptions, and personalities of the players occupy important roles. Competitive process also changes industry structure.

In subsequent chapters, we will draw heavily upon the frameworks, concepts, and techniques described in this chapter. We will also be extending the analysis to deal with some of its limitations and to make it more applicable to the dynamics of competitive situations. The next chapter examines the internal complexity of industries in terms of segmentation and the characteristics and behavior of individual competitors. Chapter 5 returns to the dynamics of competitive interactions, and chapter 9 considers the evolution of industries over time.

Notes

1   See, for example, J. P. Leemhuis, "Using Scenarios to Develop Strategies," *Long Range Planning* (April 1985): 30–7; and Pierre Wack, "Scenarios: Shooting the Rapids," *Harvard Business Review* (November-December 1985): 139–50.

2   Michael E. Porter, *Competitive Strategy: Techniques for Analyzing Industries and Competitors* (New York: Free Press, 1980), chapter 1. For a summary see his article, "How Competitive Forces Shape Strategy," *Harvard Business Review* (1979): 86–93.

3   W. J. Baumol, John C. Panzar, and Robert D. Willig, *Contestable Markets and the Theory of Industry Structure* (New York: Harcourt Brace Jovanovich, 1982).

4   "Annual Franchise 500," *Entrepreneur* (January 1993): 170–1.

5   "Brand Loyalty Is Rarely Blind Loyalty," *Wall Street Journal*, October 19, 1989: B1.

6   Robert D. Buzzell and Paul W. Farris, "Marketing Costs in Consumer Goods Industries," in *Strategy + Structure = Performance*, ed. Hans Thorelli (Bloomington, IN: Indiana University Press, 1977): 128–9.

7   For a discussion and empirical evidence see Martin B. Lieberman, "Excess Capacity As a Barrier to Entry," *Journal of Industrial Economics* 35 (June 1987): 607–27.

8   J. S. Bain, *Barriers to New Competition* (Cambridge: Harvard University Press, 1956); H. Michael Mann, "Seller Concentration, Entry Barriers and Rates of Return in Thirty Industries," *Review of Economics and Statistics* 48 (1966): 296–307.

9   See, for example, the studies by W. S. Comanor and T. A. Wilson, *Advertising and Market Power* (Cambridge: Harvard University Press, 1974); and L. Weiss, "Quantitative Studies in Industrial Organization," in *Frontiers of Quantitative Economics*, edited M. Intriligator (Amsterdam: North Holland, 1971).

10 George S. Yip, "Gateways to Entry," *Harvard Business Review* 82 (September-October 1982): 85–93.

11 Guy de Jonquieres, "Europe's New Cold Warriors," *Financial Times*, May 19, 1993, 18.

12 See "U.S. Probes Whether Airlines Colluded on Fare Increases," *Wall Street Journal*, December 14, 1989, B1; and "A Tank Full of Trouble," *Economist*, December 16–22, 1989, 57.

13 The problems caused by excess capacity and exit barriers are discussed in *Strategic Management of Excess Capacity*, ed. Charles Baden Fuller (Oxford: Basil Blackwell, 1990).

14 "When the Chips Are Down," *Business Week*, June 27, 1988, 28–9.

15 Richard Schmalensee, "Inter-Industries Studies of Structure and Performance," in Handbook of Industrial Organization, ed. Richard Schmalensee and Robert D. Willig, vol. 2 (Amsterdam: North Holland, 1988), 976.

16 For evidence on the impact of concentration in banking, airlines, and railroads see D. W. Carlton and J. M. Perloff, *Modern Industrial Organization* (Glenview, IL: Scott, Foresman, 1990), 383–5.

17 As noted in chapter 1, PIMS stands for Profit Impact of Market Strategy. The PIMS database is developed, maintained, and analyzed by the Strategic Planning Institute. The PIMS database comprises information provided by over 3,000 business units in North America and Western Europe. PIMS uses multiple regression analysis to estimate the impact of a variety of strategy and industry structure variables on business-unit profitability. The development of PIMS and the application of its analytic techniques to strategy formulation are discussed in chapter 13.

18 Robert D. Buzzell and Bradley T. Gale, *The PIMS Principles: Linking Strategy to Performance* (New York: Free Press, 1987), 273–84.

19 S. H. Lustgarten, "The Impact of Buyer Concentration in Manufacturing Industries," *Review of Economics and Statistics* 57 (1975): 125–32; and Robert M. Grant, "Manufacturer-Retailer Relations: The Shifting Balance of Power," in *Business Strategy and Retailing*, ed. G. Johnson (Chichester: John Wiley & Sons, 1987).

20 See Joe Bower, *When Markets Quake* (Boston: Harvard Business School Press, 1986).

21 Paul Abrahams, "ICI Seeks Restructure of Polyurethane Industry," *Financial Times*, July 1, 1993, 28.

22 The term was coined by Chuck Hofer and Dan Schendel (*Strategy Formulation: Analytical Concepts* [St. Paul: West Publishing, 1977], 77) who defined key success factors as ". . . those variables which management can influence through its decisions and which can affect significantly the overall competitive positions of the firms in an industry . . . Within any particular industry they are derived from the interaction of two sets of variables, namely, the economic and technological characteristics of the industry . . . and the competitive weapons on which the various firms in the industry have built their strategies."

23 Pankaj Ghemawat, *Commitment: The Dynamic of Strategy* (New York: Free Press, 1991), 11.

24 Joseph Schumpeter, *The Theory of Economic Development* (Cambridge: Harvard University Press, 1934).

25 R. T. Masson and J. Shaanan, "Stochastic Dynamic Limit Pricing: An Empirical Test," *Review of Economics and Statistics* 64 (1982): 413–22; R. T. Masson and J. Shaanan, "Optimal Pricing and Threat of Entry: Canadian Evidence," *International Journal of Industrial Organization* 5 (1987).

26 P. A. Geroski and R. T. Masson, "Dynamic Market Models in Industrial Organization," *International Journal of Industrial Organization* 5 (1987): 1–13.

27 Dennis C. Mueller, *Profits in the Long Run* (Cambridge: Cambridge University Press, 1986).

28 Richard Caves and Michael E. Porter, "The Dynamics of Changing Seller Concentration," *Journal of Industrial Economics* 19 (1980): 1–15; P. Hart and R. Clarke, Concentration in British Industry (Cambridge: Cambridge University Press, 1980).

29 "Within the Whirlwind: A Survey of the Computer Industry," *Economist*, February 27, 1993.

30 Keith Weigelt and Colin F. Camerer, "Reputation and Corporate Strategy: A Review of Recent Theory and Applications," *Strategic Management Journal* 9 (1988): 443–54; A. K. Dixit, "The Role of Investment in Entry Deterrence," *Economic Journal* 90 (1980): 95–106; P. Milgrom and J. Roberts, "Informational Asymmetries, Strategic Behavior and Industrial Organization," *American Economic Review*, 77, no. 2 (May 1987): 184–9; J. Tirole, *The Theory of Industrial Organization* (Cambridge: MIT Press, 1990); Pankaj Ghemawat, *Commitment: The Dynamic of Strategy* (New York: Free Press, 1991).

31 There are two outstanding introductions to the principles of game theory and their practical applications: Thomas C. Schelling, *The Strategy of Conflict*, 2d ed. (Cambridge: Harvard University Press, 1980); and A. K. Dixit and B. J. Nalebuff, *Thinking Strategically: The Competitive Edge in Business, Politics, and Everyday Life* (New York: W. W. Norton, 1991).

32 Dixit and Nalebuff, *Thinking Strategically*, 131–5; "Auctions," *Economist* (July 23, 1994): 70.

33 In game theory terminology, we may regard the establishment of competitive advantage through cost or differentiation advantage as a *dominant*

strategy. If all players are pursuing such dominant strategies then equilibrium in the game is simple and robust.

34 There are numerous critiques of the usefulness of game theory. F. M. Fisher ("The Games Economists Play: A Noncooperative View," *RAND Journal of Economics* 20 [1989]: 113–24) points to the ability of game theory to predict almost any equilibrium solution. Colin F. Camerer describes this as the "Pandora's Box Problem" ("Does Strategy Research Need Game Theory?" *Strategic Management Journal*, special issue, 12 [winter 1991]: 137–52). Steve Postrel illustrates this problem by developing a game theory model to explain the rationality of bank presidents setting fire to their trousers ("Burning Your Britches behind You: Can Policy Scholars Bank on Game Theory?" *Strategic Management Journal*, special issue, 12 [winter 1991]: 153–5). Michael E. Porter ("Towards a Dynamic Theory of Strategy," *Strategic Management Journal*, special issue, 12 [winter 1991]: 95–117) notes that game theory ". . . stops short of a dynamic theory of strategy . . . these models explore the dynamics of a largely static world."

35 "The Mathematics of Markets: A Survey of the Frontiers of Finance," *Economist*, October 9, 1993.

36 Terence A. Olivia, Diana L. Day, and Ian C. MacMillan, "A Generic Model of Competitive Dynamics," *Academy of Management Review* 13(1988): 374–89.

FOUR

Intra-Industry Analysis: Segmentation, Strategic Groups, and Competitor Appraisal

---

> ***Outline***
> Introduction and Objectives
> Segmentation Analysis
> The uses of segmentation
> Stages of segmentation analysis
> Strategic Groups
> Use of strategic analysis
> Competitor Analysis
> Predicting competitors' behavior: a framework
> Applying the results of a competitor analysis
> Summary and Conclusions

Introduction and Objectives

An "industry" is an artificial construct. Companies exist, but an industry is a group of companies where the boundaries depend upon the classification scheme adopted by the observer. Unlike other taxonomies, such as species of plants or birds, industry classifications identify categories that have little internal homogeneity, and there is little agreement between individuals as to the precise delineation of boundaries. The retailing sector includes J. C. Penney, Safeway Food Stores, Tiffany's, Shell filling stations, and Mad Mike's Video Emporium. Each of these retailers inhabits a different environment and none competes directly with another.

Such heterogeneity poses problems for industry analysis. In the last chapter, we viewed the industry as something real with definite structural features that determined competition and profitability. However, if the concept of the industry is a simplification of reality, then, as with all generalizations, industry analysis can be misleading. For example, industry analysis tells us that the bread industry is subject to declining demand, excess capacity, low brand loyalty, and strong buying power exerted by the supermarket chains, all of which lead to strong competition and low margins. Yet, Jean-Louis Vilgrain, president of France's leading milling group, established the Vie de France chain of minibakeries in the United States and achieved an average annual growth of sales of

53 percent and net earnings growth of 72 percent during the 1980s. Clearly, the fresh-baked, specialty bread segment of the bread industry is substantially different from the industry in general.[1] Similarly, the fierce competition and low margins in the British food retailing industry would have offered little indication of the potential for clothing retailer Marks & Spencer to have earned such high margins in retailing fresh, prepared gourmet foods.

To understand competition more intimately and to identify profit opportunities more accurately, a more detailed analysis of industries may be needed. This chapter explores on a more disaggregated level the internal structure of industries.

By the time you have completed this chapter, you will be able to:

- *segment* an industry into a number of constituent markets and deploy the tools of industry analysis to analyze the attractiveness of each segment and the key success factors within it;
- classify the firms within an industry into *strategic groups* based on similarities in their strategies;
- predict the behavior of individual competitors including the competitive moves that they are likely to initiate and their likely responses to strategic initiatives that our subject firm introduces.

Segmentation Analysis

The uses of segmentation

If the nature and intensity of competition varies within an industry, then it is useful to partition an industry into segments and analyze its structural characteristics. Such analysis is useful in appraising the attractiveness of different segments.[2] This is beneficial not only for the new entrant in determining which part of a market to enter but also for the established firm in deciding in which segments to maintain a presence and how to allocate resources between them.

Differences in structure and competition between segments may also mean differences in key success factors between segments. In the bread industry, competing effectively in the market for standard, packaged sliced bread requires cost-efficient operation in the form of large-scale, automated production with well-organized distribution through large-volume retail outlets. In the market for specialty bread, success is far more dependent upon quality, freshness, variety, and presentation. This would require small-batch, localized production of a wide variety of breads.

Stages in segmentation analysis

Segmentation analysis proceeds in five principal stages, which are summarized in figure 4.1.

- Identify Key Segmentation Variables and Categories
  - Identify segmentation variables
  - Reduce the number of segmentation variables by selecting the most significant segmentation variables and combining closely correlated segmentation variables
  - Identify discrete categories for each segmentation variable
- Construct a Segmentation Matrix
- Analyze Segment Attractiveness
  Structural analysis of competition and profitability within the segment
  Also: segment size and segment growth rate
- Identify Key Success Factors in Each Segment
- Analyze Attractions of Broad versus Narrow Segment Scope
  - Potential for sharing costs and transferring skills across segments
  - Similarity of key success factors between segments
  - Product differentiation benefits of segment specialization

Figure 4.1 Analyzing Industry Segments: The Main Stages

1 Identify key segmentation variables The first stage of segmentation analysis is to decide upon the basis of segmentation. At the outset, it is important to recognize that segment decisions are essentially choices about products and customers. Hence, the focus of segmentation analysis is market selection. Having identified the broad market that the industry supplies, the next task is to determine the most appropriate basis for subdividing it: different types of products, different groups of customers, different price ranges, or different geographical areas? For most markets, multiple criteria can be applied. These mostly relate to characteristics of the product or characteristics of the customers. Figure 4.2 lists a number of segmentation variables. The most appropriate segmentation variables are those that yield the most distinct categorization in terms of our *substitutability* criteria. Just as we used substitutability on the customer and supplier side as the basis for defining industry boundaries, the same criteria can be applied to determining market segments.

Market segments often tend to be associated with price differentials. Indeed, price itself may provide a useful basis for segmenting a market. One of the classic examples of a business strategy founded upon a price-based segmentation is that established by General Motors in the 1920s (see exhibit 4.1).

Typically, there will be many customer and product characteristics that can be used as a basis for segmentation. In order for a segmentation analysis to be manageable, we need to reduce these to two or three. To reduce the number of segmentation variables we can apply two processes:

- identify the most *strategically significant* segmentation variables. In terms of substitutability by customers and by producers, which variables are most important in creating meaningful divisions in a market?
- combine segmentation variables that are closely correlated. Among sedan automobiles, price, vehicle size, engine capacity, and features

Figure 4.2. The Basis for Segmentation: Customer and Product Characteristics

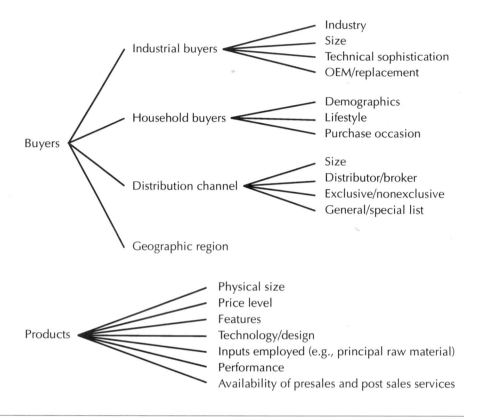

tend to be highly correlated. Hence a size categorization: full size, mid-size, compact, and subcompact can describe multiple dimensions. In the case of restaurants, possible segmentation might include price level, service (waiter service/self-service), cuisine (fast-food/full meals), alcohol (wine served/soft drinks only). However, all these variables are likely to be closely correlated with one another, and it may be possible to combine the four variables and identify just three segments: full-service restaurants, cafes, and fast-food outlets.

2 Constructing a segmentation matrix   Once the segmentation variables have been selected and discrete categories for each determined, the individual segments may be identified using a two- or three-dimensional matrix. For example, an analysis of the British frozen food industry used types of food and distribution channels as the basis for segmentation (see figure 4.3).[3] Where firms are specialized by their geographic area or where customer preferences differ by country or region, then geography may be a useful basis for segmentation.

3 Analyze segment attractiveness   Competition and the profit potential of an industry segment can be analyzed using the same structural analysis that was applied to the analysis of an industry. Just as the pressure of competition and the prospects for profit in the world automobile industry can be analyzed using Porter's "Five Forces of Competition" framework, the same analysis can be applied to evaluate the attractiveness of individual market segments (see exhibit 4.2).

However, there are a few differences. First, when analyzing the pressure of competition from substitute products, we are concerned not only with substitutes from other industries but, more importantly, with substitutes from other segments within the same industry. For example, in evaluating potential profit margins on station wagons within the American market, firms must take account of the increasing substitution between station wagons and passenger minivans.

		DISTRIBUTION CHANNELS				
		Supermarkets		Independent grocery retailers	Specialist freezer stores	Caterers
		Producers' brands	Retailers' brands			
P R O D U C T T Y P E S	Vegetables					
	Fruits					
	Meat Products					
	Desserts					
	Convenience Ready Meals					

Figure 4.3   Segmenting the British Frozen Food Industry

Exhibit 4.2 Segmenting the World Automobile Market

A global automobile producer such as Ford or Toyota might segment the world auto market by product type and geography. A first-cut segmentation might be along these lines:

	REGION						
	North America	W. Europe	E. Europe	Asia	Latin America	Australasia	Africa
Luxury sedans							
Full-size sedans							
Midsize sedans							
Compact sedans							
Subcompact sedans							
Station wagons							
Passenger minivans							
Sports cars							
Sport-utility							
Pickup trucks							

One of the most useful applications of such a segmentation would be an understanding of how profitability in the past had varied between segments and the determinants of such differentials. During the early 1990s, a number of segments are especially interesting:

- the North American market for subcompacts has always yielded low profits. Factors here include the large number of competitors (all the world's major auto producers including a number of low-cost producers such as Hyundai), comparatively low product differentiation (as indicated by the convergence of car designs, automotive technologies, and quality levels), and high level of capacity relative to demand;
- the North American market for passenger minivans has been a highly profitable segment for most participants. In particular, during the 1980s, a strong positioning within this segment (with its Dodge Caravan and Plymouth Voyager) was the primary reason for the survival of Chrysler. This segment has seen strong demand relative to capacity and comparatively few participants;
- worldwide, the market for luxury cars was highly unprofitable during the early 1990s. As a group, Rolls-Royce, Mercedes, Jaguar, and BMW suffered substantial losses. This was primarily the result of recession, which depressed demand and resulted in substantial excess capacity. But it was also the result of long-term structural trends in this segment. Historically, luxury cars have been highly profitable, reflecting the high level of profit differentiation and consequent customer price insensitivity. However, new entry by Honda (Acura), Toyota (Lexus), and Nissan (Infiniti), together with the acquisition of Jaguar by Ford, resulted in increased competition. Meanwhile enhancement in the quality and features of mass-produced family sedans, made these cars closer substitutes for luxury cars.

Second, when considering entry into the segment, the major source of entrants is likely to be producers established in other segments within the industry. Thus, in discussing the threat of entry into the segment we must focus primarily upon the barriers that restrict the incursion of firms from other segments – these are termed "*barriers to mobility*" to distinguish them from the barriers to entry that offer protection from outside the industry. Barriers to mobility are a key factor in determining the ability of a segment to offer superior returns to those available elsewhere in the industry. Unless there are significant barriers to the mobility of firms from other segments, there is no basis for the preservation of superior profitability.[4] In most industries, the increased flexibility of design and production made possible by computer-aided design and flexible manufacturing systems has had the effect of reducing barriers to mobility. In the automobile industry, high margin segments such as luxury cars, passenger vans, and sport-utility vehicles have seen a sharp rise in competition as many leading volume car manufacturers have sought to establish themselves.

Segmentation analysis can also be useful in identifying unexploited opportunities in an industry. Figure 4.4 shows a segmentation matrix of the restaurant industry in San Luis Obispo, a California town of

Figure 4.4
Segmentation of the San Luis Obispo Restaurant Industry*

	Type of Restaurant			
	Up-market waiter service	Cafes & midpriced waiter service restaurants	Bar-restaurants	Counter service & fast food
American e.g., steaks, hamburgers	Madonna Inn	Hudson's Grill Apple Farm Del Monte Cafe This Old House	SLO Brewery McLintocks The Graduate	McDonald's Burger King Bishop Burger
Californian	Brubeck's Sebastian's	Rhythm Cafe Chocolate Soup Hogy's	Spike's	////////
Italian	Cafe Roma	Upper Crust Da Vinci's Pasta House	////////	Pizza parlors, e.g., Woodstocks' Pizza Hut
French	////////	////////	////////	////////
Mexican	////////	Buona Tavola Izzy Ortega's Pete's Cafe Tacos Mexicali Maya Restaurant	TA's Cantina Tortilla Flats	Tacos Acapulco Chilie Peppers Taco Bell
Chinese	////////	Golden China China Bowl Imperial China	////////	////////
Japanese	////////	Yuji's, Sushi Tsurugi	////////	////////
Other Asian	////////	Thairrific Little Bangkok	////////	////////

* San Luis Obispo city only
⊞ = Empty segment

some 50,000 persons. The analysis reveals a number of empty segments: there exist no luxury Mexican-cuisine restaurants nor any budget-priced French bistros. Such empty segments may reflect a lack of customer demand, or they may represent unexploited opportunities. For example, in the early 1960s microwave ovens and dishwashing machines were manufactured almost exclusively for the catering trade. A segmentation analysis of the appliance industry might have alerted the firms established in these segments to opportunities for developing these products for the consumer market.

4 Identify the segment's key success factors   Differences in competitive structure and customer preferences between segments also imply differences in the basis of competitive advantage. Examination of differences between segments in buyers' purchase criteria and the ways in which firms compete can reveal clear differences in key success factors.

For example, the U.S. bicycle industry can be segmented on the basis of the age group of the customer (infants, children, youths, adults), price, branding, and distribution channel. Combining these segmentation variables, four major segments can be identified. Key success factors differ between the segments (see figure 4.5).

5 Narrow versus broad segment scope   A final issue concerning the choice of which segments to enter and how to compete in each concerns the relative advantages of segment specialization versus segment diversity. The advantages of a broad over a narrow segment focus are dependent upon two major factors: similarity of key success factors and the presence of shared costs. In an industry where key success factors are similar between segments, then a firm can adopt a similar strategic approach in relation to different segments. If different strategies need to be adopted for different segments, then not only does this pose organizational difficulties for the firm but the credibility of the firm in one segment may be adversely affected by its strategy in another. The introduction by Harley-Davidson of a range of lightweight motorcycles during the early 1970s was a failure not only because Harley-Davidson could not compete with the Japanese in this segment but also because of the damage to the firm's reputation in the heavyweight motorcycle segment.

Shared costs between segments mean that broad segment suppliers can achieve lower costs than their narrow-segment competitors. The vulnerability of narrow-segment specialists to competition from broad-line competitors is constantly being revealed:

- in soft drinks, Seven-Up's reliance on a single lemon-lime drink places it in a weak position against its broader-line competitors such as Coca-Cola, PepsiCo, and Schweppes and ultimately caused it to merge with Dr. Pepper (which faced similar problems);

Segment	Key Success Factors
Low-price bicycles sold primarily through department and chain stores, mainly under the retailer's own brand (e.g., Sears' "Free Spirit").	Access to distribution channels essential. The key requirement is low-cost manufacture combined with consistency of quality and sufficient financial security to guarantee a long-term supply relationship. Most of this segment was occupied by Taiwanese assemblers, although some U.S. manufacturers such as Murray Ohio had survived rigorous cost control and supplementing domestic production by imported components and complete bicycles.
Medium-priced bicycles sold primarily under the manufacturer's brand name and distributed mainly through specialist bicycle stores.	Survival and prosperity also requires cost efficient manufacture, which depends upon scale-efficient manufacture and either low wage rates or automated manufacturing techniques. Success here requires not just low price but also effective marketing both to dealers through the provision of information and dealer-support services and to final customers through advertising. Scale-efficient production and national (and increasingly international) distribution and advertising gave large-sized firms an advantage. Leading companies included Huffy (U.S.), Raleigh (U.K.), Peugeot (France), and Fuji (Japan).
High-priced enthusiasts' bicycles	Success requires high-quality components and assembly, innovation in design and materials (primarily in order to achieve speed by minimizing weight and wind resistance), and market appeal through competitive success in racing and through advertising in the specialist cycling press.
Children's bicycles (and tricycles) sold primarily through toy retailers (both department stores and specialist toy stores).	Manufacturers can compete either on the basis of low price (offshore manufacture) or through a strong brand name backed by good design and a reputation for safety and quality.

Figure 4.5
Segmentation and Key Success Factors in the U.S. Bicycle Industry

- the acquisition of specialist auto producers Saab, Lancia, Jaguar, AMC/Jeep, Maserati, and Lotus by broad segment carmakers resulted from the inability of the specialist manufacturers to spread their development costs over a large enough output volume.

It is impossible to generalize about the relative merits of focused and broad segment strategies. The critical issue concerns the merits of specialization versus the benefits of sharing joint costs. In service industries, William Davidow and Bro Uttal have argued that economies from specialization and differences in key success factors in different customer segments favor a narrow segment focus.[5] By specializing in hernia surgery, Shouldice Hospital near Toronto achieves remarkable levels of productivity and quality. In banking, a number of regional banks that have concentrated upon basic banking services have outperformed banks that have expanded both nationally and across a broad range of financial services.

Many of the issues that arise in relation to the relative attractiveness of broad or narrow segment strategies are identical to those that arise when considering the merits of specialization versus diversification. These issues will be discussed in more detail in chapter 14.

Strategic Groups

While segmentation analysis concentrates upon the characteristics of product markets as the basis for dividing industries, *strategic group analysis* uses the characteristics of firms as the basis for division. The strategic group concept was developed at Harvard and applied in empirical research at Purdue University.[6] A strategic group is *"the group of firms in an industry following the same or a similar strategy along the strategic dimensions."*[7] These "strategic dimensions" include those strategic decision variables that best distinguish the business strategies and competitive positioning of the firms within an industry. These may include product market scope (in terms of product range and geographical breadth), choice of distribution channels, level of product quality, degree of vertical integration, choice of technology, and so on. By selecting the most important strategic dimensions and locating each firm in the industry along with them, it is usually possible to identify one or more groups of companies that have adopted more or less similar approaches to competing within the industry. Figure 4.6 identifies strategic groups within the world automobile industry, while figure 4.7 identifies strategic groups within the world oil industry.[8]

Uses of strategic group analysis Most of the empirical research into strategic groups has been concerned with analyzing differences in profitability between firms.[9] In general, the proposition that profitability differences *within* strategic groups are less than differences *between* strategic groups has not received robust empirical support. The inconsistency of empirical findings may reflect the fact that the members of a strategic group, while pursuing similar strategies, are not necessarily in competition with one another. For example, within the world oil industry, the nationally based integrated oil companies are not competing with one another by virtue of their locational differentiation.

This is not to imply that the strategic group is not a useful concept but that the value of strategic group analysis is more as a descriptive than a predictive tool. Strategic group analysis is unlikely to offer much insight into why some firms in an industry are more profitable than others. However, as a means of gaining a broad picture of the types of firms within an industry and the kinds of strategy that have proven viable, strategic group analysis can contribute to an understanding of

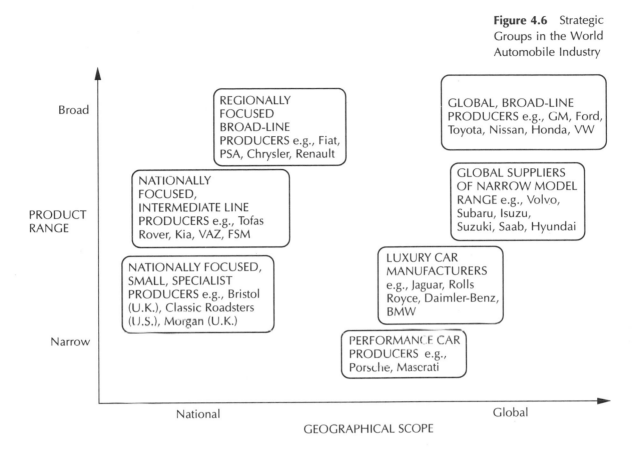

Figure 4.6 Strategic Groups in the World Automobile Industry

the structure, competitive dynamics, and evolution of an industry and to the issues of strategic management within it. This view of strategic groups as a valuable descriptive device is supported by Reger and Huff's evidence that managers within an industry have consistent perceptions of groupings of similar firms.[10]

Competitor Analysis

The purpose of competitor analysis is to predict the behavior of one's closest rivals. The importance of competitor analysis to a company depends upon the structure of its industry. In a fragmented industry where firms produce an undifferentiated product, as in the case of most agricultural commodities, market competition is the outcome of the strategies and decisions of so many producers that there is little point in analyzing the behavior of one or two individual firms. In highly concentrated industries, the competitive environment of a company depends critically upon the behavior of a few rivals. In household detergents, the industry environment is dominated by the competitive interaction of Procter & Gamble, Colgate-Palmolive, and Lever Brothers

Figure 4.7 Strategic Groups within the World Petroleum Industry

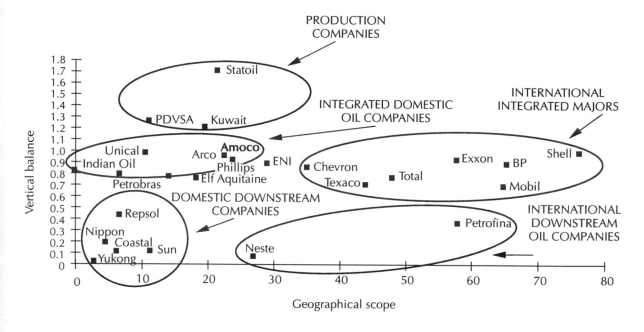

Source: Robert M. Grant, *Restructuring and Strategic Change among the World's Largest Companies*, 1980–91 (Milan: Franco Angeli, 1993).

(Unilever). In large commercial jet manufacture, the industry environment is formed primarily by the interacting competitive strategies of Boeing and Airbus Industrie.

In other industries, although concentration may be only modest, the extent of differentiation in the goods and services offered by different firms may mean that a company faces just one or two close competitors whose strategies impact substantially upon its profitability. For example:

- in the world soft drinks industry, despite the large number of national, international, and local suppliers of soft drinks, the dominant feature of competition is the struggle between Coca-Cola and PepsiCo for dominance in cola drinks. Each company maintains an obsessive interest in relative market share and is engaged in a constant quest for advantage through advertising and multimillion-dollar promotional contracts with pop stars and sports celebrities;
- in the U.S. automobile market, more than 20 manufacturers vie for market share. However, Jaguar's competitive environment is most strongly influenced by the product, pricing, and promotional policies of Mercedes-Benz and BMW.

It is not only through marketing activities that firms' competitive strategies are interdependent. In industries where plant capacity is large relative to the total market, investment decisions are highly interdependent.[11] In petrochemicals, any single firm's calculation of the returns on investment in a new plant must take careful account of other firms' investment plans. Research and development (R&D) activities show similar interactions. In pharmaceuticals, the returns to R&D depend crucially upon being the first company to apply for a patent on a new drug. Expenditures on R&D require a careful appraisal of whether other firms are pursuing similar avenues of research and, if so, what their stage of development is.

Competitor analysis has three major purposes:

1. To forecast competitors' future strategies and decisions;
2. To predict competitors' likely reactions to a firm's strategy and competitive initiatives;
3. To determine how competitors' behavior can be influenced to the benefit of the initiating firm.

For all three purposes, the key requirement is to understand competitors in order to predict their choices of strategy and tactics and likely reactions to environmental changes and any competitive moves initiated by our own company.

Predicting competitors' behavior: a framework

Figure 4.8 shows the basic framework for competitor analysis. There are four main inputs into the analysis.

1 Identifying current strategy The starting point is an identification of the competitor's current strategy. In the absence of any forces for change, a reasonable assumption is that the company will continue to compete in the future in much the same way as it competes at the present. A competitor's strategy may be identified on the basis of what the firm says and what it does. These two are not necessarily the same, as Mintzberg has pointed out: there may be a divergence between *intended strategy* and *realized strategy*.[12] Major sources of explicit statements of strategy intentions are likely to be found in the annual reports of companies, particularly in the chairman's message to shareholders and in other public statements by senior managers. With regard to realized strategy, emphasis must be given to the competitors' actions and decisions: What capital investment projects are being undertaken? What hiring is taking place? What new products are in the pipeline? What acquisitions or strategic alliances have recently been undertaken or rumored? What new advertising and promotional campaigns have been planned?

Such information can offer considerable insight into future priorities and the likely reaction of a company to our own company's competitive

Figure 4.8 A
Framework for
Competitor Analysis

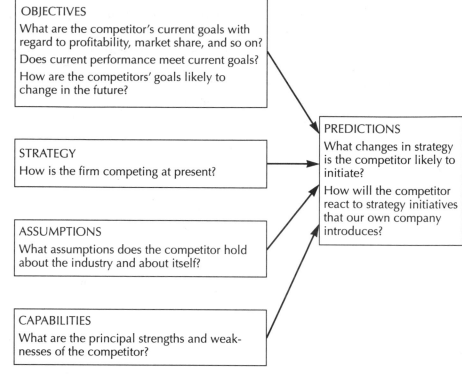

OBJECTIVES
What are the competitor's current goals with
regard to profitability, market share, and so on?
Does current performance meet current goals?
How are the competitors' goals likely to
change in the future?

STRATEGY
How is the firm competing at present?

ASSUMPTIONS
What assumptions does the competitor hold
about the industry and about itself?

CAPABILITIES
What are the principal strengths and weaknesses of the competitor?

PREDICTIONS
What changes in strategy
is the competitor likely to
initiate?
How will the competitor
react to strategy initiatives
that our own company
introduces?

Source: Adapted from M. E. Porter, *Competitive Strategy* (New York: Free Press, 1980).

initiatives. For example, Sears Roebuck's 1993 flotation of its Dean
Witter subsidiary was a clear signal to competitors and to the investment
community of a change in its strategy. Sears would no longer be able
to support its flagging retail operations with the profits from financial
services. Its traditional retailing business was now its only business, on
the basis of which Sears would either sink or swim. A more aggressive
and purposeful approach toward competing in the retail sector seemed
likely. Similarly, Zenith's sale of its computer division in 1989 was a clear
indication to its competitors of its commitment to long-term survival in
the U.S. television industry.

2 Identifying the competitor's objectives   To determine likely changes
in a competitor's strategy and competitive stance, some knowledge of
the company's goals is crucial. Identifying basic financial and market
objectives is particularly important. A company with short- and medium-term ROI objectives such as ITT or Hanson is likely to be a very
different competitor than a company with long-term market share goals
such as Procter & Gamble or Komatsu. A company with a short-
term ROI objective is unlikely to react aggressively to the competitive
initiative of a rival. Such a reaction would be financially costly. The
company is more likely to withdraw from competition and retreat to
market segments where profits are more secure. When Hanson acquired
Eveready, it withdrew from most European markets because strong

competition had made them financially unattractive. Not only did Eveready give up ground to its archrival Duracell, it actually sold several of its overseas subsidiaries to Duracell. Compare the reaction of Procter & Gamble (P&G) to competition. When meeting competition in any market, it is renowned for its willingness to finance long-lasting competitive warfare using price cuts, promotions and advertising. In the case of new products, P&G is willing to accept losses for up to nine years while building a market position.

If the competitor is a subsidiary of a larger corporation, it is important to comprehend the goals of the parent because these will be the major determinant of the goals of the subsidiary. The means by which the parent controls the subsidiary is also important. How much autonomy does the subsidiary have? In the case of a highly centralized corporation, the ability of the subsidiary to respond to competitive assaults may be restricted by slow corporate decision-making procedures.

The level of current performance in relation to the competitor's objectives is important in determining the likelihood of strategy change. The more a company is satisfied with present performance, the more likely it is to continue with the present strategy. If, on the other hand, the competitor's performance is falling well short of target, then the likelihood of radical strategic change, possibly accompanied by a change in top management, is increased.

Particular problems arise when a competitor is not subject to commercial objectives at all. Such situations are extremely dangerous because they can give rise to destructive price competition that drives the industry into sustained losses. During the early 1990s, the world aluminum industry was plagued by depressed prices resulting from heavy sales by Russian producers onto world markets. Russian producers were not subject to financial disciplines and were able to acquire energy at below world market prices.

3 Competitors' assumptions about the industry A competitor's strategic decisions are conditioned by its perceptions (of the outside world and of itself) and by assumptions concerning the industry and about business in general. Both are likely to reflect the theories and beliefs that senior managers hold about their industry and the determinants of success within it. Evidence suggests that not only do these systems of belief tend to be stable over time they also tend to converge within an industry. Hence, at any point of time, different firms tend to adhere to very similar beliefs. These industrywide beliefs about the determinants of success have been described by J.-C. Spender as "industry recipes."[13]

Industry recipes may limit the ability of a firm, and indeed an entire industry, in responding rationally and effectively to external change. The result may be that established firms have a "blind spot" to competitive initiatives of a newcomer. For example, during the 1960s, the "Big Three" U.S. automobile manufacturers firmly believed that small cars were unprofitable. This belief was based upon their own experiences – which were, in part, a consequence of their own cost allocation procedures. As a result, they were willing to yield the fastest growing segment of the U.S. automobile market to Japanese and European imports. A similar point is even more vividly illustrated by the responses of U.S. and British motorcycle manufacturers to the growing Japanese threat (see exhibit 4.3).

4 Identify the competitor's capabilities Predicting a competitor's future strategy is not enough: the key issue for a firm is evaluating the seriousness of a potential challenge. The extent to which a competitor threatens a company's market position depends upon the competitor's capabilities. Detailed analysis of resources and capabilities is deferred to the next chapter. Suffice it to say at this stage that the key elements are an examination of the firm's principal categories of resources including financial reserves, capital equipment, work force, brand loyalty, and management skills together with an appraisal of capabilities within each of the major functions: R&D, production, marketing, distribution, and so on.

Circumspection in evaluating a competitor's capabilities is essential before embarking upon a strategy that may provoke a competitor. Many brilliant and innovative new companies have failed to withstand the aggressive reactions of established, well-financed incumbents. In the U.S. airline industry, most of the new entrants of the early 1980s had been forced out of business by the end of the decade. In the British newspaper industry, several innovative new newspapers, including *Today* and the *Sunday Correspondent*, have failed, while the *Indepen-*

Exhibit 4.3 Motorcycle Madness

During the 1960s, the motorcycle markets of Britain and the United States were dominated by BSA and Harley-Davidson, respectively. At the beginning of the 1960s, Japanese manufacturers, spearheaded by Honda, began to make inroads into the market for small bikes in both countries. The leading British and U.S. manufacturers discounted the Japanese threat, principally because of their disregard for smaller motorcycles. Eric Turner, Chairman of BSA Ltd (manufacturer of Triumph and BSA motorcycles) commented in 1965: "The success of Honda, Suzuki and Yamaha has been jolly good for us. People start out by buying one of the low-priced Japanese jobs. They get to enjoy the fun and exhilaration of the open road and they frequently end up buying one of our more powerful and expensive machines."

Similar complacency was expressed by William Davidson, President of Harley-Davidson:

Basically, we do not believe in the lightweight market. we believe that motorcycles are sports vehicles not transportation vehicles. Even if a man says he bought a motorcycle for transportation, it's generally for leisure time use. The lightweight motorcycle is only supplemental. Back around World War I, a number of companies came out with lightweight bikes. We came out with one ourselves. We came out with another in 1947 and it just didn't go anywhere. We have seen what happens to these small sizes.

By the end of the 1970s, BSA and Triumph had ceased production and Harley-Davidson was barely surviving. The world motorcycle industry, including large bike segments was dominated by the Japanese.

Source: Advertising Age, December 27, 1965; R. T. Pascale, *Honda (A)*, Harvard Business School, Case 9-384-049, Boston, 1983.

dent is still fighting to sustain its position against encroachment by *The Times* and *Telegraph*.

Applying the results of a competitor analysis

1 Predicting competitors' behavior   The first question we want to answer is: "What strategy shifts is the competitor likely to make?" This requires that we carefully identify current forces that are likely to provoke a change in strategy. These may be external, such as a shift in consumer preferences or a regulatory change that may have important consequences for the firm, or they may be internal, such as a failure to achieve current financial or market share targets or factional conflict within the company. Whatever the sources, a careful identification of current strategy and goals, the company's assumptions about the industry, and its capabilities, will provide a sound basis on which to forecast the direction of change.

Second, we may wish to forecast a competitor's likely reactions to a proposed strategy change that our own company is initiating. If this strategy change involves an attack upon the competitor's market base, then his reactions may be crucial in determining the desirability of the strategy change. The same four elements will together provide useful guidance as to the nature, likelihood, and seriousness of a defensive reaction by the competitor. When Honda first attacked BSA/Triumph and Harley-Davidson directly with the introduction of a large-capacity motorcycle Honda knew that:

> *first,* both companies pursued medium-term financial goals rather than market share goals;
> *second*, that both firms were benefiting from an upsurge in motorcycle demand and hence, were not unduly sensitive to losses in market share;
> *third,* both firms believed that due to their own customer loyalty and brand image, the Japanese producers were not a serious threat in the big bike market;
> *fourth,* even if BSA/Triumph and Harley-Davidson did react aggressively, the effectiveness of their response would be limited by their weak financial positions and by their lack of innovative and manufacturing capabilities.

2 Influencing competitors' behavior: signaling and credible threats
Understanding one's competitors can assist the firm in influencing its competitors' behavior. Competitor reaction depends not upon what the firm does but also upon what the competitor believes that its rival is doing. The term "signaling" is used to describe the selective communication of information to competitors designed to influence competitors' perceptions and behavior in order to provoke or avoid certain types of reaction.[14] The use of diversionary attacks and disinformation is well developed in military warfare. In 1944, Allied deception was so good

that even after the D-Day landings in Normandy, the Germans believed that the main invasion would occur near Calais.

The principal role of signaling is to provide clear threats to competitors of the company's intention to react aggressively to any rival's competitive move. Such signals need to be credible. It has been argued that some firms deliberately overinvest in order to have available capacity that can be used to flood a competitor's market if that competitor does not toe the industry line with regard to acceptable competitive behavior. Such strategic excess capacity may be particularly valuable in deterring entrants. The classic example is Alcoa's use of capacity expansion as a warning to potential entrants into the U.S. aluminum industry (*U.S. versus Alcoa*, 1945). However, subsequent studies have suggested that this practice is far from prevalent.[15]

The credibility of threats is critically dependent upon the reputation of a company.[16] Even though carrying out threats against rivals is costly and depresses short-term profitability, such threats can build a reputation for aggressiveness that deters competitors in the future. The benefits of building a reputation for aggressiveness may be particularly great for diversified companies where reputation can be transferred from one market to another.[17] Hence, Procter & Gamble's protracted market share wars in disposable diapers and household detergents have established a reputation for toughness that protects it from competitive attacks in other markets. *Fortune* magazine identifies Gillette in razors and razor blades, Anheuser-Busch in beer, and Emerson Electric in sink disposal units as examples of companies whose aggressive quest for market share has gained them reputations as "killer competitors," has encouraged a number of rivals to give up the fight.[18]

Signaling may also be used to maintain a cozy industry environment of cooperation and restrained competition between firms. One means of avoiding price competition in an industry is for the firms to follow a pattern of price leadership. In the U.K. gasoline market, the initiation of a price increase by a firm is normally preceded by a period of consensus building during which the firm tests the water by press releases that announce "the unsatisfactory level of margins in the industry," the "need for a price increase to recoup recent cost increases," and the likelihood that "a price increase will become necessary in the near future."[19]

Summary and Conclusions

The industry analysis of chapter 3 provided a first stage analysis of a company's industry environment. However, industries are internally complex. A more detailed analysis of the industry environment is required in order to target more precisely where a firm will position itself within the industry and how it will outmaneuver rivals. Hence, segmentation analysis and competitor analysis are critical components of industry analysis.

Segmentation analysis applies the framework of industry analysis to specific portions of an industry. Such analysis permits a company to:

- identify which segments have the most attractive profit prospects within the industry;
- identify the strategies that are likely to be effective in increasing the profit potential of a segment and exploiting the key success factors within a segment;
- evaluate the merits of a niche strategy involving specialization in one or a few segments, as compared with a broad-based multisegment strategy.

The ability to identify and occupy attractive segments of an industry is critical to success. Hewlett-Packard's superior performance in the office electronics industry during the late 1980s was primarily due to its ability to identify quickly slowing sales and falling margins in the minicomputer segment and swiftly shift its emphasis toward personal computers (desktops and workstations) and PC peripherals such as laser printers.[20] Location of attractive industry segments must be supported by a clear understanding of key success factors within those segments. In apparel retailing, both Benetton and Marks & Spencer are highly successful companies, but their strategies are quite different, reflecting the different requirements of their respective market segments.

Analysis at an even more micro level may be necessary. Where a company faces a few close competitors, it is not possible to understand competition without understanding the competitors themselves. Understanding competitors requires identification of:

- The competitor's goals
- The competitor's current strategy
- The competitor's assumptions
- The competitor's capabilities

"Getting inside" competitors in order to understand and influence competitive interaction lies at the heart of strategy analysis. An essential characteristic of successful strategists, whether corporate chief executives, military commanders, political leaders, or chess players, is their ability to insightfully analyze their opponents.

Notes

1   "How America took to France's Baguettes," *Financial Times*, November 22, 1985, 26.
2   This section draws heavily upon the approach used by Michael E. Porter, *Competitive Advantage* (New York: Free Press, 1985), chapter 7.

3   Robert M. Grant, *Birds Eye and U.K. Frozen Food Industry*, mimeograph, 1986 (available from the author).

4   For a formal analysis of mobility barriers, see Richard E. Caves and Michael E. Porter, "From Entry Barriers to Mobility Barriers: Conjectural Decisions and Contrived Deterrence to New Competition," *Quarterly Journal of Economics* 91 (1977) 241–62.

5   William H. Davidow and Bro Uttal, "Service Companies: Focus or Falter," *Harvard Business Review* (July-August 1989): 77–84.

6   See, for example, Michael Hunt, *Competition in the Major Home Appliance Industry*, Ph.D. diss., Harvard University, 1973; and Michael E. Porter, "Structure within Industries and Companies' Performance," *Review of Economics and Statistics* 61 (1979): 214–27; Kenneth Hatten, Dan Schendel, and Arnold Cooper, "A Strategic Model of the U.S. Brewing Industry, 1952–71," Academy of Management Journal 21 (1978): 592–610; Karel Cool and Dan Schendel, "Strategic Group Formation and Performance: The Case of the U.S. Pharmaceutical Industry," Management Science 33 (1987): 1102–24.

7   Michael E. Porter, Competitive Strategy (New York: Free Press, 1980), 129.

8   For further discussion of strategic groups and their role in strategy analysis see John McGee and Howard Thomas, "Strategic Groups: Theory, Research and Taxonomy," *Strategic Management Journal* 7 (1986): 141–60.

9   A. Feigenbaum and H. Thomas, "Strategic Groups and Performance: The U.S. Insurance Industry," *Strategic Management Journal* 11 (1990): 197–215; Karel Cool and Ingemar Dierick, "Rivalry, Strategic Groups, and Firm Profitability," *Strategic Management Journal* 14 (1993): 47–59.

10   R. K. Reger and A. S. Huff, "Strategic Groups: Cognitive Perspective," *Strategic Management Journal* 14 (1993): 103–24.

11   For an analysis of such interdependence, see Michael E. Porter and A. M. Spence, "The Capacity Expansion Process in a Growing Oligopoly: The Case of Corn Wet Milling," in *The Economics of Information and Uncertainty*, ed. J. McCall (Chicago: University of Chicago Press, 1982).

12   Henry Mintzberg, "Opening up the Definition of Strategy," in *The Strategy Process: Concepts, Contexts and Cases*, ed. Quinn, Mintzberg, and James (Englewood Cliffs, NJ: Prentice-Hall, 1988).

13   J.-C. Spender, *Industry Recipes: The Nature and Sources of Managerial Judgement* (Oxford: Basil Blackwell, 1989). The propensity for social interaction to result in a convergence of perceptions and beliefs is commonly referred to as "group-think" and has been discussed by Anne Huff, "Industry Influences on Strategy Reformulation," *Strategic Management Journal* 3 (1982): 119–31.

14   For a review of theory and research on competitive signaling, see O. Heil and T. S. Robertson, "Toward a Theory of Competitive Market Signaling: A Research Agenda," *Strategic Management Journal* 12 (1991): 403–18.

15   Marvin B. Leiberman, "Excess Capacity as a Barrier to Entry: An Empirical Appraisal," *Journal of Industrial Economics* 35 (1987): 607–27.

16   For a survey of the strategic role of reputation, see Keith Weigelt and Colin F. Camerer, "Reputation and Corporate Strategy: A Review of

Recent Theory and Applications," *Strategic Management Journal* 9 (1988): 443–54.

17 P. Milgrom and J. Roberts, "Predation, Reputation and Entry Deterrence," *Journal of Economic Theory* 27 (1982): 280–312.

18 "Companies That Compete Best," *Fortune*, May 22, 1989, 36–44.

19 Robert M. Grant, "Pricing Behavior in the UK Wholesale Market for Petrol," *Journal of Industrial Economics* 30 (1982): 271–92.

20 "Hewlett-Packard's Screeching Turn Towards Desktops," *Business Week*, September 11, 1989, 106–12.

III
The Analysis of Competitive Advantage

FIVE

Analyzing Resources and Capabilities

Analysts have tended to define assets too narrowly, identifying only those that can be measured, such as plant and equipment. Yet the intangible assets, such as a particular technology, accumulated consumer information, brand name, reputation, and corporate culture, are invaluable to the firm's competitive power. In fact, these invisible assets are often the only real source of competitive edge that can be sustained over time.

– Hiroyuki Itami, *Mobilizing Invisible Assets*

Objectives of the Chapter

This chapter has five objectives:

- to explain the role that a company's resources and capabilities play as a basis for its strategy;
- to show how the firm can identify and appraise its resources and capabilities;
- to develop a set of criteria for analyzing the potential for the firm's resources and capabilities to establish competitive advantage and yield long-term profit returns;

- to show how strategy is concerned not only with deploying the firm's resources to yield returns over the long term but also with augmenting and strengthening the firm's resources and capabilities;
- to develop a framework for resource analysis that integrates the above themes into a practical guide to formulating strategies that build competitive advantage.

Let me begin by explaining why a company's resources and capabilities are so important.

The Role of Resources and Capabilities in Strategy Formulation

Strategy, we have observed, is concerned with matching a firm's resources and capabilities to the opportunities that arise in the external environment. So far, the emphasis of the book has been the interface between strategy and the external environment of the firm. With this chapter, our emphasis shifts to the interface between strategy and the internal environment of the firm – more specifically, with the resources and capabilities of the firm. Figure 5.1 depicts this shift of emphasis.

This emphasis on the external environment reflects the dominant themes in strategy literature during the 1970s and most of the 1980s. During this period, most developments in strategy analysis concentrated upon the industry environment of the firm and its competitive positioning in relation to rivals. The analysis of industry and competition has

Figure 5.1 Shifting from an Industry Focus to a Resource Focus

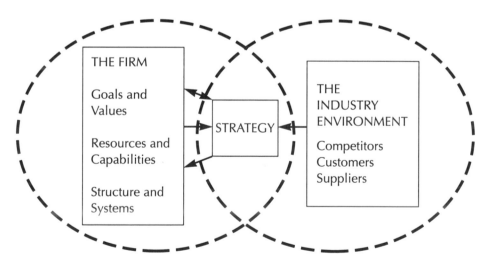

Resource Analysis: Focus on the interface between strategy and the internal resources and capabilities of the firm

Industry Analysis: Focus on the interface between strategy and the industry environment

been closely associated with the work of Michael Porter at Harvard. The analysis of competitive positioning was pioneered by consulting companies, notably, the Boston Consulting Group's use of the experience curve to analyze relative costs and the Strategic Planning Institute's PIMS project, which linked market share, quality, and other positional variables with profitability.

By contrast, strategic analysis of the firm's internal environment remained underdeveloped. Analysis of the internal environment has, for the most part, been concerned with issues of strategy implementation: appropriate organizational structure, systems of control, and top management structure and style have been viewed primarily as consequences of the strategy adopted.[1] This comparative neglect of internal resources by business strategists contrasts sharply with military strategy, which has always given primacy to resource analysis. Liddell Hart, a prominent military historian, argued that there is only one underlying principle of war: "concentration of strength against weakness."[2] During the present century, military strategy has been dominated by the analysis of relative resource strength. During the First World War, the Allied forces perceived strategic advantage in the fact that the combined population of the Allies exceeded that of the Axis countries. During the Second World War, the unease among the German High Command over Hitler's military strategy reflected recognition that Germany did not possess the resources to simultaneously wage war on the Eastern, Western, and North African fronts as well as in the sky and sea. The Cold War strategy of "nuclear deterrence" was founded upon the logic that a balance of nuclear missiles and warheads between NATO and Warsaw Pact and the expectation of "Mutually Assured Destruction" provided a stable basis for peace.

Since the late 1980s, there has been a surge of interest in the role of firm resources and capabilities as the principal basis for strategy and the primary determinants of firm profitability. These ideas have been described as *the resource-based view of the firm*.[3]

Resource-based strategy

The starting point for the formulation of strategy must be some statement of the firm's identity and purpose – conventionally, this takes the form of a *mission statement* that answers the question: "*What is our business?*" Typically, the definition of the business is in terms of the served market of the firm: "*Who are our customers?*" and "*Which of their needs are we seeking to serve?*" But in a world where customer preferences are volatile, the identity of customers is changing, and the technologies for serving customer requirements are developing rapidly, an externally focused orientation does not provide the constancy of direction to act as a secure foundation for formulating long-term strategy. When the external environment is in a state of flux, the firm itself in terms of its bundle of resources and capabilities may be on a much more stable basis on which to define its identity. Hence, a definition of the firm in terms of what it is capable of doing may offer a more durable basis for strategy than a definition based upon the needs that the business seeks to satisfy.

Theodore Levitt's solution to the problem of external change was that companies should define their served markets broadly rather than narrowly: railroads should have perceived themselves to be in the transportation business, not the railroad business.[4] But such broadening of the target market is of little value if the company cannot easily develop the capabilities required for serving customer requirements across a wide front. Was it feasible for the railroads to have developed successful trucking, airline, and car rental businesses? Perhaps resources and capabilities of the railroad companies might have been better suited to real estate development or the building and management of oil and gas pipelines. Casual empiricism suggests that serving broadly defined customer needs is a difficult task. The attempts by Merrill Lynch, American Express, Sears, and Citicorp to "serve the full range of financial needs of our customers" by diversifying across stockbroking, retail banking, credit cards, insurance, and real estate gave rise to serious problems and were not conducive to profitability.[5] Allegis Corporation's attempt to "serve the needs of the traveller" by combining United Airlines, Hertz car rental, and Westin Hotels was a costly failure. By contrast, several companies whose strategies have been based upon developing and exploiting clearly defined internal capabilities have been adept at adjusting to and benefiting from external change. Honda's strategy since its founding in 1948 has been built around its expertise in the development and manufacture of engines; this capability has successfully carried Honda from motorcycles to a number of gasoline-engined products (see figure 5.2). The expertise of 3M Corporation in the application of adhesive and thin-film technology to new product development has provided the basis for successful diversification across a broad range of products.

Figure 5.2 The Evolution of Honda

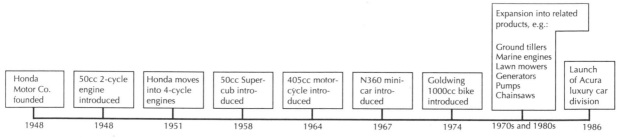

Sources: Honda (A) and (B), Harvard Business School, Boston, 1983; J. B. Quinn, *Intelligent Enterprise* (New York: Free Press, 1992).

In general, the greater the rate of change in a company's external environment, the more it must seek to base long-term strategy upon its internal resources and capabilities than upon an external market focus. In the fast-moving world of information technology, new companies are built around specific technological capabilities. The products or markets within which the technical capabilities are applied is a secondary strategic consideration. Autometric Inc. is an Alexandria, Virginia, company that specializes in 3-D imaging. The focus of the company's strategy has been the development of its technical capabilities. This development has taken the company from the entertainment industry (it was originally founded as a subsidiary of Paramount Pictures) into defense. It is currently exploiting its technical capabilities in defense, cartography, geological analysis, arcade games, and medical diagnostics.

James Brian Quinn has argued that the pervasiveness of information and communications technologies and the shift toward capability-based competition have rendered conventional notions of "industry boundaries" quite meaningless:

[T]he widespread penetration of service technologies has virtually destroyed the boundaries of all industries. . . . Airlines no longer compete just against airlines. They also compete against travel agents, tour groups, retailers (for products sold from in-flight catalogues), financial service companies (credit cards), ground transportation providers (rental cars or buses), communications companies (network and database services), and so on. . . . As a result managers can no longer define their corporation as being in a single "industry." Technology demands that they reconceptualize the "industries with which they compete" to include all functional and potential crosscompetitors for the services and products they create.[6]

The choice of whether to orient strategy around external customer needs or internal resources and capabilities was a key issue for typewriter manufacturers facing the microcomputer revolution of the late 1970s and early 1980s. With the approaching obsolescence of typewriters, there were two strategic alternatives. On the one hand, the companies could pursue their traditional market focus and attempt to acquire the electronic technology necessary to continue to serve the word processing needs of their customers. On the other, the companies could concentrate upon their existing resources and capabilities in terms of brand names, physical plant, electrical engineering, and precision and seek other markets where these resources and capabilities could be deployed. Few companies have successfully made the transition from typewriters to personal computers. Olivetti, the Italian typewriter and office equipment, invested heavily in establishing itself in PCs but achieved limited success. However, several companies have managed the transition from typewriters to printers, where the resource needs of two product areas were more similar.

Resources as the basis for corporate profitability

In chapter 2, we noted that a superior rate of profit may derive from two sources: location within an attractive industry and achieving a competitive advantage over rivals. Industry analysis has emphasized market power conferred by favorable industry structures as the primary basis for superior profitability, the implication being that strategic management is concerned with identifying attractive industries, locating favorable segments and strategic groups within industries, and adopting strategies that modify industry conditions and competitor behavior to moderate competitive pressures. The appeal of this approach has been undermined by three factors. First, the increase in competitive pressure across industries due to increased international competition and deregulation has meant that industries that once offered cozy environments for making easy profits are now subject to vigorous price competition. Second, technological and demand changes are causing industry boundaries to become increasingly ill defined. Third, empirical research has failed to confirm a relationship between profitability and the industry structures presumed to confer market power.[7]

As a result, deployment of resources and capabilities to establish competitive advantage rather than seeking shelter from the storm of competition has become the primary goal for strategy formulation. The resource-based view of the firm conceives of the firm as a unique bundle of heterogeneous resources and capabilities. These resources and capabilities are the basis upon which a firm's competitive advantage is built. As a result of its large, low-cost Alaskan oil reserves, Atlantic Richfield (Arco) has held a cost advantage in gasoline retailing on the West Coast. Singapore Airlines's passenger-service capabilities have given that company a differentiation advantage on certain trans-Pacific routes. The profits derived from these competitive advantages represent rents earned by the resources being deployed – they are returns to resources that confer the competitive advantage over and above the real costs of these resources.

Thus, while conventional approaches to competitive advantage focus upon the "generic" sources of competitive advantage – namely, cost and differentiation advantage – the resource-based view concentrates upon the resources and capabilities that underlie these advantages. Indeed, we can go further. A closer look at monopoly profits and the market power that gives rise to them suggests that they too have their source in the resources of firms. Barriers to entry, for example, have their basis in scale economies, patents, experience economies, brand awareness, or some other resource that incumbent firms possess but that entrants can acquire only slowly or at disproportionate expense. Other structural sources of market power are similarly based upon firms' resources: monopolistic price-setting power depends upon market share that is a consequence of cost efficiency, financial strength, or some other resource. The resources that confer market power may be owned individually by firms; others may be owned jointly. An industry standard (which raises costs of entry) – or a cartel – is a resource that is collectively owned by the participating firms.[8] Figure 5.3 depicts these relationships.

The remainder of this chapter outlines a resource-based approach to strategy formulation. The essence of the approach is that the firm should seek self-knowledge in terms of a thorough and profound understanding of its resources and capabilities. Such a resource-based approach to strategy comprises three key elements:

- selecting a strategy that exploits a company's principal resources and capabilities. Companies that have been successful over the long term, such as Sony, Black & Decker, Marks & Spencer, BMW, and Motorola, have achieved a close linkage between their strategies and their resources and capabilities. Companies whose strategies have strayed beyond their resource base (such as ITT during the 1970s and Saatchi and Saatchi during the 1980s) suffered loss of direction and deteriorating profitability;
- ensuring that the firm's resources are fully employed and its profit potential is exploited to the limit. Walt Disney's remarkable turn-

Figure 5.3 Resources as the Basis of Superior Profitability

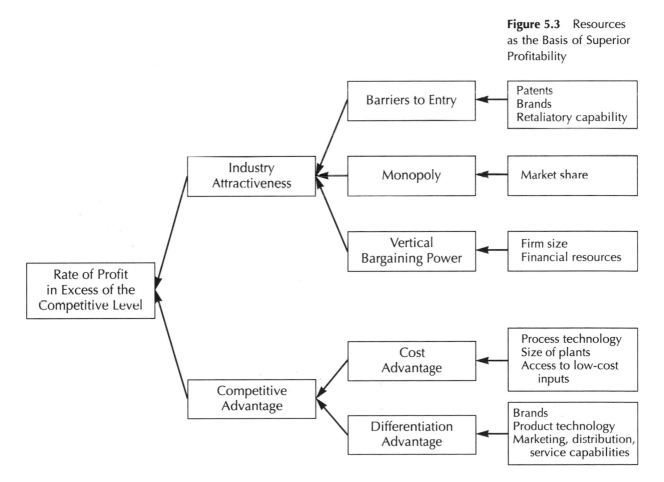

around between 1980 and 1990 involved very little change in basic strategy. The key feature was that Disney's wealth of assets and skills was being mobilized to produce profit (see exhibit 5.1);
- building the company's resource base. Resource analysis is not just about deploying assets; it is crucially concerned with filling current resource gaps and building the company's future resource base. The continuing dominance of Procter & Gamble, Johnson & Johnson, and Motorola in their respective fields of business owes much to these companies' commitment to nurturing talent, augmenting technologies, and adjusting capabilities to fit emerging market trends.

The starting point for analysis is to identify and assess the resources and capabilities that the firm has available to it.

Exhibit 5.1 The Power of Resource Analysis: The Revival of Walt Disney

When Michael Eisner arrived at Walt Disney Productions in 1984 to take over as president, the company was heading for its fourth consecutive year of decline in net income, and its share price had fallen to a level that was attracting a variety of predators. Between 1984 and 1988, Disney's sales revenue increased from $1.66 billion to $3.75 billion, net income from $98 million to $570 million, and the stock market's valuation of the company from $1.8 billion to $10.3 billion. Yet during Eisner's first three years at Disney, initially as president then as chairman, there was no obvious shift of strategy. All Disney's major strategic initiatives of the 1980s – the Epcot Center, Tokyo Disneyland, Touchstone Films, the Disney Channel, and the acquisition of Arvida – were the initiatives of the previous management.

So what happened? The essence of the Disney turnaround was the mobilization of Disney's considerable resource base.

Disney's 28,000 acres of land in Florida were put to commercial use. With the help of the Arvida Corporation, a land development company acquired in 1984, Disney began hotel, resort, and residential development of its Florida landholdings. New attractions were added to the Epcot Center, and a new theme park, the Disney-MGM Studio Tour, was added. These developments involved Disney World expanding beyond theme parks into resort vacations, the convention business, and residential housing.

In exploiting its huge film library, Disney went far beyond its usual practice of periodic rereleases of the Disney classics. It introduced videocassette sales of Disney movies and the licensing of packages of movies to TV networks. A single package of films licensed to a European TV network raised $21 million. The huge investments in the Disney theme parks were more effectively exploited through heavier marketing effort and increased admission charges. Encouraged by the success of Tokyo Disneyland, Disney embarked upon further international duplication of its U.S. theme parks with a planned EuroDisneyland.

The most ambitious feature of the turnaround was Disney's regeneration as a movie studio. As well as maintaining Disney's commitment to high-quality family movies (and cartoons in particular), Eisner began a massive expansion of Disney's Touchstone label, which had been established in 1983 with the objectives of putting Disney's film studios to fuller use and establishing Disney in the teenage and adult markets. To achieve fuller utilization of Disney Studios, Eisner quickly doubled the number of movies in production. Simultaneously, Disney engaged in aggressive recruiting of leading producers, directors, filmmakers, actors, and scriptwriters. In 1988, Disney became America's leading studio in terms of box office receipts. Studio production was further boosted by Disney's increasing TV presence, both through the Disney Channel and programs for network TV.

Above all, the new management team was exploiting Disney's most powerful and enduring asset: the affection of millions of people of different nations and different generations for the Disney name and the Disney characters.

The Resources of the Firm

Resource analysis takes place at two levels of aggregation. The basic units of analysis are the individual resources of the firm: items of capital equipment, the skills of individual employees, patents, brand names, and so on. But to examine how the firm can create competitive advantage we must look at how resources work together to create capabilities. Figure 5.4 shows the relationship between resources, capabilities, and competitive advantage.

Drawing up an inventory of a firm's resources can be surprisingly difficult. No such document exists within the accounting or management information systems of most corporations. The corporate balance sheet provides a partial and distorted picture of a firm's assets. A useful starting point is a simple classification of the principal types of resource into tangible, intangible, and human resources. Table 5.1 shows the principal categories.

Tangible resources

Tangible resources are the easiest to identify and to evaluate: financial resources and physical assets are identified and valued in the firm's financial statements. Yet balance sheets are renowned for their propensity to obscure strategically relevant information and to misvalue assets. Historic cost valuation can provide little indication of an asset's market value. A critical issue in the 1994 battle between Viacom and QVC to acquire Paramount Communications was the value of Paramount's

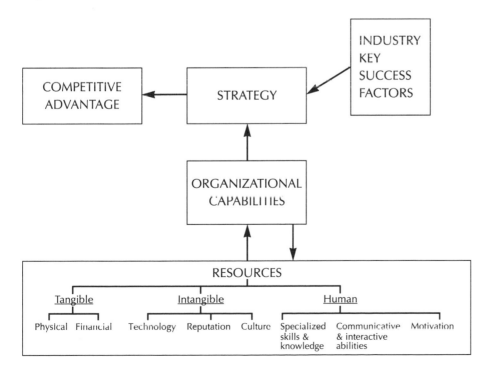

Figure 5.4 Resources, Capabilities, and Competitive Advantage: The Basic Relationships

Table 5.1 Classifying and Assessing the Firm's Resources

Resource	Main characteristics	Key Indicators
Financial resources	The firm's borrowing capacity and its internal funds generation determine its investment capacity and its cyclical resilience.	Debt/equity ratio. Ratio of net cash to capital expenditure. Credit rating.
Physical resources	The size, location, technical sophistication, and flexibility of plant and equipment; location and alternative uses for land and buildings; reserves of raw materials constrain the firm's set of production possibilities and determine the potential for cost and quality advantage.	Resale values of fixed assets. Vintage of capital equipment. Scale of plants. Alternative uses of fixed assets.
Human resources	The training and expertise of employees determine the skills available to the firm. The adaptability of employees determines the strategic flexibility of the firm. The commitment and loyalty of employees determines the firm's ability to maintain competitive advantage.	Educational, technical, professional qualifications of employees. Pays rates relative to industry average.
Technological resources	Stock of technology including proprietary technology (patents, copyrights, trade secrets) and expertise in its application of know-how. Resources for innovation: research facilities, technical and scientific employees.	Number and significance of patents. Revenue from patent licenses. R&D staff as a percentage total employment.
Reputation	Reputation with customers through the ownership of brands, established relationships with customers, the association of the firm's products with quality, reliability, etc. The reputation of the company with the suppliers of components, finance, labor services, and other inputs.	Brand recognition. Price-premium over competing brands. Percentage of repeat buying. Objective measures of product performance. Level and consistency of company performance.

movie library – valued in the balance sheet as capitalized production costs net of depreciation.

While the balance sheet provides a starting point, it is important to get behind the accounting numbers and look at basic facts pertinent to evaluating the potential of the resources for creating competitive advantage. Information that Bethlehem Steel has fixed assets with a book value of $480 million is of little use in assessing the strategic value of these assets. Where are Bethlehem's plants located, what are their capacities, what is the age and type of the equipment, and how flexible are they with regard to inputs, output variations, and product varieties?

A strategic assessment of tangible resources is directed toward answering two key questions:

1   *what opportunities exist for economizing on the use of finance, inventories, and fixed assets?*   This may involve using fewer tangible resources to support the same level of business or using the existing resources to support a larger volume of business. The success of companies that have pursued growth through acquisitions within mature industries, such as ConAgra and Hanson, has been due to management's ability to prune rigorously the cash and assets needed to support the turnover of acquired businesses.

2   *what are the possibilities for employing existing assets in more profitable occupations?*   The returns to a company's tangible resources can be increased in several ways. Resources can be utilized more productively: following its acquisition of Belridge Oil, Shell was able to greatly increase the output of Belridge's oil fields through the application of enhanced recovery techniques. Resources can often be utilized more fully through alliances with other companies: following privatization, British Telecom has sought to utilize its telephone network more fully by establishing relationships with the suppliers of value-added network services. Department stores have increasingly leased floor space to specialty retailers. Finally, resources can be sold to companies capable of deploying them more profitably. During the late 1980s and early 1990s, the major oil companies underwent thorough reviews of their oil properties, a process that involved widespread sales and swaps of "marginal" assets. At the beginning of 1990, Chevron owned 1,800 oilfield properties in the United States. By the end of 1994, these had been reduced to 400. These sales reflected the belief that because different companies have different capabilities and different infrastructure fields that were marginal for Chevron could be more valuable to other companies.

Intangible resources

Overtime, working capital, fixed capital, and other tangible assets are becoming less important to the firm both in value and as a basis for competitive advantage. Yet, intangible resources remain largely invisible in terms of company financial statements. On most firms' balance sheets, intangible items are typically restricted to "goodwill arising on acquisition" and capitalized R&D expenditure. Hence, accounting book values usually bear little relationship to the true value of a firm's resources. In some cases, the most strategically important resources of a company may be both invisible and nonobvious. In the airline industry, some of the most critical resources – takeoff and landing slots at airports – are not even owned by the companies. In industries where the qualities of products or services are not readily apparent to potential customers, *reputation* is a critically important resource. Reputation may be attached to the company. For example, Marks & Spencer earned a reputation for supplying quality products and treating customers fairly as well as being a good employer and a reliable customer to its suppliers. Reputation may also be attached to products in the form of brand recognition and loyalty. Despite the fact that the most valuable assets of many consumer goods firms are their brand names, these are typically not valued in a company's balance sheet (or are only valued on acquisition). When Nestlé acquired the British chocolate manufacturer Rowntree in 1988, the bid price exceeded the book value of Rowntree's assets by over 500 percent – an indication of the value of Rowntree's brand names such as "Kit Kat" and "After Eights."[9] Two variables are critical to the valuation of reputation: first, the size of the price premium that reputation will sustain and, second, the product and market scope over which reputation can be deployed. Thus, the increasing stock market valuation of Harley-Davidson during the period 1988–93 reflected recognition not just that the Harley name would support a price premium of about 40 percent above that of comparable motorcycles but also that the Harley reputation could be exploited in Japan and Europe and on a wide variety of products from T-shirts to coffee mugs.

A second vitally important group of intangible resources is technology. A central issue in appraising technological resources is ownership. Proprietary technology, that in which property rights are clearly established, comprises patents, copyrights, and trade secrets. However, once we stray into the broad area of know-how, the distinction between company-owned and employee-owned knowledge is vague. I will return to this issue.

The tendency to misunderstand and misvalue intangible resources is especially true for technology. Xerox Corporation's failure to recognize and exploit the advances in personal computer technology from its PARC facility is a classic example of a company squandering its critical resources. Conversely, some of the most consistently profitable companies are those that have established and safeguarded core intangible resources. Du Pont, Intel, and Motorola are companies that have protected and developed their critical technological resources. Similarly, Walt Disney Company, American Express, Coca-Cola Corporation, and Philip Morris are companies that have carefully nourished and preserved the reputational resources linked to their trademarks.

While intangible resources receive scant recognition from accountants, their values are being increasingly recognized by the stock market.

Table 5.2 lists the members of the top 200 U.S. companies (ranked by stock market valuation) with the highest ratio of stock price to book value. Two types of companies dominate the list: those with valuable technological resources (notably computer software and pharmaceutical companies) and companies with very strong brand names (mainly in packaged consumer goods).[10]

Human resources

While people are clearly tangible, the resources that they offer to the firm are their skills, knowledge, and reasoning and decision-making abilities. In economist's terminology the productive capability of human beings is referred to as "human capital." Identifying and appraising the stock of human capital within a firm is complex and difficult. Individuals' skills and capabilities can be assessed from their job performance, from their experience, and from their qualifications. However, these are only indicators of individuals' potential. The problems of recognizing individuals' abilities are exacerbated by the fact that people work together in teams where it is difficult to observe directly the contribution of the individual to overall corporate performance. As a result, firms tend to resort to indirect approaches to assessing performance – hours spent at the office, enthusiasm, "professional" appearance, and attitudes. If a company is to develop, to adjust to changing environmental

Company	Ratio of Share Price to Book Value per Share	Industry
Cisco Systems	19.50	Computer software and services
Avon Products	18.41	Personal care
Coca-Cola	12.24	Beverages
Ralston Purina	14.92	Food processing
UST	12.41	Tobacco
Oracle Systems	11.10	Computer software & services
U.S. Healthcare	10.00	Health care services
Home Depot	9.70	Retailing
Gillette	9.43	Personal care
Wal-Mart Stores	9.35	Retailing
Novell	8.68	Computer software & services
General Mills	8.44	Food processing
Microsoft	8.40	Computer software & services
Merck	7.89	Drugs
Schering-Plough	7.69	Drugs
Quaker Oats	7.21	Food processing
Tele-Communications	7.16	Broadcasting
Viacom	6.81	Broadcasting
Kellogg	6.73	Food

Table 5.2 Large U.S. Companies with the Highest Ratio of Share Price to Book Value per Share, March 1993

Note: The 20 companies among the largest 200 (ranked by market capitalization) with the highest valuation ratios.
Source: "Business Week 1000," *Business Week*, special issue, March 1993.

conditions, and to exploit new opportunities, then it must have knowledge not only of how its employees perform in their present and past jobs but also of their repertoire of skills and abilities.[11] In recent years, many companies have initiated broadly based, detailed, and systematic appraisals of employees' knowledge, skills, attitudes, and behaviors. At Amoco Production Company, reorientation of employee evaluation and promotion toward building organizational capabilities involved the identification and measurement of four categories of employee competency:

- achieving objectives, e.g., concern for improvement, risk taking or initiative, and ownership or accountability;
- problem solving, e.g., information gathering, evaluation and judgment, and systematic problem solving;
- interacting with others, e.g., organizational astuteness, effective communication, and confidence;
- teamwork, e.g., building consensus, coaching and development, and focusing on development.

Increasingly, firms are recognizing that in evaluating their human resources it is not just individuals' expertise and knowledge that is important but the ability of employees to work effectively together. As we will see, organizational capability depends not just upon the resources that are brought together but also upon the firm's ability to integrate the various resources. The ability of the firm to harness human resources effectively depends upon the *relationships* between individual employees, which is itself a product of another intangible resource: the *culture* of the organization. Building on the observations of Peters and Waterman and others that "firms with sustained superior financial performance typically are characterized by a strong net of core managerial values that define the ways they conduct business," Jay Barney identifies organizational culture as firm resource that is potentially very valuable and of great strategic importance.[12]

Organizational Capabilities

Capabilities and competences

Resources are not normally productive on their own. Productive tasks require the cooperation of teams of resources. I use the term *organizational capabilities* to refer to a firm's capacity for undertaking a particular activity. The literature uses the terms "capability" and "competence" interchangeably.[13] Thus, Selznick used *"distinctive competence"* to describe those things that an organization does particularly well relative to competitors, and Igor Ansoff used the same term in analyzing the basis of firms' growth strategies.[14] Hamel and Prahalad coined the term "core competences" to distinguish those capabilities that are fundamental to a firm's performance and strategy from those that are more peripheral.[15] Core competences, argue Hamel and Prahalad, are those that:

1 make a disproportionate contribution to ultimate customer value or to the efficiency with which that value is delivered, and
2 provide a basis for entering new markets.[16]

The value of the terms *distinctive competence* and *core competence* is that they center attention upon the issue of competitive advantage. Our interest is not in capabilities per se but in capabilities *relative to other firms*: What can the firm do *better* than its competitors? Hamel and Prahalad castigate U.S. companies for their emphasis on product management as opposed to competence management. They compare the strategic development of Sony and RCA in consumer electronics. Both companies were failures in the home video market. RCA introduced its videodisc system, Sony its Betamax videotape system. For RCA, the failure of its first product marked the end of its venture in home video systems and heralded a progressive retreat from various segments of the consumer electronics industry. RCA was eventually acquired by GE, and the combined consumer electronics division was sold to Thomson of France. Despite the failure of Betamax, Sony continues to develop its capabilities in video technology. It switched to VHS and went on to develop a highly successful range of camcorders.

A strategic focus on capabilities rather than products is also observable in Canon's development. Canon's technological capabilities lie in the integration of microelectronics, fine optics, and precision engineering. Figure 5.5 shows how these technologies are common to most of Canon's product introductions during the late 1980s.

Identifying capabilities: functions and value chain activities

Before we can identify which of the firm's capabilities are "distinctive" or "core," we need to identify what capabilities a firm possesses. To examine the firm's capabilities, some classification of the firm's activities is needed. Two main approaches are commonly used:

1 a *functional classification* identifies organizational capabilities in relation to each of the principal functional areas of the firm. Table 5.3 classifies the principal functions of the firm and identifies organizational capabilities pertaining to each function.

2 the *value chain* desegregates the firm into a sequential chain of activities. Figure 5.6 shows a typical chain of activities for a manufacturing company based upon McKinsey & Company's concept of "the business system."

Michael Porter has proposed a rather more elaborate classification of activities that distinguished between primary activities (those involved

Figure 5.5 Products as Outgrowths of Technical Capabilities: Canon

	Precision Mechanics	Fine Optics	Micro-electronics
Basic camera	■	■	
Compact fashion camera	■	■	
Electronic camera	■	■	
EOS autofocus camera	■	■	■
Video still camera	■	■	■
Laser beam printer	■	■	■
Color video printer	■		■
Bubble jet printer	■		■
Basic fax	■		■
Laser fax	■		■
Calculator			■
Plain-paper copier	■	■	■
Battery PPC	■	■	■
Color copier	■	■	■
Laser copier	■	■	■
Color laser copier	■	■	■
NAVI	■	■	■
Still video system	■	■	■
Laser imager	■	■	■
Cell analyzer	■	■	■
Mask aligners	■		■
Stepper aligners	■		■
Excimer laser aligners	■	■	■

Source: C. K. Prahalad and Gary Hamel, "The Core Competence of the Corporation," *Harvard Business Review* (May–June 1990).

with the transformation of inputs and interface with the customer) and support activities. Figure 5.7 shows Porter's conceptualization of the value chain.

However, neither a functional classification nor the value chain depicts satisfactorily the anatomy of a firm's organizational capabilities. We have observed how capabilities are formed from teams of resources working together. What is also the case in complex organizations is that capabilities are organized in a hierarchical structure. Some capabilities are highly specific, relating to a narrowly defined task; other, higher-level capabilities involve the integration of a number of more specific capabilities. For example:

- a hospital's capability in treating heart disease depends upon its integration of capabilities pertaining to patient diagnosis, cardiovascular surgery, pre- and postoperative care as well as capabilities relating to various administrative and support functions;
- Toyota's manufacturing capability – generally referred to as its system of "lean production" – is a highly complex organizational capability requiring the integration of a large number of more specific capabilities relating to the manufacture of particular components and subassem-

Functional Area	Capability	Examples
CORPORATE MANAGEMENT	Effective financial control systems	Hanson Exxon
	Expertise in strategic control of diversified corporation	General Electric ABB
	Effectiveness in motivating and coordinating divisional and business-unit management	Shell
	Management of acquisitions	ConAgra, BTR
	Values-driven, in-touch corporate leadership	Wal-Mart Stores Federal Express
MANAGEMENT INFORMATION	Comprehensive and effective MIS network, with strong central coordination	American Airlines L.L. Bean
RESEARCH AND DEVELOPMENT	Capability in basic research Ability to develop innovative new products	Merck, AT&T Sony 3M
	Speed of new product development	Canon Mazda
MANUFACTURING	Efficiency in volume manufacturing	Briggs & Stratton
	Capacity for continual improvements in production processes	Toyota Nucor
	Flexibility and speed of response	Benetton Worthington Industries
PRODUCT DESIGN	Design capability	Pinifarini Apple
MARKETING	Brand management and brand promotion	Procter & Gamble PepsiCo
	Promoting and exploiting reputation for quality	American Express Mercedes Benz
	Responsiveness to market trends	The Gap Campbell Soup
SALES AND DISTRIBUTION	Effectiveness in promoting and executing sales	Microsoft Glaxo
	Efficiency and speed of distribution	Federal Express The Limited
	Quality and effectiveness of customer service	Walt Disney Marks & Spencer

Table 5.3 A Functional Classification of Organizational Capabilities

Figure 5.6 A Simple
Value Chain:
McKinsey & Company's
"Business System"

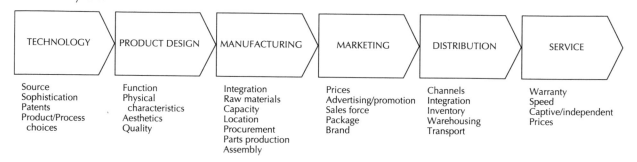

TECHNOLOGY	PRODUCT DESIGN	MANUFACTURING	MARKETING	DISTRIBUTION	SERVICE
Source	Function	Integration	Prices	Channels	Warranty
Sophistication	Physical	Raw materials	Advertising/promotion	Integration	Speed
Patents	characteristics	Capacity	Sales force	Inventory	Captive/independent
Product/Process	Aesthetics	Location	Package	Warehousing	Prices
choices	Quality	Procurement	Brand	Transport	
		Parts production			
		Assembly			

Figure 5.7 The Porter
Value Chain

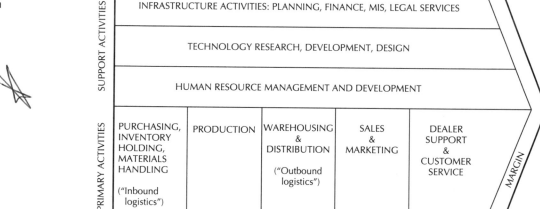

Source: Adapted from M. E. Porter, *Competitive Advantage* (New York: Free Press,
1985).

blies; welding and assembly processes; quality control procedures;
systems for managing innovation and continuous improvement; and
mechanisms for the just-in-time flow of parts and materials from
suppliers to the assembly plants and within assembly plants.

Within the firm, specialized capabilities relating to individual tasks are
integrated into broader functional capabilities: marketing capabilities,
manufacturing capabilities, R&D capabilities, and the like. At the highest level of integration are capabilities that require wide-ranging cross-
functional integration. Thus, new product development capability usually requires the integration of R&D, marketing, manufacturing,
finance, and strategic planning.[17] In many firms, customer service capability may also require integration across multiple functions to provide
customers with solutions to the diversity of problems that they experi-

ence. Figure 5.8 shows a hypothetical hierarchy of capabilities for a manufacturer of telecommunication switching equipment.

Although higher-level capabilities involve the integration of lower-level capabilities, it is important to recognize that capabilities cannot be integrated directly. Capabilities can only be integrated by integrating the knowledge of individual persons. This is precisely why higher-level capabilities are so difficult to perform. New product development requires the integration of a wide diversity of specialized knowledge and skills, yet communication constraints mean that the number of individuals who can be directly involved in the process is small. A common solution has been the creation of cross-functional product development teams. While setting up such teams is a seemingly straight-

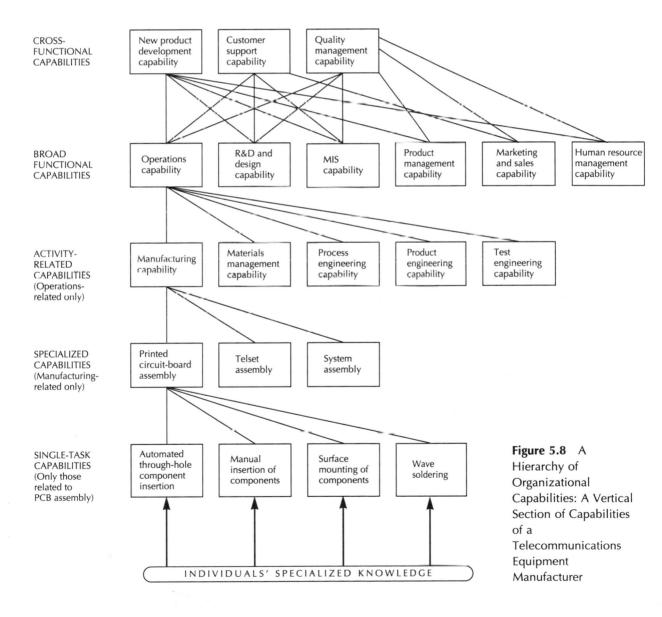

Figure 5.8 A Hierarchy of Organizational Capabilities: A Vertical Section of Capabilities of a Telecommunications Equipment Manufacturer

forward task, the research into new product development confirms that the most difficult problem is the team's ability to access the breadth and depth of functional knowledge pertinent to the product and then integrating that knowledge.[18] Probably the greatest achievement of Japanese industrial corporations during the 1980s was achieving the complex patterns of coordination necessary for integrating broad spectra of technical and functional knowledge into the development of innovative new products in remarkably short time periods. Companies such as Toyota, Sony, Matsushita, and Canon have become models for U.S. and European corporations seeking to accelerate new product development. The revival of Chrysler during the 1990s owes much to the restructuring of its new product development processes to imitate those of Honda.

Appraising capabilities: the role of benchmarking

An important problem in assessing capability is objectivity. In assessing their own competences, organizations frequently fall victim to past glories, hopes for the future, and their own wishful thinking. Among the failed industrial companies of both America and Britain are many that believed themselves world leaders with superior products and customer loyalty:

- Sheffield, England, once supplied cutlery and silverware to the world. Its belief in its superior production skills and product quality was one of the principal reasons for its near extinction in the face of foreign competition.[19]
- lack of competition between domestic producers and easy access to sources of coal and iron ore encouraged a stubborn belief among leading U.S. steelmakers in the superior quality of American steel and their own technological prowess. After several decades of neglecting new process technology and customers' needs, the leading integrated steel companies declined rapidly in the face of import competition and competition from domestic minimill producers.[20]
- during the late 1970s and early 1980s, BankAmerica's steady increase in revenues and profits and its position as the world's largest bank diverted its attention from the underlying reality of the deteriorating quality of its top and middle management, its technological backwardness, and the declining quality of its loan portfolio.[21]

Similarly, firms may be unaware of the competences they possess. In the mid-1950s, Richard and Maurice McDonald owned a single hamburger restaurant in San Bernardino, California. It was Ray Kroc, then a milk shake salesman, who recognized the merits of the McDonald's' approach to fast food and the potential for replicating the McDonald's system.[22]

To identify and appraise a company's capabilities, managers must look broadly, look deeply, and look from different perspectives. Critical to objectivity is establishing the quantifiable measures of performance that permit the comparison of the firm with other firms. During the last decade, *benchmarking* has emerged as an important tool for appraising and developing organizational capability through detailed comparisons with other firms and organizations.

Benchmarking involves four stages:

1 identifying the activities or functions of the business that need improving;
2 identifying companies that are world leaders in each of these activities or functions;
3 contacting the companies, visiting them, talking to the managers and workers, and analyzing firsthand how it does so well;
4 using the new learning to redefine goals, redesign processes, and change expectations regarding one's own functions and activities.

Benchmarking has played a critical role in upgrading organizational capability in a number of well-known companies. For example:

- *Xerox*. Benchmarking played a central role in the revitalization of Xerox during the 1980s. Detailed comparisons of Xerox copiers and those of competing manufacturers began in 1979. The comparisons found that Japanese rivals made copiers at half the cost, with product development schedules that were half as long and involved half as many people. Xerox's defects per thousand in assembly were 10 to 30 times greater than Japanese competitors. The result was the establishment of a continuous program of benchmarking in which every department within Xerox is encouraged to look globally to identify "best in class" companies against which to benchmark;
- *ICL*. The British computer subsidiary of Fujitsu benchmarks against a variety of different companies. In manufacturing processes, ICL benchmarks Sun Microsystems. In distribution, ICL benchmarks the retailer Marks & Spencer.

Every organization has some activity where it excels or has the potential to excel. For Federal Express, it is a system that guarantees next-day delivery anywhere within the United States. For the British retailer Marks & Spencer, it is the ability to ensure a high and consistent level of product quality across a wide range of merchandise through meticulously managed supplier relationships. For McDonald's, it is the ability to supply billions of hamburgers from several thousand outlets throughout the world, with each hamburger almost identical to any other. For General Electric, it is a system of corporate management that reconciles control, coordination, flexibility, and innovation in one of the world's largest and most diversified corporations. All these companies are examples of highly successful enterprises. One reason why they are successful is that they have recognized what they can do well and have based their strategies upon it. There are many other companies that are not successful. A common reason for lack of success is not an absence of distinctive competences but a failure to recognize what they are and to put them to effective use.

Integration mechanisms: direction and organizational routine

Organizational capability involves the integration of teams of resources – in particular, the knowledge and skills of individual employees. But how does this integration occur? This question takes us to the heart of organizational theory, which is not the intention of this book! However, we are concerned with the practicalities of establishing competitive advantage, which means that we must understand what organizational capability is and how it is created. The integration of nonhuman resources poses few management problems: finance, technology, brands, and machines are inanimate and, hence, passive resources. The critical management issues concern the integration of human resources. Knowledge and skill are embodied within individual employees in specialized form. Because of economies in the acquisition of skills and knowledge, it is not feasible for everyone within the company to learn what everyone else knows, hence some mechanism for integrating knowledge and skills is needed. Two primary mechanisms exist:

- *rules and directives* Specialized knowledge can be transferred and hence integrated by means of rules and directives. It is not feasible for a McDonald's restaurant manager to learn the full knowledge of the food technologists, chefs, bacteriologists, marketing experts, and milk shake design engineers whose expertise is embodied within McDonald's organizational capabilities. However, in the voluminous operating manuals that occupy every McDonald's manager's office shelf their knowledge has been distilled into a multitude of highly exacting operating practices.
- *organizational routines* Observation of any productive activity from a car assembly line to a surgical team in a hospital operating theater indicates that individuals can integrate their specialized knowledge and skills without significant direction or verbal communication. Richard Nelson and Sidney Winter have used the term "*organizational routines*" to refer to such coordination.[23] Organizational routines are regular and predictable patterns of activity that are made up of a sequence of coordinated actions by individuals. Such routines form the basis of most organizational capabilities. At the manufacturing level, a series of routines governs the passage of raw materials and components through the production process to the factory gate. Sales, ordering, distribution, and customer service activities are similarly organized through a number of standardized, complementary routines. Even top management activity consists of routines: for monitoring business-unit performance, for capital budgeting, for employee appraisal and promotion, for strategy formulation. Routines are to the organization what skills are to the individual. Just as the individual's skills are carried out semiautomatically, without conscious coordination, so organizational routines involve a large component of tacit

knowledge, which implies limits on the extent to which the organization's capabilities can be articulated. Just as individual skills become rusty when not exercised, so it is difficult for organizations to retain coordinated responses to contingencies that arise only rarely. Hence, there may be a trade-off between efficiency and flexibility. A limited repertoire of routines can be performed highly efficiently with near perfect coordination – all in the absence of significant intervention by top management. The same organization may find it extremely difficult to respond to novel situations.

Most organizational capabilities involve both types of coordination. Even in highly bureaucratized settings, such as McDonald's hamburger restaurants and aircraft maintenance shops, rules and directives tend to become translated into organizational routines. Recognizing the role and the nature of these coordination mechanisms can offer illuminating insights into the relationships between resources, capabilities, and competitive advantage:

1 *Factors conducive to integration* A focus on coordination mechanisms emphasizes the fact that the firm's competences are not simply a consequence of the collection of individual resources that the firm controls. Critical to the relationship between resources and capabilities is management's ability to achieve the cooperation and coordination between resources required for the development of organizational routines. The ability of the firm to motivate and socialize its members in order to gain their cooperation and commitment depends upon the organization's style, culture, leadership, and systems of control, reward, and communication. Peters and Waterman's "7-S" framework and their stress upon the role of "*shared values*" in promoting cooperation and commitment implicitly recognizes the importance of these issues.[24]

2 *There is a trade-off between efficiency and flexibility* Nelson and Winter regard routines as the organizational equivalent of individual skills. Just as the individual's skills are carried out semiautomatically, without conscious coordination, so organizational routines involve a large component of tacit knowledge, which implies limits on the extent to which the organization's capabilities can be articulated. Just as individual skills become rusty when not exercised, so it is difficult for organizations to retain coordinated responses to contingencies that arise only rarely. Hence, there may be a trade-off between efficiency and flexibility. An organization can perform a limited repertoire of routines highly efficiently with near perfect coordination from top management. The same organization may find it extremely difficult to respond to novel situations.[25] The art of crisis management is to achieve proficiency in the management of eventualities whose probabilities are very small but whose consequences may be devastating.

3 *Economies of experience* Just as individual skills are acquired through practice over time, so an organization's capabilities are developed and sustained through experience. The advantage of an established

firm over a newcomer is largely based upon the routines that have been perfected over time. The Boston Consulting Group's "experience curve" is a naive and mechanistic representation of this relationship of experience to performance. By inquiring into the characteristics of coordination, we can acquire a broader-based understanding of the relationship between experience and capability. Thus, in industries where technological change is rapid, we may discover that new firms possess an advantage over established firms. Because they are less committed to old routines, they have the potential for faster development of new capabilities.

Appraising the Profit-Earning Potential of Resources and Capabilities

So far, we have established what resources and capabilities are, how they can provide a long-term focus for a company's strategy, how we can go about identifying them, and on what basis we can appraise the strengths and weaknesses of the firm's resource base relative to competitors. However, if the focus of this book is the pursuit of profit, we also need to appraise the potential for resources and capabilities to earn profits for the company.

The profit returns to resources and capabilities ("rents") depend upon the extent to which a firm deploys its resources and capabilities to establish a competitive advantage over rivals. I will examine this issue in detail in the next chapter. In this section, let me identify some of the characteristics of a firm's resources that are most important in determining the profit earning potential of resources and capabilities.

The profits that a firm obtains from its resources and capabilities depend upon three factors each of which in turn depend upon a number of resource characteristics. Figure 5.9 shows the principal relationships.

The extent of competitive advantage

For a resource or capability to establish a competitive advantage, two conditions must be present. First, that resource or capability must be *scarce*. If it is widely available within the industry, then it will become a prerequisite for competing but not a source of competitive advantage. In the personal computer industry, there are a number of resources and capabilities that are critical to being able to compete effectively. Manufacturers must have access to the latest Intel microprocessors and Microsoft operating systems, they must be capable of low-cost assembly, and they must have access to distribution. The problem for the industry leaders such as Dell, Compaq, and IBM is that these resources and capabilities are available to almost any actual or potential supplier of PCs, hence competitive advantage has been difficult to establish. In the automobile industry, the capabilities of Toyota and the other Japanese automakers in the application of *total quality management* (TQM) to

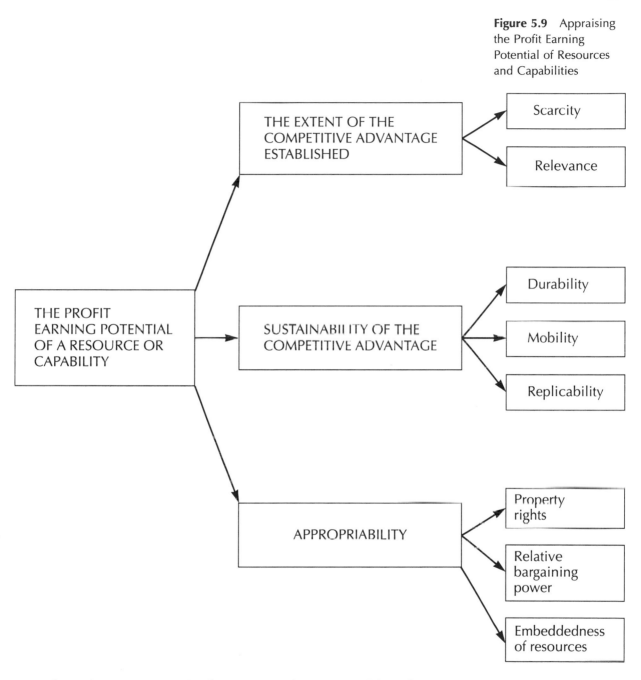

Figure 5.9 Appraising the Profit Earning Potential of Resources and Capabilities

manufacturing processes gave these companies a competitive advantage in the world auto industry. By the early 1990s, TQM had become widely diffused within the industry. With defect rates showing much lower variance, quality-based manufacturing was no longer an important source of competitive advantage in autos.

Second, the resource or capability must be *relevant*. Ted Turner may be the greatest yachtsman among the ranks of America's CEOs. However, if this capability does not correspond to any of the key success factors in the television broadcasting industry, then it is irrelevant to Turner Broadcasting's potential for achieving competitive advantage. Thus, resources and capabilities are valuable only if they can be linked with one or more of the key success factors within an industry. That is, they must, in some way, assist the firm in creating value for its customers or in surviving competition.

IBM's reputation as the world's largest and longest established computer company was critical to its initial success in the personal computer industry during 1981-6, a period when customers were concerned about continuity of customer support and uncertain over the trajectory of technological development. By the early 1990s, IBM's size, longevity, and associated reputation no longer supported significant price-premium in PCs. Customers were well informed, less risk-averse, less dependent upon manufacturer-provided customer support, and more certain about the evolution of technology.

Sustainability of competitive advantage

The profits earned from resources and capabilities depend not just upon their ability to establish competitive advantage but also on how long that advantage can be sustained. This depends upon the *durability* of the resources and capabilities upon which the competitive advantage is based, and upon rivals' ability to *imitate* the strategy of the company through gaining access to the resources and capabilities upon which the competitive advantage is built. This requires *either* that the firm purchases the resources or capabilities required, in which case they must be *mobile*, or that it *replicates* them.

Durability   Some resources are more durable than others and, hence, are a more secure basis for competitive advantage. The increasing pace of technological change is shortening the useful life span of most capital assets with the result that industrial companies are increasingly writing down or writing off the book value of fixed assets well before they are fully depreciated. Technological resources such as patents may also be rendered obsolescent before their legal life span expires. Reputation, on the other hand, can show remarkable resilience to the passage of time. Brands such as Heinz sauces, Kellogg's cereals, Campbell's Soup, Hoover vacuum cleaners, and Singer sewing machines have been market leaders for periods of a century or more. Corporate reputation is similarly long-living: the reputations of General Electric, Du Pont, and Procter & Gamble as well-managed, socially responsible, financially sound companies producing reliable products and offering good opportunities to capable employees are decades old and continue to give these companies credibility and attention in every field of business they enter.

Mobility   The simplest means of acquiring the resources and capabilities necessary for imitating another firm's strategy is to buy them. If rivals can acquire on similar terms the resources required for imitating the strategy of a successful company, then that company's competitive advantage will be short lived. The ability to buy a resource or capability depends upon its mobility – the extent to which it can be transferred between companies. Some resources, such as finance, raw materials, components, machines produced by equipment suppliers, and employees with standardized skills (such as short-order cooks and auditors) are transferable between firms and can be bought and sold with little difficulty. Some resources are not easily transferred. The principal sources of immobility are the following:

1 *Geographical immobility* The costs of relocating large items of capital equipment and highly specialized employees puts firms that are acquiring these resources at a disadvantage with respect to firms that already possess them.

2 *Imperfect information* Assessing the value of a resource is made difficult, first, by the heterogeneity of productive resources (particularly human resources), and, second, because resources work together in teams, it is difficult to observe the productivity of individual resources.[26] Because the established firm can build up information over time about the productivity of its resources, it has superior knowledge concerning its resources to that of any prospective purchaser with the potential for a "lemons" problem.[27] Jay Barney has shown how interfirm differences in expectations concerning the returns to a resource result in resources being either underpriced or overpriced and give rise to differences in profitability between firms.[28]

3 *Firm-specific resources* Apart from the transactions costs arising from immobility and imperfect information, the value of a resource may fall on transfer due to a decline in its productivity. To the extent that brand reputation is associated with the company that created the brand reputation, a change in ownership of the brand name erodes its value. The acquisition of Harrods department store in London by the Al Fayed brothers raised concerns over whether Harrods's reputation as almost a national institution might suffer from foreign ownership. Employees can also suffer loss of productivity from interfirm transfer. To the extent that a manager's performance is context-specific, then it is not clear that Lou Gerstner can be as effective a manager at IBM as he was at American Express or RJR Nabisco. Some resources may be almost entirely firm-specific – corporate reputation can only be transferred by acquiring the company as a whole and even then the reputation of the acquired company normally depreciates during the change in ownership.[29]

Organizational capabilities, because they are based upon teams of resources, are less mobile than individual resources. Even if the whole team can be transferred (e.g., the defection to Volkswagen in March 1993 of Ignacio Lopez, GM's head of worldwide purchasing, and 40 of Opel's purchasing staff) the dependence of the capability on company-specific relationships and culture may mean that capability cannot be easily recreated in the new company.[30]

Replicability   If a firm cannot buy a resource or capability, then it must build it. In retailing, competitive advantages that derive from store layout, point-of-sale technology, retailer credit card, and extended hours of opening can be copied easily by competitors. In financial services, innovations such as interest rate swaps, stripped bonds, and most other derivatives offer only temporary advantage because they can be imitated easily by competitors.

Less easily replicable are capabilities based upon complex organizational routines. Federal Express's national, next-day delivery service and Nucor's system for steel manufacturing, which combines outstanding efficiency with remarkable flexibility, are complex capabilities fused into unique corporate cultures. Some capabilities appear simple but prove difficult to replicate. Just-in-time scheduling and continuous improvement through quality circles are relatively simple techniques used to great effect by Japanese companies. Despite the fact that neither require sophisticated knowledge nor complex operating systems, their dependence on high levels of collaboration has meant that many American and European firms have encountered difficulties in implementing them.

Even where replication is possible, the dynamics of stock-flow relationships may still offer advantage to incumbent firms. Competitive advantage depends upon the *stock* of resources and capabilities that a firm possesses. These have been built up by investment over time. Dierickx and Cool show that firms that have built up strong positions in particular resources or capabilities possess advantage over imitators because of the dynamics of investing in resources and capabilities.[31] For example, *"asset mass efficiencies"* mean that an initial strong position in technology, distribution channels, or reputation may mean that subsequent accumulation of these resources can be achieved at a relatively rapid rate. Similarly, *"time compression diseconomies"* are costs that are incurred by attempting to invest in rapid accumulations of particular resources and capabilities. Thus, "crash programs" of R&D and "blitz" advertising campaigns tend to be less productive than similar expenditures made over a longer period.

The firm's ability to sustain its competitive advantage over time depends upon the speed with which rivals can acquire the resources and capabilities needed to imitate the success of the initiating firm. The primary means to acquire the resources and capabilities needed to compete is to purchase and hire the required inputs.

Appropriating resource rents

Who gains the return earned by a resource or capability? We should normally expect that such returns accrue to the owner of that resource or capability. However, ownership is often far from clear cut. Machinery, brand names, or patents are normally owned by the firm that acquired or developed these resources, but even in the case of proprietary technology, property rights are ill defined (as indicated by the amount of litigation in the area of intellectual property). Human beings normally own their own skills and knowledge, yet even with human resources issues of rent appropriation arise. First, the distinction between the technology of the firm and the human capital of the individual is not always clear. Second, employment contracts only partially specify what the firm is buying from the employee.

In the area of technology and know-how, there are enormous problems in determining what is owned by the individual employee and what is owned by the firm. When Lopez and his colleagues left General Motors for Volkswagen, to what extent were they taking their individual knowledge and expertise and to what extent were they taking GM's trade secrets? When a group of employees leaves a microelectronics company and sets up its own business, to what extent are the employees plundering the proprietary technology of their former employer? Charles Ferguson has claimed that high-tech start-ups involve employees' exploitation of corporate knowledge, which, rather than indicating the entrepreneurial dynamism of America's microelectronics and IT (information technology) sector, involves a continual leakage of the technological assets of leading U.S. companies and an impediment to their global leadership.[32]

In professional service firms, ambiguity over company versus individual ownership of knowledge, technology, customer goodwill, and reputation is similarly critical to rent allocation. The prevalence of partnership arrangements in firms of lawyers and accountants reflects the need to avoid this potential conflict. Many of the problems that have arisen in acquisitions of human capital-intensive companies are a consequence of such conflicts between the acquiring company and employees of the acquired company over property rights (see exhibit 5.2).

In the case of organizational capabilities, issues of appropriating rents are especially difficult – while capabilities are based upon employee skills and knowledge, these skills are organization-based. The degree of control exercised by a firm and the balance of power between the firm and an individual employee depends crucially on the relationship between individuals' skills and organizational routines. The more deeply embedded individual skills and knowledge are within organizational routines and the more they are dependent upon corporate systems and reputation, the greater is the firm's ability to appropriate the returns.

Where ambiguity over ownership of resources and capabilities exists, the allocation of the rents between the firm and its employees depends critically upon their relative bargaining power. If the individual employee's contribution to productivity is clearly identifiable, if the employee

Exhibit 5.2   Our Assets Just Walked Out on Us!

In the summer of 1987, Martin Sorrell, CEO of WPP Group PLC, bought Lord, Geller, Fredrico, Einstein (LGFE) – one of New York's most respected advertising agencies and best known for its Charlie Chaplin advertisements for IBM. The acquisition followed WPP's purchase of J. Walter Thompson and a string of other agencies, which had established WPP as one of the world's largest advertising agencies.

Friction between LGFE and its British parent, WPP, over issues of business and creative independence of LGFE, reached a climax in March 1988. The chairman, president, and four top executives from LGFE left to establish a new agency, Lord, Einstein, O'Neill & Partners. They were joined on March 22 by over a dozen other key employees. The exit of employees was followed by the defection of clients. One client, the president of the *New Yorker* magazine, explained: "If your used to working with someone who is generating ideas and helping you, you stay with them. This is a matter of personal loyalties." Meanwhile, the parent company, WPP, was busy taking legal action against the new agency, contending that the former LGFE employees had conspired to take away Lord Geller's business,

while at the same time trying to quash rumors that Lord Geller was about to close.

WPP obtained a temporary injunction against Richard Lord and Arthur Einstein Jr. from soliciting or accepting business from any of LGFE's clients. The new firm also took to the courts charging Martin Sorrell and WPP with libel and slander.

By the end of 1988, WPP's LGFE subsidiary was in a sorry state. Despite loyalty from a few clients – Schieffelin and Somerset decided to keep its $8 million advertising account for Hennessy cognac with LGFE – many of LGFE's largest clients switched to other agencies. IBM put its $120 million account up for competition and awarded part of it to the new agency Lord, Einstein, O'Neill & Partners. Sears Roebuck and Pan Am also withdrew their business from LGFE. Following this loss of business, LGFE was forced to lay off one-third of its employees. In the meantime, the defectors made quick progress: a $30 million advertising account was won from Saab Scania North America, and the court injunction against Lord and Einstein was lifted.

Source: Wall Street Journal, March 23, 1988, 1, 21; and subsequent issues.

---

is mobile, and if the employee's skills offer similar productivity to other firms, the employee is in a strong position to appropriate a substantial proportion of his or her contribution to the firm's value added. In 1992, Wayne Gretzky signed a new contract with the Los Angeles Kings ice hockey club, reputed to be worth $54 million over five years. To the extent that Gretzky's impact on the King's performance and attendance is quantifiable and to the extent that Gretzky can offer similar revenue enhancement to other hockey teams, Gretzky's contract reflects his ability to appropriate his contribution to the King's revenue as salary and bonuses. The strategic strength of Andersen Consulting rests not only on its leadership in the market for information technology consulting but also upon the fact that its competitive advantage is securely based upon the reputation of the firm rather than that of individual stars as gurus and upon team-based capabilities rather than individual expertise.

Developing the Resource Base of the Firm

The analysis so far has been concerned with appraising and exploiting the firm's existing pool of resources and competencies. However, the link between strategy and resources is concerned not just with designing strategies to exploit resource strengths but also investing in the preservation, upgrading, and extension of the firm's bundle of resources and capabilities in order to secure the long-term future of the firm.

The conventional approach to resource building has focused upon gap analysis. Having evaluated a company's resources and capabilities with regard to relative strengths and weaknesses, the company formulates a strategy that most effectively deploys the company's resource strengths against the key success factors in the company's industry environment. However, comparing the chosen strategy against the company's bundle of resources and capabilities may reveal certain resource gaps that will need to be closed if the strategy is to be of maximum effectiveness in building competitive advantage.

The turnaround of Walt Disney between 1986 and 1992 (exhibit 5.2) involved little in the way of new strategic directions; the principal emphasis was an adjustment of strategy in order to gain a more effective utilization of Disney's existing resources and capabilities. At the same time, these strategy adjustments also pointed to the existence of certain resource gaps. For example, the revitalization of Disney's motion picture business was achieved through heavy investment in creative talent in the form of directors, actors, scriptwriters, and cartoonists. The acquisition of the Arvida Corporation provided the real estate development skills necessary for better utilizing Disney's huge Florida landholdings. A rebuilt marketing team was instrumental in boosting attendance at Disney's U.S. theme parks.

Filling resource gaps may induce companies to seek resources and capabilities through acquisitions or strategic alliances. General Motors's strategy during the 1980s for regenerating its world auto business pointed to the need for increased automation and improved quality. These strategic thrusts were instrumental in its acquisition of Ross Perot's Electronic Data Systems (EDS) and its formation of the NUMMI (New United Motor Manufacturing Inc.) joint venture with Toyota.

However, this "resource gap" approach takes an overly static view of resource analysis. As we shall examine more fully in the next chapter, competition is a dynamic process in which a firm's competitive advantage is constantly being eroded through imitation and innovation. Michael Porter argues that it is continuous investment in resources and capabilities that is the key to competitive advantage over the long haul: "Firms create and sustain competitive advantage because of the capacity to continuously improve, innovate and upgrade their competitive advantages over time. Upgrading is the process of shifting advantages throughout the value chain to more sophisticated types and employing higher levels of skill and technology."[33]

Investment in upgrading resources and capabilities can occur naturally through organizational learning. Hiroyuki Itami has introduced the concept of *dynamic resource fit* to describe the process through which the pursuit of a strategy not only utilizes a firm's resources but also augments them through the creation of skills and knowledge that are the products of experience: "Effective strategy in the present builds invisible assets, and the expanded stock enables the firm to plan its future strategy to be carried out. And the future strategy must make effective use of the resources that have been amassed."[34]

Matsushita's multinational expansion has closely followed this principal of parallel and sequential development of strategy and resources. In developing production in a foreign country, Matsushita has typically begun with the production of batteries, then moved on to the production of products requiring greater manufacturing and marketing sophistication. Arataroh Takahashi explained the strategy:

> In every country batteries are a necessity, so they sell well. As long as we bring a few advanced automated pieces of equipment for the processed vital to final product quality, even unskilled labor can produce good products. As they work on this rather simple product, the workers get trained, and this increased skill level then permits us to gradually expand production to items with increasingly higher technology level, first radios, then televisions.[35]

This dynamic resource fit may also provide a strong basis for a firm's diversification. Sequential product addition as expertise and knowledge is acquired is a prominent feature of the strategies of Honda in extending its product range from motorcycles to cars, lawn mowers, and boat engines and of 3M in expanding from abrasives to adhesives, computer disks, video and audio tape, and a broad range of consumer and producer goods.

Summary and Conclusions

In this chapter, we have shifted the focus of our attention from the external to the internal environment of the firm. This internal environment comprises many features of the firm, including its resources; its organizational structure; its systems of information; communication, reward, and control; its style of management; its values; and its traditions. By focusing on what the firm can do, our attention is directed toward the resources of the firm and the way that resources work together in organizational routines. This is not to say that the structure and systems of the organization are not important – they are critical to the effective implementation of strategy. However, because firms possess a considerable measure of flexibility in their choices of organizational structure and management systems, we can regard these features of the internal environment primarily as consequences rather than determinants of strategy choice.

The approach of this chapter has been to emphasize a number of conceptual aspects of the firm's resources and routines in order to convey an understanding of the nature of the firm's capabilities and to explore in some depth the relationships between the firm's resource base, its competitive advantage, and its profit potential. At the same time, the approach is highly practical and applicable. To illustrate the application of this approach to specific company cases figure 5.10 summarizes the principal stages of resource analysis in a flow diagram.

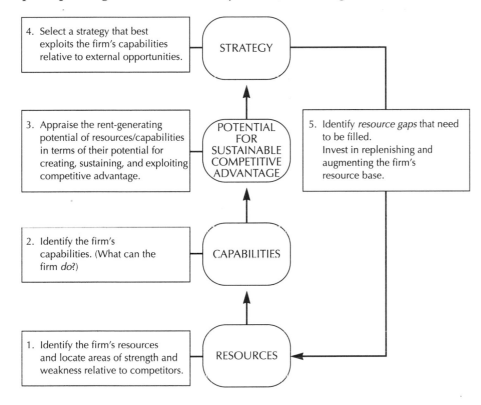

4. Select a strategy that best exploits the firm's capabilities relative to external opportunities.

STRATEGY

3. Appraise the rent-generating potential of resources/capabilities in terms of their potential for creating, sustaining, and exploiting competitive advantage.

POTENTIAL FOR SUSTAINABLE COMPETITIVE ADVANTAGE

5. Identify *resource gaps* that need to be filled. Invest in replenishing and augmenting the firm's resource base.

2. Identify the firm's capabilities. (What can the firm *do*?)

CAPABILITIES

1. Identify the firm's resources and locate areas of strength and weakness relative to competitors.

RESOURCES

Figure 5.10 Summary: A Framework for Analyzing Resources and Capabilities

Notes

1   Analysis of the internal environment of the firm has also been given prominence by researchers who have investigated the *process* of strategy formulation. Researchers who have approached strategy formulation from a behavioral science perspective view strategy formulation not as rational optimizing decisions made with objective information but either as an evolving pattern of decisions and actions (see Henry Mintzberg, "Crafting Strategy," *Harvard Business Review* [July-August 1987]: 66–75) or as a political process within the firm (see Andrew M. Pettigrew, "Strategy Formulation As a Political Process," *International Studies of Management and Organization* 7, no. 2 [1977]: 78–87).

2   B. H. Liddell Hart, *Strategy* (New York: Praeger, 1954), 365.

3   The "resource-based view" is described in J. B. Barney, "Firm Resources and Sustained Competitive Advantage," *Journal of Management* 17 (1991): 99–120; J. Mahoney and J. R. Pandian, "The Resource-Based View within the Conversation of Strategic Management," *Strategic Man-*

agement Journal 13 (1992): 363–80; and M. A. Peterlaf, "The Corner-stones of Competitive Advantage: A Resource-Based View," *Strategic Management Journal* 14 (1993): 179–92.

4   Theodore Levitt, "Marketing Myopia," *Harvard Business Review* (July-August 1960): 24–47.

5   Robert M. Grant, "Diversification in Financial Services."

6   James Brian Quinn, *Intelligent Enterprise* (New York: Free Press, 1992), 22–3.

7   R. P. Rumelt ("How Much Does Industry Matter?" *Strategic Management Journal* 12 [1991]: 167–85) found that among 2,180 business units, only 4 percent of the variance of return on assets was attributable to the influence of industry.

8   Such jointly owned resources are *"public goods"* – their benefits can be extended to additional firms at negligible marginal cost.

9   "No Accounting for Taste," *Economist*, June 25, 1988, 83.

10 An alternative explanation of the high valuation ratios of these companies might be the stock market's assessment of their potential for high growth of profits. This explanation is not entirely convincing: while the computer software and pharmaceutical companies and the two retailers have shown high rates of earnings growth, most of the brand-rich companies are comparatively slow growing.

11 In their seminal essay on the role of information within the firm, Armen Alchian and Harold Demsetz ("Production, Information Costs, and Economic Organization," *American Economic Review* 62 [1972]: 777–95) regard the monitoring of input productivity as the fundamental purpose of management.

12 Jay Barney, "Organizational Culture: Can It Be a Source of Sustained Competitive Advantage?" *Academy of Management Review* 11 (1986): 656–65.

13 While some attempts have been made to differentiate the two, Gary Hamel and C. K. Prahalad (letter, *Harvard Business Review* [May-June, 1992]: 164–5) argue that "the distinction between competences and capabilities is purely semantic."

14 P. Selznick, *Leadership in Administration: A Sociological Interpretation* (New York: Harper & Row, 1957); Igor Ansoff, Corporate Strategy (Harmondsworth, U.K.: Penguin, 1965).

15 C. K Prahalad and G. Hamel, "The Core Competences of the Corporation," *Harvard Business Review* (May-June, 1990): 79–91.

16 Gary Hamel and C. K. Prahalad, letter, *Harvard Business Review* (May-June, 1992): 164–5.

17 For an illuminating description of the integration of functional and technical capabilities to develop new automobiles, see Clark and Fujimoto (1991).

18 K. B. Clark and T. Fujimoto, *Product Development Performance* (New York: Free Press, 1991); and K. Imai, I. Nonaka, and H. Takeuchi, "Managing the New Product Development Process: How Japanese Companies Learn and Unlearn," in *The Uneasy Alliance*, ed. K. Clark, R. Hayes, and C. Lorenz (Boston: Harvard Business School Press, 1985).

19 Robert M. Grant, "Business Strategy and Strategy Change in a Hostile Environment: Failure and Success among British cutlery Producers," in

The Management of Strategic Change, ed. Andrew Pettigrew (Oxford: Basil Blackwell, 1987).

20 Paul R. Lawrence and Davis Dyer, *Renewing American Industry* (New York: Free Press, 1983), 60–83.

21 Gary Hector, *Breaking the Bank*: The Decline of BankAmerica (Boston: Little, Brown, 1988).

22 *Forbes*, January 15, 1973.

23 Richard R. Nelson and Sidney G. Winter, *An Evolutionary Theory of Economic Change* (Cambridge, MA: Belknap Press, 1982).

24 Tom Peters and Robert Waterman, *In Search of Excellence* (New York: Harper & Row, 1982).

25 This observation is supported by John Freeman and Michael Hannan ("Niche Width and the Dynamics of Organizational Populations," *American Journal of Sociology* 88 [1984]: 1116–45) who observe that, in the restaurant industry, specialists survived better than generalists (except where the environment was highly variable, in which case generalists displayed greater adaptability).

26 A. A. Alchian and H. Demsetz, "Production, Information Costs, and Economic Organization," *American Economic Review* 62 (1972): 777–95.

27 G. Akerlof, "The Market for Lemons: Qualitative Uncertainty and the Market Mechanism," *Quarterly Journal of Economics* 84 (1970): 488–500.

28 Barney, "Organizational Culture," 656–65.

29 The definition of resource specificity in this article corresponds to the definition of "*specific assets*" by Richard Caves ("International Corporations: The Industrial Economics of Foreign Investment," *Economica* 38 [1971]: 1–27.); it differs from that used by O. E. Williamson (*The Economic Institutions of Capitalism* [New York: Free Press, 1985], 52–6). Williamson refers to assets which are specific to particular transactions rather than to particular firms.

30 Christopher Parkes, "Tricky Feats at the Top," *Financial Times*, July 17, 1993, 13.

31 Ingemar Dierickx and Karel Cool, "Asset Stock Accumulation and Sustainability of Competitive Advantage," *Management Science* 35 (1989): 1504–13.

32 Charles Ferguson, *International Competition, Strategic Behavior, and Government Policy in Information Technology Industries*, Ph.D. diss., MIT, 1987. For a summary and critique, see George Gilder, "The Revitalization of Everything: The Law of the Microcosm," *Harvard Business Review* (March-April 1988): 49–61. For a reply, see Charles Ferguson, "From the People Who Brought You Voodoo Economics," *Harvard Business Review* (May-June 1988).

33 Michael E. Porter, "Towards a Dynamic Theory of Strategy," *Strategic Management Journal*, special issue, 12 (winter 1991): 111.

34 Hiroyuko Itami, *Mobilizing Invisible Assets* (Boston: Harvard University Press, 1987), 125.

35 Quoted by Itami, *Mobilizing Invisible Assets*, 25.

SIX

The Nature and Sources of Competitive Advantage

One Saturday afternoon in downtown Chicago, Milton Friedman, the famous free-market economist, was shopping with his wife.

"Look, Milton!" exclaimed Mrs. Friedman, "There's a $20 bill on the sidewalk!" "Don't be foolish, my dear," replied the Nobel laureate, "If that was a $20 bill, someone would have picked it up by now."

> – economist's anecdote of doubtful authenticity

Introduction and Objectives

In this chapter, I will draw together the ideas concerning competitive advantage that have already been introduced in the book and develop these into a wide-ranging, practical, and, I hope, insightful analysis of the nature and sources of competitive advantage. By the time you have completed this chapter, you will:

- be aware of the circumstances in which a firm can create a competitive advantage over a rival;
- appreciate the role of responsiveness and innovation in creating competitive advantage;
- understand the process through which competition erodes competitive advantage through imitation;
- be capable of identifying opportunities for competitive advantage by recognizing the role of resource conditions in creating imperfections in the competitive process;
- be familiar with the two primary types of competitive advantage – cost advantage and differentiation advantage;
- be able to apply this analysis to formulate business strategies capable of establishing and sustaining competitive advantage in different types of industry.

In chapter 2, we observed that a firm can earn a rate of profit in excess of the "normal" or "competitive" rate either by locating in an attractive industry or by establishing a competitive advantage over its rivals. We subsequently observed that, of the two sources of superior profitability, competitive advantage is of overwhelming importance. The growing intensity of competition across the business sector as a whole has meant that there are very few industries that are sheltered havens offering secure returns. Hence, the primary goal for strategy is to establish a position of competitive advantage for the firm. Kenichi Ohmae has gone as far as to define strategy as the quest for competitive advantage (see exhibit 1.3 in chapter 1).

The foundations for the analysis of competitive advantage were laid in chapters 3 and 5. Chapter 3 analyzed the *external* sources of competitive advantage. Key success factors are the requirements for success in an industry: the conditions that must be met to satisfy customers and to survive the pressures of competition. Chapter 5 analyzed the internal sources of competitive advantage: the potential offered by the firm's resources and capabilities for establishing and sustaining competitive advantage. In this chapter, I integrate external and internal sources of competitive advantage. I will show how creating competitive advantage involves managing internal resources and capabilities in order to respond to external opportunities and how sustaining competitive advantage depends upon the characteristics and availabilities of resources and capabilities. A central theme of this chapter is the competitive process. Competition provides the incentive for establishing advantage and the means by which advantage is eroded. Understanding the character of competition in an industry is fundamental to identifying the potential for competitive advantage.

The Emergence of Competitive Advantage

To understand how competitive advantage emerges, we must first understand what competitive advantage is. I define competitive advantage as follows:

When two firms compete (i.e., when they locate within the same market and are capable of supplying the same customers), one firm possesses a competitive advantage over the other when it earns a higher rate of profit or has the potential to earn a higher rate of profit.

Competitive advantage, then, is the ability to outperform rivals on what I assume to be firms' primary performance goal – profitability. Note that competitive advantage may not be revealed in higher profitability: a firm may wish to trade profit for market share gain (which may ultimately involve the destruction of a rival). Or, a firm may wish to forego profits in the interests of philanthropy, rewards to employees, or executive perks.

External sources of change

For profit differences to emerge between competing firms, *change* must take place. The source of the change may be external or internal to the industry. In the automobile industry, external changes may include a fall in the price of gasoline, a rise in the yen against the dollar, or a tightening of government emission standards. For such disturbances to result in competitive advantage requires that changes have differential effects upon companies because of differences in their resources and capabilities. Thus, the rising yen during the latter half of 1993 improved the competitive position of Ford against Toyota because Ford's production facilities are mainly in North America and Europe and Toyota's mainly in Japan. The bad winter weather in much of the United States during early 1994 benefited Chrysler against GM because of Chrysler's heavier involvement in the production of four-wheel drive vehicles.

The potential to establish competitive advantage depends, therefore, on the extent of change and the extent of differences in firms' resource bases. The more turbulent an industry's environment is, the greater will be the number of sources of change and the greater the differences in the bundles of resources and capabilities that each firm possesses – that is, the greater the dispersion of profitability within the industry. The world oil industry of the 1960s and the British brewing industry during the 1970s were industries where the environment was relatively stable and firms fairly similar; competitive advantages tended to be small and profit differentials relatively modest. The toy industry, on the other hand, experiences rapid changes in demand, technology, and fashion. The quest for novelty and the success of some companies in creating the next craze ensures a wide dispersion of interfirm profitability.

Competitive advantage through responsiveness to external change

The role of external change in creating competitive advantage is not simply in *conferring* advantages and disadvantages upon otherwise passive firms. The competitive advantage that arises from external change also depends upon a firm's ability to *respond* to external change. Any external change creates opportunities for profit. The ability to identify these opportunities and to respond to them are central components of the management activity we refer to as *entrepreneurship*. To the extent that external opportunities are fleeting or subject to first-mover advantage, speed of response is critical to exploiting business opportunity. An unexpected shower of rain creates an upsurge in the demand for umbrellas. Those street vendors who position themselves outside a busy railroad station at the onset of rain will be able to exploit this opportunity to the full.

As markets have become increasingly turbulent, so responsiveness to external change has become increasingly important as a source of competitive advantage:

- Wal-Mart's ability to consistently outperform K-Mart depends heavily upon a system that responds quickly and effectively to changes in demand. Wal-Mart's distribution and purchasing is driven by data from electronic scanning at point of sale. The speed with which Wal-Mart responds to these data results in low inventories, few stockouts, and a low level of markdowns;
- Benetton's information system plays a similar role in the company's responsiveness to franchise sales data, which are relayed daily from all its franchisees to its corporate headquarters in Polanzo, Italy. Benetton's ability to quickly adjust its manufacturing to emerging sales trends is facilitated by its practice of manufacturing its garments from undyed yarn, then dying its products in response to customers' revealed preferences.
- in the oil refining industry, the basis of competitive advantage has shifted substantially as a result of market turbulence. Superior profitability used to depend upon low cost resulting from scale-efficiency and careful operational planning of product flow. During recent years, superior performance depends more upon responsiveness to changing price differentials between different crudes and different refined products. The most profitable refineries are those that have the flexibility to make rapid changes in their crude inputs and their balance of product outputs in order to exploit short-term price changes.

Responsiveness also involves anticipating changes in the basis of competitive advantage over time. As an industry moves through its life cycle, as customer requirements change, and as patterns of competition shift, so companies must adjust their strategies and their capabilities to take account of the key success factors of the future. Monsanto's subsidiary, G. D. Searle, has shown considerable foresight in building its competitive position to outlive the expiration in 1992 of its patents on its artificial sweetener, NutraSweet. Initially, Searle successfully extended its patent protection for five years beyond the normal 17-year patent term, but as this period began drawing to a close it increasingly relied upon heavy promotion of the NutraSweet brand name and its "swirl" logo and invested in a $160 million, scale-efficient production facility in Georgia.

It has also used trade secrets to protect its production know-how.[1] Similarly, the efforts by the automobile companies to develop electric and recyclable cars are attempts to position themselves to take advantage of growing environmental concerns during the 1990s.

Responsiveness to the opportunities for competitive advantage provided by environmental change requires one key resource – *information* – and one key capability – *flexibility of response*. Information is necessary to identify and anticipate external changes. This is dependent upon a firm's *environmental scanning* capability. As the pace of change has accelerated, environmental scanning activities have changed with them: firms are less dependent upon conventional analysis of economic and market research data and more dependent on "early warning systems" through direct relationships with customers, suppliers, and competitors.

Second, flexibility of response requires that a firm is able to swiftly redeploy resources to meet changes in external conditions. Flexibility is not primarily a matter of the technical capabilities associated with plant and equipment and other types of hardware; it is primarily a result of the "organizational software" – organization structure, systems of decision making, breadth of job design, and attitudes. Flexibility typically requires fewer levels of hierarchy, greater decentralization of decision making, and informal patterns of cooperation and coordination. Benetton's remarkable responsiveness to emerging market trends and changing customer preferences is achieved through a highly flexible network. At the retail level, Benetton operates through a system of country and regional agents who coordinate the franchised retail outlets within their territories. At the production level, Benetton's own production facilities are supported by over 200 subcontractors. A remarkable feature of this vertically integrated network is an absence of formal contracts. The shifting of garment dying to the end of the production process is just one means by which Benetton has redesigned its business processes to maximize flexibility.[2]

The greater flexibility a company has in responding to changing market circumstances, the less dependent it will be upon its ability to forecast. Sony is reputed to undertake little in the way of formal demand forecasting or market research. Because of Sony's speed and flexibility in bringing to market new products, upgraded models of existing products, and adjusting production to meet sales, Sony is not dependent on forecasting in aligning its product offerings and production levels to changing market requirements.

As fast-response capability becomes an increasingly important key success factor across most industries, interest in time-based management and the role of time as a strategically important resource has grown. George Stalk views the competitive advantage of Honda, Matsushita, Toyota, and many other Japanese companies as heavily dependent on *speed*. These companies compete through time based manufacturing, time-based sales and distribution, and time-based innovation.[3] In the automobile industry, a major advantage of Japanese companies has been the speed at which they can develop new models (see table 6.1).

During the last ten years, a major preoccupation of U.S. companies has been to increase their fast-response capabilities by reducing cycle times both in manufacturing and in new product development. At Northern Telecom's PBX production plant in California, fundamental redesign of manufacturing and new-product introduction processes resulted in substantial time reductions in several activities together with cost reduction and quality improvement:

- production throughput times were reduced from two to four weeks to two to five days;
- new product introduction time (from product definition to the completion of field trials) was reduced from 24 to 13 months;
- engineering changes were approved and introduced within five days or less instead of three to four weeks.

Competitive advantage through innovation – identifying "new-game" strategies

The source of disturbance that creates the opportunity for competitive advantage may be internal as well as external. Internal change is generated by *innovation*. Innovation not only creates competitive advantage, it provides a basis for overturning the competitive advantage of other firms. Schumpeter's view of the competitive process as "a gale of creative destruction" involved market leadership being eroded not by imitation but by innovation. Innovation is typically thought of in its technical sense: the embodiment of new ideas and knowledge in new products or processes. However, within a business context, innovation also embodies new approaches to doing business. Innovative strategies involve new approaches to competing within an industry. Innovative strategies tend to be the basis of most outstanding success in most industries – far more so than product innovation alone. Many creative business strategies involve little product innovation. Consider the following examples:

Table 6.1 New Product Development Performance by U.S., Japanese, and European Auto Producers

	Japanese volume producer	U.S. volume producer	European volume producer	European high-end specialist
Average lead time (months)	42.6	61.9	57.6	71.5
Engineering hours (million)	1.2	3.5	3.4	3.4
Total product quality index	58	41	41	84

Source: Kim B. Clark and Takahiro Fujimoto, *Product Development Performance* (Boston: Harvard Business School Press, 1991), 73.

- in the North American steel industry, Nucor, Chaparral Steel, and CoSteel have achieved unrivaled productivity and flexibility producing standard steel products through process technologies, organizational structures, and management systems, which are quite different from those used by the integrated steel companies;
- in retailing, outstanding success is usually associated with innovatory retailing concepts and new approaches to organizing traditional tasks. Common to the success of Home Depot, IKEA, The Gap, and Body Shop is their entry into a traditional sector of the retailing industry with a radically different retailing strategy.

Charles Baden Fuller and John Stopford provide compelling evidence that, even in mature industries, "strategic innovation" is the primary basis for competitive advantage and the principal driving force for change in industries. They argue that a critical element of such innovation is creating customer value through the combination of performance dimensions that were previously viewed as conflicting. Thus:

- Toyota developed its "lean production system," which combined low cost and high quality;
- Courtaulds, the British acrylic fibers manufacturer, developed large-scale production of its Courtelle fiber and small-lot dying to combine low cost and product variety;
- Richardson, a Sheffield, England, manufacturer of kitchen knives, used its highly flexible management systems and its culture of entrepreneurship and customer focus to achieve low costs with a speed of customer response that was unprecedented within its industry.[4]

Innovation typically requires imagination, intuition, and creativity rather than analysis in the deductive sense. However, there are frameworks and approaches that can be useful in identifying new ways of competing. By mapping the activities that the firm performs and the linkages between these activities, the value chain provides a representation of the firm that can then be manipulated to suggest new ways of competing. On this basis, McKinsey & Company distinguish between "same game" and "new-game" strategies. New-game strategies typically take the form of new configurations of the chain of activities that are performed in the industry. The ways in which firms do business in an industry and the range of activities that they encompass are often the result of convention. By reconstructing and rearranging the value chain, a company can change the "rules of the game" so as to:

- capitalize on its distinctive competencies;
- catch competitors off guard; and
- erect barriers to protect the advantage created.

McKinsey cites Savin in the North American market for plain-paper copiers as an example of the potency of new-game strategies in challenging an established firm with a seemingly impregnable competitive position and an illustration of the application of the value chain in formulating new-game strategies (see exhibit 6.1).

The key element in the formulation of new-game strategies is to identify in which activities a firm has the potential for advantage and then to devise a strategy that achieves the maximum leverage on these advantages. Among airlines, several companies have competed successfully by redefining and reconfiguring the activities they perform:

- Southwest Airlines, and several of the other "budget airlines," have achieved unrivaled cost advantages in travel by radically pruning the number of activities that they perform and by undertaking others in nontraditional ways;
- Nike built its large and successful businesses on a business system that involved a total reconfiguration of the activities of the traditional shoe

---

Exhibit 6.1   Using the Value Chain to Help Formulate New-Game Strategies: Savin and Xerox

For most of the 1970s, Xerox possessed a near monopoly position in the North American market for plain-paper copiers. Xerox's dominance rested, first, upon the wall of patents that the company had built over several decades and, second, on the scale economies and reputation that its market dominance conferred. The first company to compete effectively with Xerox during the late 1970s was Savin. The basis of Savin's challenge was an approach that sought not to imitate Xerox's success but to compete in an entirely different manner.

Savin developed and patented a new low-cost technology. Its product design permitted the use of standardized parts that could be sourced in volume from Japan. Assembly was also undertaken in Japan. The result was a product whose cost was about half that of Xerox's. To avoid the costs of leasing and the need for a costly direct sales force, Savin distributed through existing office equipment dealers.

The principal differences between the approach of Savin and that of Xerox can be seen by comparing the main activities of the companies:

	XEROX	SAVIN
Technology and design	Dry xerography High copy speed Many features	Liquid toner Low copy speed Few features and options
Manufacture	Most manufacturing (including components) in house	Machines sourced from Ricoh in Japan
Product range	Wide range of machines	Narrow range of machines for different volumes and uses
Marketing	Machines leased to customers	Machines sold to customers
Distribution	Direct sales force	Distribution through dealers
Service	Directly operated service organization	Service by dealers and independent service engineers

Source: Roberto Buaron, "New-Game Strategies," *McKinsey Staff Paper*, March 1980.

manufacturing firm. To begin with, Nike does not manufacture shoes – indeed, it manufactures little of anything. Nike designs, markets, and distributes shoes, but its primary activity is the coordination of a vast and complex global network involving the design and market research (primarily in the United States), the production (under contract) of components (primarily in Korea and Taiwan), and the assembly of shoes in Taiwan, Malaysia, China, the Philippines, Thailand, and a number of other countries for sale throughout the world;

- Dell Computer's success in personal computers during the early 1990s was based upon an innovatory reconfiguration of the sales, distribution, and customer service activities.

Developing new configurations of conventional value chains in order to take advantage of the competitive advantages of different companies and the comparative advantages of different countries is a major force driving strategic change across large industrial corporations throughout the world. Companies are increasingly withdrawing from those activities where they do not possess a clear competitive advantage in order to concentrate upon those activities in which they do.

Sustaining Competitive Advantage

Once established, competitive advantage is subject to erosion by competition. The speed with which competitive advantage is undermined depends upon the ability of competitors to challenge either by imitation or innovation. The essence of the competitive process is the imitation by rivals of the strategy of the advantaged firm. For competitive advantage to be sustained over time requires the existence of barriers to imitation. Rumelt uses the term *"isolating mechanisms"* to describe "barriers which limit the ex post equilibration of rents among individual firms."[5] The more effective these isolating mechanisms are, the longer can competitive advantage be sustained against the onslaught of rivals. Empirical studies show that the process through which competition destroys the competitive advantage of industry leaders is slow. I have noted that considerable dispersion between the profitability of firms within the same industry exists. Equally interesting is the fact that these differentials are eroded at a slow pace. Even over periods of a decade and more, interfirm profit differentials tend to persist, with many firms sustaining rates of profit above or below the averages for their industries over considerable periods.[6]

To identify the sources of isolating mechanisms, we need to examine the process of competitive imitation. For one firm to successfully imitate the strategy of another, it must meet four conditions:

1 *Identification* The firm must be able to identify that a rival possesses a competitive advantage.

2 *Incentive* Having identified that a rival possesses a competitive advantage as evidenced by above-average profitability, the firm must believe that by investing in imitation, it too can earn superior returns on its investment.
3 *Diagnosis* The firm must be able to diagnose the features of its rival's strategy that give rise to the competitive advantage.
4 *Resource acquisition* The firm must be able to acquire through transfer or replication the resources and capabilities necessary for imitating the strategy of the advantaged firm.

At all four stages the potential for isolating mechanisms arises.

Identification: the potential for obscuring superior performance

A simple barrier to imitation by competitors is to obscure the firm's superior profitability. In the 1951 movie classic *The Treasure of the Sierra Madre*, Humphrey Bogart and his fellow gold prospectors go to great lengths to obscure their find from other prospectors.[7] The most direct means of obscuring competitive advantage in order to discourage would-be competitors is simply to forego short-term profits. The theory of *limit pricing*, in its simplest form, postulates that a firm in a strong market position will price at a level that just fails to attract entrants. A more attractive means of avoiding competition is for the firm to withhold information about its profitability. One advantage of private companies and unincorporated forms of business is that they are not obliged to make public their profit performance. Among public companies, diversification and consequent consolidation of accounts can help protect highly profitable subsidiaries from competitive entry.

Incentives to compete: deterrence and preemption

A firm may avoid competition by undermining the incentives for imitation. If a firm can persuade rivals that by imitating its strategy they will not achieve comparable profitability, it may be able to avoid competitive challenges. I discussed in chapter 4 the role of *signaling*: the manipulation of information by a firm in order to influence the behavior of competitors. *Deterrence* involves making threatening signals toward competitors that encourage the competitor to believe that a strategy of imitation will not prove profitable. The key to deterrence is the promise of retaliation against a competitor that encroaches upon the firm's strategic niche. For a threat to be effective in deterring a competitive challenge, it must be credible. Because carrying out a threat is usually costly to both the threatener and the victim, it needs to be supported by *commitment*.[8] Thus, the threat of aggressive price cuts needs to be backed either by excess capacity or by excess inventories. The credibility of a threat also depends upon the reputation of the firm that issues it. Hence, even though carrying out a threat can be costly and seemingly irrational, such punishment is an investment in reputation, which, by deterring competitive challenges in the future, will yield returns to the firm. Procter & Gamble (P&G), through its hard-fought marketing battles in disposable diapers, household detergents, toothpaste, and various other consumer markets, has built a reputation as a formidable competitor, which acts as a powerful deterrent to would-be intruders in all the markets in which P&G maintains a presence.

A firm can also deter imitation by *preemption* – occupying existing and potential strategic niches in order to reduce the range of investment opportunities open to the challenger. Preemption can take many forms:

- proliferation of product varieties by a market leader can leave new entrants and smaller rivals with few opportunities for establishing a market niche. Between 1950 and 1972, the six leading suppliers of breakfast cereals introduced 80 new brands into the U.S. market.[9]
- large investments in production capacity ahead of growth of market demand also preempt opportunities for rivals to earn satisfactory returns on new productive capacity. In 1959, Honda constructed a plant with a capacity of 30,000 motorcycles per month at a time when Honda's most popular models were selling barely one-tenth of that number. This drastically affected the opportunities for profitable expansion by other Japanese motorcycle producers.[10]
- patent proliferation can protect competitive advantage built upon proprietary technology by limiting competitors' technical opportunities. In 1974, Xerox's dominant market position was protected by a wall of over 2,000 patents. When IBM introduced its first copier in 1970, Xerox sued it for infringing 22 of these patents.[11]

The ability to sustain competitive advantage through preemption depends upon the presence of two imperfections of the competitive process. First, the market must be small relative to the minimum efficient scale of production, such that only a very small number of competitors are viable. Second, there must be first-mover advantage that gives an incumbent preferential access to information and other resources, putting rivals at a disadvantage. I will consider the sources of first-mover advantage in relation to the conditions for resource acquisition.

Diagnosing competitive advantage: "causal ambiguity" and "uncertain imitability"

If a firm is to imitate the competitive advantage of another, it must understand the basis of its rival's success. In most industries, there is a serious identification problem in linking superior performance to the resources and capabilities that generate that performance. Consider the remarkable success of Wal-Mart in the discount retailing business. It is easy for K-Mart to point to the differences between Wal-Mart and itself. As one Wal-Mart executive commented: "Retailing is an open book. There are no secrets. Our competitors can walk into our stores and see what we sell, how we sell it, and for how much." The difficult task is to identify which of those differences are critical to the different profitabilities of the two retailers. Is it Wal-Mart's store locations (typically in small towns with little direct competition)? its tightly integrated logistics of purchasing, warehousing, and distribution? its unique management system? the information system that supports Wal-Mart's logistics and its management system? or the culture that combines rural American values concerning thrift, simplicity, hard work, and customer attentiveness with company traditions that combine a sense of family with hard-driving entrepreneurship?

The problem for K-Mart and other discount retailers is what Lippman and Rumelt refer to as *"causal ambiguity."*[12] The more multidimensional a firm's competitive advantage is and the more each dimension of competitive advantage is based upon complex organizational capabilities rather than simple resources and capabilities – the more difficult will it be for a competitor to correctly diagnose the determinants of success. The outcome of "causal ambiguity" is *"uncertain imitability"*: that is, a competitor can attempt to imitate the success of another firm, but if it has been unable to overcome the ambiguity associated with the causes of success, then there will be uncertainty as to whether this imitation will be successful.

Resource acquisition

Having diagnosed the sources of an incumbent's competitive advantage, the imitator can mount a competitive challenge only by assembling the resources and capabilities necessary for imitation. The firm can acquire resources and capabilities in two ways: it can buy them, or it can make them. The period over which a competitive advantage can be sustained depends critically upon the time it takes to acquire and mobilize the resources and capabilities needed to mount a competitive challenge.

There is little to add here to the discussion of *mobility* and *replicability* in the previous chapter. The ability to buy resources and capabilities from outside factor markets depends upon their mobility. Immobility means that either the resource or capability cannot be purchased or it loses its productivity in the course of interfirm transfer. Even if resources are mobile, the market for a resource may be subject to *transactions costs* – costs of buying and selling arising from search costs, negotiation costs, contract enforcement costs, and transportation costs. Transactions costs are greater for highly differentiated (or "idiosyncratic") resources.[13]

The alternative to buying a resource or capability is to create it through internal investment. As we noted in the last chapter, where capabilities are based upon organizational routines, accumulating the coordination and learning required for their efficient operation can take considerable time. Even in the case of "turnkey" plants, developing the required operating capability can be a problem. Michael Polanyi observed: "I have myself watched in Hungary a new imported machine for blowing electric lamp bulbs, the exact counterpart of which was operating successfully in Germany, failing for a whole year to produce a single flawless bulb."[14] Businesses that require the integration of a number of complex, team-based routines may take years to reach the standards set by industry leaders. GM's attempt to transfer Toyota-style, team-based production from its NUMMI joint venture at Fremont, California, to the GM Van Nuys plant 400 miles to the south involved complex problems of learning and adjustment that remained unsolved two years after the program had begun.[15] Conversely, where a competitive advantage does not require the application of complex, firm-specific resources, imitation is likely to be easy and fast:

- in financial services, many new products such as money market checking accounts, brokerage accounts providing checking and credit card services, and foreign exchange and interest rate swaps, hedge fund partnerships, emerging market options, and the burgeoning range of other financial derivatives typically require resources and capabilities that are widely distributed among investment banks and brokerage houses. Hence, imitation of financial innovations is swift, and the competitive advantage associated with such innovation not sustainable;
- the rapid decline of Filofax, the British manufacturer (and originator) of personal organizers, similarly reflected the ease with which the resources and routines upon which its strategy was based could be replicated.[16]

First-mover advantage To understand the difficulties that face a would-be rival in acquiring the resources needed to imitate a successful firm's strategy, we need to look more closely at the nature of *first-mover advantage*. The idea of first-mover advantage is that the initial occupant of a strategic position or "niche" gains access to resources and capabilities that a follower cannot match. The simplest form of first-mover advantage is a patent or copyright. By establishing a patent or copyright, the first mover possesses a technology, product, or design from which a follower is legally excluded. Early occupancy of a strategic niche can offer other resource advantages. The old adage that "success breeds success" is confirmed by other resource-based advantages:

- initial competitive advantage offers a profit flow that permits the firm to invest in extending and upgrading its resource base. Pilkington's revolutionary float glass process was a competitive advantage whose life was limited to the term of the patent. However, Pilkington used its profits and income from patent licenses to invest heavily in new plants, expand multinationally by acquiring overseas competitors, and finance R&D into fiber optics and other new uses of glass;
- the first mover in a market establishes *reputation* with suppliers, distributors, and customers that cannot be initially matched by the follower;

- where proprietary *standards* in relation to product design and technology are important to competitive advantage, the first mover may have an advantage in setting the standard;
- economies of learning suggest that the first mover can build a cost advantage over followers as a result of greater experience.

Competitive Advantage in Different Market Settings

We have seen how earning profit from competitive advantage requires that the firm can *establish* a competitive advantage and that it can *sustain* its advantage for long enough to exploit the returns from that advantage. To identify opportunities for establishing and sustaining competitive advantage in a particular business, it is vital to understand the characteristics of the competitive process in that market. This, in turn, requires recognition of the types of resources and capabilities necessary to compete. In analyzing the competitive process and competitive advantage in different markets, I distinguish two activities that create value and offer profit opportunities: *trading* and *production*. *Trading* involves arbitrage across space (buying a $30 bottle of cognac in Hong Kong and selling it for $60 in Japan) and across time (buying heating oil in summer for sale in January). *Production* involves the physical transformation of inputs into outputs. Corresponding to these different types of business activity, I identify *trading markets* and *production markets*. Let me begin with a special type of trading market: an *efficient market*.

Efficient markets: the absence of competitive advantage

In chapter 3, I introduced the concept of *perfect competition*. Perfect competition exists where there are many buyers and sellers, no product differentiation product, no barriers to entry or exit, and free flow of information. In equilibrium, all firms earn the competitive rate of profit – which equals the cost of capital. The closest real-world examples of perfect competition are financial and commodity markets (for example, the markets for securities, foreign exchange, and grain futures). These markets are sometimes described as *"efficient."* An efficient market is one in which prices reflect all available information. Because prices adjust instantaneously to newly available information, no market trader can expect to earn more than any other. Any differences in ex post returns reflect either different levels of risk selected by different traders or purely random factors (luck). Because all available information is reflected in current prices, no trading rules based upon historical price data or any other available information can offer excess returns: it is not possible to "beat the market" on any consistent basis. In other words, competitive advantage is absent.

The absence of competitive advantage in efficient markets is a direct consequence of the types of resources required by participants in these markets. There are only two primary resources required in financial markets: finance and information. If both are equally available to all participants, then there is no basis for one to gain competitive advantage over another.

Imperfections of competition and competitive advantage in trading markets

In order for competitive advantage to exist, imperfections (or "inefficiencies") must be introduced into the competitive process. Focusing on the relatively simple case of trading markets, let us introduce different sources of imperfection to the competitive process, showing how these imperfections create opportunities for competitive advantage, and how these imperfections are closely related to the conditions of resource availability.

Imperfect availability of information Financial markets (and most other trading markets) depart from the conditions for efficiency because of imperfect availability of information. Competitive advantage, therefore, is dependent upon superior access to information. The most likely source of superior information is privileged access to private information. Trading on the basis of such information normally falls within the restrictions on "insider trading." While insider information creates advantage, such competitive advantage tends to be of short duration. Once a market participant begins acting on the basis of insider information, then other operators are alerted to the existence of the information. Even though they may not know the content of the information, they are able to imitate the behavior of the market leader. A commonly followed strategy in stock markets is to detect and follow insider transactions by senior company executives.

Transactions costs If markets are efficient except for the presence of transactions costs, then competitive advantage accrues to traders with the lowest transactions costs. A trader's transactions costs as a proportion of turnover depend upon the efficiency of his or her information and transactions processing systems and the total volume of transaction. In stock markets, low transactions costs are also attainable by traders who economize on research and market analysis and minimize the transactions required to attain their portfolio objectives. Studies of mutual fund performance show that "Net of all management fees, the average managed investment fund performed worse than a completely unmanaged buy-and-hold strategy on a risk-adjusted basis. Further, the amount by which the funds fell short of the unmanaged strategy was, on average, about the same as the management cost of the funds."[17] The observation that competitive advantage is attained through minimizing transactions costs is further supported by evidence that, over the long term, "market-index funds" outperform managed funds.

Systematic behavioral trends If the current prices in a market fully reflect all available information, then price movements are caused by the arrival of new information and follow a random walk.[18] If, however, other factors influence price movements, then there is scope for a strategy that uses an understanding of how prices really do move. Some stock market "anomalies" are well documented, notably, the "small firm effect," the "January effect" and "weekend effects."[19] More generally, there is evidence that prices in financial markets follow systematic patterns that are the result of "market psychology," the trends and turning points of which can be established from past data. Chart analysis uses hypotheses concerning the relationship between past and future price movements for forecasting. Standard chartist tools include Elliott wave theory, Gann theories, momentum indicators, and patterns such as "support and resistance levels," "head and shoulders," "double tops," and "flags." There is some evidence that chart analysis outperforms other forecasting techniques.[20] Hence, in markets where systematic behavioral trends occur, competitive advantage is gained by traders with superior skill in diagnosing such behavior.

Overshooting Inefficiencies can also arise in trading markets from the propensity of market participants to *overreact* to new information with the result that prices overshoot. The implication is that securities that have benefited from positive news will be overbought, and those that have been depressed by bad news will also be overbought. It follows that advantage may be gained through a *contrarian strategy*: selling securities that have gained in price and buying securities that have fallen in price.[21] Contrarian strategies can offer competitive advantage in any markets where competitors tend toward imitative behavior. In many industries, profit cycles are a consequence of closely correlated investment behavior among competitors, which then offers opportunity for contracyclical investment. T. Boone Pickens built Mesa Petroleum into a highly profitable oil company by buying offshore oil leases during the early 1970s when most of the industry was competing for onshore leases, then selling many of its oil properties during the boom in upstream investment in 1979-80. Warren Buffett, the billionaire chairman of Berkshire Hathaway, is another committed contrarian: "The best time to buy assets may be when it is hardest to raise money," he observed.[22]

Imperfections of competition and competitive advantage in production markets

The transitory nature of competitive advantage in trading markets is a result of the characteristics of the resources required to compete: finance and information. Because finance is a relatively homogeneous resource, it yields competitive advantage in trading markets only in the event of unusually large transactions (e.g., the acquisition of RJR Nabisco). Information is highly differentiated and offers greater potential for competitive advantage. However, because it, like finance, is easily transferable, the competitive advantage it offers tends to be fleeting.

Production markets are quite different. Production activities require complex combinations of resources and capabilities, and these resources and capabilities are highly differentiated. The result is that each producer possesses a unique combination of resources and capabilities. The greater the heterogeneity of firms' resource endowments, the greater is the likelihood that competitive advantages will arise between firms as reflected in differences in profitability. In the U.S. steel industry during the 1960s, interfirm profit differentials were small, reflecting the similarity between the companies in their technologies, human resources, plant, and management methods. During the 1980s, profit differentials had widened substantially, reflecting the greater heterogeneity of the firms within the industry following the emergence of Nucor, Chaparral, Birmingham Steel, North Star, and other companies as significant producers.[23]

Differences in resource endowments between firms also have an important impact on the process by which competitive advantage is eroded both directly through competitive imitation and indirectly through competitive innovation. Where firms possess very similar bundles of resources and capabilities, imitation of competitive advantages will tend to be relatively easy. Where resource bundles are highly differentiated between firms, imitation will depend upon the speed at which rivals can acquire the needed resources and capabilities for imitations. On the other hand, highly differentiated resource bundles may facilitate competition through innovation. Consider, for example, the following industries:

- in the supply of *messenger services* within a city, firms tend to be similar with regard to their resources and capabilities. As a result, competitive advantages can be imitated easily, and profitability differences tend not to be sustained over time;
- in the supply of *medical imaging equipment*, on the other hand, competing firms tend to be of different sizes with different technological resources and different manufacturing, marketing, and service capabilities. Competitive advantages tend to be relatively secure from imitation, but competition through innovation, both product innovation and strategic innovation, tends to be strong;
- in *telecommunication services*, imitative competition is similarly limited by the fact that firms have very different resource bases with regard to technologies, capital stocks, and government licenses. However, innovative competition is intense.

To identify in precise terms the opportunities for creating and sustaining advantage in production markets, it is important to analyze the precise characteristics of the firm and the industry in relation to processes by which competitive advantages are established and eroded through imitative and innovative competition. For example:

- *Strategic innovation*   A firm's potential for establishing a competitive advantage within a particular industry depends upon the firm's resources and capabilities, especially its top management capabilities and the extent to which top management is able to operate outside of the industry's *dominant logic* or *industry recipe*. The second set of factors relates to the *complexity* of the industry in relation to the multidimensionality of customer choice criteria and to the number of value chain activities. In general, the more complex customer requirements and value chain activities are, the greater is the potential for creating a "new-game" strategy;

- *Identification*   A firm's ability to sustain its competitive advantage simply because other rivals are ignorant of the possibility depends upon imperfect availability of information. By operating as a private company or as a diversified company, it is possible for a firm to obscure just how profitable a particular subsidiary is. In industries where barriers to imitation are low, the incentives for obscuring superior performance are especially high. Successful fishing boats often go to great lengths to obscure the size of their catch and their choice of location. One of the problems experienced in the minimill sector of the U.S. steel industry is that Nucor's presence as a NYSE-listed company that has attracted extensive publicity has contributed to excess investment through the entry of several Nucor lookalikes;

- *Incentives to compete*   The possibility that the firm can discourage potential competitors depends upon the resources at the firm's disposal and industry conditions. Deterrence depends upon a firm's retaliatory capability (dependent partly upon its financial resources) and its reputation for retaliation. The ability to preempt depends upon market circumstances (size of the market, the extent of first-mover advantages) and the firm's possessing the resources and capabilities needed to move quickly to establish an impregnable position. The last five years have seen a scramble by Western oil and gas companies to preempt exploration and production opportunities in the former Soviet Union. Advantage has been gained by those companies with substantial financial and technical resources, with expertise in doing business in emerging market economies, and with the flexibility to respond to unique opportunities in a difficult business environment;

- *Diagnosis difficulties*   The greater the complexity of a firm's competitive advantage in terms of its multidimensionality and the number and complexity of the resources and capabilities upon which it is based, the more difficult it is for rivals to imitate. The strength of Motorola in wireless telecommunications equipment lies in the multiple layers of its competitive advantage. Motorola has enormous technical and new product development capability (founded in part upon its background in radios and semiconductors); it also possesses outstanding capabilities in efficient, high-quality manufacturing and in marketing. In some industries, diagnosing the linkages between resources, capabilities, strategies, and competitive advantage may be especially difficult. In the film production business, it would appear easy for new firms to successfully enter the market by acquiring the right assemblage of film script, actors, technicians, and a director. The long-established competitive positions of Paramount, Columbia, Universal, and Disney may reflect the experiential knowledge of the "secrets of the business" – that is, what are the ingredients of a blockbuster hit?

- *Difficulties of resource acquisition* The less resource mobility a firm has and the greater its difficulties in replicating resources and capabilities, the more difficult it is to imitate the competitive advantage of the advantaged firm. These issues have been explored both in this and the previous chapter.

A second source of first-mover advantage is experience. A firm that initially gains sales can use the experience it acquires as the basis for subsequent cost reduction. Thus, cost advantages can become cumulative. We will explore economies of experience more fully in the next chapter.

Finally, firms that experience initial success may subsequently attract inputs on more favorable terms. This is most obvious in the case of human resources. It is much easier for IBM, Procter & Gamble, and Walt Disney to attract highly capable graduates and junior managers than it is for poorly performing companies such as Sears Roebuck, Chrysler, or Goodyear. Similar tendencies are apparent in other inputs. Credit terms from suppliers are typically better for profitable than unprofitable firms.

Types of Competitive Advantage

A firm can achieve a higher rate of profit (or potential profit) over a rival in one of two ways: either it can supply an identical product or service at a lower cost or it can supply a product or service that is differentiated in such a way that the customer is willing to pay a price-premium that exceeds the additional cost of the differentiation. In the former case, the firm possesses a *cost advantage*; in the latter, a *differentiation advantage*. In pursuing cost advantage, the goal of the firm is to become the cost leader in its industry or industry segment. Cost leadership is a unique position in the industry, which requires that the firm "must find and exploit all sources of cost advantage . . . [and] . . . sell a standard, no-frills product."[24] Differentiation by a firm from its competitors is achieved "when it provides something unique that is valuable to buyers beyond simply offering a low price."[25]

These two sources of competitive advantage define two fundamentally different approaches to business strategy. A firm that is competing on

Figure 6.1 The Sources of Competitive Advantage

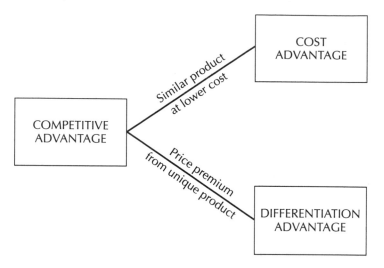

low cost is distinguishable from a firm that competes through differentiation in terms of market positioning, resource and capabilities, and organizational characteristics. Table 6.2 outlines some of the principal features of cost and differentiation strategies. By combining the two types of competitive advantage with the firm's choice of *scope* – broad market versus narrow segment – Michael Porter has defined three *generic strategies: cost leadership, differentiation,* and *focus* (see figure 6.2).

Porter views cost leadership and differentiation as mutually exclusive strategies. A firm that attempts to pursue both is "stuck in the middle":

The firm stuck in the middle is almost guaranteed low profitability. It either loses the high volume customers who demand low prices or must bid away its profits to get this business from the low-cost firms. Yet it also loses high-margin business – the cream – to the firms who are focused on high margin targets or have achieved differentiation overall. The firm which is stuck in the

Table 6.2 General Features of Cost Leadership and Differentiation Strategies

Generic strategy	Key strategy elements	Resource and organizational requirements
Cost leadership	Investment in scale-efficient plant; design of products for ease of manufacture; control of overheads, R&D; avoidance of marginal customer accounts.	Access to capital; process engineering skills; frequent reports; tight cost control; structured organization and responsibilities; incentives related to quantitative targets.
Differentiation	Emphasis on branding and brand advertising, design, service, and quality.	Marketing abilities; product engineering skills; creativity; capability in basic research; subjective rather than quantitative measurement and incentives; strong interfunctional coordination.

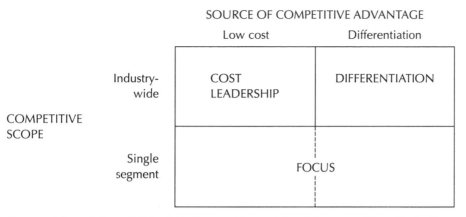

Figure 6.2 Porter's Generic Strategies

Source: Adapted from Michael E. Porter, *Competitive Advantage* (New York: Free Press, 1985).

middle also probably suffers from a blurred corporate culture and a conflicting set of organizational arrangements and motivation system.[26]

In practice, few firms are faced with such stark alternatives. Differentiation is not simply an issue of "to differentiate or not to differentiate." All firms must make decisions as to where to position their product or service in the market. Adopting a low-price, low-cost strategy generally implies a market positioning based upon a single line, limited feature, standardized offering. However, such a positioning does not necessarily imply that the product or service is an undifferentiated commodity. In the case of IKEA furniture and McDonald's hamburgers, a low-price, no-frills offering is also associated with a clear market positioning and a unique brand image. Similarly, firms that aim toward positions of differentiation advantage cannot be oblivious to cost.

In most industries, market leadership is held by a firm that achieves modest differentiation at an acceptable cost. GM, Ford, Toyota, and Volkswagen are not the lowest cost producers in their industry nor are American Airlines, United Airlines (UAL), and British Airways in theirs. In automobiles, the lowest cost producers are probably the Korean manufacturers (Hyundai, Daewoo, and Kia). In airlines, cost leadership lies with Southwest, Reno, Value Jet, and charter airlines. Across most industries, the lowest cost producers are likely to be small or fringe suppliers that have acquired cheap assets, pay low wages, and operate with exceptionally low overheads.

The reconciliation of high differentiation with low cost is one of the greatest strategic challenges facing firms in the current economic environment. Japanese manufacturers of consumer durables such as Honda, Toyota, Sony, and Matsushita, are masters in reconciling innovation, quality, and strong marketing and distribution with world-beating manufacturing efficiency. One of greatest contributions of the *total quality management* movement has been to explode the myth of the quality/cost trade-off. A host of studies show that current innovations in manufacturing technology and manufacturing management result in simultaneous increases in productivity and quality.[27] Achieving higher quality in terms of fewer defects and greater product reliability frequently involves simpler product design, fewer component suppliers that are more closely monitored, and fewer service calls and product recalls – all of which save cost. Tom Peters observes an interesting asymmetry: "Cost reduction campaigns do not often lead to improved quality; and, except for those that involve large reductions in personnel, they don't usually result in long-term lower costs either. On the other hand, effective quality programs yield not only improved quality but lasting cost reductions as well."[28]

Differentiation and cost reduction can be complementary in other ways. High levels of advertising and promotional expenditure can increase market share, which then permits the exploitation of scale economies across a wide range of functions. Moreover, the existence of scale economies in advertising and other differentiation activities means that a market share leader can improve its relative cost position by forcing rivals to compete on product differentiation. The heavy advertising campaign with which Apple launched its Macintosh computer in 1984 was partly motivated by the desire to "up the stakes" for smaller manufacturers of personal computers that did not possess a sufficient sales base for large-scale advertising. Similarly, Honda's product strategy of annual model changes increased the pressure on other motorcycle manufacturers who did not have the sales volume to justify the heavy fixed costs of annual model changes.[29]

In the next two chapters, we will develop and operationalize these concepts of cost and differentiation advantage by presenting frameworks that can diagnose the sources of cost and differentiation advantage and formulate strategies that exploit these sources of advantage.

Summary and Conclusions

Making money in business requires establishing and sustaining competitive advantage. Both these conditions for profitability require profound insight into the nature and process of competition within a market. Competitive advantage depends critically upon the presence of some imperfection in the competitive process – under "perfect" competition, profits are transitory. Our analysis of imperfections of the competitive process has drawn us back to the resources and capabilities that are required to compete in different markets and to pursue different strategies. Establishing competitive advantage is highly dependent upon creativity and luck and is, therefore, difficult to analyze systematically. Sustaining competitive advantage depends upon the existence of *isolating mechanisms:* barriers to rivals' imitation of successful strategies. While strategic ploys such as deterrence and preemption can act as isolating mechanisms, the major protectors of a firm's competitive positions are likely to be rivals' inability to access the resources and capabilities necessary to compete on equal terms with the advantaged firm. Hence, a major outcome of this analysis is to reinforce the argument made in the previous chapter: the characteristics of a firm's resources and capability are fundamental to strategic decision making and long-term success.

In the next two chapters, we will analyze the two primary dimensions of competitive advantage, cost advantage, and differentiation advantage. In both of these areas I will emphasize the importance of depth of understanding both of the firm and its industry environment. To this end, it will be useful to disaggregate the firm into a series of separate but interlinked activities. A useful and versatile framework for this purpose is the *value chain*, which is an insightful tool for understanding the sources of competitive advantage in an industry, for assessing the competitive position of a particular firm, and for suggesting opportunities to enhance a firm's competitiveness.

Notes

1 David J. Teece, "Profiting from Technological Innovation: Implications for Integration, Collaboration, Licensing, and Public Policy," in *The Competitive Challenge: Strategies for Industrial Innovation and Renewal*, ed. David J. Teece (Cambridge, MA: Ballinger, 1987).

2 See the chapters, "Benetton (A)" and "Benetton (B)" in William H. Davidson and Jose de la Torre, *Managing the Global Corporation* (New York: McGraw-Hill, 1989).

3 George Stalk Jr., "Time – the Next Source of Competitive Advantage," *Harvard Business Review* (July-August 1988): 41–51.

4 Charles Baden Fuller and John M. Stopford, *Rejuvenating the Mature Business* (London and New York: Routledge, 1992).

5 Richard P. Rumelt, "Towards a Strategic Theory of the Firm," in Competitive Strategic Management, ed. R. Lamb (Englewood Cliffs, NJ: Prentice-Hall, 1984), 556–70.

6 See John Cubbin and Paul Geroski, "The Convergence of Profits in the Long Run: Interfirm and Interindustry Comparisons," *Journal of Industrial Economics* 35 (1987): 427–42; Robert Jacobsen, "The Persistence of Abnormal Returns," *Strategic Management Journal* 9 (1988): 415–30; and Dennis C. Mueller, "Persistent Profits among Large Corporations," in *The Economics of Strategic Planning* ed. Lacy Glenn Thomas (Lexington, MA: Lexington Books, 1986, 31–61).

7 The film was based upon the book B. Traven, *The Treasure of the Sierra Madre* (New York: Knopf, 1947).

8 Thomas C. Schelling, *The Strategy of Conflict*, 2d ed (Cambridge: Harvard University Press, 1980), 35–41.

9 Richard Schmalensee, "Entry Deterrence in the Ready-to-Eat Breakfast Cereal Industry," *Bell Journal of Economics* 9 (1978): 305–27.

10   Richard Pascale, "Perspectives on Strategy: The Real Story behind Honda's Success," *California Management Review* 26, no. 3 (spring 1984): 1–29.

11   Monopolies and Mergers Commission, *Indirect Electrostatic Reprographic Equipment* (London: Her Majesty's Stationery Office, 1976), 37, 56.

12   S. A. Lippman and R. P. Rumelt, "Uncertain Imitability: An Analysis of Interfirm Differences in Efficiency under Competition," *Bell Journal of Economics* 13 (1982): 418–38. The analysis of causal ambiguity has been further developed by Richard Reed and Robert DeFillippi, "Causal Ambiguity, Barriers to Imitation, and Sustainable Competitive Advantage," *Academy of Management Review* 15 (1990): 88–102.

13   See O. E. Williamson, "Transaction Cost Economics: The Governance of Contractual Relations," *Journal of Law and Economics* 19 (1979): 153–6.

14   M. Polanyi, *Personal Knowledge: Towards a Post-Critical Philosophy*, 2d ed. (Chicago: University of Chicago Press, 1962), 52.

15   C. Brown and M. Reich, "When Does Union-Management Cooperation Work? A Look at NUMMI and GM-Van Nuys," *California Management Review* 31 (summer 1989): 26–44.

16   "Faded Fad," *Economist*, September 30, 1989, 68.

17   Frank J. Finn, "*Evaluation of the Internal Processes of Managed Investment Funds*, Contemporary Studies in Economic and Financial Analysis, vol. 44 (Greenwich, CT: JAI Press, 1984), 6.

18   Eugene F. Fama, "Efficient Capital Markets: A Review of Theory and Empirical Work," *Journal of Business* 35 (1970): 383–417.

19   Simon Keane, "The Efficient Market Hypothesis on Trial," *Financial Analysts Journal* (March-April 1986): 58–63.

20   H. Allen and M. Taylor, "Charts, Noise and Fundamentals in the London Foreign Exchange Market," *Economic Journal*, conference supplement, 100 (1990): 49–59.

21   For empirical evidence, see Werner De Bondt and Richard Thaler, "Does the Stock Market Overreact?" *Journal of Finance* 42 (1985): 793–805.

22   *Fortune*. October 23, 1989, 24.

23   "Why Steel Is Looking Sexy," *Business Week*, April 4, 1994, 106–8.

24   Michael E. Porter, *Competitive Advantage* (New York: Free Press, 1985), 13.

25   *Ibid*, 120.

26   Michael E. Porter, *Competitive Strategy* (New York: Free Press, 1980), 42.

27   See, for example, Jack R. Meredith, "Strategic Advantages of the Factory of the Future," *California Management Review* (winter 1989): 129–45.

28   Tom Peters, *Thriving on Chaos* (New York: Knopf, 1987), 80.

29   The potential for differentiation to assist the attainment of cost leadership is analyzed by Charles Hill, "Differentiation versus Low Cost of Differentiation and Low Cost: A Contingency Framework," *Academy of Management Review* 13 (1988): 401–12.

SEVEN

Cost Advantage

SEARS MOTOR BUGGY: $395

For car complete with rubber tires, Timken roller bearing axles, top, storm front, three oil-burning lamps, horn, and one gallon of lubricating oil. *Nothing to buy but gasoline....* We found there was a maker of automobile frames that was making 75 per cent of all the frames used in automobile construction in the United States. We found on account of the volume of business that this concern could make frames cheaper for automobile manufacturers than the manufacturers could make them themselves. We went to this frame maker and asked him to make frames for the Sears Motor Buggy and then to name us prices for those frames in large quantities. And so on throughout the whole construction of the Sears Motor Buggy. You will find every piece and every part has been given the most careful study; you will find that the Sears Motor Buggy is made of the best possible material; it is constructed to take the place of the top buggy; it is built in our own factory, under the direct supervision of our own expert, a man who has had fifteen years of automobile experience, a man who has for the last three years worked with us to develop exactly the right car for the people at a price within the reach of all.

– from an advertisement in the Sears Roebuck & Co. catalog, 1909

Introduction and Objectives

Historically, business strategy analysis has emphasized cost advantage as the primary basis for competitive advantage in an industry. This focus on cost advantage partly reflects the traditional view of price as the principal medium of competition between firms: the ability to compete on price depends ultimately upon cost efficiency. It also reflects some of the principal strategic preoccupations of large industrial corporations. For much of the twentieth century, large corporations have been driven by the quest for economies of scale and scope through investment in mass production and mass distribution. During the last decade, large corporations have shifted their strategic focus toward cost efficiency through restructuring, downsizing, outsourcing, "lean production," and the quest for dynamic rather than static sources of cost efficiency.

For some industries, cost advantage is the predominant basis for competitive advantage: if a product or service is a commodity, then opportunities for competing on dimensions other than cost are extremely limited. But even where competition focuses on product differentiation, intensifying competition has resulted in cost efficiency becoming a prerequisite for profitability. During the 1990s, the quest for cost efficiency spread to industries that had traditionally been relatively immune from aggressive price competition: telecommunications, health care, aerospace, and banking. Companies such as IBM, Compaq, McDonnell-Douglas, Eastman-Kodak, and U.S. Surgical have adopted the same aggressive policies of downsizing and overhead reduction as companies in mature sectors.

The objectives of this chapter are to familiarize you with the sources of cost advantage and to make you capable of applying cost analysis to a firm or business unit in order to:

- identify the determinants of relative cost within the industry or activity ("*cost drivers*");
- assess a firm's cost position relative to its competitors and identify the factors responsible for cost differentials;
- recommend cost reduction measures.

The analysis in this chapter is oriented around these objectives. We will examine concepts and techniques for:

- identifying the basic sources of cost advantage in an industry;
- appraising the cost position of a firm within its industry by disaggregating the firm into its separate activities;
- using the analysis of costs and relative cost position as a basis for recommending strategies for enhancing cost competitiveness.

The Experience Curve

We begin our analysis of costs with an outline of the *experience curve* and its role in strategy analysis. The experience curve is interesting, first, because of its pervasive influence on strategic thinking during the 1970s and early 1980s and, second, because it provides a useful introduction to the sources of cost advantage.

During the decade that followed the publication in 1968 of *Perspectives in Experience* by the Boston Consulting Group (BCG), the experience curve exercised a powerful influence not only on the analysis of costs but on strategy analysis as a whole. It is one of the best known and most influential concepts in the history of strategic management. Its basis is the observed systematic reduction in the time taken to build airplanes during the late 1930s and Liberty ships during the Second World War as more were built.[1] This concept of *economies of learning* was generalized by BCG to encompass not just direct labor hours but the behavior of all added costs as cumulative production volume increased. In a series of studies from bottle caps and refrigerators to long distance calls and insurance policies, BCG observed a remarkable regularity in reductions in costs (and prices) that accompanied increases in cumulative production. Doubling of cumulative production typically reduced unit costs (and prices) by 20 to 30 percent. BCG summarized its observations in "*The Law of Experience*": "*The unit cost of value added to a standard product declines by a constant percentage (typically between 20 and 30 per cent), each time cumulative output doubles.*"[2]

"*Unit cost of value added*" is total cost per unit of production *less* the cost per unit of production of bought-in components and materials. If suppliers of components and materials are subject to similar cost reductions as volume increases, then "unit cost" may be substituted for "unit cost of value added" in the above definition.

The Law of Experience may be expressed more precisely in algebraic form:

$$C_n = C_1 n^{-a}$$

where C_1 is the cost of the first unit of production
        C_n is the cost of the nth unit of production
        n is the cumulative volume of production
        a is the elasticity of cost with regard to output.

Graphically, the experience curve is characterized by a progressively declining gradient, which, when translated into logarithms, is linear (see figure 7.1). The size of the experience effect is measured by the proportion by which costs are reduced with subsequent doublings of aggregate production.

Experience curves may be drawn for either an industry or a single firm and may use either cost or price data. Using prices rather than

Figure 7.1 The
Experience Curve

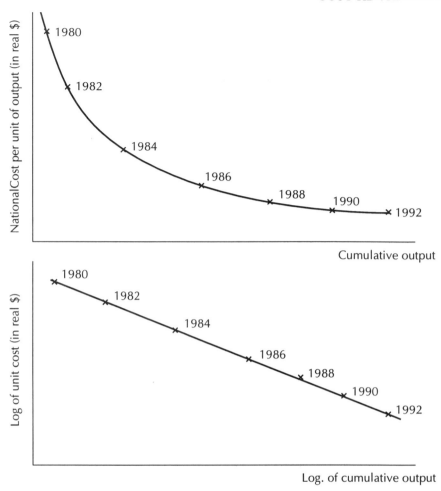

costs assumes that margins are constant. Figure 7.2 shows examples of experience curves estimated by BCG.

Plotting an experience curve

Constructing an experience curve is a simple matter once the data are available. The data required are cost per unit of production (or, ideally, cost per unit of production *less* the cost of bought-in materials and components) and production volume over time. The cost data must be expressed in constant price terms to eliminate the effects of inflation. Unit costs can be expressed either in monetary units or as an index.

The greatest single problem with drawing an experience curve is that cost and production data must relate to a *standard product*. In practice, few products remain the same over extended periods of time. As a result, unit costs must be adjusted for increases in quality over time and other changes in product features and design.

When constructing an experience curve for an industry, these difficulties of changing product characteristics make it preferable to use price rather than cost data. Official indexes of wholesale prices are

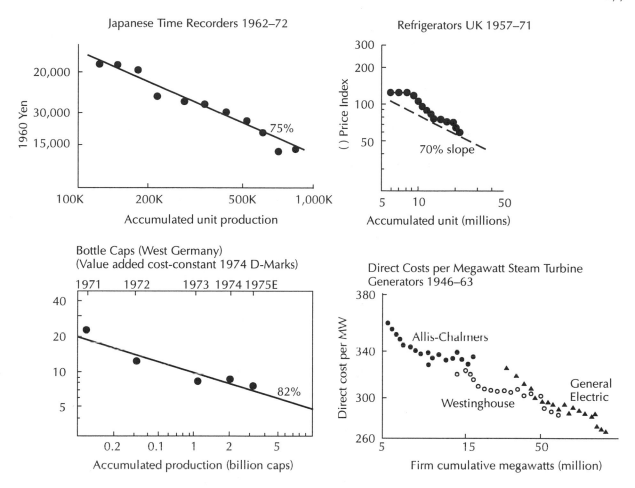

Source: Department of Trade and Industry, *A Review of Monopolies and Mergers Policy* (London: Her Majesty's Stationery Office, 1978).

Figure 7.2 Examples of Experience Curves

adjusted for changes in quality and product specifications. The availability of wholesale price indexes and output data for most manufacturing industries makes the construction of industry-level, price-experience curves easy and almost costless.

Firm-level experience curves pose more complex data problems. Obtaining a run of cost data over a sufficient period of time is difficult because of changes in accounting conventions, problems of allocating costs within a multiproduct firm, and difficulties in adjusting for changes in product characteristics. In general, the experience curve for a firm will differ in slope from the industry experience curve because of the ability of firms to *transfer* experience – that is, to learn from one another.

Strategy implications: the dubious case for market share

The significance of the experience curve lies in its implications for business strategy. If costs decline systematically with increases in cumulative output, then a firm's costs relative to its competitors' depend upon its cumulative output relative to that of competitors. If a firm can expand its output at a greater rate than its competitors, it is then able to move down the experience curve more rapidly than its rivals and can open up a widening cost differential.

The quest for experience-based cost economies implies that a firm's primary strategic goal should be *market share*. A firm's increase in cumulative output compared to a competitor's depends upon their relative market shares. If Boeing holds 60 percent of the world market for large commercial jet aircraft and McDonnell Douglas only 10 percent, then Boeing's output is six times that of McDonnell Douglas's and, over the long term, Boeing will be reducing its costs at a faster rate than McDonnell Douglas.[3]

This rationale of experience-based cost reduction was the basis of BCG's emphasis on the strategic importance of relative market share. The quest for cost leadership through market share leadership has important implications for pricing policy. The firm should price its products not on the basis of current costs but on the basis of anticipated costs.[4] BCG, in its study of the British motorcycle industry, observed that British motorcycle manufacturers adopted cost-plus pricing. Honda, on the other hand, priced to meet market share objectives on the assumption that, once sufficient sales volume had been achieved, costs would fall to a level that offered a satisfactory profit margin.[5] The quest for experienced-based economies also points to the advantages of maximizing volume by offering a broad rather than a narrow product range and expanding internationally rather than restricting sales to the domestic market.[6]

A number of empirical studies, most notably those undertaken by the PIMS program, have confirmed the positive relationship between profitability and market share.[7] The PIMS findings are summarized in figure 7.3. The efficiency benefits of market share are indicated in table 7.1. When market share is expressed as percentage of sales, market share leaders tend to have lower costs of investment, inventories, marketing, and purchases. In addition, market share leaders possess a differentiation advantage that arises from perceived higher quality.

Despite this evidence, strong doubts exist as to the wisdom of pursuing market share as a means of improving profitability. Criticisms of the traditional "market share doctrine" include the following:

1   *Causation*   Association is not the same as causation. Does market share confer superior profit or do profitable firms use their earnings to build market share? The most plausible explanation is that profitability and market share are consequences of some common underlying factor. For example, superior efficiency or innovation will result both in high profits and high market share.[8]

2   *The unprofitability of investing in market share*   Even if firms with high market shares possess cost advantages resulting in superior profitability, this does not necessarily imply that investments aimed at

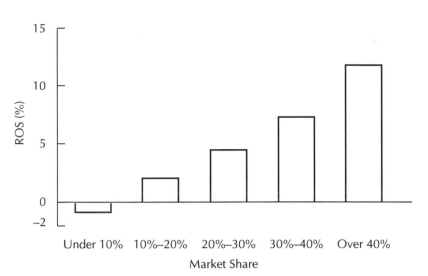

Figure 7.3 The Relationship between Market Share and Pretax Return on Sales

ROS (%)

Under 10%   10%–20%   20%–30%   30%–40%   Over 40%

Market Share

Source: PIMS

	Market Share Rank				
	#1	#2	#3	#4	#5 or below
Investment/Sales	46.3	52.1	52.5	51.4	54.9
Receivables/Sales	14.7	14.7	14.71	4.8	15.3
Inventory/Sales	18.5	19.6	20.5	20.6	22.3
Purchases/Sales	41.8	43.4	45.8	48.8	51.3
Marketing/Sales	8.9	9.5	9.5	9.3	9.2
R&D/Sales	2.1	2.3	1.9	1.8	1.9
Relative quality (%)	69.0	51.0	47.0	45.0	43.0
Relative price (%)	105.7	103.8	103.4	103.2	103.0
Pretax Profit/Sales	12.7	9.1	7.1	5.5	4.5

Table 7.1 The Relationship between Market Position, Cost Advantage, Price Advantage, and Profitability

Source: Robert D. Buzzell and Bradley T. Gale, *The PIMS Principles: Linking Strategy to Performance* (New York: Free Press, 1987), 75.

increasing a firm's market share will offer attractive returns. Once the relationship between market share and profitability is well known within an industry and if all firms have the opportunity of competing for market share through advertising, sales efforts, new capacity, and the like, then this competition for market share will quickly erode any superior profitability available from increased market share.[9]

The value of the experience curve

As a basis for making strategic decisions, the experience curve has promoted two fallacies:

1   *The fallacy of composition*   Honda's strategy of volume manufacturing backed by aggressive pricing and marketing aimed at market share goals was successful against Norton-Villiers-Triumph and Harley-

Davidson because the latter pursued cost-plus pricing directed toward short-term profit targets.[10] The fundamental fallacy of BCG's doctrine of experience economies through pricing-for-market-share is that, while it may be successful for the individual firm, it can be fatal when attempted by several competitors. During the 1970s, U.S. and European producers of steel, petrochemicals, ships, and synthetic fibers followed the lead of their Japanese competitors by investing heavily in new, scale-efficient plants while cutting margins in anticipation of lower costs. The results were disastrous: overinvestment combined with the oil crises of 1974 and 1979 resulted in chronic excess capacity and intense price competition. In all these industries, the quest for experience-based cost advantages contributed to the losses suffered by these industries during the 1970s and 1980s.

2 *Economies of experience are not automatic*   A second fallacy is that cost falls automatically with volume increases. Costs do not just fall, they must be managed down. Fundamental to the experience effect is learning, which requires the desire to learn and the capacity for change. The ability of Japanese manufacturers to achieve continuing cost reductions with increased production owes much to the persistence with which they have sought constant, incremental improvement across all aspects of their operations.

If economies of experience really comprise a stream of incremental improvements in dexterity, organization, product design, materials handling, and process innovation, why should the production of vast numbers of units be a prerequisite for conceiving and implementing such improvements? It should be possible to "short-circuit" experience-based economies by:

- acquiring experience from others. Through competitor intelligence, reverse engineering, and poaching employees from other firms, a company can assimilate many of the benefits of its competitors' experience;
- transferring experience between the divisions of a company. The experience that Honda gained as the world's leading manufacturer of motorcycles was of tremendous benefit to Honda when it entered the markets for cars, generators, and lawn mowers. Similarly, multinationals such as General Motors, Sony, and Procter & Gamble transfer the experience gained in their home markets to their overseas subsidiaries;
- innovating to leapfrog down the experience curve. Experience can perfect existing technology – it can also constrain innovation. In the U.S. steel industry, the adoption of new process technologies and new management and organizational practices has permitted the minimill producers to leapfrog the more experienced integrated steel firms such as USX (formerly U.S. Steel) and Bethlehem to become industry cost leaders.

The experience curve is simply a generalization of empirical observations. It cannot be assumed that increasing accumulated production will inevitably lead to cost reductions of some predetermined proportion, nor can it be assumed that growth of accumulated output is a prerequisite for cost competitiveness. Even if the relationship, based on past data, is strong, it cannot be assumed that past relationships can be extrapolated into the future. Moreover, any strategy based upon the quest for experience-based cost reduction must take account of the costs of growing market share.

The value of the experience curve is in demonstrating the potential for cost reduction through improvement – even in mature industries. A firm's productivity and costs are not the result of predetermined input/output relationships; efficiency depends upon the expertise of employees and how well the firm manages the production process. Appreciation of the role of experience points to the complexity of the everyday operations of most firms and the scale of the task that firms face in entering an unfamiliar industry.

The Sources of Cost Advantage

The key to cost analysis is to go beyond mechanistic approaches such as the experience curve and understand cost advantage by identifying the factors that determine a firm's cost position. The experience curve combines four sources of cost reduction: *learning, economies of scale, process innovation,* and *improved product design.* To these we can add three additional factors that influence the cost position of a firm relative to its competitors: *the cost of inputs, capacity utilization,* and *residual differences in operating efficiency.* These factors, which determine a firm's unit costs (cost per unit of output), are called *cost drivers.* Figure 7.4 lists the main cost drivers that determine cost advantage.

As we will see, the relative importance of these different cost drivers varies between different types of industry and between different activities within the firm. By identifying these different cost drivers, we will be able to:

1 diagnose a firm's cost position in terms of understanding why a firm's unit costs diverge from those of its competitors; and
2 make recommendations as to how a firm can improve its cost efficiency.

Let us examine the nature and the role of each of these cost drivers.

Economies of scale

The predominance of large corporations in most manufacturing and service industries and the confinement of small owner-proprietor and family businesses to a few sectors of the economy reflects the impact of *economies of scale.* Economies of scale exist wherever proportionate increases in the amounts of inputs employed in a production process

Figure 7.4 The Drivers
of Cost Advantage

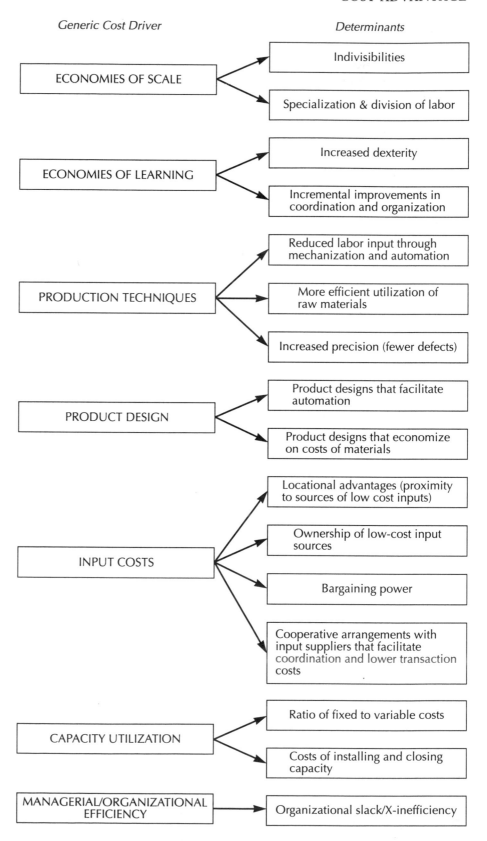

result in a more than proportionate increase in total output. Therefore, as the scale of production increases, unit costs fall. Economies of scale are conventionally associated with manufacturing operations. Figure 7.5 shows a typical relationship between unit cost and plant capacity. The point at which most scale economies are exploited is referred to as the *minimum efficiency plant size* (or MEPS). Scale economies are also important in nonmanufacturing operations, such as purchasing, R&D, distribution, and advertising.

Scale economies arise from three principal sources:

1 *Technical input/output relationships* In some activities, increases in output do not require proportionate increases in input. In the same way that a five-liter glass jar does not cost five times the cost of a one-liter glass jar, economies of capital costs exist in large-scale ships, oil refineries, and truck assembly plants. A similar relationship exists in inventory requirements: as sales and output increase, inventories do not need to be increased proportionately.

2 *Indivisibilities* Many inputs are "lumpy" – that is, they are simply unavailable in small sizes. Hence, they offer economies of scale as firms are able to amortize the costs of these items over larger volumes of output. Most units of capital equipment are indivisible below a certain size. Indivisibilities also arise in people (a plant probably needs only one gatekeeper and medical officer per shift), in activities (a company needs just one audit per accounting period), and in specialist units (there is a minimum feasible size to an effective R&D team seeking to develop anti-inflammatory drugs). In many industries, indivisibilities in marketing activities and new product development are major sources of scale economy.

3 *Specialization* Larger volumes of output require the employment of more inputs, which permits increased specialization of the tasks of individual inputs. Specialization by labor ("division of labor") is particularly important in this respect. "Mass production" (pioneered in

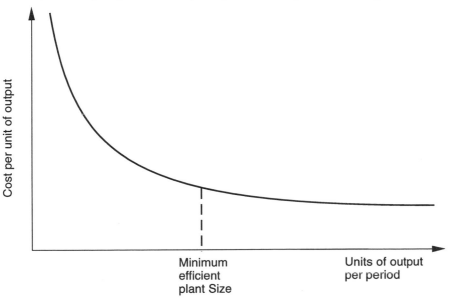

Figure 7.5 A Typical Long-Run Average Cost Curve for a Plant

automobiles by Henry Ford) involved disaggregating the production process into a series of separate tasks that can be performed by specialist workers using specialist equipment. Specialization by labor results in increased dexterity, avoids loss of time from workers switching between jobs, and assists mechanization and automation. Although conventionally associated with mass production, specialization also increases productivity in knowledge-based industries such as investment banking, management consulting, and software development where large firms can exploit economies of specialization in "knowledge workers."

Scale economies and concentration The scale economies are the single most important determinant of an industry's level of seller concentration. The extent of scale economies is indicated by MEPS as a proportion of industry size. Table 7.2 shows these relationships for U.S. industries. However, MEPS relates only to scale economies in production. In many industries, high concentration reflects scale economies in other activities. High seller concentration in cigarettes, household detergents, beer, and soft drinks is primarily a result of scale economies in marketing. A national advertising campaign is an indivisibility: producing a commercial and communicating it to the majority of potential consumers nationally involves a minimum level of expenditure, irrespective of the level of sales over which its costs are spread. Figure 7.6 shows the relationship between sales volume and average advertising costs for different brands of soft drink.

In automobile manufacture, the indivisible costs associated with new model development have been the driving force behind increasing indus-

Table 7.2 Scale Economies and Seller Concentration in U.S. Industries

	Minimum Efficient Plant Size as Percentage of U.S. Output	Percentage Increase in Unit Cost at Half MEPS	Four-firm Concentration Ratio (%)
Flour mills	0.7	3.0	18.0
Bread baking	0.3	7.5	12.0
Printing paper	4.4	9.0	23.0
Sulfuric acid	3.7	1.0	32.0
Synthetic fibers	11.1	7.0	41.0
Auto tires	3.8	5.0	56.0
Bricks	0.3	25.0	16.0
Detergents	2.4	2.5	48.0
Turbogenerators	23.0	n.a	55.0
Diesel engines	21–30.0	4–28.0	42.0
Computers	15.0	8.0	65.0
Automobiles	11.0	6.0	85.0
Commercial aircraft	10.0	20.0	89.0

Sources: F. M. Scherer, *Industrial Market Structure and Economic Performance*, 2d ed. (Chicago: Rand McNally, 1980); U. S. Department of Commerce, Washington, D.C.

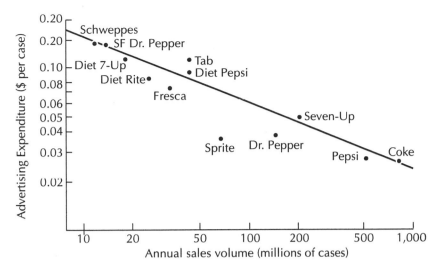

Figure 7.6 Scale Economies in Advertising: U.S. Soft Drinks in 1974

Source: Prepared by the Boston Consulting Group for the U.K. Department of Trade and Industry, 1978.

try concentration over the last decade. Total new model costs (including tooling) have escalated considerably. For example, the development cost (including plant and tooling) of models introduced during the early 1990s included:

Ford Escort (new model)	$2 billion
Ford Mondeo	$6 billion
GM Saturn	$5 billion
Chrysler Neon	$1.3 billion

Smaller producers such as Seat (Spain), Saab (Sweden), Rover (U.K.), Jaguar (U.K.), and AMC/Jeep (U.S.) have been unable to justify investment in new model development and have merged with larger producers. Other small producers have made agreements with larger auto companies to license their designs.[11]

The huge costs of product development are also the driving force behind the evolution of the aerospace sector. In both jet engines and large civilian airplanes, development costs caused the industry to concentrate around three companies: in jet engines, General Electric, Pratt and Whitney, and Rolls-Royce; in aircraft, Boeing, Airbus Industrie, and McDonnell Douglas. Boeing's 777 had absorbed $4 billion in development costs by the beginning of 1994. A proposed 500-passenger "superjumbo" would cost over $10 billion to develop and would require collaboration between Boeing and Airbus.[12] Boeing's success in amortizing its development costs over very long runs of aircraft (almost 1,000 747s built between 1970 and 1994) is critical to Boeing's position as industry cost leader. Conversely, fundamental to the supersonic Concorde being a financial disaster for its manufacturers, Aerospatiale and

British Aerospace (as well as their supporting governments), was the fact that only 16 were built.

Constraints on the exploitation of scale economies In practice, a firm's ability to exploit the full potential for cost reduction that economies of scale offer is constrained. Three factors are especially important:

1 *Product differentiation* Where customer preferences are differentiated, customers may prefer differentiated product features to lower prices. General Motors's rise to market leadership over Ford during the late 1920s was an example of this. In clothing, cosmetics, specialist cars, and a whole range of other consumer products, customer demand for variety and individuality results in firms and plants remaining far below the sizes consistent with the full exploitation of scale economies.

2 *Flexibility* A major problem with scale-efficient production facilities is their specificity and inflexibility. In a static environment, this poses few problems, but in a dynamic environment, very large plants and firms have greater difficulties than smaller units in adjusting to fluctuations in demand, in input availability, in changes in product specifications, and in changes in technology.[13] As the business environment becomes increasingly turbulent, firms' emphases shift from static efficiency toward flexibility.

3 *Problems of motivation and coordination* A key constraint on the pursuit of scale economies in many manufacturing industries are the increased difficulties of managing very large plants. Many of these problems, such as strained labor relations, increased supervision costs, and increased wastage, arise from the lower levels of motivation that accompany the more impersonal, bureaucratic environments of large organizations. As firms become more participative, less hierarchical organizations, so motivation and coordination become increasingly important for effectiveness and efficiency. VW's Wolfsburg *Halle* 54 is one of the world's largest auto assembly plants. At the same time, its costs are high, partly because of the difficulties involved in managing it.[14]

Economies of learning

The principal source of experience-based cost reduction is learning by organization members. Repetition reduces costs by decreasing the time required for particular jobs, reducing wastage and defects and improving coordination between jobs. The most interesting and persuasive evidence on efficiency through learning derives from the very long runs of military equipment produced during the Second World War.[15] For example, in 1943 it took 40,000 labor-hours to build a Convair B-24 bomber. By 1945, it took only 8,000 hours.[16] The more complex a process or product, the more substantial are economies of learning likely to be. Thus, learning effects have a dominant influence on cost economies in aircraft manufacture, shipbuilding, civil engineering, and process plant construction.

Learning efficiencies can be traced to the establishment and refinement of *organizational routines* within the firm (see chapter 5). All production processes are the result of a coordinated network of many hundreds of individual routines. Efficiency depends critically upon the quality of coordination between the people within each routine and between the various routines. The start-up of a new company involves a huge input of conscious planning and management to achieve the coordination needed for output to occur at all. With constant repetition, the need for planning and management supervision is steadily reduced to the point where the organization, when in "standard mode," can operate almost automatically.

Capacity utilization

Over the long term, firms can adjust the scale of their plants to vary output. Over the short and medium term, plant capacity is more or less fixed and variations in output are associated with variations in capacity utilization. During periods of low demand, plant capacity is underutilized; during periods of peak demand, output may be pushed beyond the normal full-capacity operation with overtime working, night and weekend shifts, faster machine operation, and cutbacks in maintenance time. Such departures from normal capacity operation are associated with higher unit costs. When there is excess capacity, fixed costs must be spread over a smaller volume of output. In capital-intensive businesses (e.g., chemicals, steel) excess capacity can raise unit costs substantially. In some businesses, virtually all costs are fixed (e.g., airlines, theme parks). Operation beyond the limits of normal capacity also raises unit costs through overtime premiums, increased costs of machine breakdowns, and loss of quality control.

In declining industries and industries subject to sharp fluctuations in demand, the ability to speedily adjust capacity to the current level of demand can be a major source of cost advantage. During the years 1985-7, Exxon's ability to increase profits despite the depressed state of the world's oil markets owed much to the speedy and drastic surgery that it performed on excess capacity in transportation, refining, and distribution. British Steel's position as Europe's most profitable steel producer during the 1980s was, in part, a consequence of the speed with which it brought capacity in line with output.

Product design

Exploiting the productivity benefits of new manufacturing technology is critically dependent upon the redesign of products:

- automated insertion of components into TV sets required the radical redesign of the TV set using all solid-state components and modular subassemblies. The redesign of TVs by U.S. and European manufacturers that accompanied their adoption of automated production methods during the mid-1970s resulted in a reduction in the number of components in a TV receiver of up to 50 percent;

- BCG's motorcycle study identified Honda's "design-for-manufacture" as opposed to the British "pure engineering" approach as a major factor in the huge cost differential between the two;
- IBM's "Proprinter" exemplifies how close attention to manufacturability in design can lead to outstanding cost reduction (see exhibit 7.1).

Redesign of products has permitted manufacturers to reconcile scale economies with product differentiation. In order to exploit scale economies in design, development, and component production, car manufacturers have reduced their number of basic "platforms," introduced single-world models, and standardized engines and major components between different models. At the same time, they have sought to increase differentiation through models that feature differences in styling and trim, and, within each model, offer a wide range of customer choices with regard to color, accessories, and optional features. Ford estimated that, on basis of the options available to customers with regard to color, trim, and accessories, it would be possible to run its U.S. plants at capacity for a full day without producing two identical cars.

Exhibit 7.1 Design for Manufacturability: The IBM Proprinter

When IBM introduced its first personal computer in 1983, the most inexpensive printer it supplied cost $5,000. Hence, the new PC was supplied with a Japanese-made printer. Facing up to the challenge of introducing an inexpensive printer for use with its PC, IBM assembled a small technical team comprising designers, manufacturing engineers, and automation specialists at Charlotte, North Carolina. The emphasis that IBM placed upon a quality machine that could be manufactured at low cost encouraged designers and manufacturing engineers to work closely together.

The emphasis in designing the printer was to reduce the number of parts from 150, found in the typical PC printer, to 60. For ease of assembly, the printer was designed in layers so that robots could build it from the bottom up. All screws, springs, pulleys, and other fasteners that required human insertion and adjustment were eliminated. The elimination of fasteners was facilitated by the use of molded plastic components that clipped together.

Ralph Gomory, former senior vice president of science and technology at IBM, reported that:

the Proprinter came out essentially as planned. It was made from only 62 parts. It printed faster and had more features than the competition – and the team developed it in half the usual time. The product was so well-designed for automated manufacture that it turned out to be easy and inexpensive to assemble by hand – so easy in fact that IBM eventually shifted a good deal of Proprinter production from the automated plant in Charlotte to a manual plant in Lexington, Kentucky. An additional benefit was that the Proprinter proved unusually reliable in the field. Fewer parts meant fewer assembly errors, fewer adjustments, and fewer opportunities for things to go wrong later.

The small number of parts and ease of manufacture – the printer could be manually assembled in three and a half minutes – established IBM as a cost leader in PC printers. Only five months after its launch, the Proprinter was the best-selling printer on the market.

Sources: Ralph E. Gomory, "From the Ladder of Science to the Product Development Cycle," *Harvard Business Review* (November-December 1989): 103; MIT Commission on Industrial Productivity, *Made in America: Regaining the Productive Edge* (Cambridge: MIT Press, 1989), 69–70.

Input costs

Where the firms within an industry purchase their inputs in the same competitive input markets, we can expect every firm to pay the same price for identical inputs. In most industries, however, differences in the costs incurred by different firms for similar inputs can be an important source of overall cost advantage. Common sources of lower input costs include:

1 *Locational differences in input prices* Most important here are differences in wage rates between different countries. In labor-intensive industries such as clothing, footwear, hand tools, and toys, international differences in wage rates give an almost unassailable cost advantage to producers in developing and newly industrializing countries. Other locational differences in input costs arise from the transport costs of raw materials and international differences in energy costs. For example, in pulp and paper, Canadian and Scandinavian producers have benefited from their access to forests and hydroelectric power. A key factor creating international differences in input costs are exchange rate movements. The rapid rise of the yen during the latter half of 1993 was a critical influence on the cost competitiveness of Japanese firms in world markets.

2 *Ownership of low-cost sources of supply* In industries where raw materials are a significant input, some firms are likely to achieve a cost advantage by possession of low-cost sources of the raw material. During the 1980s and early 1990s, Atlantic Richfield (Arco) was one of the most profitable of the U.S. oil majors as a result of its cost leadership in refined products on the West Coast based upon low-cost Alaskan oil reserves.

3 *Nonunion labor* In some industries where labor costs are important, the low-cost leaders are firms that have avoided unionization. In the U.S. airline industry, the profitability of regional upstarts such as Southwest Airlines compared to the major carriers is mainly due to differences in wages and benefits (see table 7.3).

4 *Bargaining power* Where bought-in products form a major proportion of costs and where these bought-in inputs are supplied by oligopo-

	Southwest Airlines (cents)	United Airlines (cents)
Wages and benefits	2.4	3.5
Fuel and oil	1.1	1.1
Aircraft ownership	0.7	0.8
Aircraft maintenance	0.6	0.3
Commissions on ticket sales	0.5	1.0
Advertising	0.2	0.2
Food and beverage	0.0	0.5
Other	1.7	3.1
Total	7.2	10.5

Table 7.3 Costs per Available Seat-Mile in Short-Haul Passenger Transport, 1993

Source: United Airlines

listic producers, differences in buying power between the firms in an industry can be an important source of cost advantage. The dominance of chains such as Wal-Mart, Toys-R-Us, IKEA, and Home Depot in particular areas of retail trade is, to a great extent, a result of superior bargaining power resulting in lower cost of goods sold.[17]

5 *Relationships with suppliers*   Recent developments in technology and organization have caused manufacturers to develop much closer and longer-term relationships with their suppliers. Just-in-time (JIT) methods, total quality management (TQM), and accelerated product development cycles have encouraged manufacturers to greatly reduce their numbers of suppliers, to shift responsibility for incoming quality to suppliers, to share technology, and to allow suppliers direct access to the manufacturer's production schedules. Such supplier partnerships (often based upon supplier certification procedures) have shown dramatic improvements in quality, time saving, and cost.

Process technology

In the manufacture of most goods and services a number of alternative production technologies exist. A particular production method is *technically superior* to another where for each unit of output it uses less of one input without using more of any other input. Where a production method uses more of some inputs but less of others, the relative cost efficiency of the alternative techniques depends upon the relative prices of the inputs. Thus, the lowest cost assembly of consumer electronic goods can occur in Brazil, the Philippines, and Thailand using simple, labor-intensive production techniques or in Japan using fully automated assembly techniques.

The development or adoption of a new production technique can be an important source of cost advantage. Pilkington's development of the float glass process – the manufacture of flat glass through the revolutionary process of floating molten glass on a bath of molten tin – gave it an unassailable cost advantage in glass production for a sustained period of time. The early adoption by Matsushita and Sony of automated insertion of components gave them a substantial cost advantage over RCA and Zenith in the U.S. market for TVs.

To the extent that process innovation is embodied in new capital equipment, then diffusion is likely to be rapid. Those firms that are expanding the most rapidly, and hence have the highest rates of net investment, will find it easy to establish technological leadership over their slower growing rivals. However, the effectiveness of new process technologies is likely to require systemwide changes in job design, employee incentives, product design, organizational structure, and management systems. The adoption of flexible manufacturing systems (FMS) and computer-integrated manufacture (CIM) is not simply a matter of installing new plant and equipment. Exploiting the productivity benefits depends critically upon the redesign of products, restructuring of organizations, and changes in human resource management.[18] Jaikumar found that the superior performance yielded by FMS systems in Japan compared to those in America could be attributed to the failure of American companies to adjust their management methods to the requirements of the new technology.[19] Between 1979 and 1986, General Motors spent $40 billion on new technology, new plants, and redesigned models with a view to becoming the world's most efficient volume manufacturer of automobiles. A plethora of difficulties and misfortunes has resulted in this huge investment offering only meager returns. For example, GM-Cadillac's state-of-the-art Hamtramck plant in Detroit was a nightmare of inefficiency, line stoppages, and robots run amok. After a tour of the plant, Toyota chairman Eiji Toyoda reportedly told a colleague, "It would have been embarrassing to comment on it."[20]

By contrast, other U.S. companies have made great improvements in productivity, as well as in other measures of manufacturing performance, by changing the organization and management of production – but without substantial investment in advanced capital equipment. The productivity gains at the joint GM-Toyota NUMMI plant at Fremont, California, during the 1980s were a sharp contrast to the disappointing performance at some of GM's highly automated plants. The fascinating feature of the Fremont experience is that it made heavy use of Toyota's management methods, but capital investment was modest.[21] The turn-around in productivity that was achieved at Harley-Davidson during the mid-1980s involved little automation and limited capital expenditure. The critical changes were in flexible work practices, making line-workers responsible for quality and maintenance, JIT scheduling, and training of production workers in statistical process control.[22] I will return to the role of organizational change in process innovation in the subsequent discussion of "dynamic efficiency."

Managerial efficiency

In many industries, the basic cost drivers – scale, technology, design, input costs, and capacity utilization – fail to provide a complete explanation for why one firm in an industry has lower unit costs than a competitor. Even after taking account of scale differences, differences in wage rates, and the like, there is typically some unexplained residual that I term "managerial efficiency" because it relates primarily to the ability of managers to operate the business close to its maximum efficiency. "Organizational slack" or "X-inefficiency" refer to costs that are in excess of maximum-efficiency operation.[23] They are the inevitable result of the desire of employees, both at managerial and shop-floor levels, to maintain some margin of inefficiency in preference to the strains of operating at maximum efficiency.

The ability of firms to achieve dramatic cost reductions when faced by a threat to their survival is revealing evidence of the extent of residual inefficiency. Financial crisis often results in corporate turnaround strategy involving substantial cost shedding. Chrysler's fight for survival between 1979 and 1980 is a classic case of turnaround through aggressive cost reduction. As a result of inventory reduction, plant closure, and a 40 percent cutback in white-collar employees, Chrysler's break-even level of capacity utilization fell from 80 to 55 percent.

The corporate restructurings of the last decade have involved a similar slashing of "organizational slack," especially in reducing administrative costs through aggressive cutbacks in corporate staffs. Restructuring by the oil companies resulted in such substantial reductions in corporate staffs that Exxon, British Petroleum, Texaco, Mobil, and Total all moved to smaller corporate head offices. Some of the most glaring inefficiencies of Japanese corporations lie in their administrative activities. Compared to U.S. competitors, the headquarters of many Japanese companies are characterized by large numbers of employees engaged in administrative tasks generating considerable paperwork and meetings. Nissan intends to raise white-collar productivity by 30 percent between 1993 and 1995.[24]

Using the Value Chain to Analyze Costs

Unit costs comprise the costs of many different activities. Each activity has a separate cost structure determined by particular cost drivers. For example, personal computer production involves two main activities: manufacture of components and assembly. In component manufacture, the primary cost drivers are scale of production and process technology. In assembly, wage rates are a major cost driver. Hence, for a detailed analysis of a company's cost position, the value chain is a useful framework for disaggregating the firm in order to identify:

- the relative importance of each activity in comprising total cost;
- the cost drivers for each activity and why the firm is comparatively efficient or inefficient in individual activities;
- how costs in one activity influence costs in another;
- which activities should be undertaken within the firm and which activities should be outsourced.

The principal stages of using the value chain to analyze costs are:

1 *Disaggregate the firm into separate activities* Deciding the appropriate disaggregation of the firm into value chain activities is a matter of judgment. Very often, the firm's own divisional and departmental structure is a useful guide. The principal considerations are:
   - the separateness of an activity from other activities;
   - the importance of an activity;
   - the dissimilarity of activities in terms of the factors determining cost behavior;

- the extent to which there are differences in the way that competitors perform the particular activity.

2 *Establish the relative importance of different activities in the total cost of the product* If the goal of cost analysis is to improve a firm's cost efficiency, then analysis should be focused upon activities that are important sources of cost. In disaggregating costs, Michael Porter suggests the detailed assignment of operating costs and assets to each value activity. Even with access to management and cost accounting data, this can be a major exercise. If the purpose of the study is to identify opportunities for improving cost performance, it may be possible to gain both insight and offer recommendations without a full-blown activity-costing exercise.

3 *Identify cost drivers* For each activity, what factors determine the level of cost of the firm relative to other firms? For some activities, cost drivers are evident simply from the nature of the activity and composition of costs. For capital-intensive activities, such as the operation of a body press in an auto plant, capital equipment costs, weekly production volume, and downtime between changes of dies are likely to be principal factors. For labor-intensive assembly activities, wage rates, speed of work, and defect rates are likely to be critical.

4 *Identify linkages* The costs in one activity may be determined, in part, by the way in which other activities are performed. Xerox discovered that its high service costs relative to competitors reflected the complexity of design of its copiers, which required 30 different interrelated adjustments.[25] Understanding such linkages can reveal interesting opportunities for cost reduction. Some of the most important contributions of TQM to cost reduction arise from the principle that defects need to be corrected at the source. The result is a careful tracing of linkages within the production process. As a result, cost of inspection and rework at the end of the production process can be reduced by improving accuracy at each stage of the manufacturing process.

5 *Examine the scope of reducing costs* Having identified the activities responsible for the major portions of overall costs and key factors that drive costs for each activity, the firm is positioned to identify the potential for cost reduction:
- for activities where scale economies are important, can volume be increased? One feature of Caterpillar's ambitious cost reduction strategy of the 1980s was to spread the costs of major indivisibilities such as R&D, component manufacturing plants, and dealer support over a larger volume of sales by introducing additional new models, entering the supply of forklift trucks, and expanding its OEM (original equipment manufacturer) sales of diesel engines;
- where wage costs are important, can wages be reduced either directly or by relocating production? Several airlines, notably Continental, American, and United, have sought competitiveness in the deregulated U.S. air transport market by cutting wages and benefits. The U.S. TV manufacturers vainly sought to survive Japanese and Korean competition by establishing assembly plants in Mexico, Taiwan, and Korea;

- if a certain activity cannot be performed efficiently within the firm, can the activity be contracted out or the component or service bought in? A key element of restructuring by U.S. and European corporations has been the rigorous appraisal of all production and support activities to determine whether costs can be saved through outsourcing. The initial impact of such analysis was extensive outsourcing of manufacturing activities by U.S. corporations to the extent than many were referred to as "hollow corporations." The second phase has involved increased outsourcing of support activities including distribution, payroll administration, legal services, and information technology. The growth of Ross Perot's EDS has been fueled by major U.S. corporations outsourcing their computer services. In March 1994, Xerox announced the contracting of its worldwide data systems to EDS in a contract valued at $3 billion over ten years.

Figure 7.7 shows how the application of the value chain to automobile manufacture can yield suggestions for possible cost reductions.

Cost Reduction in the 1990s: The Quest for Dynamic Sources of Efficiency

The late 1980s and early 1990s have seen a new era in managing for cost efficiency. Increased competition and pressure to create shareholder value have resulted in a new emphasis on cost reduction – especially through the quest for new sources of cost reduction. Among the mass of initiatives and new management techniques of this period, three developments can be distinguished: the move to dynamic sources of cost efficiency (including TQM), corporate restructuring, and process reengineering:

1 *The shift from dynamic to static sources of cost efficiency and the impact of TQM* Scale economies, input prices, and capacity utilization are static drivers of cost efficiency; learning and innovation are dynamic. Robert Hayes, Steven Wheelwright, and Kim Clark of Harvard Business School identify overemphasis on static efficiency at the expense of dynamic efficiency as a key determinant of America's industrial decline.[26] Since the Second World War, the marriage between scientific management, technological progress, and craftsmanship that formed the basis of American industrial dynamism for most of the twentieth century passed to Japan, while U.S. managers turned their attention from manufacturing to marketing, finance, corporate planning, and government relations. As management attention moved away from manufacturing operations to become increasingly reliant upon financial data, quantitative targets, and the technology of strategic planning, the result was a shift from a culture based around the quest for improvement to one of static optimization. Table 7.4 contrasts dynamic and static approaches to manufacturing.

Figure 7.7 Using the Value Chain in Cost Analysis: An Automobile Manufacturer

1 IDENTIFY ACTIVITIES
Establish the basic framework of the value chain by identifying the principal activities of the firm.

2 ALLOCATE TOTAL COSTS (APPROXIMATELY)
For a first-stage analysis, a rough estimate of the break-down of total product cost by activity is sufficient and indicates which activities offer the most scope for cost reductions.

3 IDENTIFY COST DRIVERS (– See diagram)

4 IDENTIFY LINKAGES
Examples include:
1. Consolidation of orders and increases inventory costs.
2. Higher-quality components reduce costs in assembly and quality control.
3. Fewer defects in manufacturing reduce warranty costs incurred in the service and dealer support.
4. Design of car models with common components exploits scale economies in components.

5 MAKE RECOMMENDATIONS FOR COST REDUCTION
Purchasing: Concentrate purchases on fewer suppliers in order to increase bargaining power. Institute just-in-time component supply to reduce inventories.

R&D/Design/Engineering: Reduce frequency of model changes. Reduce number of different models (e.g., single range of models for all countries in the world). Design for interchangeability of components.

Component manufacture: Exploit economies of scale through concentrating production of each component type on single plant. Contract out production of all components where scale of production or run lengths are suboptimal or where independent suppliers have technology advantages. For components where labor costs are important (e.g., seats, dashboards, trim) seek to relocate production in low-wage countries. Improve capacity utilization through plant rationalization or supplying components to other manufacturers.

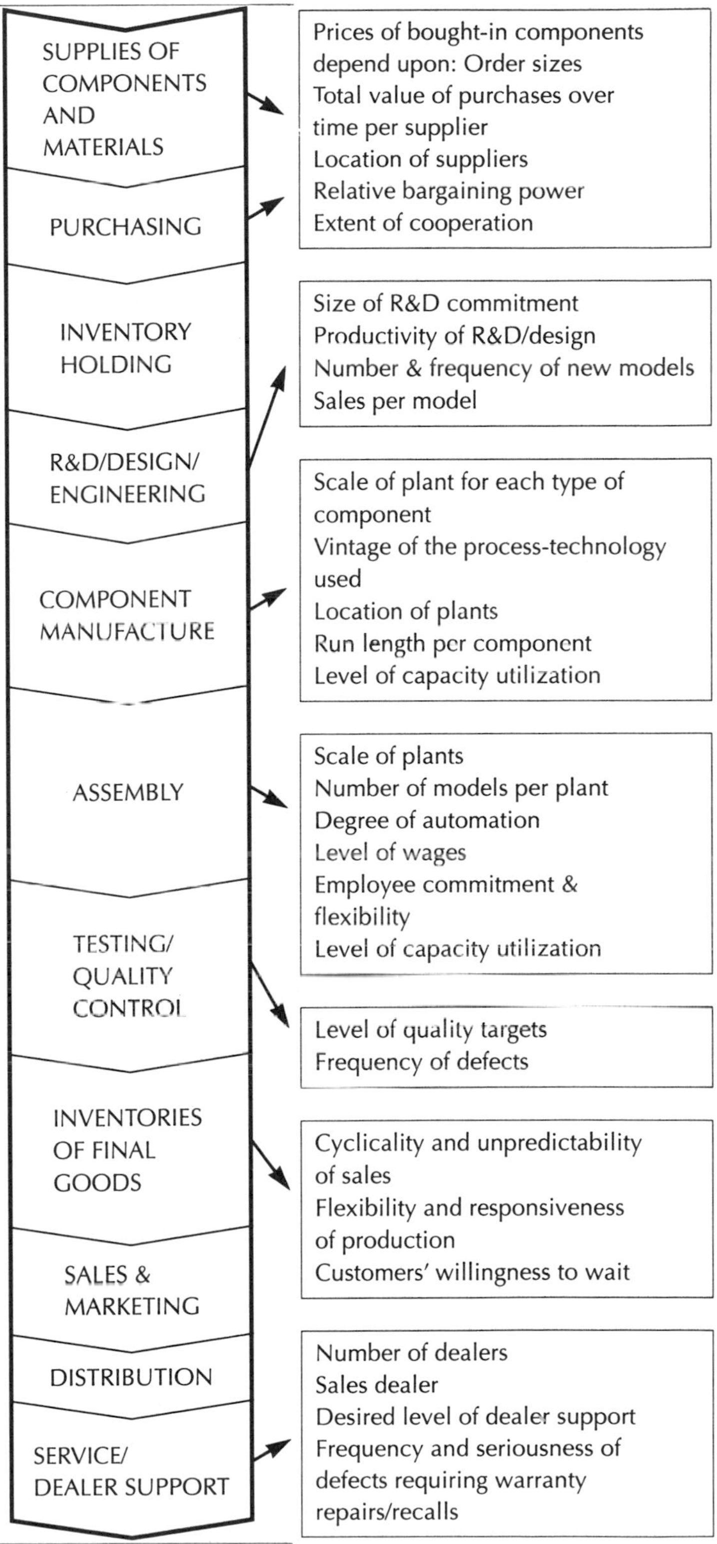

Value chain activities:

SUPPLIES OF COMPONENTS AND MATERIALS

PURCHASING

INVENTORY HOLDING

R&D/DESIGN/ ENGINEERING

COMPONENT MANUFACTURE

ASSEMBLY

TESTING/ QUALITY CONTROL

INVENTORIES OF FINAL GOODS

SALES & MARKETING

DISTRIBUTION

SERVICE/ DEALER SUPPORT

Cost drivers:

Prices of bought-in components depend upon: Order sizes
Total value of purchases over time per supplier
Location of suppliers
Relative bargaining power
Extent of cooperation

Size of R&D commitment
Productivity of R&D/design
Number & frequency of new models
Sales per model

Scale of plant for each type of component
Vintage of the process-technology used
Location of plants
Run length per component
Level of capacity utilization

Scale of plants
Number of models per plant
Degree of automation
Level of wages
Employee commitment & flexibility
Level of capacity utilization

Level of quality targets
Frequency of defects

Cyclicality and unpredictability of sales
Flexibility and responsiveness of production
Customers' willingness to wait

Number of dealers
Sales dealer
Desired level of dealer support
Frequency and seriousness of defects requiring warranty repairs/recalls

Figure 7.7 continued

Assembly: Increase labor productivity through automation. Improve capacity utilization through improved sales forecasting and bigger promotions during seasonal downturns. To lower costs of quality control and warranties, reduce defects through improved employee morale and increase employee involvement.

Table 7.4
Characteristics of Dynamic and Static Approaches to Manufacturing

DYNAMIC	STATIC
The Production System Artisan mode of production involving: • problem solving • creation of knowledge by production workers • workers' control over the product • orientation toward the product and the customer	*The Production System* Production dominated by the imperatives of Scientific Management: • quest for the "one best way" * people matched to tasks • supervise, reward, and punish to ensure conformity of individual efforts and company objectives • use staff to plan and control
Management of Technology An emphasis upon: • continual improvement in small steps • commercial needs establish the R&D agenda (technology pulled in by practical demands) • product and process innovation intimately related • teamwork and cross-functional collaboration	*Management of Technology* • science-driven – research findings seeking commercial applications • concentrated in corporate R&D departments • emphasis on product innovation and on large-scale projects

Source: Based upon the ideas and concepts in Kim Clark and Robert H. Hayes, "Recapturing America's Manufacturing Heritage," *California Management Review* (summer 1988): 9–33.

The TQM movement of the 1980s has been the principal vehicle by which dynamic approaches to manufacturing have been reintroduced into Western industry. Although the focus of TQM has been the pursuit of quality improvement, a remarkable byproduct of TQM has been the reduction of operating costs. The emphasis of TQM on the rigorous analysis of production activities, on the simplification of processes and training, and on increasing the responsibility and decision making authority of shop-floor workers has had the effect of reducing the costs of defects and rework, lowering costs of supervision and maintenance, cutting inventories and work in progress, and stimulating process innovation.[27]

Corporate restructuring

"Corporate restructuring" refers to the dramatic strategic and organizational changes that companies have undergone in order to adjust their strategies, structures, and management systems to the environment of competition, instability, and low rates of economic growth that have characterized most of the 1980s and 1990s. The primary objective of restructuring has been increasing profitability, and a major ingredient of such restructuring has been improving margins through reducing costs. Corporate restructurings have involved several types of cost reduction measures:

- plant closures to improve capacity utilization and eliminate obsolete technology;
- outsourcing of components and services wherever internal suppliers are less cost efficient than external suppliers;
- increasing managerial efficiency through "delayering" to reduce administrative overhead and the application of rigorous financial targets and control to provide incentives for aggressive cost reduction.

Exhibit 7.2 describes Chevron's efforts to reduce costs through restructuring.

Business process reengineering

One of the most successful approaches to cost reduction during the 1990s was "*business process reengineering*," which the "reengineering gurus" Michael Hammer and James Champy have defined as "the fundamental rethinking and radical redesign of business processes to achieve dramatic improvements in critical contemporary measures of performance, such as cost, quality, service and speed."[28]

The idea is to redesign business processes in ways that increase their efficiency in fundamental ways. The idea is also to abstract from the present way in which a process is organized and start from scratch with the simple question: "If we were starting afresh, how would we design this process?" Although no general theory or design framework for process reengineering has been proposed, the following "commonalities, recurring themes or characteristics" have been advanced by Hammer and Champy:

- several jobs are combined into one;
- workers make decisions;
- the steps in the process are performed in a natural order;
- processes have multiple versions, that is, processes are designed to take account of different situations;
- processes are performed where it makes the most sense; for example, if the accounting department needs pencils, it is probably cheaper for such a small order to be purchased directly from the office equipment store around the block than to be ordered via the firm's purchasing department;
- checks and controls are reduced to the point where they make economic sense;
- reconciliation is minimized;

Exhibit 7.2 Cost Cutting at Chevron

After a decade during which Chevron's profitability and returns to shareholders lagged behind those of most other U.S. oil majors, Chevron announced in January 1992 an "aggressive action plan" involving:

- capacity reduction and efficiency increases at the Port Arthur refinery including a cut in employment of 700;
- an acceleration in sales of U.S. oil and gas properties: of Chevron's 1,000 remaining fields at the beginning of 1992, Derr announced the intention to sell 600 of them;
- a program to reduce operating expenses of 50 cents a barrel of sales by mid-1993.

In fact, this cost reduction was achieved before the end of 1992. For 1992 as a whole, operating expenses were reduced by 59 cents for each barrel of product sold, adding $570 million to pretax income. Total employment was cut by 6,200 during 1992. For 1993, a further cost reduction target of 25 cents per barrel was established. A key element of the proposed cuts in costs were reductions at the corporate level where a 30 percent cost reduction was targeted. In its report for the third quarter of 1993, Chevron was able to report that it had already exceeded its cost reduction target for 1993: costs had been reduced by over 40 cents a barrel of product sold. After adjusting for special items, Chevron succeeded in cutting operating costs by 7 percent during the first nine months of 1993 compared to the comparable period in 1992. The principal cost reductions occurred in the following areas:

1   *selling, general, and administrative expenses* were cut from $459 million during the third quarter of 1992 to $359 million during the third quarter of 1993. The biggest cost savings were incurred at corporate headquarters. Between 1992 and 1993, headquarters staff was reduced from 3,600 to 2,600 and headquarters operating costs from $670 million to $470 million. Of the 1,000 headquarters positions lost, about 550 were by voluntary early retirement. The reductions were primarily in tax, treasury, public affairs, security, law, and human resources. Chairman K. Derr stated, "We regret that these changes will leave some employees without jobs. The cutbacks reflect a business environment that has required us to change our structure and eliminate work that's not absolutely essential to our business."

2   *Chevron Information Technology Company.* A combination of reorganization and outsourcing of IT services resulted in CITC's employment being cut from 2,300 in 1992 to 1,800 in 1993.

3   *E&P.* During 1992 employee innovations, sales of high-cost oil and gas fields and a 23 percent reduction in the number of employees cut operating costs by $400 million or $1.18 per barrel of oil.

4   *U.S. refining and marketing.* A key element in Chevron U.S.A. Products' target of reducing operating costs by $300 million was cutting refinery capacity to ensure full capacity utilization at both its Port Arthur and Richmond (California) refineries. In retailing, Chevron reduced its number of stations while focusing its marketing efforts on 16 key metropolitan areas in the south and west of the United States. From year-end 1988 to year-end 1992, Chevron's company-owned and company-leased stations fell from 3,400 to 2,500. At the end of 1993, Chevron was pursuing further capacity reduction. Its Port Arthur, Texas, and Philadelphia refineries were put up for sale as well as two small refineries in the Northwest and six terminals in the east.

Source: Chevron Company annual reports.

- a case manager provides a single point of contact;
- hybrid centralized/decentralized operations are prevalent; for example, through a shared database, decentralized decisions can be made while permitting overall coordination because information is available to all decentralized decision makers.

As an example of efficiency gains from process reengineering, see exhibit 7.3.

Exhibit 7.3 Process Reengineering at IBM Credit

IBM Credit provides credit to customers of IBM for the purchase of IBM hardware and software. Under the old system, five stages were involved:

- the IBM salesperson telephoned a request for financing. The request was logged on a piece of paper;
- the request was sent to the Credit Department where it was logged onto a computer, and the customer's creditworthiness was checked. The results of the credit check were written on a form and passed to the Business Practices Department;
- there the standard loan covenant would be modified to meet the terms of customer loan;
- the request was passed to the pricer who determined the appropriate interest rate;
- the clerical group took all the information and prepared a quote letter that was sent to the salesperson.

Because the process took an average of six days, it resulted in a number of lost sales and held up the sales staff in finalizing deals. After many efforts to improve the process, two managers undertook an experiment. They took a financing request and walked it around through all five steps. The process took 90 minutes!

On this basis, a fundamental redesign of the credit approval process was achieved. The fundamental change was replacing the specialists (credit checkers, pricers, and so on) with generalists who undertook all five processes. Only where the request was nonstandard or unusually complex were specialists called in. The basic problem was that the system had been designed for the most complex credit requests that IBM received, whereas in the vast majority of cases no specialist judgment was called for – simply clerical work involving looking up credit ratings, plugging numbers into standard formulas, and so on.

The result was that credit requests are processed in four hours compared to six days, total number of employees was reduced slightly, and the total number of deals increased one hundred times.

Source: Adapted from M. Hammer and J. Champy, *Reengineering the Corporation: A Manifesto for Business Revolution* (New York: HarperBusiness, 1993), 36–9.

Summary and Conclusion

Cost efficiency may no longer be a guarantee of security and profitability in today's fast-changing markets, but in almost all industries it is a prerequisite for success. In industries where competition has always been primarily price-based – steel, textiles, and mortgage loans – increased intensity of competition is requiring more intense and radical approaches to cost reduction. In industries where price competition was once muted – airlines, investment banking, and computer software – firms are for the first time being forced to reconcile the pursuit of innovation, differentiation, and service quality with vigorous cost reduction.

The foundation for cost reduction strategy must be an understanding of the determinants of a company's costs. The principal message of this chapter is the need to look behind cost accounting data and beyond simple single-factor analyses of cost efficiency to analyze the factors that drive relative unit costs in each of the firm's activities.

While detailed analysis of the firm's activities and their cost structures are critical in providing a basis for cost reductions strategies, it is important that such analysis does result in an acceptance of the prevailing activity-structure of the firm. Some of the most interesting and substantial sources of cost reduction have arisen from fundamental rethinking of the activities undertaken by the firm and the ways in which it organizes them. By focusing upon those activities in which the firm possesses a cost advantage and outsourcing others, companies such as Polaroid concentrate upon producing internally a few key products and components while buying in film medium from Kodak, electronics from Texas Instruments, and cameras from Timex and others.[29] Business process reengineering can involve the radical redesign of individual activities that can offer far more substantial cost reductions than manipulating static cost drivers such as scale economies and input costs.

The implication is that the quest for cost initiative must involve multiple initiatives at different levels. It must carefully analyze existing activities relative to competitors in order to determine where it can exploit efficiency opportunities through static sources of cost reduction. At the same time, the firm must look to opportunities for innovation and process redesign in order to exploit novel sources of dynamic efficiency. At one level, the firm must seek major cost breakthroughs through fundamental restructuring and redesign. At another level, it must utilize initiatives such as TQM to inspire employees throughout the company to seek opportunities for incremental improvement in every single task and operation.

Notes

1   Louis E. Yelle, "The Learning Curve: Historical Review and Comprehensive Survey," *Decision Sciences* 10 (1979): 302–28.
2   Boston Consulting Group, *History of the Experience Curve*, Perspective No. 125 (Boston: Boston Consulting Group, 1973).
3   A rigorous analysis of the profit gains to market share leadership under differently sloped experience curves and different competitive conditions is developed by David Ross, "Learning to Dominate," *Journal of Industrial Economics* 34 (1986), 337–53.
4   This is sometimes referred to as "*penetration*" pricing, as opposed to "*full-cost*" pricing or "*skimming*."
5   Boston Consulting Group, *Strategy Alternatives for the British Motorcycle Industry* (London: Her Majesty's Stationery Office, 1975).
6   For a discussion of the policy implications of the experience curve, see Charles Baden Fuller, "The Implications of the Learning Curve for Firm Strategy and Public Policy," *Applied Economics* 15 (1983): 541–51.
7   Robert D. Buzzell, Bradley T. Gale, and Ralph Sultan, "Market Share – A Key to Profitability," *Harvard Business Review* (January-February 1975); Robert Buzzell and Fredrick Wiersema, "Successful Share-Building Strategies," *Harvard Business Review* (January-February 1981); Robert Jacobsen and David Aaker, "Is Market Share All That It's Cracked up to Be?" *Journal of Marketing* 49 (fall 1985): 11–22.
8   Richard Rumelt and Robin Wensley, using PIMS data, found the relationship between market share and profitability to be the result of both being joint outcomes of a risky competitive process (*In Search of the Market Share Effect*, Paper MGL-63, Graduate School of Management, UCLA, 1981).

9   Robin Wensley, "PIMS and BCG: New Horizons or False Dawn?" *Strategic Management Journal* 3 (1982): 147–58.

10 Boston Consulting Group, *Strategy Alternatives for the British Motorcycle Industry* (London: Her Majesty's Stationery Office, 1975).

11 To be more precise, the economies of amortizing the costs of new product development are *economies of volume* rather than *economies of scale*. The product development cost per unit of production declines not on the *volume of production per unit of time* but upon the *total volume of production over the life of the model.*

12 "Boeing: Banking on a Big Bird," *Economist*, March 12, 1994, 73–4.

13 This argument was first made by David Schwartzman, "Uncertainty and the Size of the Firm," *Economica* (August 1963).

14 Maryann Keller, *Collision* (New York: Doubleday, 1993): 173–7.

15 Leonard Rapping, "Learning and World War II Production Functions," *Review of Economics and Statistics* (February 1965): 81–6.

16 Kim B. Clark and Robert H. Hayes, "Recapturing America's Manufacturing Heritage," *California Management Review* (summer 1988): 25.

17 Robert M. Grant, "Manufacturer-Retailer Relations: The Shifting Balance of Power," in *Retailing and Business Strategy*, ed. G. Johnson (New York: John Wiley, 1987).

18 See, for example, Robert H. Hayes and Ramchandran Jaikumar, "Manufacturing's Crisis: New Technologies, Obsolete Organizations," *Harvard Business Review* (September-October 1988): 85; and Robert M. Grant, A. B. Shani, R. Krishnan, and R. Baer, "Appropriate Manufacturing Technology: A Strategic Approach," *Sloan Management Review* 33, no. 1 (fall 1991): 43–54.

19 Ramchandran Jaikumar, "Postindustrial Manufacturing," *Harvard Business Review* (November-December 1986): 69–76.

20 Maryann Keller, Collision (New York: Doubleday, 1993), 169–71.

21 Clair Brown and Michael Reich, "When Does Union Management Coop eration Work? A Look at NUMMI and GM-Van Nuys," *California Management Review* (summer 1989): 28–9.

22 Robert M. Grant, "Roaring Back: Harley-Davidson in 1988," mimeo, 1990 (available from the author).

23 Cyert and March, *A Behavioral Theory of the Firm* (Englewood Cliffs, NJ: Prentice-Hall, 1963); H. Leibenstein, "Allocative Efficiency versus X-Efficiency," *American Economic Review* (June 1966).

24 "Japan's Struggle to Restructure," *Fortune*, June 28, 1993, 84–8.

25 Jeremy Main, Quality Wars (New York: Simon & Schuster, 1994).

26 Robert H. Hayes, Steven C. Wheelwright, and Kim B. Clark, *Dynamic Manufacturing: Creating the Learning Organization* (New York: Free Press, 1988).

27 For a review of the impact of TQM, see David A. Garvin, *Managing Quality: The Strategic and Competitive Edge* (New York: Free Press, 1988).

28 Michael Hammer and James Champy, *Reengineering the Corporation: A Manifesto for Business Revolution* (New York: HarperBusiness, 1993), 32.

29 See James Brian Quinn, *Intelligent Enterprise* (New York: Free Press, 1992), chapters 2 and 3.

EIGHT

Differentiation Advantage

If you gave me $100 billion and said, "Take away the soft drink leadership of Coca-Cola in the world," I'd give it back to you and say, "It can't be done."
– Warren Buffett, chairman, Berkshire Hathaway, and Coca-Cola's biggest shareholder

Introduction and Objectives

A firm differentiates itself from its competitors "when it provides something unique that is valuable to buyers beyond simply offering a low price."[1] Differentiation advantage occurs when a firm is able to obtain from its differentiation a price-premium in the market that exceeds the cost of providing the differentiation.

There is virtually no limit to a firm's opportunities for differentiating its offering to customers, and, because every firm is different, this set of differentiation opportunities is unique to each firm. The range of differentiation opportunities does, of course, depend upon the characteristics of the product. An automobile or a restaurant offer greater potential for differentiation than highly standardized products such as cement, wheat, or DRAM computer chips. These latter products are referred to as "commodities" precisely because they lack opportunities of physical differentiation. Yet, even commodity products can be supplied in ways that create customer value: "Anything can be turned into a value-added product or service for a well-defined or newly created market," claims Tom Peters.[2] Peters gives the example of Milliken & Company's success in the market for the lowly "shop towel" – towels and cloths for factories, hospitals, and other institutions. Milliken's customers are industrial launderers who rent the towels to the final users. Milliken supplies its customers not just with towels but with a complete service that covers ordering, distribution, inventory control, sales training, promotional materials, audiovisual sales aids, seminars, and market research data. Thus, differentiation extends beyond the characteristics of the product or the service to encompass every possible interaction between the firm and its customers.

The supply-side analysis of differentiation can tell us what the firm can do that is different, but the critical issue is whether that differentiation *creates value for customers*. Because the purpose of differentiation is to generate profit for the firm, the focus for analyzing differentiation must be the customer: it is by creating value for the customer that exceeds the costs incurred by the firm that profit is generated. Thus, our primary concern in this chapter will be the *demand side* of the market. By understanding what customers want, how they choose, and what their motivations are, we can identify opportunities for profitable differentiation. Differentiation strategies are not simply about pursuing uniqueness for the sake of being different.

Differentiation is about understanding the product or service and about understanding the customer. To this extent, the quest for differentiation advantage takes us to the heart of business strategy. The fundamental issues of differentiation are also the fundamental issues of business strategy: Who are our customers? how do we create value for them? and how do we do it more effectively and efficiently than anyone else so that we can earn profit from it?

Because differentiation is about uniqueness, differentiation advantage cannot be achieved simply through the application of standardized frameworks, techniques, checklists, and systems of classification. Differentiation advantage involves identifying new and unique opportunities and developing innovatory approaches to exploiting them. That is not to say that differentiation advantage is not amenable to systematic analysis. As I have observed, there are two elements to creating profitable differentiation: on the *supply side*, the firm must be aware of the resources and capabilities through which it can create uniqueness (and do it better than competitors); on the *demand side*, the key is to have insight into and understanding of customers and their needs and preferences. These two sides form the major components of our analysis of differentiation. This analysis is not intended to constrain or supplant intuition and creativity but to provide a framework that is capable of stimulating and guiding novel and creative approaches to generating customer value.

By the time you have completed this chapter, you will be able to:

- understand what differentiation is, its multiple dimensions, and its potential for creating and sustaining competitive advantage;
- analyze the sources of differentiation in terms of customers' preferences and characteristics and the firm's capacity for supplying differentiation;
- formulate strategies that create differentiation advantage by linking the firm's differentiation capability to customers' demand for differentiation.

The Nature of Differentiation and Differentiation Advantage

Differentiation variables

The potential for differentiating a product or service, we have seen, is only partly determined by its physical characteristics. For a product that is technically simple (a pair of socks or a brick) or that satisfies uncomplicated needs (a corkscrew or a nail) or that must meet specific technical standards (a spark plug or a thermometer), differentiation opportunities are constrained by technical or market factors. Products that are complex (an airplane), satisfy complex needs (an automobile or a vacation), or that do not need to conform to stringent technical standards (wine, toys) offer much greater scope for differentiation.

Beyond these constraints, the potential in any product or service for differentiation is limited only by the boundaries of the human imagination. In the case of simple products such as shampoo, toilet paper, and cigarettes, the proliferation of brands on any supermarket's shelves is a testimony both to the ingenuity of firms and the complexity of customer preferences. Differentiation extends beyond the physical characteristics of the product or the service to encompass everything about the product or service that influences the value that customers derive from it. This means that differentiation includes every aspect of the way in which a company does business and relates to its customers. Thus, McDonald's differentiation advantage within the fast-food business depends not just upon the characteristics of the food and drinks it serves nor just upon the services associated with its food and drinks (speed of service, cleanliness of its restaurants) but also upon the attitudes it projects of happiness and interest in children. Differentiation is likely to be built into the identity, style, and values of a company. As a result, companies that supply seemingly basic, undifferentiated offerings such as Volkswagen during the 1960s and Southwest Airlines during the early 1990s may achieve highly differentiated market positions in terms of customers' perceptions.

Hence, differentiation strategies should not be associated simply with *product* differentiation. The core of differentiation is concerned not only with products and the services that accompany them but the *relationship* between a company and its customers. Ultimately, differentiation is all about a firm's responsiveness to customer requirements. Tom Peters calls for "*total customer responsiveness*": "Every action, no matter how small, and no matter how far from the firing line a department may be, must be processed through the customer's eyes. Will this make it easier for the customer? Faster? Better? Less expensive? . . . Long-term profit equals revenue from continuously happy customer relationships minus cost."[3]

In analyzing differentiation opportunities, a basic distinction is made between *tangible* and *intangible* aspects. Tangible differentiation is concerned with the observable characteristics of a product or service that are relevant to the preferences and choice processes of customers. These include such characteristics as size, shape, color, weight, design, material, and technology. Tangible differentiation also comprises the performance of the product or service in terms of reliability, consistency, taste, speed, durability, and safety. The products and services that are complements to the product in question are also important in relation to differentiation potential. These include presales services, postsales services, accessories, availability and speed of delivery, credit, and the ability to upgrade the product in the future. For consumer products, these differentiation variables directly determine the utility that consumers gain from the product. For producer goods, differentiation variables affect the customer firm's ability to make money in their own businesses – hence, these performance variables are valuable sources of differentiation if they lower the costs of the customers' firms or increase their ability to differentiate their own products.

Opportunities for intangible differentiation arise from the fact that the value that customers perceive in a product or service is not dependent exclusively upon the tangible aspects of the offering. There are few products where customer choice is determined solely by observable product features or objective performance criteria. Social, emotional, psychological, and aesthetic considerations are present in choices over all products and services. The desire for status, exclusivity, individuality, and security are extremely powerful motivational forces in choices relating to most consumer goods. Where a product or service is meeting complex customer needs, then differentiation choices involve the overall *image* of the firm's offering. Issues of image differentiation are especially important for those products and services whose qualities and performance are difficult to ascertain at the time of purchase ("*experience goods*"). These include cosmetics, medical services, and education.

Differentiation and segmentation

Conventional strategy analysis treats differentiation and segmentation as separate strategy variables. Differentiation is concerned with *how* the firm competes: that is, in what ways the firm can offer uniqueness to its customers. Segmentation is concerned with *where* the firm competes: issues of product-market scope. While segmentation choices are concerned with selecting particular geographical, product, or customer segments, differentiation decisions are concerned with selecting the sources of uniqueness that the firm will use to distinguish its offerings from those of its competitors. These might include *consistency* (McDonald's hamburgers), *reliability* (Federal Express's next-day delivery), conferring *status* (American Express), *quality* (Marks & Spencer), and *innovation* (Philips).

While segmentation is a feature of market structure, differentiation is a strategic choice by a firm. A segmented market is one in which demand can be divided into segments with distinct demand functions. Differentiation is concerned with a firm's positioning within a market or a segment in relation to the various product characteristics that influence customer choice.[4] Simply by locating within a segment, a firm does not necessarily differentiate itself from its competitors within the same segment.

The distinction between differentiation and segmentation can also be seen from the fact that a firm may be committed to a differentiation strategy and yet position itself within the mass market. IBM, General Motors, and Burger King all aim at well-defined positions of differentiation within their markets while focusing on market share leadership. In many instances, however, it is not possible to unambiguously separate decisions concerning differentiation from the choice of which segments in which to compete. By offering uniqueness in its product or service offerings, the firm must inevitably appeal more to the preferences of some customer groups than to others. Hence, decisions about differentiation have implications for which industry segments the firm is focusing upon. By selecting performance, engineering, and style as the basis on which BMW competes in the automobile industry, it inevitably orients itself to different market segments than does Volvo or Chrysler. The same is true even for broadly targeted firms: in the personal computer market, IBM's commitment to customer service focuses it upon the business computer rather than home computer segment, and, within the business computer segment, on users requiring a high level of support rather than those seeking either low-priced student computers or technologically advanced, high-performance computers.

The sustainability of differentiation advantage

Although strategy analysis has traditionally emphasized cost advantage as the primary basis for establishing a competitive advantage over rivals, in many respects, low cost is a far less secure basis for sustainable competitive advantage than differentiation. The growth of international trade has been particularly important in revealing the fragility of seemingly well-established positions of domestic cost leadership. Across North America and Western Europe, firms whose competitive advantage was based upon cost leadership through scale economies and superior process technology have been undermined by competition from the newly industrializing countries. Moreover, in internationally competing industries, cost leadership is seldom clearly defined: movements in exchange rates can cause rapid shifts in cost competitiveness. Within the space of a few days during September 1992, the British pound plunged in value by 20 percent against the German mark. As a result, Volkswagen suddenly became cost-uncompetitive in the U.K. car market against rivals with British manufacturing plants (Rover, Ford, GM-Vauxhall).

Even in relation to domestic competition, low-cost production is an increasingly vulnerable source of competitive advantage:

- the increasing pace of technological change means that cost advantages based upon scale and experience may be undercut by a competitor's process innovation. During the 1970s, several major European and U.S. steel companies invested heavily in large, integrated iron and steel plants at coastal locations. However, it was the small minimill steel firms using a quite different technology that emerged as the cost leaders in the industry;
- where cost advantage is built upon technical capabilities, the embodiment of new technology in new equipment and the increased intercompany mobility of personnel speeds the transfer of technology and experience between firms.

The superiority of differentiation advantage over cost advantage is indicated by the strategies pursued by U.S. companies that have been consistently successful over the long term. Table 8.1 lists companies among the Fortune 100, largest U.S. corporations with the highest return to stockholders. The list is dominated by firms whose strategies have been based upon differentiation in terms of quality, brand loyalty, and innovation.

Analyzing Differentiation: The Demand Side

Successful differentiation involves a matching of customers' demand for differentiation with the firm's capacity to supply differentiation. Let's begin with the demand side. Analyzing customer demand enables us to determine the potential for differentiation in a market, the willingness of customers to pay for differentiation, and the most promising position-

	Average annual return (%)
Gillette	29.4
Coca-Cola	29.4
PepsiCo	28.0
Compaq Computer	28.0
Sara Lee	26.3
Kellogg	24.8
Philip Morris	24.6
Merck	24.2
Colgate-Palmolive	23.3
Ford Motor Company	22.3
General Mills	21.8
CPC International	21.4
Campbell Soup	21.3
Quaker Oats	21.0
ConAgra	20.6
Abbot Laboratories	20.6
Kimberly-Clark	20.3
Chrysler	20.2
Warner-Lambert	20.0
PPG Industries	19.8

Table 8.1 Companies among the Fortune 100 Top U.S. Corporations with the Highest Return to Stockholders, 1983-93

Source: "The Fortune 500," Fortune, April 18, 1994, 220–3.

ing for the firm in terms of differentiation variables and in relation to competitors.

Analyzing demand begins with understanding why customers buy a product or service. What needs and requirements are to be satisfied by a person's purchase of a personal computer or a firm's commissioning of an advertising agency? Market research seeks to explore customer preferences and customer perceptions of existing products. However, the key to successful differentiation is to *understand* customers. In gaining insight into customer requirements and preferences, simple, direct questions about the purpose of a product and its performance attributes can often be far more illuminating than objective market research data obtained from large samples of actual and potential customers. Exhibit 8.1 provides a striking example of the value of simplicity and directness in probing customer requirements.

Product attributes and positioning

Virtually all products and service serve multiple customer needs, hence understanding customer needs requires the analysis of multiple attributes. Market research has developed numerous techniques for analyzing customer preferences in relation to product attributes in order to guide the positioning of new products and the repositioning of existing products within the market. Techniques include:

Exhibit 8.1   Understanding What a Product Is About

Getting back to strategy means getting back to a deep understanding of what a product is about. Some time back, for example, a Japanese home appliance company was trying to develop a coffee percolator. Should it be a General Electric-type percolator, executives wondered? Should it be the same drip-type that Philips makes? Larger? Smaller? I urged them to ask a different kind of question: Why do people drink coffee? What are they looking for when they do? If your objective is to serve the customer better, then shouldn't you understand why that customer drinks coffee in the first place? Then you would know what kind of percolator to make.

The answer came back: good taste. Then I asked the company's engineers what they were doing to help the consumer enjoy good taste in a cup of coffee. They said they were trying to design a good percolator. I asked them what influences the taste in a cup of coffee. No one knew. That became the next question we had to answer. It turns out that lots of things can affect taste – the beans, the temperature, the water. We did our homework and discovered all the things that affect taste. . . .

Of all the factors, water quality, we learned, made the greatest difference. The percolator in design at the time, however, didn't take water quality into account

at all. . . . We discovered next the grain distribution and the time between grinding the beans and pouring in the water were crucial. As a result we began to think about the product and its necessary features in a new way. It *had* to have a built-in dechlorinating function. It *had* to have a built-in grinder. All the customer should have to do is pour in water and beans. . . .

To start you have to ask the right questions and set the right kinds of strategic goals. If your only concern is that General Electric has just brought out a percolator that brews coffee in ten minutes, you will get your engineers to design one that brews it in seven minutes. And if you stick to that logic, market research will tell you that instant coffee is the way to go. . . . Conventional marketing approaches won't solve the problem. If you ask people whether they want their coffee in ten minutes or seven, they will say seven, of course. But its still the wrong question. And you end up back where you started, trying to beat the competition at its own game. If your primary focus is on the competition, you will never step back and ask what the customers' inherent needs are, and what the product really is about.

Source: Quoted from Kenichi Ohmae, "Getting Back to Strategy," *Harvard Business Review* (November-December 1988): 154.

1   *Multidimensional scaling*, which permits customers' perceptions of competing products' similarities and dissimilarities to be represented graphically and for the dimensions to be interpreted in terms of key product attributes.[5] For example, a pharmaceutical company's survey of consumer ratings of competing pain relievers resulted in the mapping shown in figure 8.1.

2   *Conjoint analysis* is a powerful means of analyzing the strength of customer preferences for different product attributes. The technique requires, first, an identification of the underlying attributes of a product and, second, that consumers be asked to rank hypothetical products that comprise alternative bundles of attributes. On the basis of this data, trade-offs can be analyzed and the simulations can be run to determine the proportion of customers who would prefer a hypothetical new product to competing products already available in the market.[6] A conjoint analysis undertaken by BCG of potential personal computer buyers identified price, manufacturer's reputation, portability, processing capability, memory capacity, word processing capability, and styling as critical attributes. The data gathered on customer preferences and trade-offs were used to predict the share of customer preferences that the forthcoming Apple Macintosh and IBM PC Junior

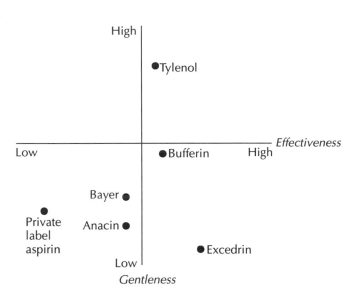

Figure 8.1 Customer Perceptions of Competing Pain Relievers Mapped by Multidimensional Scaling

Sources: Glen L. Urban and John R. Hauser, *Design and Marketing of New Products* (Englewood Cliffs, NJ: Prentice-Hall, 1980), 221; reprinted in Alan Rowe, Richard Mason, Karl Dickel, and Neil Snyder, *Strategic Management: A Methodological Approach* (Reading, MA: Addison-Wesley, 1989), 125.

would obtain and to simulate the effects of changing the design features and prices of the new products on customer preferences.[7]

3 *Hedonic price analysis* Lancaster's characteristics analysis of demand views the demand for a product as comprising customers' demand for the underlying attributes that the product provides.[8] The price at which a product can sell in the market is the aggregate for the prices charged for all the individual attributes of the product. Hedonic price analysis observes price differences for competing products, relates these differences to the different combinations of attributes offered by each product, and calculates the implicit market price for each attribute. For example, it is possible to relate price differences for automatic washing machines to differences in:

- Capacity
- Spin speed
- Energy consumption
- Features (e.g., number of programs, electronic control)
- Reliability (as indicated by consumer organizations' data)

By estimating (using multiple regression analysis) the implicit price for each attribute, it is possible to determine the price-premium that can be charged for additional units of a particular attribute. In Britain, for example, a machine that spins at 1000 rpm sells at about a $200 price-premium to one that spins at 800 rpm.[9] If the cost of adding the faster spin is only $50, it is profitable to differentiate by means of faster spin.

Hedonic price analysis allows us to estimate the price advantage that differentiation will support. In the case of producer goods, it may be possible to calculate even more directly the extent to which differentiation creates value for the customer. In the case of producer goods, creating value for the customer means increasing the customer's profit margin. Where differentiation lowers the buyer's costs, the value of differentiation can be directly calculated. For example, the increase in value to the buyer of a copier that collates and staples is equivalent to the savings in labor costs from undertaking their activities by separate means.

The role of social and psychological factors

The problem with analyzing product differentiation in terms of measurable performance attributes is that it does not delve very far into the underlying motivations for buying decisions. Very few goods or services are acquired to satisfy basic needs for survival: most buying reflects social goals and values in terms of the desire to find community with others, to establish one's own identity, and to make sense of what is happening in the world. Some purchases serve as information: they signal self-image, rank, and values. Some mark social events and bond social relationships – the giving of presents at birthdays and weddings for instance. Others – such as houses and insurance policies – confer security. The symbolic role of personal possessions is deep-seated, powerful, and extends back to the earliest human societies.

Social and psychological influences are not restricted to consumer goods: purchases of producer goods are seldom based exclusively upon objective performance criteria. A company's choice of suppliers may reflect a company's need for identity and security and also the social and organizational aspirations of individual purchasing managers.

To understand customer demand and identify potential profitable avenues to differentiation therefore requires that we analyze not only the product and its characteristics but also the customer and his or her characteristics. If purchase decisions are driven by the need to identify with others, to establish individuality, and to proclaim aspirations, it is vital to look behind the product and investigate the lifestyle, personality, and social grouping of the customer. Such analysis can be both systematic and quantitative in terms of establishing demographic (age, sex, race, location), socioeconomic (income, education), and psychographic (lifestyle, personality type) factors that correlate to patterns of buying behavior.

But, despite the statistical validity of formal market research techniques, the key to effective differentiation is to develop *understanding* of what customers want and how they behave. The answer, claims Tom Peters, is very simple: businesspeople need to *listen to their customers*. "Good listeners," says Peters, "get out from behind their desks to where the customers are. . . . Further, good listeners construct settings so as to maximize 'naive' listening, the undistorted sort. . . . Finally, good listeners provide quick feedback and act on what they hear."[10] It is important, however, that "naive listening" not be confused with naive understanding of customer needs. To really understand customer needs and preferences, listening is insufficient. Companies must observe and analyze customers' use of the product. We shall return to this issue when we examine the value chain in relation to differentiation analysis.

The most effective approaches to increasing customer responsiveness have been increasing interaction between customers and employees. Initiatives have included: customer involvement in new product development teams, periodic secondments of employees to sales and customer service departments, giving customers direct access to operations staff as part of customer support services, and involving employees in on-site visits to customers.

Figure 8.2 summarizes the above discussion in the form of some basic questions for exploring the potential for differentiation on the demand side of the market.

Broad-based versus focused differentiation

Differentiation, we have observed, may be consistent with a broad market appeal or focusing upon a specific market segment. The choice of market scope has important implications for the orientation of demand analysis. A firm that wishes to establish a broad-based position of differentiation advantage in an industry is primarily concerned with the *general* features of market demand: What general needs are being satisfied by the product? what do customers have in common in terms of their motivations and choice criteria? The firm needs to focus not

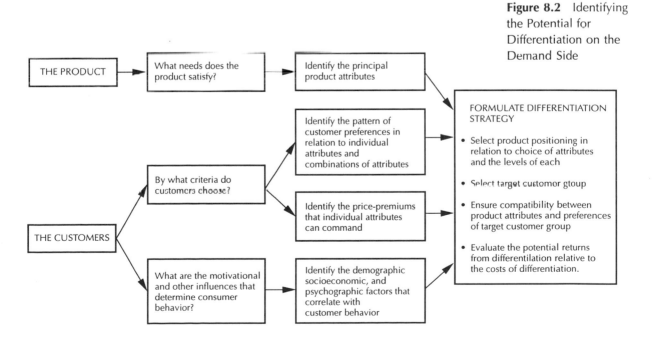

Figure 8.2 Identifying the Potential for Differentiation on the Demand Side

on the factors that distinguish customer groups and that segment their demand but on the requirements and the aspirations that they have in common. To establish a position of uniqueness while still appealing to a broad market is no easy task:

- McDonald's has extended its appeal across age groups, social groups, and national boundaries by emphasizing a few qualities with universal appeal: speed, consistency, value, hygiene, and family lifestyles;
- the British retailer Marks & Spencer has been similarly successful in establishing a reputation for product quality and fair dealing that extends across the traditional class divisions that segment British consumer markets;
- Honda and Toyota have positioned themselves within the U.S. market to achieve a broad-based market appeal in contrast to the more targeted positioning of most American and European brands within age groups and socioeconomic segments.

Establishing a differentiated niche position in a market necessitates more specific analysis: What are the differences between customers' needs and between the customer groups? what groups of customers are not being adequately served by the existing range of offerings? The emphasis is on the factors that distinguish one group from another and one set of needs from another. In principle, a focused approach to differentiation should displace a broad-based approach. If customers are presented with a wide range of highly targeted product offerings they should be able to find a targeted product that meets their preferences more closely than a product that is designed for the market as a whole. Certainly the strategy of offering a wide product range to appeal to a number of distinct product segments was successful for General Motors in displacing Ford as market leader during the 1920s and 1930s.

At the same time, segment-focused approaches to differentiation run particular risks. Apart from the higher costs that are incurred in supplying a narrow rather than a broad market, there are dangers that market segments can change over time or that a firm adopted an inappropriate segmentation in the first place. To the extent that a segmented approach is based upon existing differences in customers and their demand, it is inherently conservative. A problem with General Motors's segmented approach to the U.S. car market was that many consumers within the segments that GM had targeted no longer wanted to be identified with the segment that GM had defined for them. As a result, Buick, Oldsmobile, and Chevrolet have been engaged in strenuous efforts to redefine their brand images.

The danger with all analysis is that, instead of being a guide to understanding, it distorts through oversimplification. Nowhere is this more evident than in the application of predetermined market segmentation and customer classification to the analysis of customer demand. By focusing upon demographic and lifestyle differences between groups of customers, upon different purchase occasions and patterns of use, and the particular requirements of different distribution channels, it is possible to overlook customers' real needs and preferences. GM's concern over the positioning of each of its model ranges in relation to market segments first identified by Alfred Sloan Jr. encouraged it to overlook customers' increasing concern with economy, safety, and reliability. If differentiation is really about creating "total customer responsiveness," then analysis should bring us closer to customers and not obscure them.

Analyzing Differentiation: The Supply Side

The drivers of uniqueness

While demand analysis identifies the customers' demands for differentiation and their willingness to pay for it, creating a differentiation advantage is crucially dependent upon a firm's ability to supply differentiation and to do so at a cost that does not exceed the price-premium that it creates. Identification of the firm's potential to supply differentiation necessitates an examination of the activities that the firm performs and the resources that the firm has access to. Differentiation, I have noted, is concerned with the provision of *uniqueness*. A firm's opportunities for creating uniqueness in its offerings to customers are not located within a particular function or activity but can arise in virtually everything that the firm does. Porter identifies a number of *drivers of uniqueness* over which the firm exercises control:

- product features and the performance that the product offers;
- the services that the firm provides (e.g., credit, delivery, repair);
- the intensity of particular marketing activities (e.g., rate of advertising spending);
- content of activities (e.g., type of pre- and postsales services provided);
- the technology employed in performing an activity (e.g., the precision with which products are manufactured, computerization of order processing, and so on);
- the quality of purchased inputs;
- procedures governing the conduct of particular activities (e.g., frequency of quality control inspections, service procedures, frequency of sales visits to a customer);
- the skill and experience of employees in activities;
- the control procedures used in different activities;
- location (e.g., with retail stores);
- the degree of vertical integration (which influences a firm's ability to control inputs and intermediate processes).[11]

Differentiation of hardware and software

In analyzing a firm's potential for creating uniqueness in the market, it is useful to distinguish between differentiation of products and differentiation of services. Shiv Mathur observes that most transactions do not involve a single product or a single service but are a combination of products and services.[12] In analyzing the potential for differentiation, Mathur distinguishes between differentiation of the product ("hardware") and differentiation of ancillary services ("software"). On this basis, four transactions categories can be identified (figure 8.3).

The firm's choice of transactions categories is fundamental to its strategy within a market. Because economies of scale are usually more important in the production of goods than of services, some industries have tended to mass-produce relatively undifferentiated hardware and to differentiate through complementary services. For example, as gasoline has become a standardized product, oil companies and retailers have sought to differentiate by service, by the attractiveness of their filling stations, and by retailing a wider range of consumer products.

The predominant transactions type in a market is also influenced by the stage of maturity of the product and its industry. Mathur identifies a *transactions cycle* over which the extent and basis of differentiation shift (figure 8.4). Initially, the lack of customer knowledge and market infrastructure obliges producers to provide "systems" comprising both hardware and software. Market expansion and industry development

Figure 8.3 The Transactions Matrix

		SOFTWARE	
		Differentiated	Undifferentiated
HARDWARE	Differentiated	SYSTEM	PRODUCT
	Undifferentiated	SERVICE	COMMODITY

Source: Shiv Mathur, "Competitive Industrial Marketing Strategies," *Long Range Planning* 17, no. 4 (1984).

Figure 8.4 The Transactions Cycle

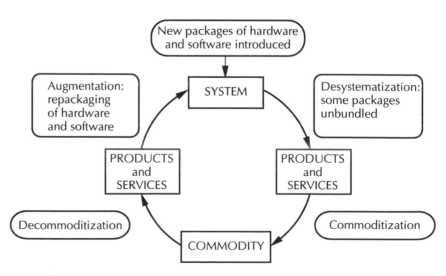

Source: Shiv Mathur, "Competitive Industrial Marketing Strategies," *Long Range Planning* 17, no. 4 (1984).

permits "desystematization" through the unbundling of packages, which may culminate in the product emerging as an undifferentiated "commodity." However, growing sophistication of customer preferences and the quest by producers for new sources of differentiation advantage encourages "augmentation" through the repackaging of hardware and software into new systems.

The personal computer has followed such a cycle. The early entrants – Apple, Commodore, Tandy, and later IBM – supplied systems comprising hardware (computers, monitors, printers) and software (computer programs, training, presales and postsales service). Subsequent entrants included specialist hardware companies and specialist software companies. By the late 1980s, standardization around Intel/MS-DOS technology caused increasing commoditization. However, such trends encouraged the quest for renewed repackaging of hardware and software into systems: desktop publishing systems, local area networks, and engineering workstations customized to particular applications.

Product integrity

For any firm, the range of differentiation opportunities is wide, and the primary issue is likely to be the determination of which forms of differentiation are likely to be most successful in distinguishing the firm in the market and which are most valued by customers. In establishing a coherent and effective position of differentiation in a market, a firm needs to assemble a complementary package of differentiation measures. If Beck's beer wishes to differentiate itself on the basis of the quality of its ingredients, then it must adopt production methods that are consistent with quality ingredients and packaging, advertising, and a distribution system that are appropriate to a quality product at a premium price.

Consistency in a firm's differentiation is referred to as *product integrity*. Clark and Fujimoto refer to product integrity as the extent to which the product achieves:

total balance of numerous product characteristics including basic functions, aesthetics, semantics, reliability, and economy. . . . Product integrity has both internal and external dimensions. Internal integrity refers to consistency between the function and structure of the product – e.g., the parts fit well, components match and work well together, layout achieves maximum space efficiency. External integrity is a measure of how well a product's function, structure and semantics fit the customers objectives, values, production system, lifestyle, use pattern, and self-identity.[13]

As Clark and Fujimoto explore in their book, simultaneously achieving high levels of internal and external integrity is the most complex organizational challenge facing the world's automobile manufacturers because it involves collaboration across all functions of the firm as well as intimate contact with customers. The organizational changes among

U.S. and European companies during the late 1980s and the move toward strengthening the role of product managers are attempts to imitate the success of Nissan, Toyota, and Honda in achieving high levels of internal/external integration.[14]

Achieving high levels of internal and external product integrity is critical to all companies seeking to establish competitive advantage on the basis of differentiation. It is especially important to those firms seeking to establish *image differentiation* where the credibility of the image depends critically upon the consistency of the image presented. Manufacturers of cosmetics and perfumes are masters in the creation of images involving a high level of integrity between all aspects of the product and its manufacturer. Exhibit 8.2 outlines a highly successful

---

Exhibit 8.2 Body Shop: An Innovatory Approach to Differentiation

While Anita Roddick scorns businessmen and management principles, the success of Body Shop reveals an insightful and sophisticated approach to differentiation strategy. In some respects, Body Shop's strategy is consistent with other manufacturers of cosmetics and toiletries: success has always been associated with the establishment of a strong product image that requires consistency between the product, the packaging, the advertising and promotion, the retail environment, and the image of the company.

To this extent, Body Shop is not novel: its products are physically differentiated and this differentiation is carried through to the packaging and to the retail environment in which the products are sold. Indeed, Body Shop goes one step further than most competitors: it only sells its products within its own franchised stores. However, in the nature of its image, Body Shop has contradicted the industry's conventions concerning differentiation advantage. The companies have sought to differentiate their products on the basis of beauty, youth, and sexual attractiveness. Body Shop rejects this "magic": "My products can only cleanse, moisten, and protect."

Rather, Body Shop appeals to traditional notions of grooming, maintaining, and enhancing faces and bodies through the use of natural ingredients, many of them associated with the traditions of ethnic peoples throughout the world. This differentiation of the product is supported by a strong commitment to research and discovery that identifies and examines the use and the potential of a whole range of natural products from oatmeal to obscure vegetable oils.

Emphasis on the natural properties of the products is encouraged by a packaging that emphasizes simplicity, economy, and information. A similar feeling is communicated by Body Shop's retail outlets, which are uniform, open, nonostentatious, and designed to encourage customers to look, read, sample, and interact with sales personnel. Despite the encouragement that Body Shop gives to individuality and free expression, the retail stores are uniform in their decor and displays and maintain common approaches to customer service.

However, unlike all other cosmetic companies, Body Shop's image is transmitted by its values rather than by advertising and promotion. While most cosmetic companies rely heavily on advertising to identify their products with beauty, stylishness, and the fount of youth, Body Shop's image is communicated through its values. In virtually all its words and actions, Body Shop communicates its commitment to environmental and social responsibility. The primary medium of this communication is Body Shop's employees and franchisees. Body Shop exerts special care in selecting its franchisees, rejecting those with prior business experience, and seeking enthusiasm and commitment to Body Shop ideals. The result is that Body Shop is not simply supplying skin creams and shampoo, it is creating an identity with its customers built around the concepts of naturalness, global environmental responsibility, economic support for indigenous people through trade, and a rejection of traditional business principles built upon exploitation of the weak and disregard for the environment.

Source: Body Shop International, Harvard Business School, Case 9-392-032, Boston, 1991.

and unorthodox approach to achieving such differentiation within this market.

Signaling and reputation

For differentiation to be effective it is essential that it is communicated to the customer. But customers are not always well informed about the qualities and characteristics of the goods they purchase. The economics literature distinguishes between *search goods* – goods whose qualities and characteristics can be ascertained by inspection – and *experience goods* – goods whose qualities and characteristics are only known after consumption. These latter class of goods include medical services, baldness treatments, frozen TV dinners, and wine. Even with experience goods, that experience may be slow in revealing itself: it is only over time that we assess the reliability of a car or the competence of our dentist.

The situation is a classic "*prisoners' dilemma.*" The producer has a choice of offering a high- or low-quality product. The customer can pay either a high or low price. If quality cannot be detected, then equilibrium is established, with the customer offering a low price for a low-quality product, even though both would be better off with a high-quality product sold at a high price (see figure 8.5).

The resolution of this dilemma is for producers to find some credible means of signaling quality to the customer. The most effective signals are those that change the payoffs in the prisoners' dilemma. Thus, an extended warranty is effective because such a warranty would be more expensive for a low-quality than a high-quality producer. Brand names

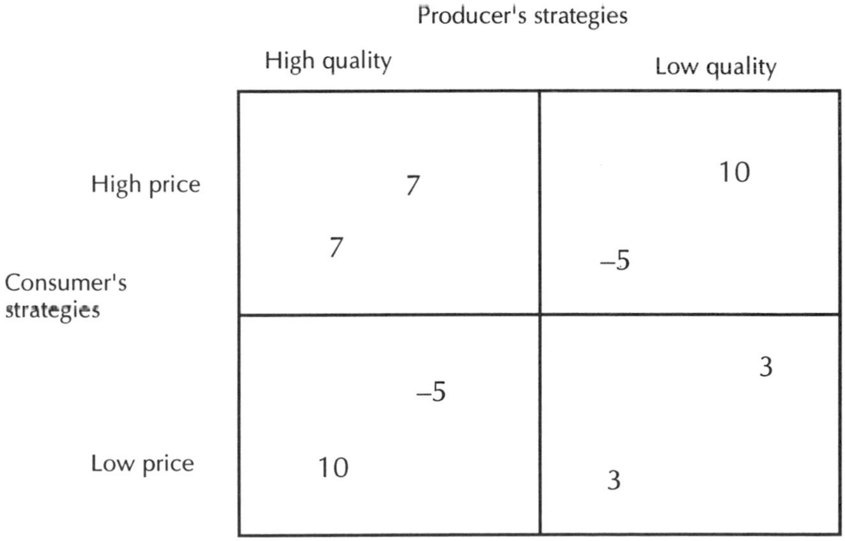

Figure 8.5 The Quality of an Experience Good: A "Prisoners' Dilemma"

In each quadrant, the benefit to the producer is shown in the top right corner, and the benefit to the consumer in the bottom left corner.

and the advertising that supports them are signals of quality and consistency: a brand is valuable as an advertisement for past customer satisfaction and because it is a valuable asset as a disincentive for providing poor quality in the future. Other signals of quality include packaging, money-back guarantees, the retail environment in which the product is sold, and the supplier's sponsorship of sports and cultural events.

The need for signaling variables to complement performance variables in differentiation depends upon the ease with which performance can be assessed by the potential buyer. A perfume can be sampled prior to purchase and its smell assessed, but it is uncertain if perfume has the ability to augment the identity of the wearer and impact upon social relationships. Hence, the key role that the brand name, the manufacturer's name, packaging, advertising, and lavish promotional events play in establishing an identity for the perfume in terms of the implied personality, lifestyle, and aspirations of the consumer.

Signaling and reputation are especially important for products and services where quality is difficult to ascertain even after purchase. In financial services, the customer cannot easily assess the honesty, financial security, or competence of a broker, fund manager, or insurance company. Hence, the emphasis that financial service companies accord to symbols of security, stability, and competence: large, well-located head offices; conservative and tasteful office decor; smartly dressed, well-groomed employees; historical associations; and perceptions of size.

Strategies for reputation building have been the subject of rigorous theoretical analysis.[15] Some of the propositions arising from this research include:

- quality signaling is primarily important for products whose quality can only be ascertained after purchase ("experience goods");
- expenditure on advertising is an effective means of signaling superior quality because suppliers of low-quality products will not expect repeat buying, hence it will not be profitable for them to spend money on advertising;
- a combination of premium-pricing and advertising is likely to be superior at signaling quality than either price or advertising alone;
- the higher are the sunk costs required for entry into a market and the greater the total investment of the firm, the greater are the incentives for the firm not to cheat customers by providing low quality at high cost.

The costs of differentiation

Differentiation adds cost. The direct costs of differentiation include elements such as the costs of higher-quality inputs, the costs of larger inventories in order to guarantee speedy filling of orders, and the costs of heavy advertising to sustain brand strength. In addition, there are indirect costs of differentiation that arise through the interaction of differentiation variables with cost variables. To the extent that differentiation narrows the product-market scope of a firm, it also limits the potential for exploiting scale economies. To the extent that differentiation requires product innovation and the introduction of new models, it hampers the exploitation of experience curve economies.

However, not all aspects of differentiation add significant costs. One of the central themes of TQM is that the elimination of product defects results in *cost savings*. The argument that quality incurs costs that are trivial in relation to its market benefits has received widespread empirical support. The PIMS program has identified quality and market share as the two most important determinants of a business unit's profitability. Figure 8.6 shows that quality adds a significant premium to price while having little or no effect on cost. As a result, quality is strongly associated with superior profitability.

The costs of differentiation can also be offset by any tendencies for differentiation to expand the market share of a firm and hence permit exploitation of scale economies. The tendency for many firms to increase their advertising budgets during recessions reflects their desire to spread fixed costs over an expanded sales base. In some instances, a differentiation strategy can improve a firm's relative cost position by shifting the basis of competition in an industry. In chapter 7, I noted how Honda's annual model changes and Apple's decision to support its new Macintosh computer with heavy TV advertising had the effect of putting smaller companies under substantial cost pressure.

One means of reconciling differentiation with cost efficiency is to *postpone differentiation* to later stages of the firm's value chain. Economics of scale and the cost advantages of standardization are frequently

Figure 8.6 The Impact of Relative Quality and Relative Market Share on Price, Cost, and Profitability

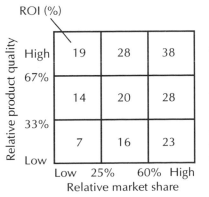

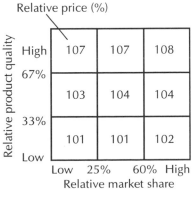

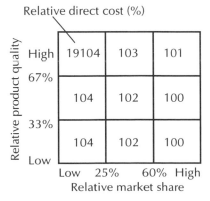

Source: Robert Luchs, "Successful Businesses Compete on Quality Not Cost," *Long Range Planning* 19 (1986): 12–24.

greatest in the manufacture of basic components. By utilizing a modular design with common components, economies of large-scale production can be achieved even if considerable product variety is offered to appeal to a broad diversity of customer requirements. The auto companies have been leaders in this process. Toyota's 1994 cost-cutting exercise, which aims to reduce expenses by $1.5 billion, involves reducing the number of basic platforms used across the Toyota model range and standardizing components: for example, the Corona and Carina models share front and rear door panels and windshield glass and use the same dashboard as the Celica.[16] The introduction of "world cars" by GM and Ford has permitted substantial cost savings in R&D, design, testing, tooling, and component production. At the same time, the companies offer distinct national features and a wide range of customer choices over color, accessories, and trim.

The effect of new manufacturing technology is causing traditional trade-offs between efficiency and variety to break down. The introduction of computer-aided manufacture (CAM), just-in-time (JIT) scheduling, and computer-integrated manufacturing (CIM) have made the objective of an "economic order quantity of one" realistic while simultaneously cutting unit costs. In the manufacture of household appliances, consumer electronic products, and a variety of other producer and consumer products, a number of different models are manufactured on the same assembly line with close to zero changeover time. At Kawasaki Motors's motorcycle plant at Lincoln, Nebraska, production was switched to mixed-model production on January 1, 1983. Previously, manufacture had been in lots of at least 200 of each model. Yet, mainly through reorganizing the production process, adopting JIT scheduling, and adapting some machinery, the plant reduced changeover time in frame production from half a day to less than ten minutes.[17]

Bringing it all Together: The Value Chain in Differentiation Analysis

There is little point in identifying the attributes that customers value most if the firm is incapable of supplying those attributes. Similarly, there is little purpose in identifying a firm's unique abilities to supply certain elements of uniqueness if these attributes are not valued by customers. The key to successful differentiation is in matching the firm's capacity for creating differentiation with customers' potential demand for it. For this purpose, the value chain provides a particularly useful framework. There are four principal steps in the analysis:

> 1   *Construct a value chain for the firm and the customer* on the basis of the importance of different activities, the separateness of different activities, and at later stages in the value chain as well. If the firm

supplies different types of customer (for example, if a steel company supplies steel strip to automobile manufacturers and domestic appliance manufacturers) draw separate value chains for each of the main categories of customer.

2 *Identify the drivers of uniqueness in each activity* Assess the firm's potential for differentiating its product by examining each activity in the firm's value chain and identifying the variables and actions through which the firm can achieve uniqueness in relation to competitors' offerings. Figure 8.7 identifies sources of differentiation within Porter's generic value chain.

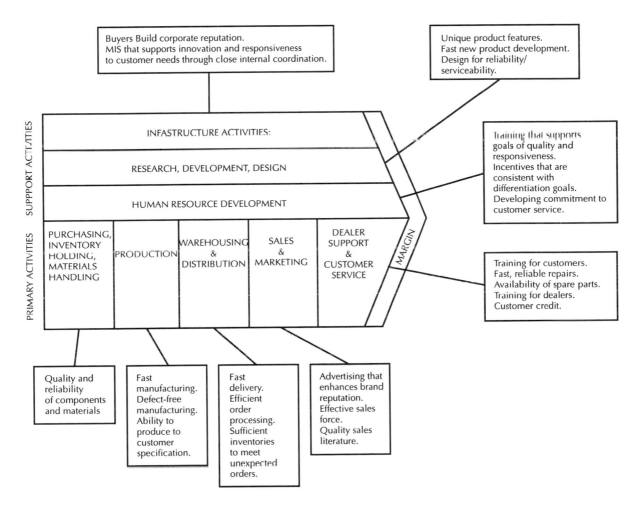

Source: Michael E. Porter, *Competitive Strategy* (New York: Free Press, 1980), 122.

Figure 8.7 Identifying the Potential for Differentiation in the Supply Side: Sources of Differentiation in Porter's Generic Value Chain

3 *Select the most promising differentiation variables for the firm*
Among the numerous drivers of uniqueness that we can identify within
the firm, which should be selected as the primary basis for the firm's
differentiation strategy? On the supply side, there are three important
considerations:

- first, we must *establish where the firm has greater potential for
  differentiating or can differentiate at lower cost than rivals.* Our
  concern is with *competitive advantage*, hence differentiation must
  be based upon the firm's internal strengths in terms of resources
  and skills;
- second, in order to determine which activities to prioritize as the
  sources of differentiation, we need to *identify linkages between
  activities.* For example, product reliability is likely to be the outcome of several linked activities: monitoring of purchases of inputs
  from suppliers, the skill and motivation of production workers,
  and the stringency of quality control and product testing. If a
  particular level of product reliability is sought, the firm must determine the least-cost means of achieving that reliability and the
  coordination between activities that is required;
- third, we need to consider the ease with which different types of
  uniqueness can be sustained. The more differentiation is based
  upon resources that are specific to the firm or skills that involve
  the complex coordination of a large number of individuals, then
  the more difficult it will be for a competitor to imitate the particular
  source of differentiation. Thus, offering business-class passengers
  wider seats and more leg room is an easily imitated source of
  differentiation. Achieving high levels of punctuality represents a
  more sustainable source of differentiation.

4 *Locate linkages between the value chain of the firm and that of the
buyer* The objective of differentiation is to yield a price-premium
for the firm. This requires that the firm's differentiation must create
value for the customer. Creating value for the customer involves one
of two activities: either the firm *lowers the costs* of the customer or
the firm *assists product differentiation* by the customer. For example,
Hotpoint lowers retailers' costs by offering a speedy delivery service
that enables retailers to hold lower stocks while enhancing retailers'
differentiation by appointing them as exclusive dealers within particular localities. To identify the means by which a firm can create value
for its customers, it must locate the linkages between differentiation
of its own activities and cost reduction and differentiation within the
customer's activities.

Locating these linkages is also useful for evaluating the potential
profitability of differentiation. The value that differentiation creates
for the customer represents the maximum price-premium that the
customer will pay. If the provision of JIT delivery by a component
supplier costs an additional $1,000 a month but saves an automobile
company $6,000 a month in reduced inventory, warehousing and
handling costs, then it should be possible for the component manufacturer to obtain a price-premium that easily exceeds the costs of the
differentiation.

As an example of the application of the value chain to the analysis of differentiation advantage, exhibit 8.3 considers the differentiation opportunities available to a manufacturer of metal containers.

Value chain analysis for consumer goods

Value chain analysis of the type outlined above is most readily applicable to producer goods where the customer is also a company with an easily definable value chain and where linkages between the supplier's and the customer's value chains are readily apparent. However, the same analysis can be applied to consumer goods with very little modification. Few consumer goods are consumed directly; in most cases, consumers are involved in a chain of activities before the total consumption of the product.

This is particularly evident for consumer durables. A washing machine is consumed over several years in the process of doing home laundry. The process begins with search activity prior to purchase. In the home laundry process, the machine is used together with water, detergent, and electricity to wash clothes, which are later dried and, possibly, ironed. Continued use of the washing machine requires service and repair. We have a complex value chain for the customer with, potentially, many linkages between the value chains of manufacturer, retailer, and consumer.

Few nondurables are consumed directly without the consumer engaging in prior productive activity. A frozen TV dinner must be purchased,

---

Exhibit 8.3 A Value Chain Analysis of Differentiation Opportunities for Manufacturer of Metal Containers

The metal container industry is a highly competitive, mature industry. Cans lack much potential for differentiation, and buyers (especially beverage and food canning companies) are very powerful. Clearly, cost efficiency is essential, but are there also opportunities for superior profitability through differentiation? A value chain analysis can help a manufacturer identify profitable opportunities for differentiation.

STAGE 1. Construct value chain for firm and customers. The principal activities of the can manufacturer and its customers are shown in the diagram.

STAGE 2. Identify drivers of uniqueness. For each can-making activity, identify differentiation variables. Examples are shown on the diagram.

STAGE 3. Select key variables. Identify the internal strengths of the firm. If the firm has strong technical capabilities, it may differentiate by meeting demanding design specifications and offering a high level of technical support to customers.

STAGE 4. Identify linkages. To determine differentiation likely to create value for the customer, linkages are made between the firm's potential for differentiation and the potential for reducing cost or adding differentiation in any of the customers activities. Five examples are shown in diagram:

1. designing distinctive can for customers may assist their own marketing activities.

2. consistent quality of can lowers customers' canning costs by avoiding breakdowns and holdups on their canning lines.

3. by maintaining high stocks and offering speedy delivery, customers can economize on their own stockholding (they may even be able to move to a just-in-time system of can supply).

4. efficient order processing can reduce customers' ordering costs.

5. capable and fast technical support can reduce the costs of breakdowns on canning lines.

Exhibit 8.3   continued

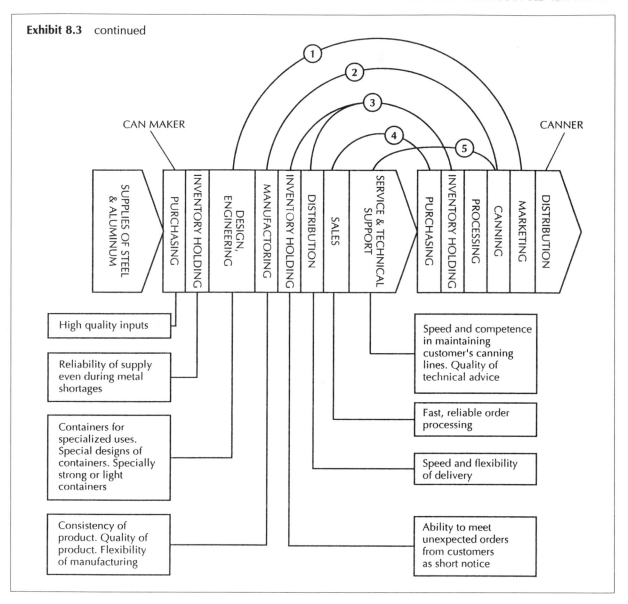

taken home, removed from the package, and heated before consumption. After eating, the consumer must clean any crockery, cutlery, or other utensils employed. Again, we have a chain of activities where the manufacturer has opportunities to create value for the consumer by eliminating or facilitating any of these activities. Takahiro Fujimoto has emphasized the need for companies to integrate their design process with the consumption process of the product.[18] For example, as the differentiation advantages of Japanese automobile companies in terms of reliability and fuel efficiency are increasingly replicated by U.S. and European producers, these companies are seeking new sources of differentiation. Toyota has undertaken detailed analysis of the wide range of activities that consumers engage in when using a car and the features associated with consumer satisfaction from each activity. The research has revealed such characteristics as the sound that car doors make when they are closed and the tone of the engine noise when the car is being driven are important to customers in their perceptions of quality.

Summary and Conclusion

The attraction of differentiation over low cost as a basis for competitive advantage is, first, that it is less vulnerable to being overturned by turbulence in the external environment, and, second, that it is more difficult to replicate.

The potential for differentiation is nearly limitless for any business: it may involve physical differentiation of the product, it may be through the services that accompany a product, or it may be tangible or intangible. The essence of differentiation advantage is to increase the perceived value of the offering to the customer either more effectively or at lower cost than do competitors. This requires that the firm match the requirements and preferences of customers with its own capacity for creating uniqueness.

The value chain provides a useful framework for analyzing differentiation advantage. By analyzing how value is created for customers and by systematically appraising the scope of each of the firm's activities for achieving differentiation, the value chain permits a matching of demand-side and supply-side sources of differentiation.

Successful differentiation requires a combination of astute analysis and creative imagination. The two are not antithetical. A systematic framework for the analysis of differentiation can act as a stimulus to creative ideas.

Notes

1 Michael E. Porter, *Competitive Advantage* (New York: Free Press, 1985), 120.
2 Tom Peters, *Thriving on Chaos* (New York: Knopf, 1987), 56.
3 *Ibid*, 185.
4 These distinctions are developed in more detail by Peter R. Dickson and James L. Ginter, "Market Segmentation, Product Differentiation and Marketing Strategy," *Journal of Marketing* 51 (April 1987): 1–10.
5 See Susan Schiffman et al., *Introduction to Multidimensional Scaling: Theory, Methods, and Applications* (Cambridge, MA: Academic Press, 1981).
6 See P. Cattin and D. R. Wittink, "Commercial Use of Conjoint Analysis: A Survey," *Journal of Marketing* (summer 1982): 44–53.
7 Alan Rowe, Richard Mason, Karl Dickel, and Neil Snyder, *Strategic*

Management: A Methodological Approach, 3d ed. (Reading, MA: Addison-Wesley, 1989), 127–8.

8   Kelvin Lancaster, *Consumer Demand: A New Approach* (New York: Columbia University Press, 1971).

9   Phedon Nicolaides and Charles Baden Fuller, *Price Discrimination and Product Differentiation in the European Domestic Appliance Market* (London: Center for Business Strategy, London Business School, 1987).

10 Tom Peters, *Thriving on Chaos* (New York: Knopf, 1987), 149.

11 Michael E. Porter, *Competitive Advantage* (New York: Free Press, 1985), 124–5.

12 Shiv Mathur, "Competitive Industrial Marketing Strategies," *Long Range Planning*, 17, no. 4: 102–9.

13 Kim Clark and Takahiro Fujimoto, *Product Development Performance* (Boston: Harvard Business School Press, 1991), 29–30.

14 Clark and Fujimoto, *Product Development Performance,* 247–85.

15 For a survey, see Keith Weigelt and Colin F. Camerer, "Reputation and Corporate Strategy: A Review of Recent Theory and Applications," *Strategic Management Journal* 9 (1988): 443–54.

16 "Toyota Retooled," *Business Week*, April 4, 1994, 54–7.

17 Richard J. Schonberger, *World Class Manufacturing Casebook: Implementing JIT and TQC* (New York: Free Press, 1987), 120–3.

18 Takahiro Fujimoto, "Managing Effective Development Projects," presentation to Strategic Management Society Conference, San Francisco, October 1989.

NINE

Competitive Advantage and Industry Evolution

No company ever stops changing. . . . Each new generation must meet changes
– in the automotive market, in the general administration of the enterprise, and
in the involvement of the corporation in a changing world. The work of creating
goes on.

> – Alfred P. Sloan Jr., president of General Motors 1923-37,
> chairman 1937-56, in *My Years with General Motors*

Outline

Introduction and Objectives

Chapter 3 followed a largely *static* approach to industry analysis. We
looked at how industry structure influences the intensity of competition,
which at the same time determines the level of profitability. The analysis
of competitive advantage in chapter 6 recognized that competition is a
dynamic process in which industry structures are transformed as a result
of the quest for competitive advantage and its subsequent undermining.
Thus, there exists a two-way relationship between industry structure
and competition: industry structure determines the intensity of competition; at the same time, competition causes the transformation of industry

structure. The result is that industries are in a constant stage of evolution. New competitors and new strategies emerge continuously, and these strategies transform products, processes, distribution channels, and marketing methods. Firms that adjust efficiently to changing circumstances prosper and grow; those that are inefficient or select inappropriate strategies are eliminated. The central thesis of this chapter is that while every industry develops differently and displays unique characteristics, within this diversity it is possible to detect similar patterns that are the result of common driving forces. In this chapter, we identify patterns of industry evolution, the forces that drive them, and explore the implications for competitive advantage.

The organizing framework for this chapter is the *industry life cycle*. The life cycle model is a simplified characterization of the principal stages in an industry's development. Each stage of an industry's development is associated with particular structural features that influence the nature of competition and, most important, determine key success factors. By examining these stages of development, we can identify the types of strategies that are likely to be successful at each stage and anticipate the strategic adaptations that the firm must make in adjusting to its evolving environment.

Thus, the industry life cycle provides us with a basis for classifying industries into distinct categories according to their stage of development. The value of such classification is controversial. Can it make any sense to classify aluminum smelting, insurance, and bakeries as "mature industries" and expect them to display any strategic similarities? The answer is yes. Despite the huge differences in the characteristics of the products and processes, these industries share relatively stable industry structures, fairly undifferentiated products, an emphasis on cost efficiency and price competition, and fairly low rates of technological change.

The process of classification is valuable for coming to grips with the key elements that determine the strategic character of an industry. The process of, first, choosing a classification scheme and, second, assigning industries to different categories forces us to consider what is important about an industry and is useful in (a) highlighting the ways in which industries are similar to one another and (b) indicating the ways in which they are different. Grouping industries on the basis of strategic similarities can assist the transfer of management ideas from one industry to another. Philip Morris has experienced considerable success in transferring business strategies and marketing techniques from its cigarette business to brewing, soft drinks, and the food industry. Hanson perceives strategic similarities between its different businesses – cement, bricks, coal, chemicals, and tobacco – in terms of their maturity, their technological stability, and their comparative lack of international competition – factors that make these businesses amenable to similar management approaches.

By the time you have completed this chapter, you will be able to:

- appreciate the nature and the uses of the industry life cycle and the factors that drive the process of industry evolution;
- recognize the key success factors associated with industries at different stages of their life cycle;
- understand the implications of the industry life cycle for strategy implementation in terms of the types of organizational structures and management systems appropriate to different stages of the cycle.

The Life Cycle Model

One of the best-known and most enduring marketing concepts is the *product life cycle*.[1] Products are born, their sales grow, they reach maturity, they go into decline, and they ultimately die. If products have life cycles, so too do the industries that produce them. The principal basis used in this book for classifying industries is their maturity. The key assumption is that industries follow a life cycle that comprises a number of evolutionary characteristics that are common to different industries. While the industry life cycle is the supply-side equivalent of the product life cycle, to the extent that an industry produces a range and a sequence of products the industry life cycle is likely to be of longer duration than that of a single product. While digital audio cassette players may have a life cycle of a decade, the life cycle of the consumer electronics industry is much longer.

The life cycle is conventionally divided into four phases: introduction, growth, maturity, and decline. Before we examine the features of each of these stages, it is important to understand the forces that are driving industry evolution. There are two factors that can be identified as fundamental to driving industry evolution: demand growth and the production and diffusion of knowledge.

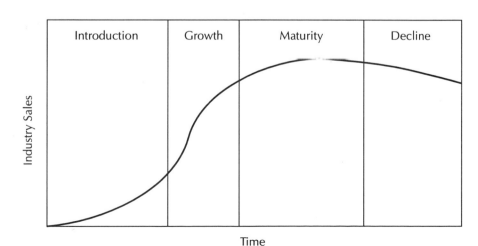

Figure 9.1 The Growth Curve and Stages of the Industry Life Cycle

Demand growth

The life cycle and the stages within it are defined by changes in an industry's growth rate over time. The characteristic profile is that of an S-shaped growth curve. At the outset, the industry's products are little known and there are a few pioneering firms and customers. The novelty of the technology and lack of economies of scale or experience in manufacture means that costs and prices are high. Product quality tends to be low because products have not benefited from the multitude of incremental innovations and modifications that accompany the passage of time and widespread use. Market penetration is initially slow. The customers for new products tend to be high income and innovation oriented. They also tend to be risk-averse because the danger of buying early is not just that one pays a high price but that one buys into a technology that is displaced. The Japanese consumers who purchased high-definition TVs during the early 1990s now face the prospect of their TVs' becoming obsolescent once Japan moves to the emerging digital standard.

As product technology becomes more standardized and product prices begin to fall, so market penetration accelerates. This is the *growth phase* during which ownership spreads from higher-income customers to the mass market. As market saturation is approached growth of demand slows as new demand gives way to replacement demand. Once saturation is reached, demand is wholly for replacement, either direct replacement (customers replacing old products with new products) or indirect replacement (new customers replacing old customers). Finally, as the industry becomes challenged by new industries that produce technologically superior substitute products, the industry enters its *decline stage*.

Creation and diffusion of knowledge

The second critical factor driving the industry life cycle is the creation and diffusion of knowledge. New knowledge in the form of product innovation is responsible for an industry coming into being, and the dual processes of knowledge creation and knowledge diffusion continue to be a major driving force of competition.

In the introduction stage, product technology advances rapidly. There is no dominant product technology, and rival technologies compete for attention. Competition is primarily between alternative technologies and design configurations. The competitive process involves the selection of the more successful from the less successful approaches, and, typically, a dominant technology and design configuration emerges. This process of elimination therefore involves *standardization*. The transition from technological heterogeneity to one of increased standardization is associated with the industry's *growth phase*. Increased standardization is associated with lower risk for customers and the ability to adopt large-scale manufacturing methods in order to achieve cost reduction. Hence, once the growth phase is underway, the focus of technological development shifts from product innovation toward process innovation. Figure 9.2 shows the typical pattern.

This pattern is evident in the development of the automobile industry. Between 1890 and 1920, cars featured a wide diversity of engine configurations and transmission designs, not to mention body designs and steering and braking systems. Not until the 1920s did a dominant design emerge involving a closed body; a front-mounted, water-cooled engine; and a transmission system based upon a gearbox, wet clutch, and rear-wheel drive. During the next half century, "outliers" in terms of nonconventional technologies and designs were gradually eliminated. Volkswagen's Beetle was the last mass-produced, rear-mounted, air-cooled engine; Citroen abandoned its pneumatic suspension system; and the unusual "Variomatic" automatic transmission system of the Dutch manufacturer Daf was eliminated at the end of the 1970s. During the 1980s, even distinctive national differences in car design tended to disappear: American cars became smaller; Japanese and Italian cars became bigger. With the tearing down of the Iron Curtain, the last outposts of nonconformity also disappeared: by 1994, East German-made, two-stroke Wartburgs and Trabants were becoming collectors' items. During the 1990s, car parks throughout the world were peopled by confused motorists searching for their cars among the ranks of bewilderingly similar vehicles.

Product innovation in automobiles continued, of course, but shifted from being radical to incremental. Most of the innovations in automobiles during the postwar era have involved the refinement of existing technologies and the application of technologies developed in other sectors (most notably the application of microelectronics and new materials such as plastics and ceramics to cars). Many of the product innovations have in fact involved the adoption of features and components that were developed many years ago. Table 9.1 identifies some of these.

As product innovation has shifted from radical to incremental, so car manufacturers have sought to increase quality and lower costs through

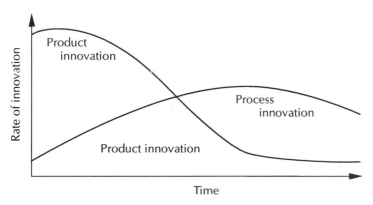

Figure 9.2 Product and Process Innovation over Time

Source: William J. Abernathy and James M. Utterback, "Dynamic Model of Process and Product Development," *Omega* 3, no. 6 (1975).

Table 9.1 From
Option to Standard: The
Diffusion of Innovations
and Features in
Automobiles

FEATURE	INTRODUCTION	GENERAL ADOPTION
Speedometer	1901 by Oldsmobile	Circa 1915
Automatic transmission	First installed in 1904	Introduced by Packard as an option, 1938. Standard on Cadillacs and other luxury cars, early 1950s
Electric headlamps	GM introduces in 1908	Standard equipment by 1916
All-steel body	Adopted by GM, 1912	Becomes standard, early 1920s
All steel, enclosed body	Dodge, 1923	Becomes standard, late 1920s
Radio	Appears as an option, 1923	Standard equipment, 1946
Four-wheel drive	Appears, 1924	Only limited availability by 1994
Hydraulic brakes	Introduced, 1924	Becomes standard, 1939
Shatterproof glass	First used in cars in 1927	Standard features in Fords, 1938
Power steering	Introduced, 1952	Adopted as standard equipment, 1969
Antilock brakes	Introduced, 1972	Standard on GM cars in 1991
Air bags	Introduced by GM in 1974	By 1994 most new cars equipped with air bags

Source: Robert M. Grant, "The World Automobile Industry," Georgetown University, mimeograph, 1994.

process innovation. Henry Ford's assembly line production method was the critical breakthrough, shifting manufacturing from small-volume, craft-based workshops to capital-intensive, mass-manufacturing. Ford's assembly line production was a process innovation that involved not only manufacturing technology but also innovation in organization and management. The second major process innovation in automobile manufacture during the twentieth century was Toyota's system of "lean production." While the basis of Ford's assembly line production was specialization, the basis of Toyota's lean production was integration and continuous improvement.

The development of the video cassette recorder (VCR) also featured a high level of technological diversity and rivalry during the early stages of the industry, with competition between five companies and a number of different technologies. The American company Ampex pioneered videotape recording for commercial use and in 1970 developed its "Instavideo" video recorder/camera. During the early 1970s, RCA worked on both a VCR product and its videodisc system. Sony developed several videotape technologies before launching first its U-Matic VCR and then its Betamax design in 1975. The Victor Company of Japan, together with its parent company Matsushita, also adopted the U-Matic standard before introducing its VHS system in 1976. RCA's videodisc was an early casualty of the competition, but not until 1987, when Sony finally abandoned its Betamax system and switched to the rival VHS system, did a single standard emerge.[2]

On the customer side, the principal factor in the development of knowledge is the diffusion of experience-based information. In the early stages of the life cycle, customers are first-time buyers and there is limited information available regarding the performance attributes of competing products. As an industry enters its maturity phase, replacement demand predominates. Most customers are experienced, they can draw upon the experiences of other customers, and they are influenced by manufacturers' reputations and independent sources of objective information.

How general is the life cycle pattern?

Even if the life cycle pattern does apply to all industries, it is clear that the duration of the various phases of the life cycle varies considerably from industry to industry. The life cycle of the railroad industry extended for about 100 years after 1840 before entering its declining phase. In the case of the U.S. automobile industry, the introduction stage lasted about 25 years: from the final decade of the nineteenth century until industry growth took off in 1913-15. The growth phase lasted about 40 years: maturity of the industry in terms of slackening of the growth rate dates from the mid-1950s. In other industries, the cycle has been much shorter. The first Apple personal computers were assembled by Steve Jobs and Steve Wozniak in 1976. By 1978, the industry was in its growth phase with a flood of new and established firms entering the industry. Toward the end of 1984, the first signs of maturity appeared: growth stalled, excess capacity emerged, and the industry began to consolidate around a few companies. In general, industry life cycles are shortening. Improved dissemination of information increases the rate of product diffusion. New production technology has increased the speed with which firms can design and establish manufacturing capability for new products. Accelerating technical change hastens the onset of obsolescence. Compact discs are a product that passed almost immediately from introduction to growth phase. By 1988, compact discs outsold conventional record albums in the United States, and by 1990, only six years since their introduction, the market displayed signs of maturity.

However, the differences between industries are not simply one of cycle duration. The patterns of industry evolution are far from uniform.

Some industries may never enter a declining phase. Industries supplying basic necessities such as residential construction, food processing, and clothing are likely to remain mature but are not likely to enter prolonged decline, simply because obsolescence is unlikely. Some industries may experience a rejuvenation of their life cycle. In the 1960s, the world motorcycle industry, which had gone into decline in the United States and Europe at the beginning of the 1960s, entered a decade-long spurt of growth as the recreational use of motorcycles developed. The TV receiver industry has experienced several revivals: the first caused by color TV, the second by the demand for multiple TV receivers within a household, and the third spurred by the demand for computer monitors and TV video games. The advent of high-definition TV promises a further cycle. What we observe is that these rejuvenations of the product life cycle are not simply a natural phenomenon – they are typically the result of company strategies that have fostered breakthrough product innovations or developed new markets and new customers for the product.

An industry is likely to be at different stages of its life cycle in different countries. Hence, even if opportunities for regenerating the whole cycle are not apparent, it may be possible for a company to exploit international differences between the stages of an industry's life cycle. U.S. multinationals have traditionally developed and introduced products for the American market; then, as growth falters and competition intensifies in the domestic market, they have exploited the more attractive growth potential overseas, where the product was at an earlier stage of its life cycle. This strategy worked particularly well for the U.S. metal can manufacturers: in a mature U.S. can market where canned food was increasingly being challenged by fresh and frozen foods, the can makers could invest domestically in new equipment while shipping their older lines overseas to the still-growing overseas markets.[3]

Industry Structure, Competition, and Success Factors over the Life Cycle

Changes in demand growth and technology over the product life cycle tend to be associated with changes in industry structure and competition, which also have implications for the sources of competitive advantage (*key success factors*). Table 9.2 summarizes the principal features of each stage of the industry life cycle. The main changes in structure and competition over the course of the life cycle are as follows:

Product differentiation

We have observed that emerging industries are characterized by a wide variety of product types that reflect the diversity of technologies and designs, lack of consensus over customer requirements, and a range

Table 9.2 The Evolution of Industry Structure and Competition over the Life Cycle

Industry characteristic	Introduction	Growth	Maturity	Decline
Demand	High-income buyers.	Readily increasing market penetration.	Mass market, replacement/repeat buying.	Customers knowledgeable.
Technology	Not standard technology.	Some technologies eliminated.	Well-diffused technical know-how: quest for technological improvements.	
Products	Poor quality. Wide variety. Frequent design changes.	Design and quality improves. Reliability of key importance.	Standardization lessens differentiation. Minor model changes predominate.	Product differentiation lessens.
Manufacture and distribution	Short production runs. High-skilled labor content. Specialized distribution channels.	Capacity shortages. Mass production. Competition for distribution.	Emergence of overcapacity. Deskilling of production. Long production runs. Reduced number of lines carried by distributors.	Heavy overcapacity. Reemergence of specialty channels.
Trade	Shift of manufacture from advanced countries to poorer countries.			
Competition	Few companies.	Entry with many mergers and failures.	Shakeout. Price competition increases.	Price wars, exits.
Key success factors	Product innovation.	Design to allow large-scale manufacture.	Cost-efficiency scale, process innovation, buyer selection.	Reduce overheads. Signal commitment. Rationalize capacity. Support services. Establishing credible image of firm and product. Access to distribution. Establishing strong brand.

of distribution channels. Technical standardization increases product uniformity, and the emphasis on differentiation shifts to marketing variables, ancillary services such as credit and postsales service, and product features in the form of "optional extras." In the course of maturity, increasing consumer knowledge is likely to hasten the elimination of inferior varieties and designs; it may also eliminate more frivolous differentiation. As a result, the product may evolve toward commodity status unless producers are effective in developing new dimensions for differentiation.[4] A feature of the markets for personal computers, credit cards, stockbroking, and short-haul air travel is their emerging commodity status. As technical standardization and customer knowledge increases, buyers select on the basis of price relative to objective performance and identifiable features.

Industry structure and competition

Market growth and technological change are the primary determinants of the structural evolution of manufacturing and distribution, although it is difficult to generalize about their patterns of development. The introduction phase is marked by product diversity, short production runs, and underdeveloped process technology involving intensive use of skilled labor. In many industries, the introduction phase is associated with fragmentation, reflecting the lack of scale economies. Prior to Henry Ford, cars were custom-built by craftsmen on a customized basis in small workshops. This "garage stage" of both development and production was also apparent in the personal computer industry. During the growth phase, there are conflicting forces: rapid sales growth creates space for new entrants, while the displacement of small-scale batch production by large-scale continuous production (or at least, large batches) encourages industry consolidation. Certainly in automobiles, personal computers, and computer software, rapid industry growth was associated with rising industry concentration.

In other industries, the development trend can be quite different. Industries that begin with patent-protected new products are likely to start out as near monopolies, then become increasingly competitive. For example, plain-paper copiers were subject to a virtual worldwide monopoly by Xerox Corporation (and its affiliates Rank Xerox and Fuji-Xerox), and it was not until the early 1980s that the industry was transformed by the entry of many competitors.

A critical factor in determining the evolution of industry concentration is the development of entry barriers over time. Where entry barriers rise due to increasing capital requirements (automobiles, commercial aircraft, telecommunications equipment) or product differentiation and access to distribution channels (soft drinks, beer, cosmetics), seller concentration is likely to increase over the life cycle. Where entry barriers fall due to technology becoming more accessible or the decline of product differentiation, concentration may decline over time (credit cards, television broadcasting, steel, frozen foods).

The critical phase in shaping industry structure is usually the transition from growth to maturity. The slowing of sales growth and additions to productive capacity result in the emergence of excess capacity, which, combined with increasing product homogeneity, can cause fierce price competition to break out. This transition is typically associated with *shakeout* – a period of intense competition in which weaker producers are squeezed out of the industry either by bankruptcy or acquisition. In many instances, shakeout may be precipitated by a cyclical downturn in demand: for example, the Great Depression of 1930-6 in automobiles, the downturn in the demand for personal computers in the last quarter of 1984, the reduction in the U.S. demand for air travel in 1990-1.

The evolving structure of distribution channels also has an important influence on the competition and the overall development of an industry. The typical pattern is for small-scale, specialized distribution channels to give way to larger-scale, more generalized distribution channels. At the retailing level, the size of individual retail units increases and independent retailers are displaced by chains. While this trend occurred in the U.S. food retailing in the 1930s, in toys and hardware it has occurred much more recently (associated with Toys-R-Us and Home Depot, respectively). As always, generalization is dangerous. While maturity is typically associated with concentration of distribution, the quest for differentiation and niche positions may result in opposing developments. Thus, while the retailing of cosmetics and toiletries is increasingly dominated by large chains of drug stores, we also observe the emergence of specialists such as Body Shop.

Location and international trade

An important feature of the structural changes that accompany industry evolution is the international migration of production. The industry life cycle is associated with changes in the pattern of trade and direct investment that together result in important locational shifts.[5] The *life cycle theory of trade and direct investment* is based upon two assumptions. First, that the demand for new products emerges first in the richer, developed countries (especially the United States) and then diffuses internationally. Second, that with maturity, products require fewer inputs of technology and sophisticated skills. The result is the following development pattern:

1 new industries begin in high-income countries (notably the United States but increasingly in Japan and Western Europe) where there are ample technical and scientific resources and affluent demand for novel goods and services. As demand grows in overseas markets (initially Western Europe) these are served by exports.
2 continued growth of overseas markets and reduced need for inputs of technology and sophisticated labor skills make production attractive in some overseas markets. As lower-cost production expands in these markets, either by subsidiaries of U.S. multinationals or by domestically owned firms, the United States begins to import.
3 continued maturity resulting in further deskilling of production, reduced product differentiation, and fewer opportunities for innova-

tion result in the growing comparative advantage of low-wage countries – initially the newly industrializing countries of the Far East, southern Europe, and Latin America and later the developing countries. Production shifts away from Western Europe, North America, and Japan, and they become wholly dependent upon imports from low-wage countries.

Thus, consumer electronics were initially produced primarily in the United States and, during the 1960s, production increased in Japan and Western Europe. By the 1980s, production was shifting increasingly to newly industrializing countries such as South Korea, Taiwan, Hong Kong, and Singapore. Increasingly, it is the next tier of emerging industrial countries such as Thailand, China, Mexico, and Brazil where the major increases in production and exports are occurring. We will return to national influences on competitive advantage in chapter 13.

The nature and intensity of competition

The structural changes associated with industry evolution have important consequences for competition. The typical pattern of development is for competition to shift from nonprice to price competition and for its intensity to increase. During the introduction stage, competitors battle for technological leadership, and competition often features a diversity of technologies and designs. In personal computers, this continued into the early 1980s when the IBM/Intel/MS-DOS technical standard was established with Apple as the only viable nonconformist.

Once technological competition wanes, the quest for competitive advantage shifts to low-cost, quality, brand leadership and strength within distribution channels. Technological competition may still be important, but the emphasis is on the use of technology to obtain cost and quality advantage. With the onset of maturity and narrowing product differentiation, the emphasis on price competition tends to increase. How intense this price competition is depends heavily upon the evolution of industry structure. In particular:

- the extent to which capacity expansion overtakes demand growth;
- whether seller concentration rises or falls;
- the trends in entry barriers;
- the rise in buying power as a result of the consolidation of distribution channels.

In some industries, maturity is associated with the emergence of intensely competitive industry environments in which profit margins become severely pressured. In the oil industry, petrochemicals, U.S. domestic airlines, and car rental, relatively low levels of seller concentration combined with an overhang of excess capacity has produced aggressively price-competitive market environments. In other industries that have reached their mature stages – magazine publishing, soft drinks, fast food, household detergents, breakfast cereals, and toothpaste – high levels of seller concentration and a commitment to heavy investment in branding and image differentiation have resulted in more benign market environments with attractive margins. The most important shift is from nonprice competition to price competition. In the introduction and growth stages, technical progressiveness, product performance, reliability, brand reputation, and securing channels of distribution are paramount. In the course of maturity, these dimensions of competition give way to price competition, driven by increasing cost efficiency of manufacture, emerging excess capacity, and growing international competition. The onset of price competition can be traumatic. As we have already observed, an unexpected slowdown in demand or the emergence of a firm with a clear cost advantage can precipitate an industry "shakeout" involving the elimination of weaker companies and consolidation of the industry around a few leaders. Once the industry enters its decline phase, then, depending upon the height of exit barriers and the strength of international competition, price competition may degenerate into destructive price wars.

The pattern of changes in industry structure and competition is summarized in figure 9.3. The structural changes that drive increased price competition are also responsible for a deterioration in industry attractiveness in the course of maturity. As industries evolve and mature, the range of available competitive weapons declines, and the increasing intensity of price competition erodes margins. Table 9.3 shows the profitability of businesses at different stages of the life cycle and experiencing different rates of growth.

Maturity in an industry usually corresponds to maturity of the individual firms. The membership of a mature industry tends to be stable, with most firms long established. Lack of radical innovation and limited opportunities for differentiation also lead to stability of market shares for the leading firms. This stability is partly a product of the heavy investments that leading firms have made in their market positions over long periods of time. The acquisition of experience, reputation, distribution channels, and brand recognition makes it difficult for newcomers to easily dislodge incumbents from their leadership positions. The world oil industry continues to be dominated by the "Seven Sisters," although one sister (Chevron) has acquired one of the others (Gulf). For seven decades, Ford and General Motors have led the ranks of the world's largest automakers.

Key success factors and industry evolution

The different stages of the industry life cycle are associated with different business strategies. Table 9.4 shows some of the principal differences. The changes in business strategy over the life cycle arise from the fact that the changes in competitive structure and customer requirements

Figure 9.3 The Evolution of Industry Structure and Competition

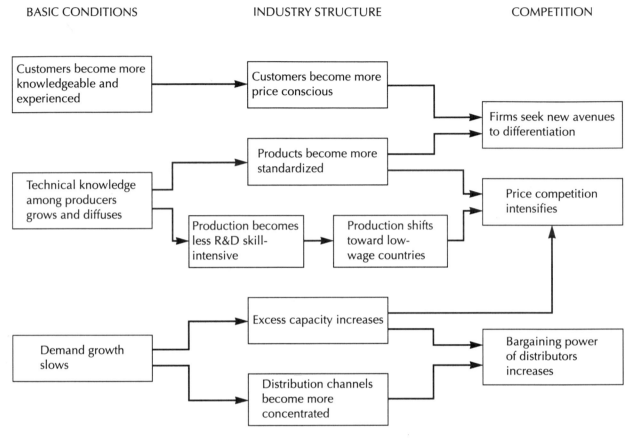

Table 9.3 Average ROI at Different Stages of the Industry Life Cycle

	Real rate of growth		
	Less than 3% (%)	3% to 6% (%)	Over 6% (%)
Growth (%)	22.8	24.4	24.3
Maturity (%)	21.7	22.0	24.1
Decline (%)	16.4	22.3	

Note: These results are for 6,600 business units on the PIMS database over a four-year period.
Source: Robert D. Buzzell and Bradley T. Gale, *The PIMS Principles: Linking Strategy to Performance* (New York: Free Press, 1987), 58.

associated with industry evolution have important consequences for key success factors:

- During the *introductory phase,* product innovation is the primary basis for success. In a new industry, the essential condition for being able to compete is to possess the technology necessary to produce the

	GROWTH	MATURITY	DECLINE
Efficiency Variables			
ROI	.005	.008	−.233*
Capacity utilization	−.100*	.061*	.107
Employee productivity	.308*	.127	−.087
Value added/Revenue	.155	.063	−.428*
Industry & Product Variables			
Technological change	.580*	−.159*	−.044
Customization	.185	.151	.035
Relative product breadth	−.055	.032*	−.341*
Relative price	.018	−.049	−.047
Market share	.030	.062	−.064
R&D Variables			
Sales from new products/Total sales	.499*	−.179*	−.383*
Product R&D/Revenue	.537*	.042*	−.365*
Process R&D/Revenue	.484*	−.029*	.003
Production & Investment Variables			
Total inventory/Revenue	.045	.107	.081
Newness of plant & equipment	.323*	−.211*	−.676*
Investment/Revenue	.305*	.028*	−.052*
Backward vertical integration	.026	−.043	.001
Forward vertical integration	−.030	.029	−.023
Marketing Variables			
Sales force/Revenue	.278*	−.049*	−.279*
Advertising & promotion/Revenue	−.250*	−.328*	−.384*

Table 9.4 Strategic and Performance Differences between Businesses at Different Stages of the Life Cycle

Notes

1 The table shows the standardized means for each variable for businesses at each stage of the life cycle. Category means that are significantly different from the average for all categories at the 0.05 probability level are indicated by an asterisk.

2 The data were obtained from 1,234 industrial products manufacturing businesses included in the PIMS database during the period 1970–80.

Source: Carl Anderson and Carl Zeithaml, "Stage of the Product Life Cycle, Business Strategy and Business Performance," *Academy of Management Journal* 27 (1984): 5–24.

product or service. In all new industries – whether virtual reality-based arcade games, laser beam surgical equipment, or interactive home shopping services – the essential requirement is the *knowledge* to enter the industry. Soon, however, knowledge alone is not enough. As the industry begins its evolution and technological competition intensifies, other requirements for success emerge. In moving from the first generation of products to subsequent generations, investment requirements tend to grow, and financial resources become increasingly important. Capabilities in product development soon need to be matched by capabilities in manufacture, marketing, and distribution. Hence, in an emerging industry, firms need to support their innovation by a broad array of vertically integrated capabilities. At the same time, potential customers need convincing and they need support. Hence, success during the introduction phase also requires that firms establish a credible image for themselves and their product and establish the means to market the product and provide postsales service;

- Once the *growth stage* is reached, the key challenge is scaling up. As the market expands, the firm needs to adapt its product design and its manufacturing capability to large-scale production. To utilize increased manufacturing capability, access to distribution becomes critical. At the same time, the tensions that organizational growth imposes create the need for internal administrative and strategic skills. I will consider the strategic issues presented by emerging and technology-based industries in the next chapter. Let us turn to the process of maturity and its implications for competitive advantage;

- With the *maturity stage*, competitive advantage is increasingly a quest for cost efficiency – or at least, this is the case in those mature industries that tend toward less and less product differentiation. The key success factors thus tend to be those cost drivers that are most important within that particular industry. I will consider these further in chapter 11;

- The transformation from maturity in the *decline phase* raises the potential for destructive price competition. Whether or not a firm has a competitive advantage tends to be secondary to the importance of maintaining a stable industry environment. Hence, company strategies tend to focus upon encouraging the orderly exit of industry capacity and the building of a strong position in relation to residual market demand.

Anticipating industry evolution

Critical to sustaining competitive advantage is not simply protecting one's competitive position against competitive imitation but also ensuring that one's competitive advantage is not rendered obsolete by changes in the industry environment. IBM did not *lose* its competitive advantage in the world computer industry; the problem was that changes in the market meant that its enormous investments in internal resources and capabilities, such as its research labs, its sales and marketing organization, and its customer support capabilities, no longer matched industry key success factors as well as they did during the early 1980s.

The evolution of industries, and with it the changing requirements for success, creates a dilemma for the firm. The firms that are successful at one stage of the life cycle are unlikely to be successful at a subsequent stage because the resources and capabilities that provided the foundation for their success at one stage are not appropriate to the subsequent stage. Thus, Birds Eye Ltd's national distribution network for frozen foods, which was fundamental to its competitive advantage in the U.K. frozen foods market during the 1960s and 1970s, became a source of high costs and inflexibility in the mature, price-competitive market of the 1980s.[6] The solution identified by Derek Abell is for firms to pursue *dual strategies*: they must manage to maximize performance under today's circumstances, but strategy must also be involved with *change* in order to meet the circumstances of the future.[7] Abell cites Nestlé as a company that, at the beginning of the 1990s, was concerned with maximizing returns to its present products and brands within the many countries of the world in which it distributes while simultaneously pursuing its "Nestlé 2000" project aimed at repositioning Nestlé to meet the challenges of a more global, dynamic, and price-competitive marketplace.[8]

Summary and Conclusions

Classifying industries according to their stage of development fulfills three purposes. First, it acts as a shortcut in strategy analysis. Categorizing industries and applying generalizations concerning the type of competition likely to emerge and the kinds of strategy likely to be effective provide a quick and useful first-cut analysis for the purposes of strategy formulation. Second, classifying an industry requires comparison with other industries. Such comparisons, by highlighting similarities and differences with other industries, can form the basis for a deeper understanding of its structure, competitive character, and sources of advantage. Third, it directs attention to the forces of evolution within the industry and encourages us to look ahead to the future circumstances of the industry. However, while the life cycle approach is useful because it helps us to identify and understand the common forces that drive the evolution of markets and industries, we must recognize that industries do not follow a common development path.

In the next two chapters, I will discuss strategy formulation and strategy implementation in industries at different stages of their development: emerging industries and those characterized by technology-based competition and mature industries.

Appendix: Other Approaches to Industry Classification

The life cycle is the most common approach to industry classification used in strategy analysis. However, other bases of classification are available. For example, industries can be classified by type of customer (e.g., into producer goods and consumer goods), by the principal resources used (e.g., into capital-intensive, technology-intensive, and marketing-intensive professional skill industries), or by the geographic scope of the industry (local, national, global). The critical issue in evaluating the usefulness of any means of classification is whether it can offer insights into the similarities and differences between industries for the purposes of formulating business strategies. The first, Jeffrey Williams' classification of strategic environments, recognizes that industries follow different development paths. In particular, some industry environments are fairly stable over time while others exhibit high rates of change. The second approach, that of the Boston Consulting Group, uses the sources and nature of competitive advantage as the basis for classification. BCG's "*Strategic Environments Matrix*" offers insight into different sources of competitive advantage and is an illuminating example of the value of "2 × 2" classification matrices to generate strategy prescriptions.

BCG's Strategic Environments Matrix

In the industry life cycle, the stage of maturity of an industry determines the key structural characteristics of an industry, which, in turn, determine the nature of competitive advantage. BCG's Strategic Environments Matrix reverses this direction of causation: it is the nature of competitive advantage in an industry that determines strategies that are viable in an industry, which in turn determine the structure of the industry.

BCG classifies industries in relation to two variables: the number of viable strategy approaches that is available and the size of the industry leader's potential competitive advantage. The number of strategy approaches depends upon the complexity of the industry in terms of the diversity of sources of competitive advantage. Thus, in commodity products where there is no opportunity for differentiation, competitive advantage must be achieved through cost leadership. Furthermore, if all firms face identical input costs and technologies, then scale is a dominant strategic variable. If an industry's products and customers' requirements are complex – as in the case of automobiles, fashion clothing, and restaurants – the sources of competitive advantage are several, and a number of strategies are viable.

The second variable, the size of the competitive advantage available, depends primarily upon the cost and demand characteristics of the industry. Where substantial economies of scale are available (either through production efficiencies or through the ability to spread large indivisible costs of R&D or advertising over increasing sales volume), substantial cost advantage may accrue to the market leader. In other industries, such as computers or soft drinks, substantial differentiation advantages may accrue to firms with the leading brand positions.

Four industry categories can be established (see figure 9.A1).

1   *Volume businesses*   Businesses with few sources of advantage but for whom the size of the available competitive advantage is large are termed *volume businesses*. Competition is cost-based, and scale economies are typically of key importance. Thus, in jet engines, scale economies in R&D and production have reduced the number of global players to three. The key success factor in a volume business is market share. Market share confers economies of scale; the firm that achieves the largest market share and greatest growth in market share will also achieve the greatest cost reduction through economies of learning.

	FRAGMENTED	SPECIALIZATION
Many	apparel, housebuilding, jewelry retailing, sawmills	pharmaceuticals, luxury cars, chocolate confectionery
	STALEMATE	VOLUME
Few	basic chemicals, volume grade paper, ship owning (VLCCs), wholesale banking	jet engines, food supermarkets, motorcycles, standard microprocessors
	Small	Big

SOURCES OF ADVANTAGE

SIZE OF ADVANTAGE

Figure 9.A1 Boston Consulting Group's Strategic Environments Matrix

Source: Boston Consulting Group.

2 *Stalemate businesses* These are businesses in which the sources of advantage are few, and the size of potential advantage is small. As a result, the environment is highly competitive: firms compete with similar strategies, but none is able to obtain significant advantage over another. The consequence is low profitability all around. Typical industries in this category are those producing commodity products where firms have similar input costs, similar technologies, and limited opportunity for scale advantage. Examples include wholesale banking, bulk marine transportation, and volume grades of paper. Volume businesses tend to evolve into stalemate businesses as growth slackens, technology becomes diffused, and firms' cost advantages become eroded. A critical strategic issue is the ability to perceive the emergence of stalemate early on so that a timely exit can be executed. Once a business is embroiled in a stalemate industry, survival and profitability are crucially dependent upon a high level of operational efficiency, low administrative overheads, and a corporate management that is ruthlessly cost conscious. As demonstrated by Crown, Cork and Seal in metal containers and ConAgra in poultry and meat packing, such a strategy can offer attractive returns even in the most unpromising industry environments.

3 *Fragmented businesses* These are businesses whose sources of competitive advantage are many, but the potential size of the advantage is small. These fragmented industries often supply differentiated products in markets where brand loyalty is low, technology is well diffused, and minimum efficient plant size (MEPS) is small relative to total market size. Fashion clothing, restaurants, and video rental stores are examples of such industries. Success factors may include low costs through operational efficiency, focusing on attractive market segments, responding quickly to change, and establishing novel forms of product differentiation. Large companies tend to be at a disadvantage relative to small companies. Successful large companies tend to be

entrepreneurial and organized like small firms. Franchising is one way of matching the advantages of size with those of flexibility and decentralization. An alternative strategy is to attempt to transform the business into a specialized or volume business. McDonald's transformed the fast-food industry from a fragmented industry into a specialized/volume industry. Starbucks appears to be achieving a similar feat among gourmet coffee shops.

4 *Specialized businesses*   These are businesses for whom the sources of advantage are many and the size of the potential advantage is substantial. The characteristics of a typical specialization business include:
   - varied customer needs;
   - the presence of first-mover advantages, brand loyalty, and scale economies that create barriers against competitors seeking to serve the same need;
   - there are large specific costs associated with serving each market niche and shared costs are few – hence, there are no major advantages to firms with a broad market or product scope.

The key feature of specialization businesses is strategic differentiation. Each firm does something different and, as a result, competition is indirect rather than direct. The focus of competitive activity is product design, innovation, and brand promotion rather than price. Specialized businesses include pharmaceuticals, luxury cars, perfumes, and management consulting.

BCG's analysis of the strategies appropriate to specialization businesses focuses upon two variables: the degree of *environmental stability* and the *ability to systematize* customer and competitor behavior. On the basis of these two variables, figure 9.A2 defines four types of businesses and four strategic approaches:

   - where the market environment is stable and market behavior is sufficiently regular to permit systematization, an *analytic* approach to

Figure 9.A2
Specialization
Businesses: Strategic
Characteristics and
General Management
Skills

ABILITY TO SYSTEMATIZE		
low	CREATIVE fashion general publishing	EXPERIMENTAL toiletries magazines food products
high	PERCEPTIVE high-tech	ANALYTICAL luxury cars confectionery paper towels
	high	low
	ENVIRONMENTAL VARIABILITY	

Source: Boston Consulting Group.

strategy formulation is possible. In luxury cars, concepts of style and quality change slowly. Success depends upon the careful analysis of customer requirements and competitors' positioning;

- an environment that is stable but where customers' and competitors' behavior cannot be systematized is conducive to *experimental* approaches to new product introduction and strategy adjustment. The food industry is stable, but it is difficult to predict the market's acceptance of new products. In developing and marketing new convenience food products, a meticulous experimental approach is called for;

- where the environment is variable but where behavior is systematic, *perceptive* skills are the key to competitive advantage. Hence, in high-tech environments, the key is to perceive how new technological opportunities can better serve existing customer needs;

- environmental variability combined with inability to systematize requires *creativity* in order to establish competitive advantage. In fashion clothing, not only do markets change quickly but fashion trends and cycles are not amenable to techniques of market analysis. Success in fashion clothing accrues to those that, through creativity and style, become trendsetters.

Classifying industries according to competitive dynamics

Focusing upon dynamic aspects of competition, Jeffrey Williams has identified the rate of new product introduction, duration of product life cycles, the rate of decline of unit costs, geographical scope, and the stability of supplier-customer relations as the key strategic features of industries.[1] Williams identifies three industry types. Table 9.A1 summarizes the key characteristics of these three categories.

Local monopoly markets sell specialized products to relatively few customers. They are "the 20th century equivalent of the early craftsmen's guild . . . regional businesses with negligible focus on productivity and little direct price competition. Each monopolized its immediate geographical area and hand-produced whatever goods the local population needed, maintaining personal contact with the customer."[2] In these markets, firms use highly specialized resources and capabilities to meet highly specific customer requirements. Examples include high-tech defense contractors (North American Rockwell, Grumman Aerospace), professional service companies that rely upon close client contact such as corporate law firms and private bankers, and more traditional local monopolists such as the Baby Bells. Product differentiation tends to be high: customers are resistant to standardization and elasticity of demand is low, reflecting the fact that customers prefer a higher-priced specialty product to a lower-priced mass-produced product (e.g., designer clothing, Rolls-Royce cars, military equipment, defense-related communication equipment).

The strategies of these shielded monopolists tend to be oriented toward maintaining close customer relations, often supported by a

Table 9.A1 Williams's Classification of Market Types

	Local Monopoly	Traditional industrial	Schumpeterian
Economies of experience	Small.	Moderate.	Substantial.
Customer relations	Stable and long term. Based upon close personal contact.	Moderately stable. Emphasis on defending market share.	Unstable with volatile market shares.
Market scope	Narrow. Firms' markets are local or a few customers.	Markets defined broadly: national or global mass markets.	Typically broad geographically but often segmented by product/customer type.
Competition	Sheltered markets; competition weak.	Market share battles; competition on price and advertising.	Intense rivalry in product and process innovation.
Key success factors	Dominate local markets and build barriers through close customer ties.	Exploit economies of scale and mass marketing. Market share key.	Fast product innovation. Move quickly down the experience curve. Adopt novel strategies.

Source: Jeffrey R. Williams, *"I Don't Think We're in Kansas Any More . . ."*: *A Perspective on Our Expanding Markets,* Working Paper 20-86-87, Graduate School of Industrial Administration, Carnegie Mellon University, January 1988.

strong emphasis on product and service quality. High-quality, low-volume production with lack of competition encourages craft-based production that is vertically integrated, makes intensive use of highly skilled labor, and places little emphasis on attaining economies of scale or experience. Typically, the experience curve for these industries is shallow, and, in the absence of volume gains and process innovation, annual reductions in real unit costs are usually less than 2 percent.

Traditional industrial markets are those where market size is large and not heavily segmented and the rate of product innovation is modest. Competition in these markets is dominated by the quest for the benefits of size: economies of scale from standardized production and the reputation benefits of brand leadership. Market domination, though sought, is seldom achieved: products are close substitutes in these markets and market shares respond both to price and advertising. The strategy of cost-leadership/brand-awareness/product-variety is exemplified by McDonald's, Sears Roebuck, and General Motors. For these strategies to be effective, organizations must emphasize efficiency through control, competence through experience and specialization, and perfection through the elimination of problems and defects. The quest for cost advantage through scale efficiency, process technology, and product design improvement typically results in continuous cost reduction over time in the order of 2 to 8 percent a year, despite the fact that many of these industries are highly mature (e.g., cars, glass, appliances, tires).

Schumpeterian markets are those driven by a "gale of creative destruction" in the form of a stream of innovation. Established products are constantly being displaced by new products that, if successful, show rapid rates of growth. Industries where product innovation is the dominant form of competition include semiconductors, telecommunications, computers, consumer electronics, financial services, recorded music, entertainment, and certain fashion goods. At the same time, innovations are quickly imitated, and speed in exploiting new products is essential. Hence, success in these industries does not depend exclusively upon product innovation – manufacturing and marketing capabilities are important in establishing competitive advantage by moving down the experience curve ahead of competitors. Annual average reductions in real unit costs in excess of 8 percent are typical for these products. Table 9.A2 shows the rapid rate of price reduction for several products within this category. Successful firms in Schumpeterian markets are innovators that can establish first-mover advantage (exemplars include Hewlett-Packard in calculators, Intel in microprocessors, and Sony in consumer electronics) but also those firms that are fast-followers and can achieve cost reduction through process innovation (exemplars include Texas Instruments and Motorola in semiconductors and Matsushita in consumer electronics).

The implications of these fast-moving Schumpeterian markets for companies' organizational structures and management systems are far-reaching. The large-scale, scale-efficiency-oriented, hierarchical organization appropriate to traditional industrial markets is quite inappropriate for Schumpeterian markets (as Exxon found when it tried to establish Exxon Office Systems as a major player in the market for office computer systems and printers). The key requirements for success in these industries are organizations that can nurture innovation and use *speed* to respond to market changes and outmaneuver competitors.

It is important to recognize that industries may move from one class to another. Over time, technology and the opening of the "mass market" have caused many industries to move from craft-based local monopolies to scale-oriented industrial markets. Saville Row, the center for bespoke tailoring in London, is one outpost of "local monopoly" in a now-industrialized market. In other industries, such as local telephone services, trucking, and banking, deregulation has been instrumental in the shift from local monopoly market to traditional industrial market. In other industries, corporate restructuring is driven by the need to adjust to a transition from traditional industrial to Schumpeterian market structures. Shoes and toys are both traditional industries where product

Table 9.A2 Classifying Industries According to Rate of Productivity Growth (as Indicated by Changes in Real Prices)

Industry	Period	Average annual real change in producer price index (%)
Local monopoly industries		
Surgical, orthopedic, and prosthetic appliances	1983–9	+4.9
Boat repair	1981–8	+2.8
General job printing	1982–9	+2.6
Musical instruments	1985–9	+2.6
Map, atlas, and globe cover printing	1982–9	+2.3
Entertainment	1980–7	+1.8
Highway construction	1970–88	+1.7
Burial caskets	1982–9	+1.7
Residential construction	1970–88	+1.6
Traditional manufacturing industries		
Passenger cars	1982–9	+0.3
Wheeled tractors	1982–9	0.0
Metal cans	1981–9	−0.1
Electric lamps	1983–9	−0.7
Gasoline engines (under 11 hp)	1982–9	−0.8
Household refrigerators	1981–9	−0.9
Dynamic, Schumpeterian industries		
Home electronic equipment	1982–9	−3.6
Microprocessors	1981–9	−4.6
Microwave cookers	1982–9	−4.6
Analog integrated circuits	1981–9	−4.8
Digital PBXs	1985–9	−4.9
Color TVs (more than 17-inch)	1980–9	−6.0
Memory integrated circuits	1981–9	−6.0
Digital computers	1988–9	−10.3

Source: U.S. Bureau of Labor Statistics, Bulletin (Washington, D.C.: U.S. Government Printing Office), various issues.

innovation and compression of product life cycles have transformed competitive conditions.

The use of this classification is complicated by the fact that some industries may be hybrids, that is, they may combine the productivity characteristics of more than one market category. Williams observes that in personal computer industries, the production of basic components such as keyboards, cabinets, and power supplies are traditional, high-volume industries; components such as microprocessors and microcomputers themselves are dynamic, Schumpeterian industries; while applications software and customer support are craft-based, sheltered industries.[3] Similarly, in telecommunications equipment, electronics and fiber optics provide Schumpeterian competition on the technological front. Manufacturing of switching equipment is subject to important scale economies, while the presence of government-owned national telephone companies provides close customer contact typical of local monopoly markets. The differences between competition and competitive advantage between different activities within the personal computer and telecommunications industries pose considerable difficulties for strategy and organization. In particular, they may make it desirable for the firm to specialize in activities that are located within an industry category. For a firm to span activities that fall into different categories, it may be desirable to carry these out within separate operating units.

Notes

1 The concept of the product life cycle is associated with the work of Everett M. Rogers, *The Diffusion of Innovations* (New York: Free Press, 1962); and Theodore Levitt, "Exploit the Product Life Cycle," *Harvard Business Review* (November-December 1965): 81–94. For a contemporary discussion, see Philip Kotler, *Marketing Management: Analysis, Planning, and Control,* 5th ed. (Englewood Cliffs, NJ: Prentice-Hall, 1984), chapter 11.

2 Richard S. Rosenbloom and Michael A. Cusumano, "Technological Pioneering and Competitive Advantage: The Birth of the VCR Industry," *California Management Review* 29, no. 4 (1987).

3 "Crown Cork and Seal Company, Inc.," in C. R. Christensen, K. R. Andrews, Joe L. Bower, R. G. Hamermesh, and Michael E. Porter, *Business Policy: Text and Cases,* 5th ed. (Homewood, IL: Irwin, 1982).

4 In Mathur's "transaction cycle," differentiation reemerges as products and service are recombined into new systems (see chapter 7).

5 R. Vernon, "International Investment and International Trade in the Product Cycle," *Quarterly Journal of Economics* 80 (1966): 190–207.

6 D. Collis and Robert M. Grant, *Birds Eye Foods Ltd.*

7 Derek F. Abell, *Managing with Dual Strategies* (New York: Free Press, 1993).

8 *Ibid*, 8–12.

9 This section draws upon the work of Jeffrey R. Williams, which is contained in the following papers: *The Productivity Base of Industries,* Working Paper 1983-84, Graduate School of Industrial Administration, Carnegie Mellon University, May 1984; Jeffrey R. Williams, *"I Don't Think We're in Kansas Any More . . ."*; "How Market Settings Influence CIM Strategies," *Long Range Planning,* 23(February 1990); "How Sustainable is your Competitive Advantage," *California Management Review* (Spring 1992).

TEN

Competitive Advantage in Technology-Intensive Industries and the Management of Innovation

The best way to predict the future is to invent it.
> – John Scully, chairman, Apple Computer

Outline
Introduction and Objectives
Some Characteristics of Emerging and Technology-Intensive Industries
   The evolution of technology
   Cost reduction
   Uncertainty
Competitive Advantage in Technology-Intensive Industries
   The profitability of innovation
   Legal protection of innovation
   Complementary resources
   The characteristics of the technology
   Lead time
   Some empirical evidence
Strategic Decisions Concerning Technology Management
   Forecasting
   The timing of entry and innovation: To lead or to follow?
   Managing risks
   Exploiting innovation: Licensing versus internal development
Strategy Implementation in Emerging Industries: Creating the
Conditions for Innovation
   From strategy formulation to conditions for innovation
   The conditions for creativity
   From invention to innovation: The need for coordination and
   leadership
   Managing the evolution of industries and markets
   The implications for organizational change
   Innovation and maturity
Summary and Conclusions

Introduction and Objectives

The distinguishing characteristic of emerging industries – those in the introductory and growth phases of their life cycle – is the central role that technology plays in competition. Indeed, technology is typically responsible for the creation of these industries. New markets are created through the development of new technology (biotechnology, fiber optics, digital wireless communication) through the application of existing technology to new products (personal computers, diagnostic imaging) and through the environmental problems created by technology (pollution control and waste management). Technological intensity is not exclusively a feature of industries in the early phases of their life cycles. While maturity is generally associated with a shift from technology-based to cost-based competition, in industries such as pharmaceuticals, chemicals, communications, and electronics, technology continues to be the driving force of competition. These industries retain many of the features of emerging industries. Innovation also plays a continuing role in other industries that are clearly mature – in food processing, fashion goods, and automobiles – constant new product development, market changes, and technological change in related industries provide important innovative opportunities.

In this chapter, we explore market environments in which technology is the driving force of competition and derive insights and principles for the strategic management of technology. Our focus is on innovation. Innovation is responsible for the creation of new industries, and it is the primary source of both cost and differentiation advantage.

By the time you have finished reading this chapter, you will be able to:

- appreciate the role of technology both as a weapon of competition and as the driving force behind industry evolution;
- understand the characteristics of competitive advantage in technology-intensive industries and the extent to which technological advantage can be appropriated and sustained;
- appraise the returns to innovation;
- formulate strategies appropriate to technology-intensive environments;
- identify the organizational conditions conducive to the implementation of such strategies.

First, I will examine competition and the characteristics of competition and competitive advantage in technology-intensive industries. Second, I will explore central issues in the formulation of strategies in such industries, with a particular emphasis on the management of technology for competitive advantage. Third, I will examine the organizational conditions for the successful management of technology.

Some Characteristics of Emerging and Technology-Intensive Industries

The evolution of technology

Knowledge creation, invention, and innovation   In the previous chapter, we examined patterns of product and process innovation over the industry life cycles and observed the progression toward standardization over time, first, of product technology and design and, second, of process technology. Let me examine in a little more detail the development and dissemination of technology. The pattern is shown in figure 10.1.

Invention is the creation of new products and processes through the development of new knowledge or, more typically, from new combinations of existing knowledge. *Innovation* is the initial commercialization of invention by producing and marketing a new good or service or using a new method of production. Once the innovation has occurred, if successful, it becomes diffused: on the demand side, through customers purchasing the good or service; on the supply side, through imitation by competitors. At each of these stages, substantial lags may occur. For example:

- xerography was invented by Chester F. Carlson in 1938 by combining established basic knowledge concerning electrostatics and printing. The first patents were awarded in 1940. Patent rights were purchased by Xerox Corporation, which launched its first office copiers in 1958. By 1974, the first competitive machines were introduced by IBM, Kodak, Ricoh, and others;
- the jet engine, employing Newtonian principles of forces, was patented by Frank Wittle in 1930. The first commercial jet airliner, the Comet, flew in 1957. Two years later, the Boeing 707 was introduced.

The trend over time is for the lags between knowledge generation, invention, innovation, and diffusion to become shorter. The mathematics of *fuzzy logic* were developed by Lofti Zadeh at Berkeley during the 1960s. By the early 1980s, Dr Takeshi Yamakawa of the Kyushu Institute of Technology had registered patents for integrated circuits embodying fuzzy logic, and, in 1987, a series of fuzzy logic controllers for

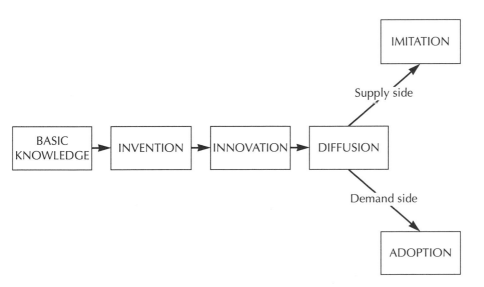

Figure 10.1 The Development of Technology

industrial machines was launched by Omron of Kyoto. By 1991, the world market for fuzzy controllers was estimated at $2 billion.[1]

The early stages of technological development typically involve competition between different technologies and different design configurations. Technological and design variety is promoted because most new products involve a combination of different technologies, with the result that different combinations of core technologies, different configurations of key components, and different choices with regard to performance trade-offs can result in quite different products. For example, the wide variety of personal computers available in 1981 reflected different choices with regard to microprocessors, data storage, and operating systems; different approaches to integrating the various key components; and different emphases with regard to speed versus user-friendliness, innovation in hardware versus availability of software, and price versus power.

The emergence of standards   Competition between rival technologies and designs results in the elimination of approaches that are less preferred by customers, not simply because they are technologically inferior but because they offer an inferior price-performance combination. Over time, a *dominant design paradigm* emerges. This dominant design is that which is able to meet a whole set of user needs in a complete and economical manner. Examples of such dominant design paradigms are the Model T Ford in autos, the IBM 360 in mainframe computers, and the Douglas DC3 in passenger aircraft.[2] These dominant designs become a model for imitation and subsequent, usually incremental, technological development.

Once established, standards that form around the dominant design are difficult to displace. There are two chief reasons: learning effects and network effects. Learning effects are associated with continuing product development and increasing volumes of products. Once a design and associated technical standards become dominant, product innovation does not stop but tends to become incremental with the result that considerable improvements in product performance are achieved. At the same time, the emphasis of technological development shifts to process innovation with the result that huge increases in efficiency occur.[3] As a consequence, the dominant design achieves a combination of price and performance that is difficult to match by any alternative design embodying significantly different technology.

Consider, for example, the four-cycle internal combustion engine. Although the basic technology was well established by the time of the First World War and the dominant technology was in place during the 1920s, continued refinement has made the engine resistant to displacement. Although the Wankel rotary engine was believed to offer potential advantages in technical efficiency and licenses were purchased by many of the world's leading auto manufacturers, only Mazda persisted in taking the engine to market. Even with further technical development, the engine was unable to meet the performance of the standard four-cycle engine. A similar fate may await other challengers to the conventional four-cycle engine, notably the improved two-cycle engine and electric propulsion.

Network effects Network effects arise whenever *externalities* exist between users. Such demand-side externalities arise where the benefit a customer derives from a product depends upon the number of other customers of the product that exists. The classic case is a telephone service. The benefits from owning a telephone connection depend almost entirely upon the number of other people connected to the same service. The key here is *connectability*. Thus, the success of the new personal communication networks (PCNs) in challenging the established cellular networks in the field of wireless communication requires connectability between PCN telephone users and those using other forms of wired and wireless telephones.

Network effects may also exist on the supply side. The dominant position of IBM/Intel/MS-DOS personal computers since 1982 is not so much the desire of computer users to be connected to one another within networks as the recognition that the dominant design in personal computers will also possess the widest range of applications software. In the move toward standardization, only Apple's Macintosh has survived as an alternative design paradigm. A key element in the survival of a second network is achieving compatibility or connectability. Thus, the risks facing Mac users of becoming isolated with a narrower range of applications were reduced by modifications that permitted the Macintosh to run DOS-based applications software. Similarly, other new operating systems, such as Windows and IBM's PS/2, have only been able to establish themselves through compatibility with a DOS environment. Such supply-side network effects also contributed to customer resistance to rotary-engined cars. A factor discouraging their acceptance was the limited availability of trained mechanics and service points compared with conventionally engined cars.

The issue of which technology and design configuration will eventually dominate is a critical risk factor for customers in markets where network effects are important. The fear of becoming isolated with an obsolete design may delay large-scale market acceptance of an innovation to the point at which a standard emerges. If a standard does not emerge quickly, a product may never achieve its growth phase. Steve Postrel has shown how the failure of quadraphonic sound to displace stereophonic sound resulted from competing technologies among audio manufacturers, with each hardware technology needing compatible "software" from the recording companies.[4] The uncertainty over these competing technologies discourages investment by the recording companies in quadraphonic records and tapes, which reinforced the reluctance of consumers to invest in quadraphonic systems.

This type of "chicken-and-egg" dilemma may be emerging in high-definition TV (HDTV) even despite the adoption of a technical standard for HDTV in the United States. There is little incentive for consumers to purchase HDTV receivers until HDTV broadcasts are available from broadcasters and producers. But until there is a clear indication that customers will adopt HDTV, there is inevitably reluctance on the part of producers and broadcasters to switch.[5]

Cost reduction

Once a dominant design does emerge, the rapid growth in demand and the advances in process technology associated with the growth phase of the product life cycle tend to result in rapid cost reductions. Unit costs are initially high for new products, reflecting heavy development costs and inefficiently small production runs. Hence, experience-related cost reductions tend to be substantial. The ballpoint pen, invented by a Hungarian, Ladislao Biro, in 1940, is a classic example. In the 1945 Christmas season, Gimbel's New York store was selling the pens for $12.50. By the early 1950s, the price had fallen to 15 cents.[6] Rapid cost reduction is a characteristic feature of many products that feature low differentiation, high demand elasticity, and limited service content (see chapter 8). Moreover, significant cost reduction may continue for many years, led by process innovation and design modification. For example, over the 17-year period 1965-82, the prices of black-and-white TVs fell by an average of 4.32 percent per annum.[7] An office microcomputer such as the Xerox Star cost $3,950 in 1980 – equivalent to $8,500 in 1994 dollars. In 1994, microcomputers with the vastly increased performance of 486 processors were retailing for $1,000.

Uncertainty

A general feature of emerging and technology-intensive industries is the high level of uncertainty that firms have to bear. Uncertainty over which technology and product design will ultimately emerge as the industry standard is exacerbated by the fact that different approaches offer different advantages and disadvantages, and even if one approach is clearly superior, this does not guarantee its acceptance. In the mid-nineteenth century, the 3.5-foot railway gauge was accepted as the standard for British railways, despite the technical superiority of Brunel's 6-foot gauge. In VCRs, the displaced Betamax system offered higher quality image reproduction than the ultimately dominant VHS system. In typewriter keyboards, the QWERTY arrangement of keys is dominant despite the inconvenience of this layout compared to DSK (the Dvorak Simplified Keyboard).[8] Microsoft DOS, largely because it was selected by IBM for its personal computer launched in 1981, has dominated microcomputer operating systems, despite general recognition of its fundamental imperfections.

One consequence of the uncertain outcome of competition between rival technologies is that technological forecasting, always a hazardous game, is especially difficult in new industries. The implications of this technological uncertainty for business risk is made more serious by the fact that establishing a particular approach as the industry standard requires heavy investment in development, production facilities, and marketing. These investments may prove to be worthless for the runner-up.

Technological uncertainty is compounded by market uncertainty. The successful transition from the introduction phase to the growth phase is far from certain. When Xerox introduced its first plain-paper copier in 1959 and when Steve Jobs and Steve Wozniak introduced their first personal computer in 1977, the success of the companies, or of the industries they spawned, was far from certain. Technological achievement and a successful introduction of a new product do not guarantee commercial viability:

- the Concorde was a technically superb aircraft, but airlines' doubts over their ability to operate it profitably were such that the only sales made were to the British and French state-owned airlines;
- Du Pont's "Corfam" was a technically superb product: the first synthetic leather substitute that could "breathe" like leather. But the product failed to gain acceptance either from the shoe manufacturers or their customers, and after running up losses of almost $100 million, Du Pont ceased production of Corfam in 1971.[9]

Market risks exist not just for entirely new innovations. Many types of new market entries involve transferring an existing product to a new market. EuroDisney involved the transfer of Disney's theme park concept from Disneyland and Disney World to Europe. Despite detailed market research, the popularity of Disney's U.S. theme parks with visiting European tourists, and the success of Tokyo Disneyland, EuroDisney's revenues during 1993 and 1994 fell substantially below those forecast.

The business risks arising from technological and market uncertainty are exacerbated by the investment requirements of innovation. Typically, substantial up-front investment must be made in technology and product development and in manufacturing facilities well before any returns are generated. To the extent that components or distribution and customer support facilities are not available, the innovator's investment requirements are increased by the need for vertical integration. Early entrants into the home computer industry faced the problems of finding distribution outlets, software availability, and providing customer education and customer support. In both North America and Europe, the early involvement of the oil companies in establishing filling stations was a consequence of the apparent inability of the existing retail sector to provide gasoline service to a rapidly expanding population of users.

The combination of high risk and substantial capital requirements represents a powerful entry barrier into many emerging and technology-intensive industries. It is also true, however, that new industries lack many of the barriers that restrict entry into more mature industries. In the early stages of an industry's life, established firms are unlikely to have built substantial advantages over potential entrants. Brand loyalty is not well entrenched, distribution channels are still developing, capital requirements are comparatively modest, and no firms have traveled far down the experience curve. Industry development is typically accompanied by rising entry barriers as the scale of production increases and firms establish clear market positions.

Competitive Advantage in Technology-Intensive Industries

The profitability of innovation

Emerging and technology-based industries offer considerable opportunities for profit. In terms of our two primary sources of superior profitability (see chapter 2), these industries score highly on both: they are growing industries with substantial product differentiation, hence, conducive to attractive margins, and, second, innovation offers considerable scope for establishing competitive advantage. The commercial potential of innovation was clearly recognized by Emerson: "If a man . . . make a better mousetrap than his neighbor, though he build his house in the woods, the world will make a beaten path to his door." Yet, how profitable in practice are investments in innovation?

The empirical evidence is mixed. PIMS data show a negative relationship between R&D expenditure (as a percentage of sales) and ROI and ROS. New product introductions also appear to depress profitability.[10] However, the relationship may be obscured by lags between R&D investments and returns being generated. A 1986 study of profitability in the longer term showed that high market share companies in research-intensive industries earned above-average returns, but firms in these industries with above-average patents-to-sales ratios did not earn significantly higher returns.[11]

The absence of general relationships between innovation and profitability probably reflects the fact that the profitability of innovation is highly dependent upon competitive conditions within particular industries. There are two sets of issues that are of fundamental importance in determining the returns to innovation. The first concerns the innovator's ability to generate financial returns from the innovation, which is termed *appropriability*; the second is the innovator's ability to sustain those returns in the face of imitation. The discussion here closely parallels that of chapters 5 and 6 where we examined the extent to which firms could utilize their resources and capabilities to establish and sustain competitive advantage. The critical issue here is that of *imitation*: if an innovation can be easily imitated by competitors, the returns will be few and brief; if the innovation can be protected against imitation, then returns can be substantial and long term.

- *Appropriability* The literature on innovation uses the term *appropriability* to describe the extent to which an innovator can capture the value from an innovation in profit returns. Innovation creates value. The critical issue for the innovator is how that value is distributed between the different parties to innovation. Figure 10.2 shows the parties to an innovation and a possible distribution of benefits from the innovation. In a strong *"regime of appropriability,"* the innovator is able to capture a substantial share of the value created. Thus, innovations such as Monsanto's NutraSweet artificial sweetener, Glaxo's Zantac, and Pilkington's float glass process generated huge profits for the innovators. Other innovations occur within weak

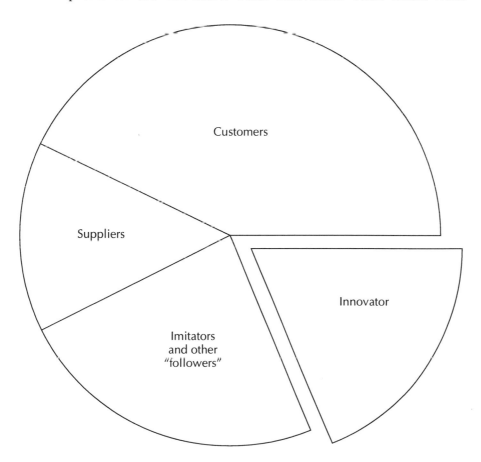

Figure 10.2 The Distribution of the Benefits from Innovation

Source: David J. Teece, "Profiting from Technological Innovation: Implications for Integration, Collaboration, Licensing, and Public Policy," in *The Competitive Challenge: Strategies for Innovation and Renewal*, ed. D. J. Teece (Cambridge, MA: Ballinger, 1987).

regimes of appropriability. In the case of the personal computer, the benefits generated were huge, but the primary beneficiaries were not the innovators, MITS and Apple Computer, but imitators such as IBM, Compaq, and Hewlett-Packard; suppliers such as Intel and Microsoft; and, above all, users.

- *Sustainability*   Over the longer term, the returns to innovation depend critically upon the extent to which the innovator can protect the innovation against imitation. The analysis here closely parallels our analysis of the sustainability of competitive advantage in chapter 6. In that chapter, we observed that imitating a competitive advantage depended upon the ability to diagnose the sources of the competitive advantage and to assemble the resources and capabilities necessary for imitation, either by purchasing them or replicating them. Similar issues arise in the specific case of innovation.

In relation to both appropriability and sustainability, four factors are especially important: legal protection, complementary resources, the characteristics of the technology with regard to complexity and transferability, and lead time.

Legal protection of innovation

The innovator's ability to appropriate the returns to innovation depend critically upon the ability to establish property rights. The importance of appropriability in providing incentives for innovation has been recognized since the English Parliament passed the 1623 Statute of Monopolies, which established the basis of patent law. Property rights exist in relation to patents, copyrights, trademarks, and trade secrets:

- *Patents* are exclusive rights to a new and useful product, process, substance, or design. Obtaining a patent requires that the invention is novel, useful, and nonobvious. Patent law varies from country to country. In the United States, a patent exists for 17 years (14 for a design);
- *Copyrights* give exclusive production, publication, or sales rights to the creators of artistic, literary, dramatic, or musical works. Examples include articles, books, drawings, maps, photographs, and musical compositions;
- *Trademarks* are words, symbols, or other marks used to distinguish the goods or services supplied by a firm. In the United States, they are registered with the Patent Office. Trademarks provide the basis for brand identification;
- *Trade secrets* offer less well-defined legal protection. Trade secret protection chiefly relates to chemical formulas, recipes, and industrial processes.

The effectiveness of these legal instruments of protection depends upon the type of innovation being protected. The advantage of patents and copyrights is that they establish clear property rights. Their disadvantage is that they make information public. For some new chemical products and basic mechanical inventions, patents can provide effective protection. For products that involve new configurations of existing components or new manufacturing processes, patents may be less effective because of opportunities to innovate around the patent. In this latter case, the act of patenting may facilitate competitive patents.

Complementary resources

Critical to the linkage between innovation and profitability – and hence to appropriability – are the resources needed to commercialize an innovation. Few, if any, innovations are capable of generating returns on their own. Whether it is a jet engine or digital audio tape, the product must be manufactured, marketed, and distributed. Moreover, developing a market for the product may be dependent upon complementary innovations: for example, the adoption of jet engines required the technical development of wings, fuselages, fuel systems, instrumentation, and control systems. Figure 10.3 shows these complementary resources.

The characteristics of the complementary resources required to commercialize an innovation are critical to the appropriability of the returns to an innovation. If the exploitation of an innovation is dependent upon the use of other resources, then the returns from that exploitation will be shared between the owner of the innovation and the owner of the other resources. The issue here is one of bargaining power, which in turn hinges upon dependence. If the complementary resources are *specialized*, then the owners of these resources are in a much more powerful position than if the complementary resources are *generic*. For example, the introduction of quick frozen foods into the European market during the early 1950s required investment in cold stores, refrigerated trucks, and frozen food retail cabinets, all of which reduced the value of the basic patents on the quick-freezing process. On the other hand, the inventor of a new additive that improves the clean-burning of gasoline by motor vehicles can expect to appropriate a major part of the value of the innovation because the commercialization of the innovation requires only existing resources in refineries and gasoline distribution, which are not firm-specific.

A special case of the relationship between innovation and complementary resources is where *co-specialization* exists. That is, the innovation is dependent upon the use of certain specialized assets, but assets are also dependent upon the innovation. For example, the introduction of electric cars will be dependent upon service stations investing in facilities for recharging batteries. In this situation, how the returns will be shared between the different owners of the key resources is not easily determined.

The role of complementary resources also affects the ease of imitation. If imitation requires not only access to the innovation but also access to a range of specialized complementary resources, this creates a more

Figure 10.3 The Complementary Resources Needed to Commercialize an Innovation

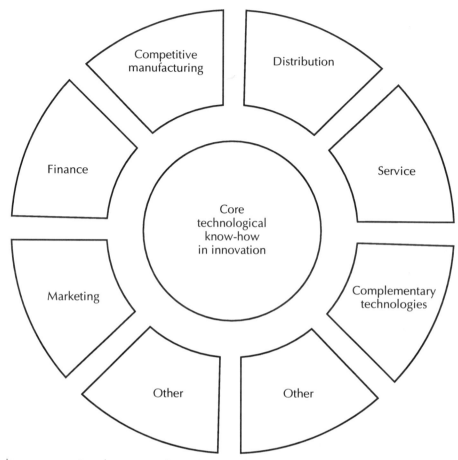

Source: David J. Teece, "Profiting from Technological Innovation: Implications for Integration, Collaboration, Licensing, and Public Policy," in *The Competitive Challenge: Strategies for Innovation and Renewal*, ed. D. J. Teece (Cambridge, MA: Ballinger, 1987).

substantial barrier to imitation. For example, Polaroid's leadership in instant photography is protected by a package of co-specialized resources relating to the technology embodied in the camera and the film, the brand name, the manufacturing facilities and know-how, and Polaroid's strong position in distribution channels.

The characteristics of the technology

The extent to which an innovation can be copied depends not just upon legal protection through patents and copyrights but also upon the characteristics of the technology. Two characteristics are especially important. The first is whether the knowledge embodied in the innovation is *tacit* or *codifiable*. Codifiable knowledge, by definition, is that which can be written down. Hence, if it is effectively protected by patents or copyright, diffusion is likely to be rapid and the competitive advantage not sustainable. Financial innovations such as mortgage-backed securities, zero-interest bonds, and new types of index options embody readily codifiable knowledge. As such, they only confer sustainable competitive advantage if supported by complementary resources such as human skills in designing and trading them and the ability to offer liquidity by developing secondary markets with sufficient volumes of trade. Similarly, Coca-Cola's recipe is codifiable and, in the absence of trade secret protection, is easily copied. Hence, the sustainability of Coca-Cola's market position is based much more on the company's brand position than upon its recipe. Tacit knowledge, such as Toyota's systems for assembling its cars and Nucor's advanced process technologies in minimill manufacturing of steel products, is embodied within the skills of employees and within the organizational routines that link employees. Experience shows that these innovations are not readily imitable.

The second characteristic is *complexity*. Whether based upon tacit or codifiable knowledge, some innovations are simply more complex than others, and the more complex an innovation, the more difficult it is to unravel and, probably, the more difficult it is to replicate. A supersonic airplane is a difficult innovation to copy because of the number and complexity of the technologies involved. A Rubik's Cube (a popular toy of the early 1980s) was a simple innovation to copy. The simpler an innovation, the more important patents and copyrights are likely to be for its protection. For complex innovations, secrecy is likely to be the more effective means of protection. However, even complex innovations can be copied through reverse engineering. During the Second World War, British and German armaments producers became especially adept at reverse-engineering captured military hardware. During the 1970s, the rapid closing of the technological gap between Japanese and U.S. industry was achieved in part through Japanese reverse-engineering of state-of-the-art U.S. products.

Lead time

These characteristics of tacitness and complexity do not provide lasting barriers to imitation; the protection they provide is that of time. Hence, innovation should be viewed not so much as conferring a monopoly position as offering a window of opportunity. This opportunity is a period of time during which the innovator has the chance to extend the initial competitive advantage. This time advantage is referred to as *lead time*. Thus, Microsoft and Motorola have never waited around to enjoy the fruits of their technological leadership in microcomputer operating systems and wireless communication equipment, respectively. Microsoft has continually pushed ahead to extend its competitive advantage both through frequent upgrading of MS-DOS and branching into applications software, networking software, and new operating systems (Windows). Similarly, despite its leadership in cellular communications equipment, Motorola is investing in a variety of competitive wireless technologies.

The innovator's lead-time advantage can be reinforced by cost advantages deriving from a leadership position on the learning curve. Thus, companies that seek to clone Intel's 486 and Pentium microprocessors face not only the legal barriers of circumventing Intel's patents and copyrights and the task of perfecting the production technology but also the cost advantages that Intel possesses as a result of its manufacturing experience.

Some empirical evidence

How effective are these different mechanisms in protecting technological advantage and permitting innovators to appropriate the returns to their innovations? Empirical evidence shows tremendous variability across industries, but the principal conclusion is that patent protection is less important than commonly supposed. One survey found that, across 12 industries, patents were judged essential to the development of commercially important inventions in:

- 65 percent of pharmaceutical inventions
- 30 percent of chemical inventions
- 10-20 percent of inventions in petroleum, machinery, and metal products
- less than 10 percent of inventions in electrical equipment, instruments, primary metals, office equipment, motor vehicles, rubber, and textiles

In another study, lead-time advantages, learning curve advantages, and sales and service networks were found to be more effective at protecting both process and product innovations than were patents (see table 10.1).

Strategic Decisions Concerning Technology Management

Having reviewed the characteristics of emerging and technology-intensive industries and the sources of competitive advantage within them,

Table 10.1 Protecting Innovation: The Effectiveness of Different Barriers to Imitation

Method of Appropriation	Overall sample means	
	Processes	Products
Patents to prevent duplication	3.52	4.33
Patents to secure royalty income	3.31	3.75
Secrecy	4.31	3.57
Lead time	5.11	5.41
Moving quickly down the learning curve	5.02	5.09
Sales or service efforts	4.55	5.59

The means show responses from 650 individuals across 130 lines of business. The range was from 1 (= not at all effective) to 7 (= very effective).
Source: R. C. Levin, A. K. Klevorick, R. R. Nelson, S. G. Winter, "Appropriating the Returns from Industrial Research and Development," *Brookings Papers on Economic Activity* 3 (1987): 794.

let us turn now to some of the critical strategic decisions concerning the management of technology for competitive advantage. This section focuses upon four issues:

- Forecasting
- Timing
- Managing risks
- Licensing versus internal exploitation of innovation

I will deal with each in turn.

Forecasting

The decision to enter an emerging industry and to develop and exploit an innovation must be based, first and foremost, upon a view of how the product and the market for it will develop over time. Forecasting is important given the extent of technological and market risk but is also made difficult by the presence of these fundamental uncertainties. Essential elements of such a forward look are ideas about the potential size and growth rate of the market, the technology and design that are likely to dominate the industry, the most likely distribution channels, the likely entrants, and the most powerful competitors that will emerge.

Most conventional techniques for forecasting the environment are of limited value in emerging industries for two reasons. First, most conventional forecasting techniques are based upon some kind of extrapolation of existing data into the future. In the case of new technologies and products, few data are available, and those that are are of limited value in predicting the future. How could it have been possible for Sony to have forecast the demand for its Walkman if the product only existed as a prototype?[12] Hence, to forecast technological changes and the future development patterns of emerging industries, qualitative analysis that draws upon imagination and expert opinion tends to be superior to quantitative forecasts based upon data analysis. Among useful forecasting techniques are:

- *Scenario building*   Over the last decade, scenarios, pioneered by Herman Kahn's Hudson Institute, have gained increasing popularity as a tool for strategy formulation.[13] A scenario is an internally consistent view of what the future may turn out to be. The value of scenarios is in being able to combine the interrelated impacts of a wide range of economic, technological, and social factors into a number of distinct alternative pictures of the future. Scenarios are conducive to the exercise of the imagination and have been shown to be valuable in identifying possible threats and opportunities, generating flexibility of thinking by managers, and developing highly practical approaches to the management of risk. Industry scenarios can be used to develop alternative views of how the market and industry structure may develop and what the implications for competition and competitive advantage might be. The Royal Dutch/Shell Group of companies has pioneered the use of scenarios as a basis for long-term strategic planning in an industry subject to rapid and discontinuous change.[14]

- *The Delphi Technique,* developed at the RAND Corporation, draws upon the coordinated views of a panel of experts to reach agreed forecasts about future developments. While the technique is a powerful method for synthesizing and probing the knowledge and experience of leading experts within a field, there is always a risk that group processes will result in an irrational judgment.[15] Delphi techniques have been used extensively by computer, electronics, and pharmaceutical companies.[16]

A second reason for the failure of conventional forecasting techniques in the area of technological change is their emphasis on predicting the future values of exogenous variables: levels of market demand, the costs of raw materials, exchange rates, government policy interventions, and so on. In the case of an emerging industry, the future is determined by the firms that develop the industry. If a company is to be an industry leader, strategy must be developed not in response to industry changes but in order to shape industry changes.

Predicting the shape of technological change in fast-moving industries has to do more with perception than with technique. The critical management requirement is to recognize the potential that emerging technologies offer for meeting customers' real needs. There is ample evidence that established firms' vested interests in current technologies can prevent the objective appraisal of competing technologies. As a result, industry leaders become incapable of anticipating change, and they are overtaken by competitors. In tire cords, the shift from cotton to rayon to nylon to polyester was associated with a shift of industry leadership, first, to the American Viscose Company (rayon), then to Du Pont (nylon), and then to Celanese Corporation (polyester). In electronic components, Sylvania, a leader in vacuum tubes, continued to invest in vacuum tube technology and discounted the advantages of the emerging solid-state technology. Richard Foster refers to this phenomenon as "technological myopia" and points to the need for top management to be alert to (1) the role of new technologies in redefining served markets, (2) the cultural factors that encourage a company to defend its established technological expertise, and (3) evidence of decay in the company's technological position.[17]

The timing of entry and innovation: To lead or to follow?

Timing represents probably the most critical and the most difficult issue in strategy formulation in emerging and technologically intensive industries. The central issue is the choice of leadership or "followership." The leader in entry and innovation can be the first to grab the prize. However, the leader also bears the highest risks and the costs of pioneering. Optimal timing of entry into an emerging industry and the introduction of new technology is a complex issue. The relative costs and benefits of pioneering depend upon a large number of variables that can be classified into three main groups: the characteristics of the technology, the structure of the industry, and the resources of the firm. Examples of success and failure in innovation point to no clear pattern (see table 10.2).

The advantages associated with pioneering are referred to as first-mover advantages, which depend upon the following factors:

(1) *The extent to which innovations can be protected by legal instruments, lead time, learning-curve advantages, and the like* If an innovation is appropriable and confers sustainable advantage, there are likely to be substantial advantages in being an early mover. Where patent protection is important, such as in pharmaceuticals, competition can take the form of a patent race where the rewards are of a winner-take-all character. Thus, in following a potentially interesting avenue of research or seeking a cure for fatal diseases such as AIDS or cancer, competition takes the form of a patent race where the rewards for being second are likely to be nonexistent.

(2) *The importance of complementary resources* The more important are complementary resources to the effective exploitation of an innovation, the greater will be the costs of pioneering and the attractions of being a follower. Thus, the costs of developing an electric car are enormous, partly because of the need to orchestrate the development of a number of technologies – particularly batteries – and the need to establish facilities for service and recharging. Investment requirements often fall as an industry develops, especially when these complementary resources are not specific to a single firm. Thus, in the British frozen foods industry, Birds Eye, the pioneer, was forced to make huge invest-

PRODUCT	INNOVATOR	FOLLOWER	WINNER
Jet airliners	De Havilland (Comet)	Boeing (707)	Follower
Float glass	Pilkington	Corning	Leader
X-ray scanner	EMI	General Electric	Follower
Office PC	Xerox	IBM	Follower
VCRs	Ampex/Sony	Matsushita	Follower
Diet cola	R.C. Cola	Coca-Cola	Follower
Instant cameras	Polaroid	Kodak	Leader
Pocket calculator	Bowmar	Texas Instruments	Follower
Microwave oven	Raytheon	Samsung	Follower
Plain-paper copier	Xerox	Canon	Not clear
Fiber optic cable	Corning	many companies	Leader
Video game players	Atari	Nintendo/Sega	Followers
Disposable diapers	Procter & Gamble	Kimberly-Clark	Leader

Table 10.2 Leaders, Followers, and Success in Emerging Industries

Source: Based in part upon David Teece, ed., *The Competitive Challenge: Strategies for Industrial Innovation and Renewal* (Cambridge, MA: Ballinger, 1987), 186–8.

ments in a frozen foods distribution network, including the leasing of frozen food cabinets to retailers. However, by the mid-1970s, the growth of public cold stores and refrigerated trucking companies meant that newcomers to the industry could enter at much lower levels of capital cost. Thus, in some industries, it would seem that companies that lack critical complementary resources can wait until the necessary industry infrastructure appears. In the European microcomputer industry, for example, the failure of Sir Clive Sinclair's Sinclair Electronics was partly due to the company's inability to assemble the necessary complementary resources: reliable sources of components and software, manufacturing capabilities, and distribution channels. By the time Amstrad entered in 1983, it was able to rely upon the highly efficient manufacturing facilities of Far Eastern manufacturers and well-developed distribution channels.

However, there are also forces working in the opposite direction. The pattern of industry development in the early stages is for competition to be highly technologically focused initially, but once a dominant design emerges, competition shifts toward other dimensions. It is this shift to competing on price, quality, brand name, and the like that puts increased emphasis on many of these complementary resources. Thus, established firms that are well endowed with the complementary resources needed to compete in a new industry are often late entrants, choosing to delay their entry to the point where uncertainties are diminished, and they are able to bring their complementary resources to bear with maximum impact. Consider the following examples:

- In personal computers, Apple was a pioneer, IBM a follower. The timing of entry was probably optimal for each. Apple's resources were its imagination and its technology. Its strategic window occurred at the very beginnings of the industry when these resources could make the biggest impact. IBM had enormous strengths in manufacturing, distribution, and brand reputation. It could use these resources to establish competitive advantage even without a clear technological advantage. The important thing for IBM was to delay its entry to the point when market and technological risks had been reduced and the industry had reached a stage of development where strengths in large-scale manufacturing, marketing, and distribution could be brought to bear;
- Although General Electric entered the market for CT scanners some four years after EMI, GE was able to overtake EMI within the space of three years because of its ability to apply vast technological, manufacturing, sales, and customer service capabilities within the field of medical electronics.

(3) *Controlling industry standards* A feature of industry evolution is the convergence over time of technology and design around a single dominant approach. In relation to the optimal time of entry, therefore, a key issue is the trade-off between the risk of early entry with the

possibility of backing the wrong technological horse and the risk of being too late to influence or establish a strong early position in the dominant technological approach. Returning to IBM's entry into personal computers, important to the success of this entry was the fact that a dominant technology or design had not emerged by 1981. IBM was able to establish a dominant *de facto* standard for the industry around the Intel microprocessor and the MS-DOS operating system.

The ownership of proprietary standards is one of the most valuable resources in technologically dynamic markets. IBM's problem was that, although it was successful in setting the standard for the industry, it did not *own* the standard. It was Intel and Microsoft that owned the critical parts of the dominant configuration and that, over the long term, were able to appropriate the major part of the returns for the highly successful IBM PC and its many clones. Morris and Ferguson refer to the technical standards that are critical components of a dominant design paradigm as *"architectural standards."*[18] An *"architectural controller"* is a company that controls one or more of the architectural standards by which the entire information package is assembled. Even in an "open systems" environment, these architectural standards play an important role. Thus, in a typical in-company computer network:

- Intel owns the microprocessor design
- Microsoft or Sun owns the operating system
- Novell owns the network software
- Adobe or Hewlett-Packard owns the printer page description system

Maximizing the rents from architectural standards requires managing a difficult trade-off. On the one side, profiting from a technical standard requires maintaining ownership of the critical technology. On the other, establishing the technology as a standard may require giving general access to it. In the personal computer industry, IBM and Apple made opposite errors. IBM was incredibly successful in getting a standard set as a result of the general availability of Intel chips and MS-DOS software but failed to establish any ownership of the critical technologies. Apple was successful in owning the critical technologies but failed to get its technology established as an industry standard because of its unwillingness to license its graphical user interface to other manufacturers.

Managing risks

The presence of technological and market uncertainties, difficulties of forecasting, frequency of entry by new competitors, and the need for heavy up-front investment in research, product development, manufacturing facilities, and marketing imply high risks in emerging industries. Two indicators of the riskiness of emerging industries are the high cost of capital for firms and projects in new industries and the frequency of corporate failure. Hence, effective management of risk is a vital ingredient of survival and success in emerging industries. Given the limited financial resources of most of the firms that pioneer innovation, a critical strategic issue is the effective management of risk. Three methods of coping with risk have been suggested:

(1) *Cooperating with lead users*   During the early phases of industry development, careful monitoring of and response to market trends and customer requirements is essential to avoid major errors in technology, design, and performance. Von Hippel argues that lead users provide a vital source of market data for developing new products.[19] Hence, identifying users whose present strong needs will become general market trends in the future and developing close ties with such customers can be vital to maintaining technological progressiveness. Cooperation with lead users yields three major benefits:

- an "early warning system" for emerging needs and technological trends;
- assistance in the conception and development of new products and processes. In electronic instruments, customers' ideas initiated most of the successful new products introduced by manufacturers.[20] Similarly, in aluminum refining, fabricators have been the source of the majority of innovations;[21]
- by targeting early adopters, the firm can achieve an early cash flow to contribute to further development expenditures.

In industrial products, the most innovative and technologically conscious customers are easy to identify, and their own decisions may have an important influence on the technological choices of other firms too. In consumer products, early adopters are frequently young, educated, affluent consumers in urban areas – although this is not always the case. A key element in Nike's recapturing of market leadership from Reebok in the U.S. market for sports shoes was Nike's market research and new product testing with street gangs in inner-city areas. In electronics and aerospace, governments (the military in particular) play a crucial role as early adopters. In the United States, Britain, and France, government contracts are major sources of finance for R&D into innovative, sophisticated products (although dependence upon government contracts to support R&D may encourage overengineering and inattentiveness to design-for-manufacturability).

(2) *Limiting risk exposure*   The high level of risk in emerging industries requires that firms adopt financial and investment practices that minimize their exposure to adversity. Uncertainties over development costs and the timing and amount of future cash flows require a strong balance sheet with limited debt financing:

- Apple's ability to survive a severe revenue slump in 1984-5 and the ensuing industry shakeout owed much to its strong cash position and absence of debt;
- Hewlett-Packard's commitment to financing all expansion out of retained profits has been an important source of strength for the company in navigating a course through technological and market turbulence;
- Similarly, the cost of developing a second generation of X-ray scanners combined with an unexpected fall in revenue was sufficient to bring down the diversified music and electronic company EMI. EMI's scanner business was acquired by GE; the remainder of EMI was taken over by Thorn.

One reason for EMI's financial vulnerability was the heavy investment needed to set up its own manufacturing, marketing, and servicing facilities for developing its scanner innovation. Innovators can reduce their exposure to risk by relying upon the investments of other companies. This might include the leasing of capital equipment, buying in major components, and contracting out wherever possible. In the electronics and communications sectors, a dominant feature of the last ten years has been the growing role of collaboration in the development of new technologies and new products. Thus, in developing software for "personal communicators," the Silicon Valley start-up General Magic has built a web of alliances that include AT&T, Apple, Motorola, Sony, Matsushita, and Philips.[22] In developing the Teledisc global system of direct satellite communication, McCaw Cellular has teamed up with Microsoft;

(3) *Flexibility* The high level of uncertainty in emerging industries makes flexibility critical to long-term survival and success. Because technological and market changes are difficult to forecast, it is essential that top management closely monitors the environment and that the organization responds quickly and effectively to demand fluctuations, changing preferences regarding technology and design, changing patterns of distribution, and the emergence of new customer segments. According to Tom Peters, a vital element in flexibility is recognizing and responding to failures. Peters quotes Sichiro Honda, the founder of Honda Motor Company: "Many people dream of success. To me success can only be achieved through repeated failure and introspection. In fact, success represents the 1 per cent of your work which only comes from the 99 per cent that is called failure."[23] An example is Honda's responsiveness to the disappointments that accompanied its entry into the U.S. motorcycle market. Although motorcycles were hardly a new product, Honda's U.S. venture shares many of the pioneering characteristics of innovation. Mr Kawashima, part of Honda's initial two-man team in the United States, recounted the experience:

By the first week of April 1960, reports were coming in that our machines were leaking oil and encountering clutch failure. This was our lowest moment. Honda's fragile reputation was being destroyed before it could be established. As it turned out, motorcycles in the U.S. are driven much farther and much faster than in Japan. We dug deeply into our precious cash reserves to air freight our motorcycles to the Honda testing lab in Japan. . . . Our lab worked 24-hour days bench testing the bikes to replicate the failure. Within a month, a redesigned head gasket and clutch spring solved the problem. But in the meantime events had taken a surprising turn. Throughout our first eight months we had not attempted to move the 50cc Supercubs. While they were a smash success in Japan, they seemed wholly unsuitable for the U.S. market where everything was bigger and more luxurious. . . . We used the Honda 50s ourselves to ride around Los Angeles on errands. They attracted a lot of attention. One day we had a call from a Sears buyer. While persisting in our refusal to sell through an intermediary, we took note of Sears' interest. . . . When the larger bikes started breaking, we had no choice. We let the 50cc bikes move. And surprisingly, the retailers who wanted to sell them weren't motorcycle dealers, they were sporting goods stores. The excitement created by the Honda Supercub began to gain momentum.[24]

A similar responsiveness to customer requirements and market opportunities is apparent in the success of Apple's Macintosh. The original Macintosh launched in 1984 was a technologically brilliant product in search of a market. During 1985 and 1986, Apple initiated a host of strategic initiatives including cooperation with Microsoft on business applications software, opening the Mac to third-party developers, upgrading speed and memory, and targeting the desktop publishing market. The result was a transformation in the Macintosh's market positioning and appeal.[25]

Managing the risks associated with innovation also requires that investment criteria are adjusted so that investments are not biased against R&D projects. One of the problems of discounted cash flow analysis of investment projects is that such appraisal fails to take account of the *option value* of R&D. Research into a promising technology is unlikely to generate financial returns directly. Its value is that it gives a company a position within an emerging technology that offers the potential for further investment in new products that may generate high profits. Merck's Financial Evaluation and Analysis Group uses a variant of the Black-Scholes option-pricing model to evaluate investments in external research being undertaken by universities or small biotechnology companies.[26]

Exploiting innovation: Licensing versus internal development

One of the greatest difficulties in managing the development of new technology and new products is the extent to which companies should specialize in technology development or invest in all the complementary resources necessary to take their innovations to market. Different approaches predominate in different industries and in different countries. In the United States, a large part of new technology and many new products is the work of small start-up companies, many of which either license their technology to larger established concerns or are acquired by these larger companies. In Japan, the development and commercialization of innovations tend to occur within individual corporations.

The case for licensing   The key success factors for innovation are different from those needed for large-scale commercialization. Innovation requires creativity, imagination, technical brilliance, and insight into customer needs. Commercialization requires the whole range of "complementary resources" required for manufacturing, marketing, distributing, and financing. These activities typically require different strategies and organizational conditions. In particular, most major inventions are associated either with individuals or small organizations, while commercialization typically requires large organizations. A survey of major innovations of the twentieth century revealed that a surprisingly large proportion were contributed by individual inventors, frequently working in their garage or garden shed.[27] A study of 27 important inventions during the postwar period found that only seven emerged from the R&D departments of established corporations.[28] Hence, in biotechnology and electronics, a two-stage model for innovation is common: the technology is initially developed by a small, technology-intensive start-up, which then licenses to a larger concern. In the small British semiconductor sector, several small, research-intensive firms have been successful in developing new products that have been licensed to bigger players. Acorn RISC Machines designed the microprocessor used in the Apple Newton, which was licensed to Sharp and Texas Instruments (TI).[29] Similarly, MEJ Electronics of Guildford, England, specializes in designing application-specific integrated circuits (ASICs), which are licensed to NEC, Hitachi, Fujitsu, TI, and other companies.[30]

The essential condition for the success of these arrangements is the ability to appropriate the value of the innovation through licensing. This depends upon the ability to establish proprietary rights through enforceable patents and copyrights. The effectiveness of patents in pharmaceuticals has meant that small biotechnology start-ups specialize in the development of new drugs, leaving testing, manufacturing, and marketing to established pharmaceutical companies.

The merits of internal commercialization   While George Gilder has praised the dynamism and inventiveness of the Silicon Valley model of entrepreneurial innovation involving small technology-based start-ups, spin-offs, and venture capitalists, Charles Ferguson argues that entrepreneurial start-ups often involve individual exploitation of the technologies developed within large corporations with the result that the large-firm capabilities in the long-term development of areas of technology and the linking of R&D with complementary resources are seriously weakened.[31] The case for the internal development and exploitation of technologies rests upon two key assumptions.

The first is that to fully appropriate the returns to innovation, innovation and complementary assets need to be brought together within the same company. This is especially important where close interdependencies exist between technology development, marketing, product development, and manufacturing.

The second is that innovation is not about single innovations but the generation of a stream of innovations that flow from building capability within a particular area of technology. Thus, Motorola's success in semiconductors and wireless communication equipment should not be viewed in terms of particular products or innovations but as the development of technological and manufacturing capability within electronics and communication. Thus, "technology leakage" as a result of Motorola's engineers' leaving to start their own companies would represent a weakening of these core capabilities.

While established corporations offer strategic advantage in developing technology and appropriating its returns, the fact remains that many of the most important and radical innovations of this century have their origins in the creative brilliance of individuals, often without significant institutional support.

Start-up companies are highly effective vehicles for fostering the creativity necessary for pioneering new technology. Even when innovation takes place within established firms, very often it is first exploited by new companies that spin off from the corporation. Such spin-offs may occur either because the established company is uninterested in exploiting the technology, because the innovators seek to exploit the technology for their own gains, or because a strategic decision was made by the parent company to obtain external equity financing while providing the autonomy needed for development. Among the large number of start-up companies in California's Silicon Valley are many that were set up by engineers and managers from Hewlett-Packard, Xerox's Palo Alto Research Center (PARC), Stanford University, and the University of California at Berkeley.

The different resource requirements of the various stages of the innovation process imply that different types of company are likely to excel at each stage. While small start-up companies may possess advantages in harnessing the expertise and enthusiasm that are key ingredients in the early creative phase, larger established companies are likely to possess the finance, development skills, marketing knowledge, and manufacturing capability necessary for successfully taking the innovation to market. Hence, success in technology-based industries is likely to depend upon establishing organizational arrangements which exploit the advantages of different types of firm at these different stages. They waited until the market was relatively well developed and the trajectory of technological development was better defined before committing their resources and reputations. Specialization by companies according to their comparative advantages implies that large companies whose strengths are in the commercialization stages of innovation should not seek to be self-sufficient in innovation. In consumer electronics, the success of Matsushita, Samsung, and several other Japanese and Korean companies reflects their willingness to license technology from all over the world and then to develop, integrate, and commercialize that technology internally. By contrast, one source of the poorer performance of Philips and RCA in the same markets may be their propensity to look internally for new product innovation. The apparent unwillingness of U.S. companies to exploit technologies developed by other companies has been termed the "Not-Invented-Here" syndrome, which is the consequence of well-established, tightly knit project groups believing that they have a monopoly on relevant knowledge in their field.[32] The strategic alliances between biotechnology start-up and major drug companies, and the strategic networks formed by Apple, Sun Microsystems and HP in Silicon Valley are examples of interorganizational arrangements to harness the advantages of different types of company.

Strategy Implementation in Emerging Industries: Creating the Conditions for Innovation

From strategy formulation to conditions for innovation

The preceding analysis of the characteristics of emerging and technology-intensive industries, the conditions or competitive advantage from innovation, and the strategic decisions in relation to innovation tell us something about generating profits out of innovation but tell us little about the conditions under which innovation is achieved in the first place. Indeed, strategic management in technology-intensive environments faces difficult challenges. If the primary source of competitive advantage in these environments is innovation and if innovation is characterized, first, by new ideas, and, second, by uniqueness, it is difficult to apply systematic analysis to the formulation of "innovation strategies," and such strategies are likely to fail in their implementation. If the essence of innovation is creativity and one of the key features of creativity is its resistance to planning, it is evident that strategy formulation must pay careful attention to the organizational processes through which innovations emerge and are commercialized. Because the features of new products and processes are unknown at the time when resources are committed to R&D and there is no predetermined relationship between investment in R&D and the output of innovations, the productivity of R&D depends heavily upon the organizational conditions that foster innovation. Hence, the most crucial challenge facing firms in emerging and technology-based industries is: *How does the firm create conditions that are conducive to innovation?*

To answer this question we must return to the critical distinction between invention and innovation. Invention is dependent upon creativity. Creativity is not simply a matter of individual brilliance; it depends upon the organizational conditions that are conducive to the generation of ideas and imagination at the individual and group levels. Similarly, innovation is not just a matter of acquiring the resources necessary for commercialization; innovation is a cooperative activity that requires interaction and collaboration between technology development, manufacturing, marketing, and various other functional departments within the firm.

The conditions for creativity

Invention has two primary ingredients: knowledge and creativity. Only by understanding the determinants of creativity, then fostering it through the appropriate organizational environment, can the firm hope to innovate successfully. Creativity is an individual act that establishes a meaningful relationship between concepts or objects that had not previously been related such that a new insight or invention is produced. Such reconceptualizing is triggered by accidents: an apple falling on Isaac Newton's head or James Watt observing a kettle boiling. Creativity also requires personal qualities. Research shows that creative people share certain personality traits: they are curious, imaginative, adventurous, assertive, playful, self-confident, risk-taking, reflective, and uninhibited.

Motivating creativity presents a further challenge. Creatively oriented people are typically responsive to different incentives than those who are effective in motivating other members of the organization: "They desire to work in an egalitarian culture with enough space and resources to provide the opportunity to be spontaneous, experience freedom, and have fun in the performance of a task that, they feel, makes a difference to the strategic performance of the firm. Praise, recognition and opportunities for education and professional growth are also more important than assuming managerial responsibilities."[33]

Creativity is likely to be stimulated by interaction with other people. Michael Tushman's research into communication in R&D laboratories concludes that developing communication networks is one of the most important aspects of the management of R&D.[34] An important catalyst to interaction is *play*, which creates an environment of inquiry, liberates thought from conventional constraints, and provides the opportunity to establish new relationships by rearranging ideas and structures at a safe distance from reality.[35] John Scully describes Apple's attempts to create such an atmosphere of playfulness:

Almost every building had its own theme, so meeting and conference rooms aren't identified by cold, impersonal numbers. Instead they are named by employees who decide upon the theme of their building. In our "Land of Oz" building, the conference rooms are named Dorothy and Toto. Our Management Information Systems Group has meeting rooms named "Greed," "Envy," "Sloth," "Lust," and the remaining deadly sins. It's not an accident that many of these are the symbols of childhood (popcorn included). William Blake believed that in growing up, people move from states of innocence to experience, and then, if they're fortunate, to "higher innocence" – the most creative state of all.[36]

These conditions for creativity have far-reaching organizational implications. Anita Roddick of Body Shop talks about a culture of "benevolent anarchy – encouraging questioning of established ways and going in the opposite direction to everyone else."[37] In particular, creativity requires an organizational structure and management systems that are quite different from those appropriate to the pursuit of cost efficiency. Table 10.3 contrasts some characteristics of the two types of organizations.

Although innovation is stimulated by creativity, it is vital for creativity to be stimulated by and directed toward *need*. The incentive for creativity is frequently the desire to solve problems. Few important inventions have been the result of spontaneous creative activity by technologists; almost all have resulted from grappling with practical problems. James

	Operating Organization	Innovating Organization
Structure	Bureaucratic. Specialization and division of labor. Hierarchical control.	Flat organization without hierarchical control. Task-oriented project teams.
Processes	Operating units controlled and coordinated by top management, which undertakes strategic planning, capital allocation, and operational planning.	Processes directed toward generation, selection, funding, and development of ideas. Strategic planning flexible; financial and operating controls loose.
Reward systems	Financial compensation, promotion up the hierarchy, power and status symbols.	Autonomy, recognition, equity participation in new ventures.
People	Recruitment and selection based upon the needs of the organization structure for specific skills: functional and staff specialists, general managers, and operatives.	Key need is for idea generators which combine required technical knowledge with creative personality traits. Managers must act as sponsors and orchestrators.

Table 10.3 The Characteristics of "Operating" and "Innovating" Organizations

Source: Based upon Jay R. Galbraith and Robert K. Kazanjian, *Strategy Implementation: Structure, Systems and Processes*, 2d ed. (St. Paul: West, 1986).

Watt's conceptualization of an improved steam engine was triggered by repair work on an early Newcomen steam engine owned by Glasgow University. The basic inventions behind the Xerox copying process were the work of Chester Carlson, a patent attorney who became frustrated by the problems of accurately copying technical drawings. The stimulus provided by problems explains the earlier observation that customers are the most fertile sources of innovation: it is customers who use products and services and consequently are most closely in touch with the problems of matching existing products and services to their needs.[38] The problem of "ivory tower" R&D departments is their isolation from outside stimulation. Thus, the poor innovatory performance of large corporate R&D departments may partly reflect the stultifying influence of bureaucracy on creativity, but it may also reflect the effect of large, highly structured organizations in isolating technologists and designers from the needs and problems of customers and manufacturing operations. Monsanto goes to great lengths to guide development teams toward areas with the greatest commercial potential. Monsanto's concern is to avoid what they term "trombone-oil projects" – wonderfully innovatory products for which the market is tiny. "Let them know you're in the research business not for the pursuit of knowledge but for the pursuit of product," says Monsanto CEO Richard Mahoney.[39]

From invention to innovation: The need for coordination and leadership

Once a company moves from invention to innovation, the additional resource requirements become substantially greater and more complex: in addition to creative ideas, innovation requires a product design and production equipment that permits cost-efficient manufacture, adaptation to customer preferences, marketing strategies that ensure a successful introduction of the product, and the establishment of distribution and customer-support facilities. Engineer-inventor John Endacott observes: "Having the idea is the easy bit. My advice to anyone coming up with a new invention is: Think about it, enjoy thinking about it, and then throw the idea in the bin."[40] The complex, multifunctional character of innovation poses awkward organizational problems. If different organizational arrangements are established between different functions – for example, a loosely structured R&D department and a more bureaucratically structured production department – a high level of *differentiation* may inhibit the *integration* that is the essence of successful innovation.

Dangers of isolation at corporate R&D departments   One problem of corporate R&D departments is their isolation from the stimulus of customer need. An even greater danger is that their output fails to be transferred into marketable, manufacturable new products. The classic case is that of Xerox Corporation's PARC facility, which, during the early 1980s was responsible for important breakthroughs in custom chips, computer-aided design, artificial intelligence, computer graphics, laser printing, and many of the features of the Apple Macintosh and Microsoft Windows (including the graphical interface, mouse, icons, and drop-down menus). Lack of coordination and cooperation between PARC and Xerox's operating divisions resulted in only a fraction of PARC's innovations being successfully exploited by Xerox. PARC initiated its own projects rather than working on those brought by internal clients. The innovations that emerged sometimes competed with existing Xerox products and frequently lacked the "product champions" to take them to market. The result was a flow of PARC engineers and innovations to Apple, Sun, Novell, Hewlett-Packard, and several other Silicon Valley companies.[41]

An important reason for the failure to effectively commercialize the fruits of research may be the resistance to new change that is inherent in virtually all organizations. Innovation upsets established organizational routines, imposes adjustment costs, increases the insecurity of organizational members, interferes with the pursuit of internal efficiency, and threatens established power positions. The more stable the administrative hierarchy, the greater is the resistance to innovation. Elting Morrison's analysis of the opposition by the U.S. naval establishment to the remarkable improvements in gunnery accuracy made possible by continuous-aim firing provides a fascinating anatomy of organizational resistance to innovation.[42]

Product development teams   One approach to the more effective integration of the fruits of R&D into the development of new products has been the creation of cross-functional new product teams. The basis of the current vogue for cross-functional teams is the success of many Japanese companies. Imai et al show how new product development teams have been a powerful mechanism for integrating knowledge, for learning, and for developing innovatory new products in remarkably short time periods.[43] In U.S. industry, Ford's successful experience with the development of its Taurus model was especially influential (see exhibit 10.1). Research by Clark and Fujimoto into the world automobile industry attributed the shorter new product development cycles of Japanese auto companies to their overlapping stages of product development and deployment of "heavyweight" cross-functional product development teams led by a product manager.[44]

The role of the "product champion"   While Clark and Fujimoto emphasize the role of integrated teams in developing new products, they also draw attention to individual leadership. They emphasize the critical role of the "heavyweight product manager": a team leader whose power and influence is equal to or greater than that of the heads of functional departments. Such a product manager is important both in achieving the overall "integrity" of the product through effective integration of

---

Exhibit 10.1   Product Development at Ford: From a Sequential to a Team Approach

The Sequential Approach: Pre-Taurus

"Designers designed a car on paper, then gave it to the engineers, who figured out how to make it. Their plans were passed on to the manufacturing and purchasing people. . . . The next step in the process was the production plant. Then came marketing, the legal and service departments, and finally the customers. If a glitch developed, the car was bumped back to the design stage for changes. The farther along in the sequence, however, the more difficult it was to make changes."

The Team Approach: The Taurus

"With Taurus . . . we brought all disciplines together, and did the whole process simultaneously as well as sequentially. The manufacturing people worked with the design people, engineering people, sales and purchasing, legal, service and marketing. . . . In sales and marketing we had dealers come in and tell us what they wanted in a car to make it more user-friendly. . . . We had insurance companies – Allstate, State Farm, American Road – tell us how to design a car so when accidents occur it would minimize the customer's expense in fixing it. . . . We went to all stamping plants, assembly plants and put layouts on the walls. We asked them how to make it easier to build. . . . It's amazing the dedication and commitment you can get from people."

– Taurus project leader, Veraldi

Source: Quoted from, Mary Walton, *The Deming Management Method* (New York: Dodd, Mead, 1986), 130–1.

---

the various functional members and in providing the leadership and drive for the project to achieve its goals.

Other studies have recognized the key role of leadership in innovation in terms of the impetus it provides for carrying the innovation from research lab to the market. A general characteristic of companies that are consistently successfully in innovation is their ability to capture and direct individual's drive for success by offering some kind of entrepreneurial role to these "product champions." Given the propensity of organizations to resist change, innovations need leadership by committed enthusiasts in order to overcome the organization's vested interest in stability and the status quo. Schon's study of 15 major innovations concluded that "the new idea either finds a champion or dies."[45] This vital role of this product champion (or in their terminology "business innovator") was confirmed by the SAPPHO project's comparative analysis of 43 pairs of successful and unsuccessful innovations.[46]

A prominent example of the role of product champions in leading team efforts to develop new products in a large, mature organization is provided by 3M Corporation. Exhibit 10.2 outlines 3M's approach to conceiving, developing, and marketing new products.

Managing the Evolution of Industries and Markets

The implications for organizational change

As products and industries move from their introductory into their growth stages, the heavy emphasis on product innovation shifts toward developing complementary resources and capabilities: manufacturing, marketing, distribution, and customer support. The need for the firm to balance innovation with efficiency and the increasingly differentiated managerial and organizational requirements of the different functions

Exhibit 10.2   Innovation at 3M: The Role of the Product Champion

"Start Little and Build"

"We don't look to the president or the vice-president for R&D to say, all right, now Monday morning 3M is going to get into such-and-such a business. Rather, we prefer to see someone in one of our laboratories, or marketing or manufacturing, or new products bring forward a new idea that he's been thinking about. Then, when he can convince people around him, including his supervisor, that he's got something interesting, we'll make him what we call a 'project manager' with a small budget of money and talent, and let him run with it. . . . In short, we'd rather have the idea for a new business come from the bottom up than from the top down. Throughout all our 60 years of history here, that has been the mark of success. Did you develop a new business? The incentive? Money, of course. But that is not the key. The key . . . is becoming the general manager of a new business . . . having such a hot project that management just has to become involved whether it wants to or not."

– Bob Adams, vice president for R&D, 3M Corporation

Scotchlite

"Someone asked the question, "Why didn't 3M make glass beads, because glass beads were going to find increasing use on the highways? . . . I had done a little work in the mineral department on trying to color glass beads we'd imported from Czechoslovakia and had learned a little about their reflecting properties. And, as a little extracurricular activity, I'd been trying to make luminous house numbers – and maybe luminous signs as well – by developing luminous pigments. . . . Well, this question and my free-time lab project combined to stimulate me to search out where glass beads were being used on the highway. We found a place where beads had been sprinkled on the highway and we saw that they did provide a more visible line at night. . . . From there, it was only natural for us to conclude that, since we were a coating company, and probably knew more than anyone else about putting particles onto a web, we ought to be able to coat glass beads very accurately on a piece of paper. . . . So, that's what we did. The first reflective tape we made was simply a double-coated tape – glass beads sprinkled on one side and an adhesive on the other. We took some out here in St. Paul and, with the cooperation of the highway department, put some down. After the first frost came, and then a thaw, we found we didn't know as much about adhesives under all weather conditions as we thought. . . .

We looked around inside the company for skills in related areas. We tapped knowledge that existed in our sandpaper business on how to make waterproof sandpaper. We drew on the expertise of our roofing people who knew something about exposure. We reached into our adhesive and tape division to see how we could make the tape stick to the highway better."

The resulting product became known as "Scotchlite"; its principal application was in reflective signs – only later did 3M develop the market for highway marking. The originator of the product, Harry Heltzer, interested the head of the New Products Division in the product and encouraged Heltzer to go out and sell it. Scotchlite was a success and Heltzer became the general manager of the division set up to produce and market it. Heltzer later went on to become 3M's president.

Source: "The Technical Strategy of 3M: Start More Little Businesses and More Little Businesses," *Innovation*, no. 5 (1969).

within the firm impose heavy adjustment pressures upon the firm. During the introductory phase, the firm can exist in a purely entrepreneurial form where the entrepreneur-technologist can act both as technical and the business leader, and the firm can prosper as an organic, informal group of creative and cooperative individuals. Lack of formal controls or organizational structure is possible because of the shared values of organization members, personal loyalty to the company founder, and, frequently, equity participation in the venture.

As the firm and the industry develop, management becomes increasingly complex. Among the important issues that transition from introductory to growth phases raises for management are:

- pressure for cost efficiency at the production level that encourages standardization of products and design, establishment of scale-efficient production units, and the quest for process innovation. All are likely to result in greater formalization of production systems. Hayes and Wheelwright observe a shift from "job shop" production methods to batch-flow production and subsequently to assembly line production;[47]

- in terms of *organizational structure*, growing firm size and the increasing importance of manufacturing, marketing, and distribution functions encourage the establishment of functional company structure. However, within the more structured organization, the close interfunctional cooperation that is essential to successful innovation must be maintained. The essential ingredient is a high level of lateral communication with problem solving taking place at the operational level through cooperation across functional boundaries without directly involving the managerial hierarchy. Lateral cooperation can occur through loosely defined teams and project groups, or, more formally, through a matrix structure;

- the *R&D agenda* also changes. Once the firm has successfully established itself with an innovatory product or process, it must then maintain its position through a stream of innovations over time, where later innovations build upon the firm's technological base and strengthen the competitive position of the company within its existing markets. The R&D priorities shift from novelty and the quest for discontinuous performance leaps toward dependability, design modification, and cost efficiency. Ensuring that new product development is headed in the right direction and that it meets the requirements of customers and those of the manufacturing system requires that the innovation process be closely integrated within overall strategy formulation.

Typically, the new demands on management necessitate changes in the top management team. This may mean augmenting top management with seasoned executives from other companies, or it may require a chief executive with a different repertoire of skills. The replacement of Steve Jobs by John Scully as chairman of Apple Computer in 1984 was an example of this process.

Innovation and maturity

As industries evolve toward maturity, continuing innovation must coexist with strong pressures for cost efficiency. Managing innovation poses particular problems of differentiation and integration for mature corporations. In certain functions and certain product areas, the firm needs to pursue efficiency through a bureaucratic system and rigorous financial and operational controls. In developing new products and revitalizing established products, it needs to foster creativity.

Different firms have established different approaches to resolving this dilemma. The 3M Corporation represents one approach to the problem of reconciling creativity and operational efficiency within the mature organization. The essence of 3M's system is a duality that runs through the organization and through each employee's activities. The organization is oriented toward the management of 3M's existing activities, yet all employees are encouraged to seek opportunities for developing new products and new business ideas beyond the scope of their position within the corporation. Employees have the opportunity to "bootleg" time, equipment, and materials to pursue their own pet projects and are encouraged to do so by the rewards that are given for successfully developing new businesses. These include career advancement, the recognition and creative satisfaction associated with initiating a new business, and attractive financial rewards.

Other established companies have sought to separate their mature businesses from those that are in their innovatory stages and apply very different organizational structures and systems to each. Many large, mature industrial enterprises have created new venture divisions that become reservations where creativity and innovation can take place in an entrepreneurial context removed from the stifling influence of the corporate bureaucracy. Such new venture divisions typically have a two-way relationship with the more mature operating divisions. Innovations and ideas initiated within the mature divisions can be nurtured and developed in the new venture division, and innovations in the new venture division may have spin-offs for the more established businesses. While the major oil companies experienced little success in their technology-based, new venture divisions, Xerox Corporation's Xerox Technology Ventures has experienced considerable success in spinning off new companies established to exploit technologies developed at its PARC facility.[48]

Summary and Conclusions

The central feature of emerging industries is the role of innovation as the basis for competition and as the determinant of industry evolution. For this reason, this chapter groups together industries that are in the early stages of their life cycles and industries in which technology continues to be the primary basis of competition.

As a result, the primary strategic issues in these industries concern the management of technology. At a general level, strategy making in technology-oriented industries is no different from that in other industries: the basic requirements are an intimate understanding of the nature of competition and the requirements for success in the industry together with identification of the particular strengths and weaknesses of the enterprise. However, the peculiar properties of innovation with respect to the determinants of success in technology-based competition and the characteristics of technological competence give rise to particularly complex issues.

A fundamental problem of strategy formulation in technology-based industries concerns difficulties of forecasting technological change, market conditions, and the evolution of industry structure. While certain generic trends are evident in the shift from discontinuous to incremental product innovation and the transition from product and process innovation, the essence of the competitive process in these industries is one of "creative destruction" where forecasting is extremely hazardous. The inherent volatility and unpredictability of technological competition play havoc with traditional approaches to strategic planning. In contrast to technologically stable environments, where the ability to make realistic medium-term forecasts permits the detailed planning of resource allocation and product introduction, strategy formulation in fast-moving industries must concern itself with developing vision and imagination that can be used to establish a sense of direction for the company. The ability to combine consistency of direction with the alertness, responsiveness, and flexibility to take advantage of technological uncertainty and turbulence are the keys to competitive advantage in emerging and technology-based industries.

At the same time, long-term strategic investment decisions must be made. In some areas of technology the time horizons are long. In pharmaceuticals, the time span between initial research and product introduction is typically a decade, while at the frontiers of research, in superconductivity for example, the outcomes of research are unknown. This combination of environmental turbulence together with the need for long-term investment means that risk management lies at the heart of successful strategies in emerging and technology-based industries. One advantage of large firms is their ability to hedge their technological bets: at this level, technology strategy may be viewed as the management of a portfolio of options on a number of risky technological opportunities.

Timing is critical: should a firm be a pioneer or a fast-follower? Analysis of the characteristics of the innovation in terms of the ability to appropriate the returns to innovation, the role of complementary resources, and the firm's ability to influence industry standards can guide timing.

These issues raise complex problems in terms of resource requirements. Resource requirements of firms vary substantially between stages of the innovation process and with different types of technology. More important, however, to the ultimate success of companies in these industry environments are not the resources that a firm has access to but its ability to integrate and motivate these resources in order to exploit their inherent potential for innovation. If innovation is the basic determinant of success in emerging and technology-based industries, the primary role of strategy is to create the conditions for innovation. Yet here lies the most daunting challenge for management: how can a company create the organizational conditions conducive to innovation while planning the course of the company's development? As John Scully of Apple has observed, "Management and creativity might even be considered antithetical states. While management demands consensus, control, certainty, and the status quo, creativity thrives on the opposite: instinct, uncertainty, freedom, and iconoclasm."[49]

Fortunately, the experiences of companies such as Apple, 3M, Sony, Merck, and Honda point to solutions to these dilemmas. The need for innovation to reconcile individual creativity with coordination points toward the advantages of cross-functional team-based approaches over the isolation of R&D in a separate "creative" environment. Moreover, the need to reconcile innovation with efficiency points toward the advantage of parallel organizational structures where, in addition to the "formal" structure geared to the needs of existing businesses and products, an informal structure exists, which is the source of new products and businesses. The role of top management in balancing creativity with order and innovation with efficiency becomes critical. The success of Japanese and German companies in the management of technology in several electronics and engineering-based industries compared to the propensity of many U.S. and British companies both to invest in what later proves to be the wrong technological solution and to fail in the commercialization of technology may reflect the greater level of technological training and awareness among Japanese and German senior management teams than is typical in the United States and Britain.

With the increasing pace of technological change and the intensification of international competition, the demands upon Western European and American companies for improved innovatory performance will continue to increase. The challenge to mature industries in Europe and North America from low-cost production in the newly industrializing world implies that advanced industrialized nations must increasingly rely upon their advantages in new and technology-based industries. But here the technological leadership of North American and European companies is being lost to Japanese companies, while companies in Singapore and South Korea increasingly narrow the gap. We will explore aspects of these competitive issues in the next two chapters.

Notes

1   "The Logic That Dares Not Speak Its Name," *Economist*, April 16, 1994, 89–91.
2   David J. Teece, "Profiting from Technological Innovation: Implications for Integration, Collaboration, Licensing and Public Policy," in *The Competitive Challenge: Strategies for Industrial Innovation and Renewal*, ed. D. J. Teece (Cambridge, MA: Ballinger, 1987), 190.
3   William J. Abernathy and James M. Utterback, "Patterns of Technological Innovation," *Technology Review* 80 (June-July 1978): 40–7; and Utterback and Abernathy, "A Dynamic Model of Product and Process Innovation," *Omega* 3 (December 1975): 639–56.
4   Steve Postrel, "Competing Networks and Proprietary Standards: The

Case of Quadraphonic Sound," *Journal of Industrial Economics* 24 (December 1990): 169–86.

5   "Bandwagons and Barriers," *Economist*, February 27, 1993, 69.

6   "Bic and the Heirs of Ball-Point Builder Are No Pen Pals," *Wall Street Journal*, May 27, 1988, 1, 27.

7   Jeffrey R. Williams, *The Productivity Base of Industries*, Discussion Paper, Carnegie Mellon University, 1984, 19A.

8   Stephen Jay Gould, "The Panda's Thumb of Technology," *Natural History* 96, no. 1 (1986).

9   Robert F. Hartley, *Management Mistakes*, 2d ed. (New York: John Wiley & Sons, 1986), 56–66.

10   Robert D. Buzzell and Bradley T. Gale, *The PIMS Principles: Linking Strategy to Performance* (New York: Free Press, 1987), 274.

11   Dennis C. Mueller, *Profits in the Long Run* (Cambridge: Cambridge University Press, 1986), 111–42.

12   One approach is to use *analogies* – the experiences of similar products – to forecast the demand for a new product. For example, data on rates of market penetration and price decline for household appliances such as electric toothbrushes and compact disc players were used to forecast the market demand for high-definition TVs in the U.S. ("High-Definition Television: Assessing Demand Forecasts for the Next Generation Consumer Durable," *Management Science* 39 (1993): 1319–33).

13   C. A. R. McNulty, "Scenario Development for Corporate Planning," *Futures* (April 1977).

14   For an outline of Shell's approach, see J. P. Leemhuis (Corporate Planning Manager, Shell Netherlands), "Using Scenarios to Develop Strategies," *Long Range Planning* 18 (April 1985): 30–7; Pierre Wack, "Scenarios: Uncharted Waters Ahead," *Harvard Business Review* (September-October 1985): 72 and "Scenarios: Shooting the Rapids," *Harvard Business Review* (November-December 1985): 139; Arie de Geus (Shell Head of Planning), "Planning as Learning," *Harvard Business Review* (March-April 1988): 70–4. Drawing upon his experience at Shell, Paul Schoemacher has discussed the cognitive features of scenario planning that make it such a powerful technique ("Multiple Scenario Development: Its Conceptual and Behavioral Foundation," *Strategic Management Journal* 14 (1993): 193–214).

15   The classic example of group decisions leading to an undesirable and irrational outcome is the "*Abilene Paradox*." See Jerry Harvey, "Managing Agreement in Organizations: The Abilene Paradox," *Organizational Dynamics* (summer 1974).

16   For a discussion of techniques of technological forecasting, see B. C. Twiss, *Managing Technological Innovation*, 2d ed. (New York: Longman, 1980).

17   Richard N. Foster, "Timing Technological Transitions," in Michael Tushman and William Moore, *Readings in the Management of Innovation*, 2d ed., (Cambridge, MA: Ballinger, 1988), 215–28.

18   Charles R. Morris and Charles H. Ferguson, "How Architecture Wins Technology Wars," *Harvard Business Review* (March-April 1993), 86–96.

19 Eric von Hippel, "Lead Users: A Source of Novel Product Concepts," *Management Science* 32 (July 1986).

20 Eric Von Hippel, "Users As Innovators," *Technology Review*, no. 5 (1976): 212–39.

21 M. J. Peck, *Competition in the Aluminum Industry* (Cambridge, MA: MIT Press, 1968).

22 "Rebels Turned Diplomats," *Financial Times*, February 8, 1993, 7.

23 Tom Peters, *Thriving on Chaos* (New York: Knopf, 1987), 259–66.

24 Richard T. Pascale, *Honda (B)*, Harvard Business School, Case No. 384–050, Boston, 5–6.

25 John Scully, *Odyssey* (Toronto: Fitzhenry and Whiteside, 1987), 323–59.

26 Nancy Nicholls, "Scientific Management at Merck: An Interview with CFO Judy Lewent," *Harvard Business Review* (January-February 1994): 89–105.

27 J. Jewkes et al, *The Sources of Invention*, 2d ed. (London: Macmillan, 1969).

28 D. Hamberg, *Essays in the Economics of Research and Development* (New York: John Wiley, 1966).

29 "Texas to Make UK-Designed Chip," *Financial Times*, May 24, 1993, 16.

30 "Putting the Chips on the Table," *Business Age* (July 1992): 120–1.

31 George Gilder, "The Revitalization of Everything: The Law of the Microcosm," *Harvard Business Review* (March-April 1988), 49–66; Charles H. Ferguson, "From the People Who Brought You Voodoo Economics," *Harvard Business Review* (May-June 1988).

32 Ralph Katz and Thomas J. Allen, "Investigating the Not-Invented-Here (NIH) Syndrome: A Look at the Performance, Tenure, and Communication Patterns of 50 R&D Project Groups," *R&D Management* 12, no. 1 (1982): 7–19.

33 Louis W. Fry and Borje O. Saxberg, "Homo Ludens: Playing Man and Creativity in Innovating Organizations," Discussion Paper, Department of Management and Organization, University of Washington, 1987.

34 Michael L. Tushman, "Managing Communication Networks in R&D Laboratories," *Sloan Management Review* (winter 1979): 37–49.

35 See Fry and Saxberg, "Homo Ludens," 9. See also Joline Godfrey, *Our Wildest Dreams: Women Entrepreneurs Making Money, Having Fun, Doing Good* (New York: HarperCollins, 1992).

36 John Scully, *Odyssey*, 187–8.

37 L. Grundy, J. Kickel, C. Prather, "Building the Creative Organization," *Organizational Dynamics* (spring 1994): 22–37.

38 Eric Von Hippel (*The Sources of Innovation* [New York: Oxford University Press, 1988]) provides strong evidence of the dominant role of users in the innovation process.

39 "The Innovators," *Fortune*, June 6, 1988, 52.

40 "Making Bright Ideas Shine," *Financial Times*, March 25, 1993, 12.

41 "The Lab That Ran Away from Xerox," *Fortune*, September 5, 1988; "Barefoot into PARC," *Economist*, July 10, 1993, 68.

42 Elting Morrison, "Gunfire at Sea: A Case Study of Innovation," in *Readings in the Management of Innovation*, ed. Michael Tushman and William L. Moore (Cambridge, MA: Ballinger, 1988), 165–78.

43 K. Imai, I. Nonaka, and H. Takeuchi, "Managing the New Product Development Process: How Japanese Companies Learn and Unlearn," in *The Uneasy Alliance*, ed. K. Clark, R. Hayes, C. Lorenz (Boston: Harvard Business School Press, 1985).

44 Kim Clark and Takahiro Fujimoto, *Product Development Performance: Strategy, Organization, and Management in the World Auto Industry* (Boston: Harvard Business School Press, 1991).

45 D. A. Schon, "Champions for Radical New Inventions," *Harvard Business Review* (March-April 1963): 84.

46 R. Rothwell et al., "SAPPHO Updated – Project SAPPHO Phase II," *Research Policy* 3 (1974): 258–91.

47 Robert H. Hayes and Stephen C. Wheelwright, "Matching Process Technology with Product/Market Requirements," in *Restoring Our Competitive Advantage* (New York: John Wiley, 1984), chapter 4.

48 "Barefoot into PARC," *Economist*, July 10, 1993 68.

49 John Scully, *Odyssey*, 184.

ELEVEN

Competitive Advantage in Mature Industries

We are a true "penny profit" business. That means that it takes hard work and attention to detail to be financially successful – it is far from being a sure thing. Our store managers must do two things well: control costs and increase sales. Cost control cannot be done by compromising product quality, customer service, or restaurant cleanliness but rather by consistent monitoring of the "vital signs" of the business through observation, reports, and analysis. Portion control is a critical part of our business. For example, each Filet-O-Fish sandwich receives 1 fluid ounce of tartar sauce and 0.5 ounces of cheese. Our raw materials are fabricated to exacting tolerances, and our managers check them on an ongoing basis. Our written specification for lettuce is over two typewritten pages long. Our french fries must meet standards for potato type, solid and moisture content, and distribution of strand lengths.

– Edward H. Rensi, president and chief operating officer, McDonald's U.S.A.
in *Strategies . . . Successes . . . Senior Executives Speak Out*

> **Outline**
> Introduction and Objectives
> Key Success Factors in Mature Environments
> Cost advantage
> Segment and customer selection
> The quest for differentiation
> The role of innovation in mature industries
> Strategy Implementation in Mature Industries: Structure, Systems, and Style
> Efficiency through bureaucracy
> The bureaucratic model in decline
> Strategies for Declining Industries
> Adjusting capacity to declining demand
> The nature of demand
> Strategy options in declining industries
> Summary and Conclusions

Introduction and Objectives

Despite the technological revolutions that have spawned new industries such as aerospace, petrochemicals, computers, consumer electronics, biotechnology, and wireless communication, the greater part of national product and employment in the industrialized countries continues to be located within industries that can be broadly described as mature. Although mature industries form a heterogeneous group ranging from fast-food restaurants to the production of agricultural tractors, from a strategic perspective they present several similarities. The purpose of this chapter is to examine the characteristics of mature industries, the strategies that are likely to be successful in establishing competitive advantage, and the implications of these strategies for organizational structure, management systems, and leadership style.

By the time you have completed this chapter, you will be:

- familiar with the principal strategic characteristics of mature industries;
- capable of identifying key success factors within mature industries and formulating strategies directed toward the exploitation of such success factors;
- able to recognize the potential for strategic innovation in mature industries and appreciate the potential for such innovation to establish competitive advantage;
- capable of designing organizational structures and management systems that can effectively implement such strategies.

Key Success Factors in Mature Environments

Maturity has two principal implications for competitive advantage: it reduces the opportunities for establishing competitive advantage; second, it shifts these opportunities from differentiation-based factors to cost-based factors. Diminishing opportunities for competitive advantage in mature industries stem from:

- less scope for differentiation advantage resulting from increased buyer knowledge, product standardization, and less product innovation;
- diffusion of technology means that cost advantages through superior process technology or more advanced capital equipment methods are difficult to obtain and sustain;
- a highly developed industry infrastructure together with the presence of powerful distributors makes it easier for new or established firms to attack firms that have highly differentiated market positions or strong positions in particular segments;
- the vulnerability of cost advantage to exchange rate movements and the emergence of low-cost overseas competitors.

Cost advantage

If cost is the dominant success factor in mature industries, what are its primary sources? The following tend to be especially important:

- *Economies of scale*   In industries that are capital-intensive or where advertising, distribution, or new product development are important elements of total cost, economies of scale are likely to be important sources of interfirm cost differences. The increased standardization that accompanies maturity greatly assists the exploitation of such scale economies. The significance of scale economies in mature industries is indicated by the fact that the association between ROI and market share is stronger in mature industries than in emerging industries;[1]

- *Low-cost inputs* Where small competitors are successful in undercutting the prices of market leaders in mature industries, it is frequently through their access to low-cost inputs. Established firms can become locked into high-cost positions through unionization of their workforces or through inertia. The decline in the market shares of the U.S. steel majors over the last three decades is partly the result of union agreements over wages, benefits, and working practices that guaranteed high cost production. During the 1970s and 1980s, they steadily lost ground to overseas suppliers and domestic minimills, both of which operated with substantially lower labor costs. Recent entrants into mature industries may gain cost advantages by acquiring plant and equipment at bargain basement levels. Many of the lowest cost producers of oil in the United States are small operators that purchased the oil properties divested by major oil companies during the late 1980s and early 1990s. Similarly, the acquisition of financially troubled savings and loan institutions by major U.S. banks during 1988-92 represented a remarkably low-cost method of retail expansion;

- *Low overheads* During the early 1990s, the most profitable companies in mature industries tended to be those that had achieved the most substantial reductions in overhead costs. During 1992-4, Chrysler was the most profitable of the world's largest auto producers, primarily because it had gone furthest in slashing its costs during the 1980s. The resurgence of British Steel vividly illustrates the scale of the cost reductions that can be obtained by pruning administrative overheads, rationalizing capacity, and abandoning restrictive working practices (see exhibit 9.1). Inefficiency in mature firms can be pervasive and institutionalized. Its elimination then requires shock treatment in the form of a threat to the existence of the firm or a change in management through acquisition. In the oil industry, it was not until the oil price collapse of 1986 that the oil companies began to address the fundamental issues of cost reduction and restructuring. During the late 1980s and early 1990s, the most profitable oil companies were those that were the most aggressive in cost cutting, notably Exxon, Arco, and Texaco.

The effectiveness of cost efficiency in improving profit performance in mature industries is supported by research into performance turnarounds among mature businesses. Hambrick and Schecter's study of U.S. businesses that had experienced sharp improvements in ROI over a four-year period identified three successful turnaround strategies:

- *Asset and cost surgery* aggressive cost reduction through reduction of excess capacity, halting of new investment in plant and equipment,

Exhibit 11.1   Cost Reduction and Regeneration at British Steel

The history of the British Steel Corporation from its nationalization in 1967 up until 1980 is a case history in the failure of public enterprise. In an effort to achieve the productivity gains experienced by Japanese companies, the corporation tried to exploit scale economies by investing in large-scale integrated iron and steel plants. Between 1970 and 1979, BSC invested more heavily in new plant than almost any other steel company in the world. The results were disappointing to say the least. Output per worker scarcely changed over the period and labor productivity in the British steel industry remained about one-half that of West Germany and nearly one-third that of the United States. Inefficiency and inept management characterized all levels of the organization. At senior management level, strategies were based upon wildly optimistic forecasts of the growth of world steel demand. At the operating level, inefficiency and inflexibility became institutionalized in wasteful manning agreements and a host of restrictive practices concerning working practices. The power of the steel unions ensured the continued operation of a number of small, outdated, and poorly located plants. Between 1967 and 1980, public expenditure on BSC in terms of capital investment operating losses and other forms of support totaled over $15 billion.

With the election of Mrs Thatcher's Conservative Government in 1979 and in the face of mounting financial losses, a program of capacity and cost reduction was adopted and Mr Ian MacGregor was hired as BSC's new chairman from the New York investment bank Lazard Frères. Between 1980 and 1984, BSC underwent a revolution. Plant capacity was cut ruthlessly and new investment was almost halted. Working practices were reorganized with lower manning levels, increased job flexibility, and increased worker involvement in plant management and production target setting. Heavy redundancies among managerial and support staff were implemented. Employment was cut from 210,000 in 1976 to 81,000 in 1983 to 53,000 in 1988. Several layers of management hierarchy were eliminated and, at the same time, decision making was devolved to plant level. Simplified, quantitative performance targets were introduced throughout the corporation. The results were outstanding. In the two years between mid-1980 and mid-1982, labor productivity rose 40 percent and energy consumption per ton of steel fell 13 percent. By 1987, it required five man-hours to produce a ton of steel compared to 14.5 in 1980. The turnaround in BSC's financial performance is shown in the table below. By 1987, BSC was one of the world's most profitable steel companies. Most remarkable was the emergence of BSC as one of the lowest cost producers of steel in the world, with costs per ton of steel lower than the average for firms in the United States, Japan, Germany, and even Korea and Brazil.

British Steel's Financial Performance

	Pretax profit/(loss) ($ million)	Sales
1980	(3,174)	5,576
1981	(1,811)	5,290
1982	(822)	6,168
1983	(1,553)	5,792
1984	(411)	6,025
1985	(679)	6,706
1986	75	6,706
1987	317	6,204
1988	751	7,387

British Steel's Relative Costs Per Ton of Steel

	Labor	Materials	Finance	Total
BSC	110	280	25	415
U.S.	156	274	40	470
Germany	173	295	45	513
Japan	170	190	95	555
Korea	54	265	100	419

(Data from *World Steel Dynamics,* 1988)

Sources: Jonathan Aylen, *International Competitiveness and Industrial Regeneration: The Case of British Steel,* mimeo, Salford University, 1983; *Sunday Times* (of London), September 4, 1988, D1; *Wall Street Journal,* November 16, 1988, A14.

and cutbacks in R&D, marketing expenditures, receivables, and inventories;

- *Selective product and market pruning* refocusing upon segments that were most profitable or where the firm possessed distinctive strength;
- *Piecemeal productivity moves* adjustments to current market position rather than comprehensive refocusing or reorganizing, including reductions in marketing and R&D expenditures, higher capacity utilization, and increased employee productivity.[2]

The importance of cost reduction is confirmed by Grinyer, Mayes, and McKiernan's study of substantial and sustained performance improvements by a sample of British companies (most of which were long-established companies in mature industries). Apart from changes in management, the factor that most frequently distinguished the "sharp-benders" from the control group of companies was the intensive efforts by the former to reduce production costs.[3]

Segment and customer selection

In general, the profitability of mature industries is constrained by sluggish demand growth and lack of product differentiation and customers' bargaining power. However, sharp differences in profit rates can arise between industry segments. Not only do growth rates of demand vary between segments but the structure of segments with regard to concentration, buyer power, and potential for differentiation varies considerably. As a result, choice of segments is likely to be a key strategy issue in mature industries.

In the chemical industry, for example, the principal determinant of profit differences between the world's leading chemical producers during the mid-1980s and again in the early 1990s was the extent to which they refused their activities from bulk chemicals to specialty chemicals. Companies that invested heavily in specialty chemicals such as Du Pont, ICI (U.K.), BASF (West Germany), and Ciba-Geigy (Switzerland) outperformed Union Carbide and the chemicals businesses of oil companies that were heavily committed to bulk chemicals.[4]

Some of the most widespread and far-reaching segment refocusing was undertaken by the major oil companies between 1986 and 1993. Upstream, all the leading oil companies engaged in substantial divestment and intercompany trading of oil assets as they sought to focus on those oilfields where they possessed a competitive advantage (either through technical capabilities or the presence of existing production infrastructure). Between 1991 and the end of 1993, Atlantic Richfield (Arco) sold over 2,400 of its 3,000 U.S. oil properties. Similar refocusing among other oil majors resulted in quite different repositioning. Thus, during the early 1990s, Shell increasingly shifted to exploration and production of deep-sea oil fields – reflecting its expertise in undersea drilling and platform building, while Texaco increasingly concentrated upon mature oil fields where it could exploit its expertise in enhanced oil recovery techniques. Similar refocusing occurred downstream. By 1994, not one of the oil majors could claim to be a national marketer. Arco had withdrawn to the West Coast, Texaco sold a major share of its U.S. downstream assets to Saudi Aramco as well as withdrawing from Canada and Germany, and Amoco limited its retailing to the Midwest and East.

The quest for differentiation

Cost leadership, we have noted, is difficult to sustain, particularly in internationally competitive industries. Maintaining a low-cost position requires constant attention to operational efficiency and an unrelenting search for small cost reductions across the whole range of the firm's activities. Hence, attaining some insulation from the constant threat of price competition through some degree of differentiation is particularly attractive in mature industries. The problem is that the trend toward standardization narrows the scope for differentiation and reduces customer willingness to pay a substantial premium for differentiation. Hence, the creation of meaningful differentiation in mature industries represents one of the greatest challenges to managers in mature industries.

Standardization of the physical attributes of a product and convergence of consumer preferences constrain but do not eliminate the potential for differentiation. Product standardization is frequently accompanied by increased differentiation of complementary services and image. In office equipment, particularly copiers, increased product standardization has encouraged firms to compete on maintenance, training services, and speed of repair. In consumer goods, maturity is often associated with the focus of differentiation shifting from physical product characteristics to image. Deeply entrenched consumer preferences for Coke and Pepsi are a tribute to the capacity of heavy advertising over a long period of time to differentiate near identical products.

Across a broad range of mature industries we can observe firms attempting to escape from the treadmill of price competition among standardized offerings through a multitude of differentiation variables. The intensely competitive retail sector has produced some particularly interesting examples. The dismal returns on invested capital and on equity earned by many of the leading food chains (e.g., Kroger, A&P, Vons) and by old, established variety chains and department stores (Sears, J. C. Penney, Macy's, Montgomery Ward, Federated Department Stores) contrasts sharply with the sales growth and profitability of stores that have established clear differentiation through variety, style, and ambience (The Limited, Toys-R-Us, Nordstom, The Gap). Table 11.1 lists large U.S. retailers with the highest and lowest returns to investors during the 1980s. A similar pattern is evident for British retailers. During the mid-1980s, those that adopted innovative approaches to differentia-

	Average annual total return to investors, 1983-93, %	Sales 1993 $ millions
TOP TEN		
The Gap (California)	32.7	3,296
Home Depot (Georgia)	31.4	9,239
Circuit City Stores (Virginia)	27.2	3,270
Wal-Mart Stores (Arkansas)	26.8	66,345
Albertson's (Idaho)	25.1	11,284
Dillard Department Stores (Arkansas)	23.7	5,131
Kroger (Ohio)	23.2	22,384
Lowe's (North Carolina)	20.1	4,538
May Department Stores (Missouri)	20.0	11,020
McDonald's (Illinois)	19.8	7,408
BOTTOM TEN		
Mercantile Stores (Ohio)	−1.9	2,730
U.S. Shoe (Ohio)	0.6	2,626
Price (California)	2.1	7,821
Tandy (Texas)	2.8	4,471
Service Merchandise (Tennessee)	8.7	3,093
Longs Drug Stores (California)	5.9	2,499
Rite Aid (Pennsylvania)	6.1	4,085
Great Atlantic & Pacific Tea (New Jersey)	9.8	10,500
K-Mart (Michigan)	11.1	34,156
Sears, Roebuck (Illinois)	11.1	54,873

Table 11.1 The Highest and Lowest Performing Top-50 U.S. Retailers, Measured by Return to Investors

Source: Fortune, May 30, 1993, 214.

tion show the highest rates of sales growth and profitability even though several of them were unable to sustain their performance into the 1990s (see figure 11.1).

The role of innovation in mature industries

I have characterized mature industries as industries where the pace of technical change is slow. Yet I have also noted that the quest for differentiation in mature industries requires innovation – finding new approaches to uniqueness in terms of image creation, the addition of new features, or the provision of supporting services. The potential for innovation to create competitive advantage in mature industries extends beyond the differentiation of products and services. Steel, textiles, food processing, insurance, and hotel services are industries where the pace of product and process innovation is modest. In none of these industries does R&D expenditure as a percentage of sales revenue exceed 0.8 percent.[5] But it is precisely the strong competition in these mature industries and the limited opportunities for establishing sustainable competitive advantage that creates impetus for innovation in marketing, product design, customer service, and organization. This quest for new ways of

Figure 11.1
Innovation, Sales
Growth, and Growth of
ROI among British
Retailers, 1984-7

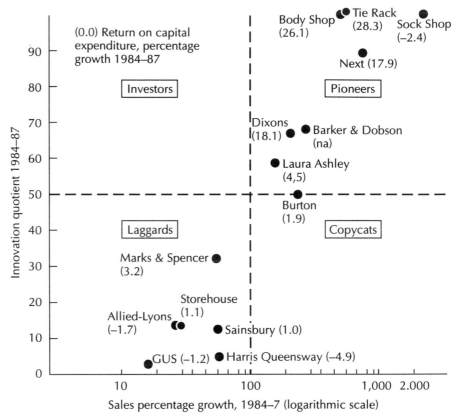

Note: Innovation is measured as the proportion of sales attributable to the introduction of new products and new strategies between 1984 and 1987. The figures shown in parentheses show change in return on capital, 1984-7.
Source: Piper Trust, Management Consultants and *Economist*, July 23, 1988, 59.

doing business is what I referred to in chapter 6 as "strategic innovation." In relation to the industry life cycle, what we may be observing is the third phase of strategic innovation, which reaches its peak at a time when technological innovations – both product and process – are slackening (see figure 11.2).

Figure 11.2 Product,
Process, and Strategic
Innovation

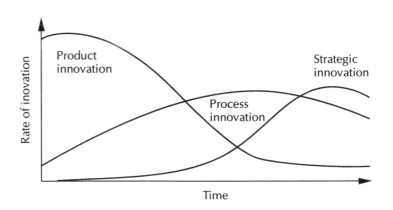

Because every strategic innovation is unique, it is difficult to adopt a systematic approach to analyzing opportunities for new strategic approaches. In chapter 6, I suggested value chain analysis as a means of identifying the potential for "new-game strategies." Understanding the sequence of activities currently being undertaken by the firm (and by competitors) may facilitate the search for a reconfiguration of the sequence of activities in a new strategic format. Benetton and Dell Computer may both be viewed as companies whose success has involved reconfiguring the conventional value chain in terms of establishing novel systems for the production of products and their distribution to the customer.

Derek Abell points to the redefinition of markets and market segments as offering important opportunities for new strategies.[6] Market boundaries may be redefined by means of:

- inclusion of *new customer groups* – thus fashion houses such as Georgio Armani and Christian Dior have progressively expanded their customer base;
- the *addition of products or services* that perform new but related functions – thus, Atlantic Richfield has redefined its retailing business from the retailing of gasoline and lubricants to the provision of a wide range of goods and services to motorists through its "*am-pm*" outlets.

Baden Fuller and Stopford's analysis of strategic innovation in mature industries focuses upon the reconciliation of multiple (often opposing) performance goals in order to create new options. They also point to the need for selectivity in defining business scope – both in terms of product and geographical breadth.[7]

It is notable that across many mature industries, the strategic innovators are often newcomers or established firms led by an outsider to the industry:

- in U.S. network broadcasting, newcomer Fox Broadcasting Company owned by Australian newspaper entrepreneur Rupert Murdoch was the major innovatory force of the last decade;[8]
- in the archaic Sheffield cutlery industry, the innovative Richardson Sheffield was owned first by an American and then by an Australian company;[9]
- in the U.S. steel industry, the outstanding strategic innovator was Nucor, created by Ken Iverson out of Nuclear Corporation of America, a technology-based, industrial materials producer. Although Iverson was a trained engineer with experience in metallurgy, his experience was in metal casting rather than steel making. Iverson traveled the world in search of new steel making and casting technology. Not only did Nucor minimills feature innovatory processes but they achieved a level of computer integration and flexibility of working practices that was unheard of in the U.S. steel industry. A critical element of Nucor's success was pushing minimill technology into new product

areas. Nucor was the world's first minimill to manufacture flat rolled steel.[10]

This propensity for strategic innovation in mature industries to be led by outsiders may reflect the tendency for long-established firms and their executives to be trapped within conventional thinking concerning key success factors and business practices within their own industries. I noted in chapter 4 how the ability of established firms to respond effectively to competitive threats may be limited by systems of belief that converge within the industry. J.-C. Spender refers to these common cognitive patterns among managers within an industry as "industry recipes."[11] Studies of *cognitive maps*, the mental frameworks through which managers perceive and think about their environments and their companies, yield fascinating insights into why some firms are able to adapt better than others to a changing business environment. One study of organizational renewal among railroad companies found that the ability of managers to *learn* by changing their mental models of the business was critical to explaining the ability of firms to renew themselves.[12]

The propensity for well-entrenched industry recipes to hamper strategic innovation and so cause deteriorating international competitiveness was apparent in the U.S. steel and automobile industries during the 1970s and early 1980s. Maturity in these industries during the period 1930-60 was associated with emphasis on scale efficiency, increasing organizational rigidity, and a growing inability to respond to opportunities for product and process innovation. While U.S. firms in these industries continued to lead the world in terms of output per employee, they steadily lost market share to firms that were more adaptable, more innovatory, and more customer driven. In the steel industry, the major integrated steel companies lost sales to the minimills, which were more technologically progressive, more flexible to market requirements, and more responsive to the interests of managers and workers. In the automobile industry, the U.S. Big Three lost sales to the more technically innovatory, design-driven, and quality-conscious Japanese and European competitors. Not until the 1980s did the U.S. firms initiate a broad-based response involving product redesign, new process technology with restructured working practices, drastic cutbacks in administrative staff, and cooperative arrangements with overseas auto producers.[13] To understand this apparent conflict between, on the one hand, efficiency and, on the other, innovation and flexibility, we need to look at the structures, organizational systems, and management styles through which strategies are implemented.

Strategy Implementation in Mature Industries: Structure, Systems, and Style

Efficiency through bureaucracy

To the extent that maturity is associated with environmental stability, lack of technological change, and an emphasis on efficiency as the key criterion for success, particular organizational and managerial characteristics are called for. At the beginning of the 1960s, Burns and Stalker argued that, while dynamic environments require "organic" organizational forms characterized by decentralization, loosely defined roles, and a high level of lateral communication, stable environments required a "mechanistic" organization characterized by centralization, well-defined roles, and predominantly vertical communication.[14] Henry Mintzberg describes this highly formalized type of organization dedicated to the pursuit of efficiency as the *"machine bureaucracy."*[15] The principal requirement for efficiency is the specialized operation of routine tasks through division of labor closely controlled by management. Such forms of organization are typically found in industries devoted to large scale production where the basis for efficiency is the application of Frederick Taylor's *principles of scientific management*. Division of labor extends to management as well as operatives. The machine bureaucracy displays a high level of vertical and horizontal specialization. Vertical specialization is reflected in the concentration of strategy formulation at the apex of the hierarchy, while middle and junior management supervises and administers through the application of standardized rules and regulations. Horizontal specialization in the company is organized around *functional departments* rather than *product divisions*.

The *machine bureaucracy* as described by Mintzberg is a caricature of actual organizations and probably the closest approximations are found in government departments performing highly routine administrative duties. However, in most mature industries, the features of bureaucracy that Mintzberg describes are familiar. Even in dynamic, fast-moving companies such as McDonald's, operating procedures are formulated into a set of precise written rules that govern virtually every part of the business (see the quotation that introduces this chapter). The organizational characteristics of bureaucracy are clearly apparent among some of the huge industrial enterprises found in automobiles, steel, and the oil industry. The key features of these mature organizations are summarized in table 11.2.

The bureaucratic model in decline

During the 1980s, the machine bureaucracy has been on the retreat in almost all mature industries. Four factors have caused this reversal:

- *Increased environmental turbulence* Bureaucracy is conducive to efficiency in stable environments. However, the centralized, structured

Table 11.2 Strategy Implementation in Mature Industries: Traditional Features of Organization and Management	STRATEGY	Primary goal is cost advantage through economies of scale, capital-intensive production of standardized product/service. Dichotomization of strategy formulation (the preserve of top management) and strategy implementation (carried down the hierarchy).
	STRUCTURE	Functional departments (e.g., production, marketing, customer service, distribution). Distinction between line and staff. Clearly defined job roles with strong vertical reporting/delegation relationships.
	CONTROLS	Performance targets are primarily quantitative and short term and are elaborated for all members of the organization. Performance is closely monitored by well-established, centralized management information systems and formalized reporting requirements. Financial controls through budgets and profit targets are particularly important.
	INCENTIVES	Incentives are based upon achievement of individual targets and are in the form of financial rewards and promotion up the hierarchy. Penalties exist for failure to attain quantitative targets, for failure to adhere to the rules, and lack of conformity to company norms.
	COMMUNICATION	Primarily vertical for the purposes of delegation and reporting. Lateral communication limited – sometimes achieved through interdepartmental committees where needed.
	MANAGEMENT	Primary functions of top management are control and strategic decision making. Two predominant top management styles appear to be effective: *the politician* – the organizational head who can effectively wield power through understanding of the organization and can formulate and implement strategy through consensus (e.g., Alfred Sloan Jr. of General Motors); and *the autocrat* – the CEO who is able to lead and control through aggressive use of power and sheer force of personality (Lee Iacocca of Chrysler).

organization cannot readily adapt to change. Achieving flexibility to respond to external change requires greater decentralization, less specialization, and looser controls;

- *Increased emphasis on innovation* The organizational structure, control systems, management style, and interpersonal relationships conducive to efficiency are likely to hinder innovation. As mature industries increasingly recognize the potential for innovation in the form of technological transfer from other industries (e.g., electronics, biotechnology) and new approaches to differentiation and competition, so the disadvantages of formalized, efficiency-oriented organizations have become increasingly apparent;

- *New process technology* The efficiency advantages of bureaucratized organizations arise from the technical virtues of highly specialized, systematized production methods. The electronics revolution has changed the conditions for efficiency. Computer-integrated manufacturing processes permit cost efficiency with greater product variety, shorter runs, and greater flexibility. As automation displaces labor-intensive, assembly line manufacturing techniques, there is less need for elaborate division of labor and greater need for job flexibility. Simultaneously, the electronic revolution in the office is displacing the administrative bureaucracy, which control and information systems once required;

- *Alienation and conflict* A consequence of specialization, mechanistic approaches to work, and the emphasis on control is the emergence of conflict between unions and management, between white collar and blue collar, between top management and middle management, and between different functional areas. Bureaucratic organizations are likely to foster conflict and provide no highly effective mechanisms for their resolution;

- *The Japanese example* Across a range of mature industries from motorcycles and steel to banking and brokerage, Japanese firms have demonstrated remarkable success with organizations that feature many of the hierarchical characteristics of Western mature corporations but fewer of the rigidities. The ability of leading Japanese firms to reconcile efficiency with innovation and control with opportunism has been an important factor in the rethinking that is taking place in North America and Europe.

In response, firms in mature industries have undergone substantial adjustment over the last decade. At Exxon, General Motors, Mobil, and Citicorp, management hierarchies have been radically pruned, decision-making processes have been transformed, and more participative working relationships have been encouraged. Among the most important features of change have been:

- greater decentralization of decision making. As well as moving operational decision making further down the line, strategy formulation has typically moved out of the top echelon of management and become more of an exercise in participation and consensus-building. Greater involvement of operational management in decision making has been encouraged by a breaking down of line-staff distinctions accompanied by pruning of head office staffs and relocation of head office functions to operational units;

- less emphasis on economies of large-scale production and increased responsiveness to customer requirements together with greater flexibility in responding to changes in the marketplace;

- increased emphasis on lateral cooperation and communication particularly through increased teamwork. The need for increased responsiveness to customer requirements and to changing market conditions has necessitated less functional separation and increased interfunctional cooperation;

- wider use of profit incentives, both through bonuses and employee stock ownership, to encourage closer identification of employees with organizational goals and to help overcome traditional conflicts between labor and capital, management and labor, and blue-collar and white-collar employees.

These trends amount to a closer convergence between the organizational and managerial characteristics of firms in mature industries and those located in the newer, more technologically oriented industries. At the same time, the primary emphasis on cost efficiency remains. It is not that the goal of cost efficiency has been superseded but rather that the conditions for cost efficiency have changed. The most powerful force for organizational change in mature industries has been the inability of highly structured, centralized organizations to maintain their cost efficiency within an increasingly turbulent business environment. The requirements for *dynamic efficiency* are different from the requirements for *static efficiency*. Dynamic efficiency requires the displacement of bureaucratically controlled, highly specialized routines by more flexible working practices. Flexibility requires higher levels of autonomy not only for divisional and plant managers but also for individual employees to permit them to adjust their work to meet changing circumstances.

Achieving dynamic efficiency through increased flexibility and autonomy does not mean less control but a change in control mechanisms. By relying more upon cost controls and profit targets, firms can permit greater autonomy to unit managers while maintaining rigorous demands for cost efficiency. The corporate restructuring initiated by Rawl at Exxon, Iacocca at Chrysler, and Walters at British Petroleum involved a dismantling of a major part of corporate bureaucracy combined with the imposition upon business units of demanding financial targets with draconian sanctions for failure to meet targets. A key element of these sanctions is a greater willingness by the corporate headquarters of mature corporations to divest underperforming divisions and to fire senior executives associated with poor financial performance.

Strategies for Declining Industries

Many mature industries degenerate into declining industries as a result of technological substitution, changes in consumer preferences, or demographic shifts. Shrinking market demand gives rise to strategic issues that are different from those encountered in other mature industries. Among the key features of declining industries are:

- excess capacity;
- lack of technical change, which is reflected in a lack of new product introduction and stability of process technology;
- a declining number of competitors but some entry as new firms acquire cheaply the assets of exiting firms;
- high average age of both physical and human resources;

- aggressive price competition.

Yet, despite the inhospitable environment that declining industries normally offer, research by Kathryn Harrigan has uncovered several examples of declining industries where at least some participants earned surprisingly attractive rates of profits. These included electronic vacuum tubes, premium cigars, and leather tanning. However, in other industries such as prepared baby foods, rayon, and economy cigars, decline was accompanied by aggressive price competition, company failures, and instability.[16]

The consequences of decline for competition and profitability depend upon two key factors: the balance between capacity and output during decline and the nature of demand for the product or service.

Adjusting capacity to declining demand

The smooth adjustment of industry capacity to declining demand is the key to stability and profitability during the decline phase. In industries where capacity exits from the industry in an orderly fashion, decline can occur without trauma. Where a substantial overhang of excess capacity persists, as has occurred in the steel industries of America and Europe and in oil tankers during 1974-84, the potential for an industry bloodbath exists. The ease with which capacity adjusts to declining demand is dependent upon:

1 *The predictability of decline* If decline can be forecast, the more likely it is that firms can plan for it. The problems of the steel industry, oil refining, and oil transport during the late 1970s were exacerbated by the unpredictability of the oil price shock of 1974. The more cyclical and volatile is demand, the more difficult it is for firms to perceive the trend of demand even after the onset of decline.

2 *Barriers to exit that impede the exit of capacity from an industry* The most important sources of barriers to exit are:
- *Durable and specialized assets* Just as capital requirements impose a barrier to entry into an industry, those same investments also discourage exit. The longer they last and the fewer opportunities there are for using those assets in another industry, the more companies are tied to that particular industry. The intensity of price competition in steel, acetylene, and rayon during the 1970s was partly a consequence of the durability and lack of alternative uses for the capital equipment employed;
- *Costs incurred in plant closure* Apart from the accounting costs of writing off assets, substantial cash costs may be incurred in plant closure arising from redundancy payments to employees, compensation for broken contacts with customers and suppliers, and costs incurred in dismantling and demolishing plants;
- *Managerial commitment* In addition to financial considerations, firms may be reluctant to close plants for a variety of emotional and moral reasons. Resistance to plant closure and divestment

arises from pride in a company's traditions and reputation, managers' unwillingness to accept failure, loyalties to employees and the local community, and the desire not to offend government;

3 *The strategies of the surviving firms*   Smooth exit of capacity ultimately depends upon the decisions of the industry players. The earlier companies recognize and address the problem, the more likely it is that independent and collective action can achieve capacity reduction. In the European petrochemical industry, for example, the problem of excess capacity was partially solved by a series of bilateral exchanges of plants and divisions. Thus, ICI swapped its polyethylene plants for BP's PVC plants.[17] Stronger firms in the industry can facilitate the exit of weaker firms by offering to acquire their plants and take over their postsales service commitments.

The nature of demand

Where a market is segmented, the general pattern of decline can obscure the existence of pockets of demand that are not only comparatively resilient but also price inelastic. For example, despite the obsolescence of vacuum tubes after the adoption of transistors, Harrigan observed that GTE Sylvania and General Electric earned excellent profits supplying vacuum tubes to the replacement and military markets.[18] As late as 1994, it was noted that the U.S. system of air traffic control depended upon vacuum tubes supplied by a few specialist companies.[19] In fountain pens, survivors in the quality fountain pen market, companies such as Cross and Mont Blanc, have achieved steady sales and high margins by appealing to high-income professionals and executives. By contrast, where the product is undifferentiated and where customer switching costs are low, the outlook is far less favorable.

Strategy options in declining industries

Conventional strategy recommendations for declining industries are either to divest or to harvest, that is, to generate the maximum cash flow from existing investments without reinvesting. However, these strategies assume that declining industries are inherently unprofitable. Once we recognize that there may be considerable profit potential within a declining industry, then other strategies may be attractive. Harrigan and Porter identify four strategies that can be profitably pursued in declining industries.[20] These strategies can be pursued either individually or sequentially:

1 *Leadership*   By gaining leadership, a firm is well placed to outstay competitors and play a dominant role in the final stages of the industry's life cycle. Once leadership has been attained, the firm is in a good position to switch to a harvest strategy and yield a strong profit stream from its market position. Possible maneuvers in establishing leadership are:

- build market share and encourage exit by aggressive competition;
- buy market share through takeovers of competitors;
- purchase competitors' plants;
- reduce competitors' exit costs by producing spare parts and private label goods for them;
- demonstrate commitment to the industry;
- develop and disclose credible market information that reduces uncertainty about future decline of the industry and helps dispel overoptimistic hopes that some firms may cling to;
- raise the stakes. Take initiatives such as product or process improvements that pressure competitors to follow and make it costly for them to stay in the business.

2 *Niche* Identify a segment that is likely to maintain a stable demand and other firms are unlikely to invade; then use the initiatives of a leadership strategy to establish dominance within the segment. The most attractive niches are those that offer the greatest prospects for stability and where demand is most inelastic.

3 *Harvest* A harvesting strategy is one that seeks to maximize the firm's cash flow from its existing assets, while avoiding, as far as possible, further investment. Harvesting strategies are typically oriented toward the short and medium term and seek to maximize cash flow by raising prices wherever possible and cutting costs by rationalizing the number of models, number of channels, and customers. Note, however, that a harvest strategy can be difficult to implement effectively. If competition is strong, harvesting may result in an unintended acceleration of decline, particularly if employee morale is adversely affected by a strategy that offers no development or long-term future for the business.

4 *Divest* If the future looks unattractive, the best strategy may be to divest the business. In general, the best price for a business, or for individual plants, is obtained in the early stages of decline before a consensus has developed as to the inevitability of decline. Once industry decline is well established, finding buyers may be extremely difficult.

Choosing the most appropriate strategy requires a careful assessment both of the profit potential of the industry and the competitive position of the firm. Harrigan and Porter pose four key questions:

- can the structure of the industry support a hospitable, potentially profitable decline phase?
- what are the exit barriers that each significant competitor faces?
- do your company's strengths fit the remaining pockets of demand?
- what are your competitors' strengths in these pockets? How can their exit barriers be overcome?

Selecting an appropriate strategy requires matching the opportunities remaining in the industries to the company's competitive position. Figure 11.3 shows a simple framework for strategy choice.

Figure 11.3 Strategy
Selection in a Declining
Industry: A Simple
Framework

COMPANY'S COMPETITIVE POSITION

		COMPANY'S COMPETITIVE POSITION	
		Has strengths in remaining demand pockets	Lacks strengths in remaining demand pockets
INDUSTRY STRUCTURE	Favorable to decline	LEADERSHIP or NICHE	HARVEST or DIVEST QUICKLY
	Unfavorable to decline	NICHE or HARVEST	DIVEST QUICKLY

Source: Kathryn R. Harrigan and Michael E. Porter, "Endgame Strategies for Declining Industries," *Harvard Business Review* (July–August 1983), 119.

Summary and Conclusions

Mature industries present challenging environments for the formulation and implementation of business strategies. Competition – price competition in particular – is usually strong and the opportunities for building and sustaining positions of clear competitive advantage are normally limited: cost advantages are vulnerable to imitation and instability, and opportunities for differentiation are limited by the tendency for maturity to be associated with standardization. Traditionally, mature industries have displayed high levels of environmental stability where the key to competitive advantage was cost efficiency through large-scale production of standardized products or services, experience curve cost advantages, and low overheads. Such conditions encouraged highly centralized, bureaucratically organized companies directed toward maximizing the efficiency with which routine operations were performed.

Today such conditions no longer prevail. The stability of mature industries has been upset by increased international competition, increased economic turbulence, and process innovation. The consequences are twofold. First, the conditions for cost efficiency have changed. In a dynamic environment, cost efficiency is no longer uniquely associated with scale, specialization, and rigid hierarchical control. The essence of dynamic is smooth, rapid adjustment to change. Second, in addition to being cost efficient, companies in the advanced industrialized countries have been forced to seek new sources of competitive advantage through innovation and differentiation. Reconciling the pursuit of scale economies with the need for responsiveness and flexibility and the requirements of cost efficiency with the growing need for innovation and differentiation is a complex challenge facing mature businesses. Many of the most successful companies in mature industries are ones that have achieved flexibility through a dismantling of bureaucratic structures and procedures, exploited the potential that new process technology offers for combining variety and flexibility with efficiency, encouraged high levels of employee commitment, and rigorously imposed cost efficiency through tight financial controls.

Notes

1 Robert D. Buzzell and Bradley T. Gale, *The PIMS Principles: Linking Strategy to Performance* (New York: Free Press, 1987), 279.

2 Donald C. Hambrick and Steven M. Schecter, "Turnaround Strategies for Mature Industrial-Product Business Units," *Academy of Management Journal* 26, no 2 (1983): 231–48.

3 Peter H. Grinyer, D. G. Mayes, and P. McKiernan, *Sharpbenders* (Oxford: Basil Blackwell, 1988).

4 "European Chemicals: Industry Profile," *Economist,* July 16, 1988, 68–9.

5 "R&D Scoreboard," *Business Week,* June 20, 1988, 139–60.

6 Derek Abell, *Managing with Dual Strategies* (New York: Free Press, 1993), 75–8.

7 Charles Baden Fuller and John M. Stopford, *Rejuvenating the Mature Business* (London and New York: Routledge, 1992), especially chapters 3 and 4.

8 *Fox Broadcasting Company,* Harvard Business School, Case Series, 1989.

9 Robert M. Grant and Charles Baden Fuller, *The Richardson Sheffield Story,* London Business School Case Series, no. 2, 1987.

10 Frank C. Barnes, "Nucor," in *Strategic Management,* ed. G. G. Dess and A. Miller (New York: McGraw-Hill, 1993), 804–32.

11 J.-C. Spender, *Industry Recipes: The Nature and Sources of Managerial Judgement* (Oxford: Basil Blackwell, 1989). On a similar theme, see also Anne S. Huff, "Industry Influences on Strategy Reformulation," *Strategic Management Journal* 3 (1982), 119–31; and Gerry Johnson, "Strategic Frames and Formulae," *Strategic Management Journal* 8 (1987).

12 P. S. Barr, J. L. Stimpert, and A. S. Huff, "Cognitive Change, Strategic Action, and Organizational Renewal," *Strategic Management Journal,* special issue, 13 (summer 1992): 15–36.

13 Paul R. Lawrence and Davis Dyer, *Renewing American Industry* (New York: Free Press, 1983), chapter 2, "Autos: On the Thin Edge," and chapter 3, "Steel: The Slumping Giant."

14 T. Burns and G. M. Stalker, *The Management of Innovation* (London: Tavistock Institute, 1961).

15 Henry Mintzberg, *Structure in Fives: Designing Effective Organizations* (Englewood Cliffs, NJ: Prentice-Hall, 1983), chapter 9.

16 Kathryn R. Harrigan, *Strategies for Declining Businesses* (Lexington, MA: D.C. Heath, 1980).

17 Joe Bower, *When Markets Quake* (Boston: Harvard Business School Press, 1986).

18 Kathryn R. Harrigan, "Strategic Planning for Endgame," *Long Range Planning,* 15 (1982): 45–8.

19 "U.S. to Shake Up Air Traffic Bureaucracy," *The Washington Post,* May 2, 1994, A1, A11.

20 Kathryn R. Harrigan and Michael E. Porter, "Endgame Strategies for Declining Industries," *Harvard Business Review* (July-August 1983): 111–20.

IV

Corporate Strategy

TWELVE

The Scope of the Firm: Vertical Integration

The idea of vertical integration is an anathema to an increasing number of companies. Most of yesterday's highly integrated giants are working overtime at splitting into more manageable, more energetic units – i.e., de-integrating. Then they are turning around and re-integrating – not by acquisitions but via alliances with all sorts of partners of all shapes and sizes.

— Tom Peters, *Liberation Management*

> ### *Outline*
> Introduction and Objectives
> Transactions Costs and the Scope of the Firm
> The Costs and Benefits of Vertical Integration
>   Defining vertical integration
>   Technical economies from the physical integration of processes
>   The sources of transactions costs
>   Administrative costs of internalization
> Designing Vertical Relationships
>   Long-term contracts and "quasi-vertical integration"
>   Some recent trends
> Summary and Conclusions

Introduction and Objectives

In chapter 2, I introduced the distinction between *corporate* and *business* strategy. Corporate strategy is concerned primarily with the decisions about scope: over what range of vertical, geographical, and product markets should a firm spread its activities? Business strategy (otherwise known as *competitive strategy*) is concerned with how a firm competes within a particular market. The distinction may be summarized as follows: corporate strategy is concerned with *where* a firm competes; business strategy is concerned with *how* a firm competes.[1] The major part of this book has been concerned with issues of business strategy. For the next four chapters, the emphasis will be on corporate strategy: decisions that involve the *scope of the firm*.

I begin with vertical integration because it takes us to the heart of many of the issues relevant to determining the optimal scope of the firm and, in particular, the role of *transactions costs* in drawing the boundaries of the firm and the types of relationships between firms. Also, issues of vertical integration are among some of the most prominent strategic questions that companies face during the 1990s. For example, *vertical deintegration* has become a powerful trend in most industrial sectors and a prominent element of corporate restructuring. The redefinition of vertical relationships – between parts makers and auto manufacturers, between chip designers and fabricators, and between consumer goods manufacturers and retailers – has involved firms in seeking to combine the benefits of both vertical integration and market transactions to yield new sources of competitive advantage.

The objectives of this chapter are as follows:

- to examine the relative efficiencies of firms and markets in organizing economic activity and apply the principles of *transactions cost economics* to determining the boundaries of firms;
- to examine the relative merits of vertical integration and market transactions in organizing vertically related activities and the circumstances that determine the attractions of each;
- to identify a range of possible relationships between vertically related firms, including spot market transactions, long-term contracts, franchise agreements, and the relative merits of each.
- to make you capable of applying the above principles and analyses in order to
  - explain why some types of vertically related activities are integrated within a single company, while others are performed by separate companies;
  - identify the critical considerations pertinent to make-or-buy decisions and the extent to which a firm should vertically integrate;
  - design the most advantageous form of relationships between a firm and its suppliers and customers.

Transactions Costs and the Scope of the Firm

Corporate strategy decisions involve the determination of the scope of the firm and the allocation of resources between the different businesses that the firm encompasses. There are three principal dimensions:

- *Product scope* How specialized should the firm be in terms of the range of products it supplies? Cummins Engine is a specialized company: it is involved almost exclusively in manufacturing diesel engines. British American Tobacco is highly diversified with interests in cigarettes, retailing, insurance, cosmetics, and engineering.
- *Geographical scope* Most new companies begin by serving a local market. Over time, many companies expand nationally and then internationally. In the next chapter we shall examine the strategic issues presented by globalization and international competition.
- *Vertical scope* What range of vertically linked activities should the firm seek to encompass? In the computer industry, quite different vertical strategies exist. IBM has traditionally been highly vertically integrated: it has in-house sources of semiconductors and software

and manages its own direct sales and service organization. Packard Bell is the reverse: it relies heavily upon third-party suppliers and distributors.

The general pattern of development over time is for an expansion in the scope of firms along all three dimensions. Alfred Chandler's research has documented over a century of growth in the vertical, geographical, and product scope of firms in response to technological change, the development of transport and communications systems, and managerial and organizational innovation.[2] What these changes involve is a shift in the relative roles of markets and firms in the organization of economic activity.

Although we typically refer to the capitalist economic organization as a "market economy," in fact, there are two forms of economic organization. One is the *market mechanism* where individuals and firms make independent decisions that are guided and coordinated by market prices. The other is the *administrative mechanism* of firms where decisions over production, supply, and the purchases of inputs are made by managers and imposed through hierarchies. The market mechanism is characterized as the "*invisible hand*" because its coordinating role does not require conscious planning. The administrative mechanism of company management is characterized as the "*visible hand*" because it is dependent upon coordination through planning.

One of the fundamental issues in organizational economics is why firms exist in the first place. If the firm is characterized as an organization involving a number of individuals bound by employment contracts with a central contracting authority, it is clear that firms are not essential for conducting complex economic activity. When I recently remodeled my house, I contracted with a self-employed builder to undertake the work. He in turn subcontracted parts of the work to a plumber, an electrician, a joiner, a drywall installer, and a painter. Although the job involved the coordinated activity of 12 individuals, these self-employed workers were not linked by employment relations but by market contracts ("$4,000 to install wiring, lights, and sockets"). What determines which activities are undertaken within a firm or between individuals or firms coordinated by market contracts? Ronald Coase's answer was *relative cost*.[3] If the transactions costs associated with organizing across markets are greater than the administrative costs of organizing within firms, we can expect the coordination of productive activity to be internalized within firms.

The growth in the scope of firms over the last hundred years is a result of the decline in the administrative costs of firms relative to the transactions costs of markets. This has resulted from technological advances, including more complex production techniques, improvements in management technology (accounting systems, decision science, and organizational structures), and advances in information and communication technologies. By the mid-1960s, this displacement of the coordinating role of markets by the internal management systems of vertically integrated, diversified, multinational corporations had amounted to the replacement of the "*market* economy" by the "*corporate* economy." For example, J. K. Galbraith's *The New Industrial State* analyzed the disadvantages of markets as coordinating mechanisms when compared to long-term planning and resource allocation within large industrial corporations.[4]

During the 1980s and the 1990s, there has been a reversal in the trend of the previous century and a refutation of the predictions of Galbraith and other economists who foresaw an increasing dominance of industrial economies by a handful of giant corporations. Although the majority of large companies have continued to expand their geographical scope, the dominant trends of the last 15 years have been "*downsizing*" and "*refocusing*." Faced with a more turbulent business environment and more intense competition, large industrial companies have reduced both their product and vertical scope. They have divested "peripheral" businesses in order to focus upon their "core" businesses and vertically "deintegrated" by increasingly "outsourcing" their requirements for components and business services. The implication seems to be that during periods of instability and intense competition, the costs of administrative planning tend to increase relative to the transactions costs of markets.

Oliver Williamson's contribution to economics has been his analysis of the nature and sources of the transactions costs of markets, which forms the basis for a theory of economic organization.[5] His analysis offers startling insights into corporate strategy decisions concerning the scope of the firm and the design of relationships between firms. I proceed by applying his analysis to vertical integration and, in doing so, introduce concepts and ideas that are also relevant to decisions concerning multinational growth and product diversification.

The Costs and Benefits of Vertical Integration

Defining vertical integration

Vertical integration is a firm's ownership of vertically related activities. Vertical integration can occur in two directions:

- *backward integration* where the firm takes ownership and control of producing its own inputs (e.g., Henry Ford's upstream expansion from automobile assembly to the production of his own components and back to the production of basic materials including steel and rubber);
- *forward integration* where the firm takes ownership and control of its own customers (e.g., Coca-Cola acquiring many of its local bottlers within the United States).

We introduced the concept of the *value chain* in chapter 5 as a framework for diagnosing competitive advantage. The value chain shows the vertical sequence of activities within the firm. However, we can extend the value chain to show the vertical chain of activities across companies. For example, a bakery producing bread may be viewed as one stage of a vertical chain involving the farmer (who produces wheat), the miller (who produces flour), the baker (who produces bread), and the retailer (who distributes to consumers).

Vertical integration may also be *full integration* or *partial integration*:

- *full integration* exists between two stages of production A and B when all stage A's production is sold internally and all stage B's requirements are obtained internally. Thus, at most integrated steel plants, all pig iron production goes into steel making, and none is purchased from outside;
- *partial integration* exists when stages A and B are not internally self-sufficient. Thus, car manufacturers have traditionally been partially backward-integrated into components. For example, most of General Motors's spark plugs, instruments, and ignition equipment are supplied externally, although for many of these items a portion is produced by its AC-Delco division. Partial integration is also typical of the oil industry. "Crude rich" companies (such as Statoil) are net sellers of crude oil; "crude poor" companies such as Exxon have to supplement their own production with purchases of crude to keep their refineries supplied.

Technical economies from the physical integration of processes

Analysis of the benefits of vertical integration has traditionally emphasized economies arising from the physical integration of processes. Thus, most steel production is undertaken by integrated steel producers that construct plants that first produce pig iron from iron ore and convert iron to steel. The advantage of such integration is the efficiencies that arise in transportation and energy costs from physically integrating the two stages of production at a single location. Similarly, with pulp and paper, there are economies in transportation, energy, and effluent control from producing pulp and paper in a single location with closely linked processes.

However, although these considerations explain the need for a single or closely adjacent plants, they do not explain why vertical integration in terms of common ownership is necessary. Why cannot iron and steel production or pulp and paper production be undertaken by separate firms owning facilities that are physically integrated with one another?

Technical economies are not a sufficient rationale for vertical integration. The key to understanding how technical factors cause vertical integration is to understand how the exploitation of technical economies causes heavy transactions costs between firms that offer economies from integration.

The sources of transactions costs

Between the production of iron and steel, most production is vertically integrated. Between the production of steel and steel cans, there is very little vertical integration: the can producers such as Crown, Cork and Seal, and Metal Box are specialist packaging companies that purchase steel strip from steel companies.

The absence of significant benefits from vertical integration between steel companies and can companies reflects the market conditions in the supply of steel strip. The market for steel strip is highly efficient: it is supplied under competitive conditions, information is readily available, and the switching costs for buyers and suppliers are low. Hence, the transactions costs associated with dealing across the market are low. This is the case for most commodity products: few jewelry companies own gold mines; few flour milling companies own wheat farms.

But pig iron is also a commodity product with potentially competitive supply conditions. However, because of the technical economies of physical integration, the nature of the market becomes very different. If iron production and steel production are owned by separate firms although the facilities are integrated, several problems arise in negotiating market contracts:

1   The *small numbers problem* If there is one iron producer and one steel producer at the integrated facilities, one is a monopoly supplier and the other a monopoly buyer. Price depends upon bargaining power and negotiating ability, and there is no obvious equilibrium. The result is likely to be unproductive investments whose aim is only to improve the bargaining power of one party relative to the other.

2   Disincentives for *transaction-specific investments* The iron producer and the steel producer must each make investments that are specific to the particular transaction. This is a source of risk. The iron producer may be discouraged from upgrading its facilities for fear that the steel producer may be considering shifting production to a lower-cost location and leaving the iron producer stranded.

3   *Opportunism and strategic misrepresentation* The small numbers problem and presence of transaction-specific investments can lead to opportunistic behavior. Thus, in the knowledge that the steel producer is a captive customer, the iron producer may be tempted to bargain for better terms of sale. If information is not readily available, such opportunism may in turn encourage misrepresentation. For example, the iron producer may be encouraged to transfer substandard pig iron.

4   *Taxes and regulations on market transactions* Transactions costs may be imposed through government taxes or regulations on an intermediate market. Thus, a tax on sales of pig iron or the introduction of quotas designed to reduce excess production of iron may encourage vertical integration as a means of avoiding these costs. OPEC's crude oil quotas on its members have encouraged the national oil companies

to forward-integrate into refining and petrochemicals as a means of cheating on their quotas.

These conditions increase the transactions costs of market contracts. Faced with small numbers, transaction-specific investments, and imperfect information, vertical integration can reduce transaction costs. That is not to say that market contracts cannot be adjusted to take account of these circumstances. For example, long-term contracts can avoid opportunism, inspection and quality-control procedures can avoid some forms of misrepresentation and opportunism, and provisions for arbitrating disputes can be built into contracts. But all these solutions impose costs. Thus, long-term contracts must take account of changing circumstances. In writing a long-term contract, provision needs to be made for inflation, the changing quantities demanded and supplied by each party need to be reconciled, quality and technical specifications must be established, and the circumstances of *force majeure* must be specified. Not only does this increase the initial costs of the contract, it may also give rise to continuing costs for contract enforcement and interpretation as well as opportunism on the part of one or other of the parties.

Administrative costs of internalization

The presence of transactions costs in intermediate markets is not enough to justify vertical integration. Vertical integration avoids the costs of using the market, but internalizing the transactions means that there are now costs of administration. The efficiency of the internal administration of vertical relations depends upon several factors, among the more important of which are the following:

1   *Differences in the optimal scale of operation between different stages of production*   Federal Express is a major purchaser of trucks and vans, but it has never considered setting up its own truck manufacturing company or acquiring an existing producer. To begin with, the transactions cost associated with buying trucks is low – Federal Express can purchase trucks very efficiently using either spot or long-term contracts. A second factor is the difference in the optimal scale of operation. Although Federal Express purchases over 25,000 trucks each year, these purchases are far below the output needed for efficiency as a manufacturer. Ford, one of the world's most efficient manufacturers, produced 2 million commercial vehicles in 1992. The risk, therefore, is that vertical integration may therefore result in suboptimal scale and high costs in those activities where minimum efficient size is very high. This fact explains why specialist vehicle producers are much less backward-integrated than volume producers. In car manufacture, an assembly plant can be fairly efficient at 250,000 units a year; however, efficiency in engine manufacture requires a scale of production in excess of 1 million units a year. As a result,

Rover Cars became highly dependent upon Honda engines during the 1980s, and most small auto manufacturers buy in engines.

2   *Managing strategically different businesses*   One of the major sources of administrative costs of internalizing vertically related businesses arises from coordinating businesses that, in strategic terms, are very different. A major disadvantage to FedEx of owning a truck manufacturing company is that the types of management and manufacturing capabilities required for truck manufacturing are very different from those required for express delivery. This consideration may explain why vertical integration between manufacturing and retailing companies is rare. Manufacturing and retailing are quite different types of businesses. Success in manufacturing requires manufacturing capabilities, technological strengths, and competence in product development. Retailing requires rapid adjustment to consumer demand and competition, astute buying practices, and constant attentiveness to managing the customer interface. Managing across such different businesses is a difficult challenge for top management not just in terms of the required knowledge and insight but also in designing corporate systems that are appropriate to both.

Such considerations are a factor in a good deal of recent vertical deintegration. For example, Marriott's decision to split into two separate companies, Marriott International and Host Marriott, was influenced by the belief that *owning* hotels is a strategically different business from *operating* hotels.

3   *Flexibility*   Both vertical integration and market transactions can claim advantage with regard to different types of flexibility. Where the required flexibility is rapid responsiveness to uncertain demand, there may be advantages in market transactions. The lack of vertical integration in the construction industry reflects, in part, the need for flexibility in adjusting both to cyclical patterns of demand and to the different requirements of each project. A vertically integrated construction company would encompass design and engineering capabilities, general building contracting, and the provision of specialist services such as steel fixing, plumbing, air conditioning, electrical work, and carpentry. Such vertical integration would mean greater complexity in adjusting to demand cycles and problems in adjusting to meet the specific requirements of different projects.

Market relations between independent firms may also be preferable to vertical integration in achieving fast-response flexibility to new product opportunities that require new combinations of technical capabilities. Ever since IBM outsourced most of the components for its PC in 1981, outside contracting has become the dominant organizational mode in the electronic sector. The main reason has been to shorten the new product development cycle. Thus, not only did Apple outsource most of the components for its Newton personal digital assistant, it also contracted the manufacturing to Sharp. During the 1990s, some of the most rapidly growing companies in the electronics sector have been contract electronics manufacturers.[6]

However, where *systemwide flexibility* is required, a vertically integrated set of activities may offer a more effective means of achieving simultaneous adjustment at every level. For example, in introducing unleaded gasoline and natural gas for motor vehicles, the integrated oil majors with their company-owned filling stations have led independent filling stations supplied by independent refiners and gas companies.

4 *Compounding of risk* To the extent that vertical integration ties a company to its internal suppliers, vertical integration represents a compounding of risk insofar as problems at any one stage of production threaten production and profitability at all other stages. In the production of sports shoes, the reliance by Nike and Reebok on contracts with independent manufacturing companies in Asia and elsewhere reduced Nike's exposure to exchange rate, political, and quality risks.

Table 12.1 summarizes the factors that are important in determining the merits of vertical integration compared to market transactions.

		Table 12.1 Vertical Integration (VI) versus Market Transactions: Some Relevant Considerations
How many firms are there in the vertically related activity?	The fewer the companies, the greater the attraction of VI.	
Do transaction-specific investments need to be made by either party?	The greater the requirements for specific investments, the more attractive is VI.	
Does limited availability of information provide opportunities to the contracting firm to behave opportunistically (i.e., cheat)?	The greater the difficulty of specifying and monitoring contracts, the greater the advantages of VI.	
Are market transactions subject to taxes and regulations?	VI is attractive if it can circumvent taxes and regulations.	
How much uncertainty exists with regard to the circumstances prevailing over the period of the contract?	Uncertainty raises the costs of writing and monitoring contracts, and provides opportunities for cheating, therefore increasing the attractiveness of VI.	
Are the two stages similar in terms of the optimal scale of operations?	The greater the dissimilarity in scale – the more difficult is VI.	
How strategically similar are the different stages in terms of key success factors and the resources and capabilities required for success?	The greater the strategic dissimilarity – the more difficult is VI.	
How uncertain is market demand?	The greater the demand uncertainty – the more costly is VI.	
Does VI increase risk through requiring heavy investments in multiple stages and compounding otherwise independent risk factors?	The heavier the investment requirements and the greater the independent risks at each stage – the more risky is VI.	

Designing Vertical Relationships

Long-term contracts and "quasi-vertical integration"

So far we have contrasted vertical integration with market transactions where market transactions have been mainly identified with spot contracts. However, spot contracts are not the only, nor even the most common, type of market transaction between companies. The supply of components and raw materials to manufacturing firms usually involves a long-term relationship between the supplier and the manufacturer. Similarly, most supply relationships between manufacturers, distributors, and retailers are long term. In some cases, long-term relationships are formulated into written contracts that specify the terms of the agreement and the responsibilities of each party; in other cases, the relationship may be based upon trust and implicit understandings. Figure 12.1 shows a range of different vertical relationships.

As already indicated, spot transactions work well where there are many buyers and sellers, a standard product, and little need for transaction-specific investment by either party. Where there are few buyers and sellers, where a customized product or service is being supplied, or where transaction-specific investments are needed, long-term vertical contracts can be a viable alternative to full vertical integration. Where

Figure 12.1   Different Types of Vertical Relationships

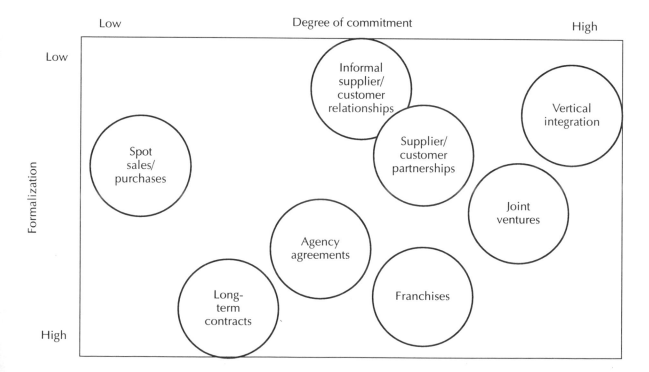

the vertical relationships are especially close and long term, they have been referred to as *"quasi-vertical integration"* or as *"value-adding partnerships."*[7]

In selecting between different types of relationships and designing the contractual form, two considerations are critical to efficiency:

1 *Allocation of risk* Any arrangement beyond a spot contract must cope with uncertainties over the course of the contract. A key feature of any contract is that its terms implicitly imply an allocation of risks between the parties. How risk is shared is dependent partly upon bargaining power and partly upon efficiency considerations. In the case of contracts between automobile manufacturers and component suppliers, prices are often fixed for six or twelve months, resulting in the component supplier accepting the risks of uncertain future costs. In the case of supply agreements between an oil company and a filling station, the price is not specified, although if the oil company has superior bargaining power it is better able to accept the risk of an uncertain future price for its product.

2 *Incentive structures* For a contract to minimize transactions costs it must provide an appropriate set of incentives to the parties. Thus, a contract for the supply of ready-mixed concrete to construction projects must specify the proportions of cement, sand, and gravel or there is an incentive to supply substandard concrete. However, achieving completeness in the specification of contracts also bears a cost. The $400 toilet seats supplied to the U.S. Navy may reflect the costs of meeting specifications that filled many sheets of paper. Very often, the most effective incentive is the promise of future business. Hence, some of the most successful long-term vertical relationships are supplier agreements where there is no formal agreement but an understanding that satisfaction and responsiveness will lead to a long-term business relationship. But for such "relational contracts" there must be some disincentives to opportunism. The presence of sunk costs in the form of transaction-specific investments by each party will act as a disincentive to opportunism.

Exhibits 12.1 and 12.2 describe two examples of long-term vertical contracts that succeed in combining the close cooperation associated with vertical integration, while avoiding some of the administrative costs and rigidities that vertical integration can impose.

Some recent trends

The ability for long-term "relational contracts" to offer the flexibility of market transactions while avoiding many of the transactions costs of spot contracts has resulted in a trend toward deintegration throughout most industries in Western Europe and North America. This has been stimulated in part by observation of the close collaborative relationships that many Japanese companies have with their suppliers. During the late 1980s, Toyota and Nissan directly produced about 20 to 23 percent

Exhibit 12.1 McDonald's Restaurants Franchise System

A franchise agreement is a contract between the franchisor who owns a brand name and other associated trademarks and has developed a system for supplying a product or service and the franchisee who purchases the right to use the trademarks and the business system at a specified location. The purpose of the franchise is to offer the coordination advantages of vertical integration while maintaining the flexibility advantages associated with independent contracting companies. Many of the transactions costs associated with market exchanges are avoided by a contract that is long term, comprehensive, and supported by a close relationship between franchisor and franchisee. The reputation that McDonald's has established through many thousands of franchise agreements over a long period gives the new franchisee trust in the relationship and also provides a disincentive for McDonald's to engage in opportunistic behavior. Cooperation is also fostered through the comprehensive training program for franchisees in which McDonald's instills its philosophy and values within the new franchisee. At the same time, because the relationship is between separate firms, the franchise relationship avoids several of the problems of vertical integration. The franchisee brings his own capital, hence reducing financial requirements and risk for the franchisor. McDonald's Restaurants Inc. and the individual franchised restaurant are very different businesses. In terms of scale, one is global and the other local. In terms of strategy, McDonald's is involved in managing a complex system requiring sophisticated management information systems, new product development, and highly sophisticated marketing. The individual restaurant is involved in flipping burgers, serving milk shakes, avoiding waste, and keeping the premises clean. The franchise system in which the franchisee works for profit provides direct incentives for increasing revenue and reducing costs.

It is interesting to note that McDonald's, along with other fast-food suppliers, has moved from franchising its restaurants toward increased direct ownership and management. This development reflects two factors. First, in the United States, at least McDonald's no longer needs the financial and managerial resources and the local knowledge of its franchisees. It is primarily in new overseas markets that McDonald's prefers franchises or joint ventures in order to tap local expertise and market knowledge. Second, developments in McDonald's management information systems, communication network, staff training methods, and operating techniques have lowered the costs of internal administration as compared to the costs of managing and monitoring franchise agreements.

---

of the value of their cars, while Ford accounted for 50 percent of its production value and GM for about 70 percent. Yet, Toyota and Nissan have achieved close technological collaboration with their suppliers, close collaboration on quality, and intimate cooperation in the scheduling of deliveries.

The response of Western companies has been twofold:

1 Companies have redefined their relationships with their suppliers. Rather than rely upon competitive tendering and written agreements, manufacturers are increasingly seeking the improved flexibility and closer coordination that can occur through long-term cooperation. In the automobile manufacturing and electronics industries, large companies have drastically reduced their number of vendors and have introduced supplier certification programs under which suppliers show that they can meet the standards required by the manufacturer, after which relationships are based more upon trust and mutual interest in continued business than upon legally enforceable contracts.

2 Companies have become focused upon a smaller number of vertical activities and increasingly *outsourced* components and business ser-

Exhibit 12.2 Managing Supplier Relations at Marks & Spencer PLC

Marks & Spencer PLC is undoubtedly the most successful retailer in Britain in the twentieth century. Established in the 1890s, M&S has achieved near continuous growth in revenue and profit over the last half century. The company is primarily a supplier of clothing but in the 1970s expanded into gourmet and convenience foods. Central elements of M&S strategy are its commitment to high quality and value for money and its policy that all its merchandise is sold under its own "St. Michael" brand name and is exclusive to M&S. The foundation of M&S's achievement of unique products of high quality and moderate prices is its system of supplier relations.

The interesting feature of these relationships is that they are long term (often extending over decades), and they are based upon a common understanding, but there is no written contract. The absence of a formal contract permits a high degree of flexibility, and the potential for highly sophisticated patterns of cooperation between M&S and its suppliers. For example, M&S involves itself in numerous aspects of the supplier's business including product design, quality control, purchasing of inputs, manufacturing methods, human resource policies, and delivery schedules. The supplier is encouraged to make substantial investments in equipment and know-how that are specific to the needs of M&S. Why is it that suppliers are willing to become dependent upon M&S and invest in adapting their business system to meet the specific needs of this single customer? Surely this is very risky for the supplier. The critical factor is the incentive structure. M&S procurement policies have been developed over a century. They are well known, and M&S has developed an unparalleled reputation for fair dealing. Any new supplier has the knowledge that previous suppliers have been treated well, and the long-term relationship that M&S is willing to build has made many of its suppliers highly profitable. Because M&S's reputation is its greatest asset, it is unlikely to engage in behavior that might put that reputation at risk.

Source: K. K. Tse, *Marks & Spencer: Anatomy of Britain's Most Efficiently Managed Company* (New York: Pergamon, 1985).

vices. This trend has been driven primarily by the quest for cost savings. Increasingly, companies have questioned every activity within their value chains and asked: Do we need to undertake this activity internally? If not, what is the best quality, lowest-cost source for this input? For many companies, this has involved a fundamental reassessment of the business. The continued domination by U.S. companies of the world computer industry owes much to the flexibility of U.S. firms in sourcing disk drives, microprocessors, memory chips, monitors, and software from external suppliers. The tendency for Western companies to increasingly outsource manufacturing activities has been followed by increased reliance upon external suppliers for critical business services. Technology-intensive services such as management information systems are increasingly subcontracted to specialists such as EDS and Andersen Consulting. Capital-intensive services such as distribution are similarly being subcontracted. In frozen-food storage and distribution, Christian Salvesen is a leader in Western Europe. A wide range of companies have shown that they can reduce costs and improve speed of delivery by subcontracting delivery to specialists such as Federal Express.

The flexibility possible from the ability to access the technology and know-how of external suppliers can also assist innovation. The resurgence of Hewlett-Packard (H-P) in computers and printers during the late 1980s and early 1990s owed much to the company's ability to reduce its new product development cycles by relying upon partnerships with other companies. H-P's Kittyhawk Personal Storage Module was brought to market in just ten months, thanks largely to the collaborative nature of product development. AT&T developed the microcircuitry, Read-Rite Inc. the read-write head, and Citizen Watch undertook manufacturing.

While the "*virtual factory*" and the "*virtual corporation*" have advantages of flexibility and access to external capabilities, there is a danger that overreliance upon external suppliers of manufacturing and technology causes degeneration into the "*hollow corporation*."[8] The risk is that, while incremental moves to outsource can be justified on the basis of cost efficiency, in the long run, companies lose the ability to innovate and develop.[9] This argument is closely linked to the concept of *core competences* discussed in chapter 5. The most valuable and difficult to replicate capabilities of a company are those that involve integration across different technologies and knowledge bases: as more and more activities are outsourced, the company's know-how becomes narrower. Hamel and Prahalad argue that core competences are embodied in "core products" that, in many cases, are components (e.g., the engine of a car, the microprocessor of a personal computer). If industrial companies increasingly outsource and are reduced to the role of being assemblers and marketers, their long-term competitiveness becomes increasingly jeopardized.[10]

Summary and Conclusions

Decisions over the vertical range of activities encompassed within the firm raise critical issues concerning the basis of a firm's competitive advantage both now and in the future as well as about the linkages between different vertical activities. In determining whether a firm should undertake a particular activity or rely upon an outside supplier, the most common question is whether the firm possesses a competitive advantage in that activity. However, the essence of any vertical chain of activity is that activities cannot be appraised individually. In determining whether to undertake any activity, the firm must compare the transactions costs of buying from or supplying to another firm, as compared with the administrative costs of managing the internal relationship. Vertical linkages are not just about the costs of managing the transaction; there are also implications for competitive advantage. To what extent is the firm's competitive advantage at each stage enhanced by its involvement in adjacent stages? This is especially relevant with regard to the ability to extend and upgrade competitive advantage in the future and respond to external changes. The danger is that decisions made with respect to today's market and technological circumstances may be suboptimal with regard to tomorrow's competitive circumstances. Hewlett-Packard sources a substantial portion of its specialized integrated circuits from its internal IC unit. In determining whether to maintain a presence in IC development and production, the issues for H-P are not simply relative costs and the transactions costs of outsourcing highly specialized ICs. The critical strategic issue is the contribution of in-house IC technology to H-P's remarkable ability to adapt its product market strategy to changing market circumstances by deploying its considerable product development capabilities.

Hence, the choice of vertical arrangements including the activities to be conducted internally and the nature of vertical arrangements with external suppliers and buyers – whether spot contracts, long-term contracts, or some form of strategic alliance – are critically dependent upon the firm's competitive strategy and its perception of its "core competences": that is, those capabilities that are fundamental to its competitive advantage over the long term. Hence, in the same industry, we are likely to see very different vertical arrangements across different firms. In microwave ovens, Samsung is highly vertically integrated, while Emerson Electric is heavily dependent upon external suppliers. Within the same company, very different vertical relationships are likely between different activities. H-P's highly successful range of laser printers use some internally sourced ICs, other components purchased on both spot and long-term contracts, and a printing mechanism that was the result of a long-established alliance with Canon for critical technologies and components.

Notes

1 In practice, determining where business strategy ends and corporate strategy begins is far from clear. Issues of scope are important in determining how a firm competes within a particular market, and issues of competitive advantage are critical in determining whether a firm should backward-integrate, diversify, or expand overseas. For example, we have considered segmentation decisions (PepsiCo's introduction of Diet Pepsi) to be business strategy, while diversification decisions (PepsiCo's acquisition of Kentucky Fried Chicken) to be corporate strategy. Outsourcing decisions (PepsiCo's outsourcing of certain transportation services) we consider within business strategy. Vertical integration (PepsiCo's acquisition of many of its bottlers) we view as corporate strategy. In all these examples, the critical issue is where we draw industry boundaries.

2 Alfred Chandler Jr., *Strategy and Structure* (Cambridge: MIT Press, 1962); *The Visible Hand: The Managerial Revolution in American Business* (Cambridge: MIT Press, 1977); and *Scale and Scope: Dynamics of Industrial Capitalism* (Cambridge: Harvard University Press, 1990).

3 R. H. Coase, "The Nature of the Firm," *Economica* 4 (1937): 386–405.

4 J. K. Galbraith, *The New Industrial State* (Harmondsworth, U.K.: Penguin, 1969).

5 Oliver E. Williamson, *Markets and Hierarchies: Analysis and Antitrust Implications* (New York: Free Press, 1975); and Oliver E. Williamson, *The Economic Institutions of Capitalism: Firms, Markets and Relational Contracting* (New York: Free Press, 1985).

6 "Financial Times Survey: Contract Electronics Manufacture," *Financial Times*, March 16, 1993.

7 R. Johnston and P. R. Lawrence, "Beyond Vertical Integration – The Rise of the Value-Adding Partnership," *Harvard Business Review* (July-August 1988): 94–101.

8 Arnoud De Meyer, *Creating the Virtual Factory* (Fontainebleau: INSEAD, 1993); and W. H. Davidow and M. S. Malone, *The Virtual Corporation* (New York: HarperCollins, 1992).

9 In the semiconductor industry, there is evidence that the trend toward separation between chip design and chip fabrication is reversing. This is driven by, first, a shortage in worldwide foundry capacity and, second, the need for close coordination between the design and fabrication of advanced chips. ("Real Men Have Fabs," *Business Week*, April 11, 1994, 108–12.)

10 C. K. Prahalad and G. Hamel, "The Core Competences of the Corporation," *Harvard Business Review* (May-June 1990): 79–91.

THIRTEEN

Strategy Formulation and Implementation in Global Industries

ABB is a company with no geographic center, no national ax to grind. We are a federation of national companies with a global coordination center. Are we a Swiss company? Our headquarters is in Zurich, but only 100 professionals work at headquarters and we will not increase that number. Are we a Swedish company? I'm the CEO, and I was born and educated in Sweden. But our headquarters is not in Sweden and only two of the eight members of our board of directors are Swedes. Perhaps we are an American company. We report our financial results in U.S. dollars and English is ABB's official language. We conduct all high-level meetings in English. My point is that ABB is none of those things – and all of those things. We are not homeless. We are a company with many homes.

    – Percy Barnevik, CEO, Asea Brown Boveri (from William Taylor, *Harvard Business Review*)

Outline

Introduction and Objectives
Implications of International Competition for Industry Analysis
   Competition from potential entrants
   Rivalry among existing firms
   The bargaining power of buyers
   Defining market boundaries: National or global?
Analyzing Competitive Advantage in an International Context
   National influences on competitiveness: Comparative advantage
   Porter's *Competitive Advantage of Nations*
   Consistency between strategy and national conditions
Applying the Framework (1): International Location of Production
   Location and the value chain
Applying the Framework (2): Overseas Market Entry Decisions
   International alliances and joint ventures
Multinational Strategies: Globalization versus National Differentiation
   The benefits of a global strategy
   Strategic strength from global positioning
Strategy and Organization within the Multinational Corporation
   The evolution of multinational strategies and structures
   Matching global strategies and structures to industry conditions
   Emergence of the "transnational corporation"
Summary and Conclusions

Introduction and Objectives

Among the forces that have transformed the business environment since 1960, the most traumatic and pervasive is the growing internationalization of the world economy. Internationalization has involved two main developments. Foremost is the growth in world trade. The growth rate of trade has consistently outstripped that of production, with the result that import penetration of most industries has increased sharply, and firms have looked increasingly to overseas markets to provide their main opportunities of sales growth. For the United States, the observation by older Americans that "I can't find anything in this store that is made in the United States!" is partly supported by data on import penetration: between 1960 and 1992, the share of imports in sales of manufactured goods in the United States rose from less than 4 percent to almost 20 percent.

The second aspect of internationalization has been overseas direct investment by corporations. By 1992, the United Nations identified 35,000 multinational corporations (MNCs) – that is, companies with subsidiaries in more than one country. The U.S. TV-manufacturing industry has been transformed by inward direct investment. By 1987, Zenith was the only U.S.-owned player in the industry. All the other manufacturers were subsidiaries of overseas corporations: Magnavox by Philips of the Netherlands, RCA and General Electric's TV businesses by Thomson of France, Motorola's TV businesses by Matsushita, and Warwick by Sanyo. A similar situation had emerged in tires. With the exception of Goodyear, the leading U.S. tire makers were foreign owned: Firestone by Bridgestone of Japan, Goodrich-Uniroyal by Michelin of France, General Tire and Rubber by Continental of Germany. Table 13.1 shows the world's leading MNCs.

The net inflow of direct investment into the United States during the last two decades is a sharp reversal of the pattern of most of the twentieth century when U.S. corporations threatened to dominate the industrial sectors of many overseas countries.[1]

The driving force for internationalization, both trade and direct investment, is twofold: first, the desire to exploit market opportunities in other countries, and, second, to exploit production opportunities by establishing production activities wherever they can be conducted most efficiently.

The result has been the "globalization of business": the creation of networks of international transactions comprising trade flows, flows of services (including technology), flows of people (especially those with highly developed skills), flows of factor payments (especially interest, profits, and licensing and royalty income), and flows of capital. Some of the clearest examples of the globalization of business are found in the strategies of the major automobile companies. Figure 13.1 illustrates

Rank	Industry	Country	Foreign assets $bn	Total assets $bn	Foreign sales $bn	% of total sales
1 Royal Dutch/Shell	Oil	Britain/Holland	n.a.	106.3	56.0	49
2 Ford Motor	Cars and trucks	United States	55.2	173.7	47.3	48
3 General Motors	Cars and trucks	United States	52.6	180.2	37.3	31
4 Exxon	Oil	United States	51.6	87.7	90.5	86
5 IBM	Computers	United States	45.7	87.6	41.9	61
6 British Petroleum	Oil	Britain	39.7	59.3	46.6	79
7 Nestlé	Food	Switzerland	n.a.	27.9	33.0	98
8 Unilever	Food	Britain/Holland	n.a.	24.8	16.7	42
9 Asea Brown Boveri	Electrical	Switzerland/Sweden	n.a.	30.2	22.7	85
10 Philips Electronics	Electronics	Holland	n.a.	30.6	28.6	93
11 Alcatel Alsthom	Telecoms	France	n.a.	38.2	17.7	67
12 Mobil	Oil	United States	22.3	41.7	44.3	77
13 Fiat	Cars and trucks	Italy	19.5	66.3	15.8	33
14 Siemens	Electrical	Germany	n.a.	50.1	15.1	40
15 Hanson	Diversified	Britain	n.a.	27.7	5.6	46
16 Volkswagon	Cars and trucks	Germany	n.a.	41.9	27.5	65
17 Elf Aquitaine	Oil	France	17.0	42.6	12.2	38
18 Mitsubishi	Trading	Japan	16.7	73.8	41.2	32
19 General Electric	Diversified	United States	16.5	153.9	8.3	14
20 Mitsui	Trading	Japan	15.0	60.8	43.6	32
21 Matsushita Electric Industrial	Electronics	Japan	n.a.	59.1	16.6	40
22 News Corporation	Publishing	Australia	14.6	20.7	5.3	78
23 Ferruzzi/Montedison	Diversified	Italy	13.5	30.8	9.1	59
24 Bayer	Chemicals	Germany	n.a.	25.4	21.8	84
25 Roche Holding	Drugs	Switzerland	n.a.	17.9	6.8	96

Note: $ bn = billions of dollars.
Source: United Nations and *Economist*, March 27, 1993, p. 9.

the role of overseas subsidiaries, overseas suppliers, and joint venture partners in the production of a recent General Motors model of car.

This chapter examines the implications of the internationalization of the business environment for the formulation and implementation of company strategy. The objectives of this chapter are the following:

Table 13.1 The 25 Largest Multinational Corporations Ranked by Value of Foreign Assets, 1990

- to explore the impact of trade and direct investment upon industry structure and competition;
- to revise our framework for the analysis of competitive advantage to take account of international competition – in particular, to take account of national influences on the sources of competitive advantage;
- to recognize the relative merits of different approaches to exploiting overseas business opportunities and to be able to select an appropriate overseas entry strategy;
- to be able to select the appropriate degree of globalization or national differentiation in formulating an international strategy;

Design: West Germany (by Opel)

Steel sheet: Japan

Stamping of exterior body parts: South Korea

Engines: 1.6 liter – South Korea
2.0 liter – Australia

Fuel injection system: U.S.A.

Fuel pump: U.S.A.

Transmission: Canada and U.S.A.

Rear axle components: U.S.A. and South Korea

Steering components: U.S.A.

Brake components: France, U.S.A., South Korea

Tires: South Korea

Windshield glass: South Korea

Battery: South Korea

Electrical wiring harness: South Korea

Radio: Singapore

Final assembly: South Korea (by Daewoo)

Major market: U.S.A. and Canada

Source: General Motors Corporation; *Los Angeles Times,* Sunday, February 10, 1989.

- to be able to determine the optimal international location of production activities in a firm;
- to be able to recommend the types of organizational structure appropriate to different international strategies.

Our first task is to extend the framework of strategy analysis that has been constructed to take account of international competition. Let me begin by outlining the implications of international competition for the analysis of industry and competition. Let me then examine the implications of international competition for competitive advantage.

Implications of International Competition for Industry Analysis

Consider the U.S. and British markets for automobiles in 1970 and 1992. Two changes stand out. First, competition has increased. In the United States, CR_3 (the combined market share of the three largest suppliers) was 0.78 in 1970 and 0.65 in 1992. For the United Kingdom, the corresponding figures were 0.66 and 0.54. Second, the principal players have increasingly become the same. Nationally focused companies (such as Rover and American Motors) have either declined or been absorbed by global players.

The trends we observe in autos are replicated in other industries – in some cases, much more dramatically. In automobiles, international-ization began early this century. During the 1900s, cars manufactured in Britain, France, and the United States were exported all over the world. During the 1920s, Ford and GM established subsidiaries in Europe, Asia, and Australia. The consequences of the international-ization of competition for industry attractiveness are mostly adverse. While internationalization offers increased investment and marketing opportu-nities to companies, it also means increased intensity of competition. Thus, the growth of international trade has been accompanied by a decline in the return on invested capital in the corporate sectors of the United States and most other Western nations (see figure 13.2).

The impact of internationalization on competition and industry profit-ability can be analyzed within the context of Porter's Five Forces of Competition framework. If we define markets as nationally bounded and industries as the set of suppliers to a national market, then interna-tionalization has its major impact on the forces of competition described in the next four sections.

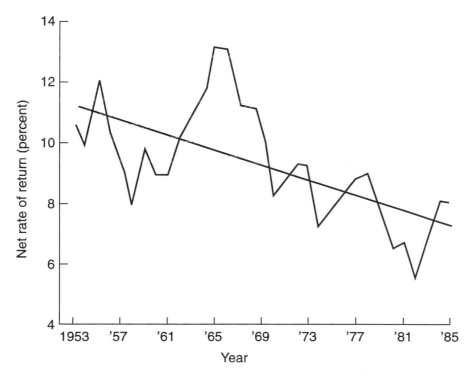

Figure 13.2 The Rate of Return on Capital Invested in U.S. Nonfinancial Corporations, 1953–85

Note: Rate of return is measured as the ratio of pretax profits, net depreciation, plus net interest, to the net stock of fixed capital plus inventories.
Source: David A. Aschauet, "Government Spending and the Falling Rate of Profit," *Federal Reserve Bank of Chicago Economic Perspectives* 12 (May-June 1988): 12.

Competition from potential entrants

The growth of international trade indicates a substantial lowering of barriers to entry into national markets. Multilateral tariff reduction during successive GATT rounds, falling real costs of transportation, the removal of exchange controls, internationalization of standards, and convergence between customer preferences have made it much easier for producers in one country to supply customers in another. Many of the entry barriers that were effective against potential domestic entrants may be ineffective against potential entrants that are established producers in overseas countries.

Rivalry among existing firms

1 *Seller concentration* International trade typically means that more suppliers are competing for each national market. Consider the U.S. auto market. In 1970, GM, Ford, and Chrysler together held 84 percent of total sales, and there were just five manufacturers with market shares greater than 2 percent. By 1993, the combined share of the Big Three had fallen to 67 percent, and there were eight manufacturers with market shares greater than 2 percent. In European countries, the fall in market shares of the national leaders (Fiat in Italy, Renault and Peugeot-Citroen in France, British Leyland in the United Kingdom, Seat in Spain) was even more dramatic. However, the trend to lower concentration in national markets is far from universal; in markets once dominated by a few national producers (the markets for TV receivers, computers, and plain-paper copiers, for example) concentration has typically fallen. In others, the very growth of international competition has resulted in a shakeout in which smaller, nationally based producers have been squeezed out or absorbed by larger international players.

2 *Diversity of competitors* Lower entry barriers and concentration ratios only partly explain the increasing intensity of competition between established firms. Equally important is the increasing diversity of competitors, which causes them to compete more vigorously while making cooperation more difficult. During the 1960s, price competition in oligopoly industries such as steel, automobiles, and domestic appliances was restrained. Price leadership patterns were well established, and firms viewed price competition as self-defeating in the long run. Such parallelism was partly a consequence of the similarities between competitors and their cost structures and the well-developed understandings that had grown between them. The entry of overseas competitors into domestic markets upsets such patterns of coordination. Mistrust tends to be high, different cost structures make aggressive competition more likely, and communication becomes more difficult. This is not to say that coordination, even collusion, is impossible on a global scale, but most instances of international collusion involve very small numbers of firms.[2]

The bargaining power of buyers

A further implication of the internationalization of business is that large customers can exercise their buying power far more effectively. Automobile manufacturers increasingly look worldwide in sourcing components. Large retailers can use the threat of shifting their purchases to overseas manufacturers in order to negotiate favorable terms from domestic suppliers.

Defining market boundaries: National or global?

The increase in international trade and direct investment raises the issue of whether it makes sense to define industries on the basis of national markets or whether industry boundaries need to be defined on a broader regional or global basis. For many industries, it is clear that national markets are simply segments within a broader global market. For industries such as aircraft manufacture, computers, telecommunications equipment, and earth-moving equipment, competition can only be understood by defining these industries on a global basis. In commercial aircraft, Boeing's principal competitor is Airbus Industric; in copiers, Xerox's leading competitor is Canon; in color film, Kodak's leading competitor is Fuji.

What about automobiles? Ford, Toyota, General Motors, and Volkswagen compete with one another in most of the countries of the world. Other companies are more geographically focused: 80 percent of Chrysler's sales are in North America; 71 percent of Fiat's sales are in Italy. Does this make automobiles a single global market? The criteria to be applied in determining the geographical boundaries of an industry are the same as those that were applied in chapter 2 to determine the boundaries of an industry in terms of product range. The criteria of *demand substitutability* and *supply substitutability* can be applied equally well to determining geographical boundaries as to determining product boundaries. An industry is international in its scope, if, on the demand side, customers are willing and able to substitute imported for domestically produced goods and, on the supply side, if producers are willing and able to shift supply from the domestic to export markets.

In the case of automobiles, demand substitutability is limited by customer immobility, by national product differences (e.g., cars for the Japanese, Australian, and British markets have the steering wheel on the right side), and by dealership and warranty restrictions that discourage the flow of cars between distributors in different countries ("grey imports"). On the supply side, substitutability is higher, but national differences in specifications and customer preferences and the need to establish dealership networks also restrict the auto producers' ability to switch between markets.

Thus, while some industries are unambiguously global (jet engines and diamonds) and others unambiguously national (the markets for nontraded goods such as hairdressing, office cleaning, and ice cream), others such as automobiles are ambiguous. For these industries, as I noted in chapter 3, industry definitions need to be adapted to the analysis being undertaken. Defining the industry in national terms is sensible for companies such as Rover and Hindustan Motors or in dealing with issues such as marketing and distribution strategies. Defining the market globally is more sensible for companies such as Toyota or Ford or for exploring issues concerning capacity additions and new product development.

Whether the boundaries are drawn narrowly (around national markets) or broadly (the global market) should not matter too much to the outcome of the analysis. If we are analyzing the competitive environment of Chrysler and choose to define this as the North American market, this market includes most of the world's auto producers as rivals, and those companies that are not present as competitors (e.g., Kia, Proton, Fiat, and Daewoo) can be regarded as potential entrants.

Analyzing Competitive Advantage in an International Context

The growth of international competition has been associated with some stunning reversals in the competitive positions of different companies. Consider again the world auto industry. In 1966, British Leyland produced 800,000 cars, ahead of Ford of Europe with 732,000, Toyota with 316,000, and BMW with 98,000. By 1992, British Leyland, then the Rover Cars subsidiary of British Aerospace, produced 405,000 cars, compared with 4.2 million by Toyota, 1.6 million by Ford of Europe, and 598,000 by BMW (which in 1994 acquired Rover).

To understand how competitive advantage has shifted over time in internationally competitive industries, we need to extend our framework for analyzing competitive advantage. Establishing competitive advantage, we observed, requires that the firm match its internal strengths in resources and capabilities to the key success factors of the industry. When firms are located within the same country, they are acquiring resources from the same factor markets, and their differences depend upon their internal investments in firm-specific resources and capabilities. Once we deal with an industry where different firms are located in different countries, the analysis becomes more complex. Differences between the resources available to firms depend not only upon their internal stocks of resources but also upon the conditions of resource availability within the country. Figure 13.3 shows this extended framework for the determination of competitive advantage.

National influences on competitiveness: Comparative advantage

The role of national conditions in affecting the internationally competitive position of industries and firms is described by the "Theory of

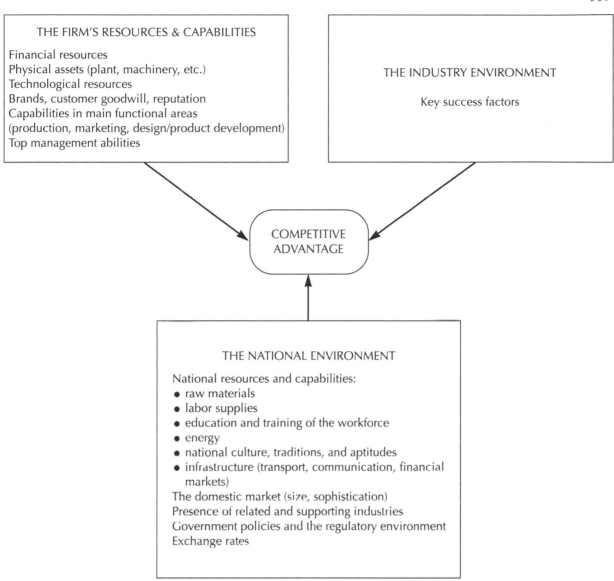

THE FIRM'S RESOURCES & CAPABILITIES

Financial resources
Physical assets (plant, machinery, etc.)
Technological resources
Brands, customer goodwill, reputation
Capabilities in main functional areas
(production, marketing, design/product development)
Top management abilities

THE INDUSTRY ENVIRONMENT

Key success factors

COMPETITIVE ADVANTAGE

THE NATIONAL ENVIRONMENT

National resources and capabilities:
- raw materials
- labor supplies
- education and training of the workforce
- energy
- national culture, traditions, and aptitudes
- infrastructure (transport, communication, financial markets)

The domestic market (size, sophistication)
Presence of related and supporting industries
Government policies and the regulatory environment
Exchange rates

Figure 13.3. The Determinants of Competitive Advantage in International Markets

Comparative Advantage." The Philippines has an abundant supply of unskilled labor. The United States has an abundant supply of technological resources – trained scientists and engineers, research facilities, and universities. The Philippines has a comparative advantage in the production of products that make intensive use of unskilled labor, such as clothing, handicrafts, toys, and other products requiring manual assembly of components. The United States has a comparative advantage in products that require heavy inputs of technological expertise, for example, advanced microelectronic products, pharmaceuticals, medical diagnostic equipment, and management consulting services.

The term "*comparative advantage*" is used to describe these national efficiency differences because what we observe is that, *compared with* the United States, the Philippines is relatively more efficient in the production of clothing than in the production of pharmaceuticals. Whether comparative advantage is turned into an actual *competitive advantage* depends upon a number of factors, most importantly, whether exchange rates are well behaved and are close to their purchasing power parity levels.

The role of factor endowments in determining comparative advantage among countries is evident in the pattern of international trade. The advanced industrialized nations tend to be net importers of labor-intensive products and products requiring low levels of technical and scientific skills (typically products in the mature phases of their life cycles). The principal exports of the advanced countries are products whose production is capital- and skill-intensive and also those services, such as business consulting and financial services, that require highly sophisticated human skills. Table 13.2 shows revealed comparative advantage, as measured by trade performance, for several product groups and several countries.

Conventionally, the theory of comparative advantage has focused upon natural resource endowments – mineral deposits, population, and climate – and the stock of capital. However, empirical research has pointed to the critical role played by intangible resources, some of which are exogenously determined (national culture, religion, and social structure) but are mostly endogenous: knowledge, skills, research facilities, management capabilities, the regulatory climate, and so on. These latter resources owe their existence to investment at the individual, company, and national levels.[3] Especially influential has been the remarkable economic success of several Far Eastern nations, notably South Korea, Taiwan, Hong Kong, Malaysia, and Singapore. Despite enormous differences in political conditions and industrial structure, these countries have in common very heavy investments in education and training and a strong Confucian influence. Conversely, a central issue in the current debate over U.S. educational policy is whether the level and the quality of public investment in education is consistent with the maintenance of America's international position as a high-wage, high-skill economy at the forefront of innovation.[4]

Table 13.2 Indexes of Revealed Comparative Advantage for Certain Broad Product Categories, 1980-85

	USA	Canada	W. Germany	Italy	Japan
Food, drink & tobacco	.31	.28	−.36	−.29	−.85
Raw materials	.43	.51	−.55	−.30	−.88
Oil & refined products	−.64	.34	−.72	−.74	−.99
Chemicals	.42	−.16	.20	−.06	−.58
Machinery and transportation equipment	.12	−.19	.34	.22	.80
Other manufactures	−.68	−.07	.01	.29	.40

Note: Revealed comparative advantage for each product group is measured as: (Exports less Imports)/Domestic Production.
Source: OECD.

Government policies are also important influences on the development of comparative advantage. The success of Hong Kong in industries that require swift adjustment to change, such as finance, fashion clothing, and electronic toys, owes much to the entrepreneurial flexibility encouraged by an absence of government regulation of business. Similarly, the emergence of Bermuda and the Cayman Islands as offshore banking centers is due to the combination of political stability, lack of regulation, and favorable taxation law.

The size of a country's domestic market can be a vital determinant of comparative advantage in industries where the minimum efficient size of operation is large or where demand is so segmented that a large total market is required for niches to be of a viable size.[5] A vast home market has been a major advantage for U.S. firms in the aircraft, automobile, computer, and pharmaceutical industries. The availability of similar scale advantages was an important motivation behind the European Community's *Project 1992* initiative to remove internal barriers to trade.

Porter's *Competitive Advantage of Nations*

In a major study of the pattern and determinants of comparative advantage among 13 industrialized nations, Michael Porter has offered an important extension of our understanding of the impact of national conditions upon firms' competitive advantage.[6] Porter's analysis is built upon three principles:

- a firm's national environment exerts a powerful influence upon its development – in particular, upon the profile of resources and capabilities that it develops. Porter views the nation as the home base within which the firm establishes its identity and critical managerial behaviors.[7]
- sustained competitive advantage at the international level depends upon *dynamic* aspects of competitive advantage. Countries that achieve sustained advantage in particular sectors are those where firms are successful in broadening and extending the basis of their competitive advantage through *innovation* and *upgrading* their resources and capabilities. Thus, Japanese success in automobiles reflects their companies' ability to continuously advance the basis of their competitive advantage. By contrast, Britain's failure across many manufacturing sectors displays a tendency for firms to attain positions of competitive advantage but to allow that advantage to atrophy through a lack of continuous innovation and upgrading.
- the principal impact of the national environment upon firms' competitive performance is not so much the resources available within the country as the *dynamic conditions* that influence innovation and the upgrading of competitive advantage.

Porter's analysis of how national conditions influence firms' competitive advantage in internationally competing industries is summarized in his *national diamond framework* (figure 13.4).[8]

Figure 13.4 Porter's
National Diamond
Framework

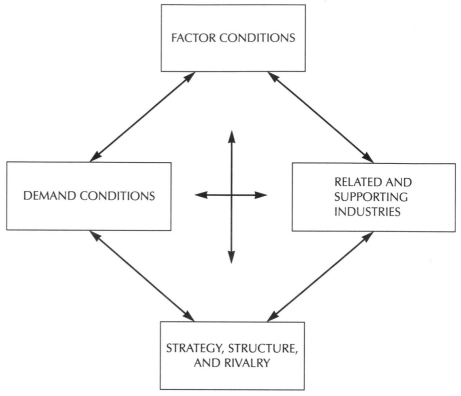

Source: Michael E. Porter, *The Competitive Advantage of Nations* (New York: Free Press, 1990).

1 *Factor conditions*   While the conventional advantage of comparative analysis emphasizes endowments of broad categories of resource, Porter's analysis emphasized, first, "home grown" resources and, second, the role of highly specialized resources. For example, in analyzing Hollywood's preeminence in film production, Porter points to the availability of skilled labor from the UCLA and USC schools of film; in explaining Japanese companies' success in cameras, printers, and video cameras, Porter points to Japanese capabilities in the integration of electronic and optical technologies and the benefits of particular training programs. Also, resource constraints may encourage the development of substitutes: in Japan, lack of raw materials has spurred innovation; in Italy, restrictive labor laws have stimulated automation.

2 *Related and supporting industries*   One of the most important national resources for some industries is the presence of related and supporting industries. One of the most striking of Porter's empirical findings is that national competitive strengths tend to be associated with "clusters" of industries. One such cluster is U.S. strength in semiconductors, computers, and computer software. For each of these industries, critical resources are the other related industries. In Germany, a mutually supporting cluster exists around chemicals, synthetic dyes, textiles, and textile machinery.

3 *Demand conditions*   Demand conditions in the domestic market are likely to exercise a powerful influence on companies in terms of their

drive for innovation and quality improvement. Porter attributes the international preeminence of Swiss and Belgian chocolate makers to the presence of highly discerning domestic customers. Similarly, the dominance by Japanese companies of the world market for cameras probably owes much to Japanese enthusiasm for amateur photography and their eager adoption of innovation in cameras. Why are German companies so prominent as producers of high-performance cars, yet comparatively weak in the mass market for autos? Presumably, this is not unrelated to German love of quality engineering and their irrepressible urge to drive on autobahns at terrifying speeds.

4 *Strategy, structure, and rivalry*   In this catchall category, let me isolate the role of rivalry. Porter argues that competition between domestic companies exerts a powerful influence upon innovation and the upgrading of competitive advantage. Domestic competition is usually more direct and personal than that between companies from different countries. As a result, the maintenance of strong competition within domestic markets is likely to provide a powerful stimulus to innovation and efficiency. The most striking feature of the Japanese auto industry is the presence of nine companies all of which compete fiercely within the domestic market. Japanese dominance of the world market for facsimile machines may also have been driven by the intensely competitive home market for these products. By contrast, the sluggish European computer and electronics industries partly reflect the propensity for national governments to create and protect their "national champions."[9]

Consistency between strategy and national conditions

The relevance of national comparative advantage to strategy formulation is that the establishment of competitive advantage in internationally competing industries requires congruence between business strategy and the pattern of the country's comparative advantage. For example, in the British cutlery industry, competition from South Korean manufacturers benefiting from low wage and low steel costs means that it was virtually impossible for companies such as J. Billam to survive in the mass market for stainless steel cutlery. The only firms to prosper, or even survive, were those that relied upon technology (such as Richardson) or concentrated upon the high-quality silverware segment.

In the personal computer industry, Malaysian and Thai manufacturers will have difficulty in establishing a competitive advantage in supplying state-of-the-art computers under their own brand names. Because the competitive advantage of these manufacturers is likely to be in low assembly costs, the obvious strategy is to assemble computers on behalf of Japanese and U.S. computer companies.

Referring back to figure 13.3, national-level and firm-level resources are not separate but are closely linked. The resources and capabilities of the individual firm have been acquired and developed within the context of a national economy. Inevitably, they will reflect the characteristics of the national economy, its society, and its culture. The issue for management, therefore, is not simply to devise a strategy that effectively combines the firm's resources and capabilities with the conditions of the national economy but also to achieve a closer and deeper understanding of the firm and its capabilities through an understanding of the environment in which the firm developed.

For example, consider the world's two largest oil companies, Exxon and the Royal Dutch/Shell Group. Both are sufficiently large and multinational that they are independent of their national environments. Yet, to fully understand their different strategies and their different organizational capabilities and management styles, it is important to examine national conditions at the time of their early development. Royal Dutch Petroleum and Shell Transport and Trading both developed in small countries that were colonial powers, and both companies had their major operations in the Far East. Royal Dutch/Shell developed as a highly decentralized corporation with a strong orientation toward local adaptation but with a pervasive sense of identity and integration. The career management system bore several resemblances to that of the British and Dutch colonial service. Exxon, on the other hand, developed as a more nationally based company, which (as Standard Oil New Jersey) was the financial center of Rockefeller's Standard Oil Trust. In common with the United States during the early decades of the twentieth century, Exxon became ethnocentric, internally competitive, and financially oriented, with a management style that was comparatively blunt and aggressive.

Applying the Framework: (1) International Location of Production

To examine the role of firm resources and country resources in international strategy decisions, let us take two types of decision that face internationalizing companies: first, the decision of where to locate their production activities and, second, the decision of how to enter a foreign market.

Whether a firm markets its product in many countries or only in its domestic market, it must decide where it is to produce it. Some firms market globally but concentrate production in their home country (Honda, Toyota, and Matsushita were like this for most of the 1970s). Other multinationals establish self-sufficient subsidiaries in each country in which they operate, where each country operation supplies its local market. Such companies have been called "multidomestic" corporations (Unilever and Philips followed this pattern).

The decision of where to manufacture requires consideration of the relative importance of national resource conditions against firm-specific resources and capabilities, together with an evaluation of the advantages of production in close proximity to the market. Let us consider these three issues:

1 *National resource conditions* Where national resource conditions exert a dominant influence on a firm's competitive advantage, it must locate where national resource conditions are favorable. For Nike and Reebok, low labor costs are of prime importance in competitive manufacturing, hence, these companies seek out locations where labor costs are low – China, Thailand, India, and the Philippines. Similarly, computer and telecommunications equipment manufacturers throughout the world have, almost invariably, established R&D facilities in the United States (very often in California's Silicon Valley) in order to exploit U.S. microelectronic expertise. In the automobile industry, high labor costs in Germany have provided a big incentive for moving automobile assembly operations to other countries – including the United States, where BMW and Mercedes-Benz have recently established plants (see table 13.3).

2 *Firm-specific competitive advantages* For firms whose competitive advantage is based upon internal resources and capabilities, location depends upon where those resources and capabilities can best be deployed. The competitive advantages of Toyota, Nissan, and Honda rest primarily upon their own technical, manufacturing, and product development capabilities. Traditionally, these companies concentrated production within Japan where they could exploit scale economies. During the 1980s, they have demonstrated the ability to transfer these competitive advantages to overseas locations.

3 *Tradeability issues* The ability to locate production away from markets depends upon transportability. High transport cost may necessitate local production, and differences in national customer preferences may encourage local production. Production close to the market may also result from governments' import restrictions as a means of forcing global corporations to establish manufacturing operations in local markets.

| | (U.S. dollars) | | | | | |
	1975	1981	1984	1986	1988	1991
United States	9.55	17.03	19.02	20.09	20.80	24.21
Mexico	2.94	5.27	2.55	2.03	1.96	3.33
Brazil	1.29	2.53	1.79	–	–	–
Japan	3.56	7.61	7.90	11.80	16.30	18.15
Korea	0.45	1.33	1.74	1.84	3.20	6.42
Taiwan	0.64	1.86	2.09	2.23	3.50	5.72
France	5.10	9.11	8.20	11.06	13.54	15.89
Germany	7.89	13.34	11.92	16.96	23.05	28.65
Italy	5.16	8.21	8.00	11.03	14.51	19.10
Spain	3.04	7.03	5.35	7.74	10.85	15.93
United Kingdom	4.12	8.10	7.44	9.22	11.95	13.84

Table 13.3 Hourly Compensation for Motor Vehicle Workers (Including Benefits)

Source: Ward's Yearbook (Detroit: Ward's Communications Inc.), various issues.

Location and the value chain

Location decisions must take account of the fact that the production of any good or service is composed of a vertical chain of activities and the input requirements of each varying considerably. The result is that different countries are likely to offer differential advantage at each stage of the value chain. These conditions help to explain the multinational production arrangements we observe in the car industry (see the example of the Pontiac Le Mans in figure 13.1). At a more aggregated level, the pattern of international trade shows an increasing tendency toward specialization, not only in specific products but in specific stages of production. Table 13.4 offers two examples.

In electronic products such as TVs and computers, the production of components is capital- and research-intensive and subject to substantial scale economies. Component production is concentrated in the advanced countries, notably the United States and Japan. Assembly is labor-intensive and is concentrated in the newly industrialized and developing countries.

A similar pattern is evident in the textile and clothing sector. Fiber production is concentrated in the countries with comparative advantage in agricultural production (for cotton and wool) and chemical production (for synthetic fibers). Spinning and weaving of cloth tend to be relatively capital-intensive and occur both in the newly industrialized and in the mature industrialized countries. Clothing production is labor-intensive; here the developing countries have a clear comparative advantage. As a result, globalization involves an examination by companies of their value chains to identify the optimal location for individual activities. This analysis involves two stages: first, determining the optimal location for each activity when viewed independently; second, consideration of *linkages* between activities to determine the benefits from close geographical proximity of linked activities. Figure 13.5 outlines a framework for considering these issues.

The benefits of geographical dispersion of activities To determine the best location for each activity, the firm needs to identify the principal inputs into each stage and then match these to the costs and availabilities of these inputs in different countries. Consider the production of sports shoes by Nike. There are three main stages: design, manufacture of components, and assembly into finished shoes. The principal inputs into the design stage are technical expertise, design and fashion expertise, and information from marketing. These inputs are most readily available in an advanced country – which is also Nike's largest market – the United States. Component production requires both skilled and unskilled labor, machinery (component production is moderately capital-intensive), and supplies of leather, canvas, rubber, and plastics. On the basis of availability and cost, newly industrializing countries such as Taiwan and South Korea are the most suitable locations. Assembly is labor-intensive,

Industry	Country	Stage of Processing	Index of Revealed Comparative Advantage
Textiles and Apparel	Hong Kong	1	−0.96
		2	−0.81
		3	−0.41
		4	+0.75
	Italy	1	−0.54
		2	+0.18
		3	+0.14
		4	+0.72
	Japan	1	−0.36
		2	+0.48
		3	+0.78
		4	−0.48
	United States	1	+0.96
		2	+0.64
		3	+0.22
		4	−0.73
Consumer Electronic Products	Brazil	1	−0.62
		2	+0.55
	Hong Kong	1	−0.41
		2	+0.28
	Japan	1	+0.53
		2	+0.97
	South Korea	1	−0.01
		2	+0.73
	United States	1	+0.02
		2	−0.65

Table 13.4

Comparative Advantage in Textiles and Apparel, and in Consumer Electronic Products by Stage of Processing

Notes:
[1]Revealed comparative advantage is measured as (Exports − Imports)/(Exports + Imports).
[2]For textiles and apparel, the stages of processing are: (1) fiber (natural and man-made), (2) spun yarn, (3) textiles, (4) apparel.
[3]For consumer electronics, the stages of processing are: (1) components, (2) finished products.
Source: United Nations.

requiring only simple machinery and little technical sophistication. The lowest-cost locations for assembly are developing countries with large pools of labor such as China, India, the Philippines, and Thailand.[10]

Similar international fragmentation of the value chain is common among electronics MNCs. Both European and North American companies tend to have R&D located in the United States. Components are typically manufactured in the United States, Japan, and Western Europe. Assembly may take place in Mexico, Taiwan, South Korea, or Brazil, depending, in part, upon the technical and capital requirements of the assembly process. Where assembly can be highly automated (as with

Figure 13.5 The International Location of Individual Activities within the Value Chain: The Key Issues

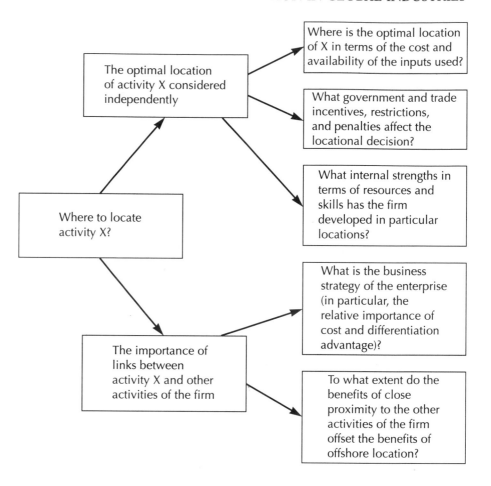

Apple's production of its Macintosh PC), location within the United States can be viable.

Locational decisions must also take account of a firm's existing geographical spread of production facilities. Once the firm is already established with plants in specific locations, the competitive advantages created by these operations will modify and even supersede those associated with national factors. If General Motors were redesigning its production activities from scratch, it would probably choose to establish auto assembly plants in Mexico, Southeast Asia, and greenfield sites in the United States. However, GM's existing concentration of plants in Michigan, Ohio, and Ontario means that, first, economies of experience have been realized, and, second, the costs associated with plant closure are likely to outweigh the benefits of relocation.

Optimal location is also dependent upon the business strategy of the firm. For the firm that is competing on the basis of cost, the primary consideration must be selecting locations that minimize cost. For a firm that strives for a differentiation advantage, the availability of quality materials and components, technical skills, and design and marketing expertise are likely to be the major considerations in selecting location.

The role of linkages   The benefits derived from breaking the value chain and locating individual activities in different countries must be traded off against the costs of weaker linkages between stages in the chain. Transport costs are one consideration. Another is increased inventory costs. In many industries, the move to JIT systems of component supply has increased the attractions of geographically concentrated component manufacture and assembly. The labor cost advantages of producing cars for the U.S. market in Mexico are offset by the costs of importing components, the cost of shipping the finished car, and increased inventory (see table 13.5).

Equally important are linkages between operational and support activities for the purposes of coordination and control. Innovation, we have noted, requires close coordination and communication between R&D, manufacturing, and marketing. Geographical dispersion is a severe handicap to such coordination. Quality control requires coordination and swift feedback between sales activities, assembly, and component manufacture. Overall cost efficiency requires that management is able to monitor and quickly respond to cost variances anywhere within the corporation. Several U.S. and European companies that established plants in low-wage countries subsequently discovered that the benefits of low wages were offset by the problems of low productivity; lack of coordination between supplies of materials, production, and market requirements; and poor quality control. The experiences of Nike and Jeep in China are extreme examples of the difficulties of achieving cost-efficient production in faraway places.[11]

Applying the Framework (2): Overseas Market Entry Decisions

Many of the same considerations are also relevant to choosing the mode of foreign market entry. A firm enters an overseas market because it believes that it will increase its profitability by doing so. This requires, first, that the overseas market is profitable – that is, the structure of the industry is conducive to profitability – and, second, that the firm is able to establish a competitive advantage vis-à-vis local producers and other MNCs. This issue of competitive advantage is the primary

	U.S. $	Mexico $
Parts & components	7,750	8,000
Labor	700	140
Shipping costs	300	1,000
Inventory	20	40
Total	8,770	9,180

Table 13.5 The Cost of Producing a Compact Automobile, United States and Mexico, 1992

Source: U.S. Office of Technology Assessment, October 1992.

consideration and is the focal point of our analysis of its competitive advantage.

In exploiting an overseas market opportunity, a firm has a range of options, in which the basic distinction is between market entry by means of *transactions* and market entry by means of *direct investment*. Figure 13.6 shows a spectrum of market exploitation options ranged according to the degree of commitment by the firm. Thus, at one extreme there is exporting through individual spot-market transactions; at the other, there is the establishment of a fully owned subsidiary that undertakes a full range of functions.

How does a firm weigh the merits of different market entry modes? Among the critical considerations are the following:

1   *Is the firm's competitive advantage based on firm-specific or country-specific resources?* If the firm's competitive advantage is country-based, then the firm must exploit an overseas market by means of exports. Thus, to the extent that Hyundai's competitive advantage in the U.S. car market is its low Korean wage rates, it must produce in Korea and export to the United States. If Toyota's competitive advantage is company-specific, then, assuming that advantage is transferable, Toyota can exploit the U.S. market either by exports or by direct investment in U.S. production facilities.[12]

2   *Is the product tradeable and what are the barriers to trade?* If the product is not tradeable because of costs or artificial trade barriers, then either the firm must invest in production facilities in the export market or it must license the use of its resources to firms within the export market.

3   *Does the firm possess the full range of resources and capabilities for establishing a competitive advantage in the overseas market?* Whether the firm is exporting or directly investing, it is likely that it will not possess the full range of resources and capabilities needed to exploit effectively the overseas market. If this is the case, then it must rely upon the resources of companies within the exploit market. Such arrangements may include appointing an overseas distributor or agent, licensing the brand or technology to a local manufacturer, striking a franchise agreement, or forming a joint venture with a local manufac-

Figure 13.6 Alternative Modes of Foreign Market Entry

TRANSACTIONS					DIRECT INVESTMENT			
Exporting: Spot transactions	Exporting: Long-term contract	Exporting: with foreign distributor/agent	Licensing technology and trademarks	Franchising	Joint venture		Fully owned subsidiary	
					Marketing and distribution only	Fully integrated	Marketing and distribution only	Fully integrated

turer. Joint ventures, such as those that many U.S. companies have with local companies in Japan (e.g., Fuji-Xerox, Caterpillar-Mitsubishi), are typically aimed at combining the product technology and brand names of the overseas partner with the local market knowledge and distribution system of the local partner. In technology-based industries, such as pharmaceuticals and semiconductors, firms exploit their innovations by licensing their technology to local companies.

4   *Are the firm's resources appropriable?* Whether or not a firm licenses the use of its proprietary resources or chooses to exploit them directly (either through exporting or direct investment) depends upon how easy it is to appropriate the returns to these resources. Trademarks and patents are often highly appropriable, which encourages their exploitation by licensing. Thus, Cadbury-Schweppes licenses the trademarks and product recipes for its Cadbury's range of chocolate bars to Hershey for sale in the United States. Similarly, Texas Instruments licensed its memory chip technology to joint venture companies including Kobe Steel in Japan, Acer in Taiwan, and the Singapore government. *Franchising* involves a licensing of trademarks and technology within a fully packaged business system.

5   *What transactions costs are involved?* A key issue that arises in the licensing of a firm's trademarks or technology concerns the *transactions costs* of negotiating, monitoring, and enforcing the terms of such agreements as compared with internalization through a fully owned subsidiary. It is notable that McDonald's first outlets in the United Kingdom were directly managed rather than franchised. The primary reason was that it was believed that, given British traditions of poor service and indifferent cuisine, direct management would avoid the difficulties of monitoring and guiding British franchisees. Issues of transactions costs are fundamental to the choices between alternative market entry modes. Barriers to exporting in the form of transport costs and tariffs are forms of transaction costs; other costs include exchange rate risk and information costs. The existence of transactions costs is fundamental to explaining the existence of the MNC. In the absence of transaction costs in the markets either for goods or for resources, companies would exploit overseas markets either by exporting their goods and services or by selling the use of their resources to local firms in the overseas markets.[13] Thus, multinationals tend to predominate in industries where:

- customer preferences are reasonably similar between countries;
- firm-specific intangible resources such as brands and technology are important (transactions costs in licensing the use of these resources favor direct investment);
- exporting is subject to transactions costs in product markets.

International alliances and joint ventures

During the last decade and a half, one of the most striking features of the development of international business has been the upsurge in the numbers of joint ventures and other forms of strategic alliance across national borders. Consider for example the U.S. and Japanese automobile companies: despite the intense competition between them, which extends from the marketplace into government policies and international relations, there has been a remarkable growth in collaborative arrangements between them (see figure 13.7).

International joint ventures are scarcely a new phenomenon. The Royal Dutch/Shell Group, a joint venture between Royal Dutch Petroleum and Shell Transport and Trading, dates from the turn of the century. The interesting feature of the current wave of cross-border

Figure 13.7
Collaboration between U.S. and Japanese Automobile Companies

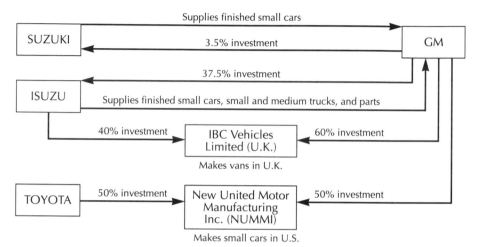

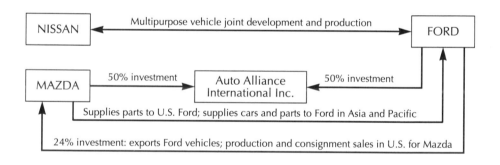

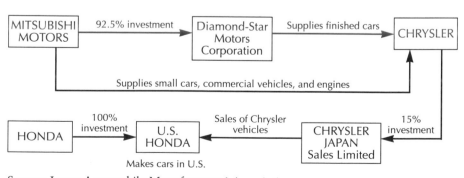

Source: Japan Automobile Manufacturers' Association.

collaborative agreements is their pervasiveness – with automobiles, information technology, communications, pharmaceuticals, and aerospace in the forefront. In many developing and emerging market countries, joint ventures are a consequence of government policy: host governments require foreign multinationals to take a local partner. Between the industrialized countries (which account for about 90 percent of alliances), cross-border alliances offer the overseas partner a means to exploit its critical internal resources while gaining access to the resources of the local partner, which are needed to access the local market. While a firm could assemble the needed resources itself, alliances can achieve this objective quicker, at lower cost, and with less uncertainty. Thus, the reason so many Western companies have formed joint ventures with Japanese firms in order to access the Japanese market is the belief that local knowledge, local manufacturing, and local distribution networks are important ingredients of success in Japan. Evidence on the success of international joint ventures and other forms of strategic alliance is mixed. Certainly these ventures have proven highly successful for some firms in gaining access to markets and technology in much shorter time than would result from a firm "going it alone." There have also been spectacular failures, and most international joint ventures are short lived, reflecting management difficulties and disagreements between the partners. Joint ventures that share management responsibility are far more likely to fail than those with a dominant parent or with independent management.[14] However, short life spans do not necessarily imply failure. A joint venture may be a useful stopgap measure for the parties until superseded by a wholly owned subsidiary or some other form of arrangement.

The greatest problems arise in cooperation between firms that are also competitors. In cooperative partnerships between Japanese and Western firms, the Western partner frequently emerges as the disappointed partner. Often the Western company makes available its key resources of technology or distribution to its Japanese partner in return for short-term benefits, only to see its Japanese collaborator reemerge as a resurgent competitor.[15] Such experiences point to Japanese companies' more systematic approach to managing complex relationships, which involve both competitive and cooperative dimensions. In the U.S. auto parts industry, 126 companies entered into joint ventures with Japanese parts suppliers in order to supply the U.S. plants of Honda, Nissan, and Toyota. Conflicting objectives, divergent management styles, and disputes over quality and labor practices resulted in widespread failure.[16] The critical issues appear to be (a) having objectives that are realistic and explicit and (b) having a willingness to learn from experience. Corning Glass, a veteran of international joint ventures, derives over half its profits from joint ventures. Ford's collaboration with Mazda has helped it enter South Korea as well as enhance its competitive position within the U.S. and Japanese markets.[17]

The effective strategic management of international alliances, argue Hamel, Doz, and Prahalad, depends upon a clear recognition that *"collaboration is competition in a different form."*[18] Naturally, one partner will tend to benefit more than the other from collaboration, but Hamel et al. argue that the sharing of benefits will depend upon three key factors:

- *The strategic intent of the partners*   Japanese companies have entered partnerships with the clear intent of gaining global dominance, and in this respect strategic partnerships are just one step on the road to global expansion. By contrast, Western companies have often entered partnerships with the goal of giving up manufacturing to more efficient Japanese producers. The willingness of Western companies to yield major items of value-added to former competitors limits their ability to learn from their partners and is likely to lead to a cumulative abandonment of activities and capabilities;
- *Appropriability of the contribution*   The ability of each partner to capture and appropriate the skills of the other depends upon the nature of each firm's skills and resources. Where skills and resources are tangible or explicit, they can easily be acquired. Where they are tacit and people-embodied, they are more difficult to acquire. To avoid the unintended transfer of know-how to partners, Hamel *et al.* argue the need for a "gatekeeper" to monitor and administer contacts with strategic partners;
- *Receptivity of the company*   The more receptive a company is in terms of its ability to identify what it wants from the partner, to obtain the required knowledge or skills, and to assimilate and adapt them, the more it will gain from the partnership. In management terms, this requires the setting of performance goals of what the partnership is to achieve for the company and managing the relationship to ensure that the company is deriving the maximum of learning from the collaboration.

Multinational Strategies: Globalization Versus National Differentiation

So far, we have viewed international expansion, whether by exports or by direct investment, as a means by which a company can exploit its competitive advantages not just in its home market but in foreign markets too. However, there is more to internationalization than simply extending the geographical boundaries of a company's market. International scope may also be a source of competitive advantage over nationally based competitors. In this section, I explore whether, and under what conditions, firms that operate on an international basis, either by exporting or by direct investment, are able to gain a competitive advantage over nationally focused firms. If such "global strategies" have potential for creating competitive advantage, in what types of industry are they likely to be most effective? and how should they be used in order to maximize their potential?

The benefits of a global strategy

A global strategy is one that views the world as a single market. Theodore Levitt of Harvard Business School has argued that companies that compete on a national basis are highly vulnerable to companies that treat the world as a single global market.[19] The basic thesis of globalization is this:

1 National and regional preferences are disappearing in the face of the homogenizing forces of technology, communication, and travel. "Everywhere everything gets more and more like everything else as the world's preference structure is relentlessly homogenized," observes Levitt. Nor is this trend restricted to technology-based products such as computer, aircraft, and consumer electronics; it is just as prevalent in branded consumer goods such as Coca-Cola, Levi jeans, and McDonald's hamburgers.

2 Firms that produce standardized products for the global market can access scale economies in production, distribution, marketing, and management that permit them to offer a price-quality combination that nationally based competitors cannot match. In automobile manufacture, we have already noted how new model development costs of over $1 billion have forced the exit of nationally based companies.

Globalization does not necessarily mean that companies became multinationals – that is, establish operations in different countries. The key is their approach to national markets: they view national markets as simply segments of a broader world market. Thus, the primary exponents of global marketing, the Japanese automobile and consumer electronics companies during the 1970s, concentrated almost all their production activities in Japan. Their overseas subsidiaries were primarily marketing and distribution offshoots. Conversely, many European and American corporations were multidomestic corporations rather than global corporations in the sense that each country was served by a fairly autonomous national subsidiary that managed a full range of functional activities. For example, until the late 1970s, General Motors's overseas subsidiaries, Opel in Germany, Vauxhall in Britain, and Holden in Australia, produced their own range of models, under their own brand names, for their own domestic markets. The advantage of this strategy is that it permitted flexibility in relation to local conditions, particularly in allowing differentiation on the basis of local preferences, while avoiding the administrative complexities associated with centralized control from a remote corporate head office.

Levitt's thesis is not that customers are the same the world over. National and regional differences exist and cannot be ignored. But underlying these differences is a commonality of goals: the alleviation of life's burdens and an expansion of leisure and spending power. When presented with a choice, it is likely that customers will select the lower-priced, standardized product that meets the basic need in preference to the higher-priced, nationally differentiated alternative.

Levitt's globalization thesis is a subject of continuing controversy. Critics have attacked his assumptions both of global homogenization of preferences and the benefits of scale economies. National differences in customer preferences continue to exert a powerful influence on the markets for packaged groceries, drinks, clothing, and furniture. Also, costs of national differentiation can be surprisingly low if common basic designs and common major components are used. As manufacturing systems become increasingly flexible, costs of customizing products to meet the preferences of particular groups of customers are falling. In the market in which Levitt developed this thesis – washing machines – national preference has remained remarkably impervious to the globalization of firms; French washing machines are primarily top-loading, elsewhere in Europe machines are mainly front-loading, the Germans prefer higher spin speeds than the Italians, U.S. machines feature agitators rather than revolving drums, and Japanese machines are small. National market differences are especially important for products and services supplied to governments and public agencies. As Volker Jung, a director of Seimens, noted: "All politics are local politics. Politicians will always find a way not to buy nonlocal products."[20]

Even among the primary examples of global products there are distinct national differences. McDonald's offers teriyaki chicken burgers in Japan, pizzas in some parts of the United States and Canada, and beer in Germany. Coca-Cola's Hi-C soy milk is popular in Southeast Asia and its Georgia coffee drink is consumed mainly in Japan. The key lies in exploiting the cost economies of globalization while making concessions to cultural and language differences.

Strategic strength from global positioning

The competitive advantage from a global approach to manufacturing, marketing, and distribution extends beyond the cost advantages from

---

Exhibit 13.1   Overseas Market Entry in the U.S. Beer Market

During the 1980s and 1990s, the number of overseas brands of beers sold in the United States – and their market shares – have expanded enormously. Some of these beers are imported directly into the United States; others are brewed under license by U.S. brewers. In practice, almost all imported beer is imported with some form of collaboration with U.S. brewing companies, primarily because the brewing companies control wholesale distribution. However, the arrangements vary widely. The Dutch beer Grolsch, with its distinc-tive bottles, is brewed and bottled in Holland and exported to the United States. Most English beers are brewed and bottled in England and exported to the United States. Guinness is brewed in Dublin and exported in bulk to the United States where it is bottled by U.S. brewing companies. Other foreign brands are brewed under license in the United States. Thus, Lowenbrau, Fosters, and Amstel are all brewed and distributed by major U.S. brewing companies.

What characteristics of the beers, and the overseas companies that brew them, might explain the different market entry modes?

scale economies. Even in the absence of cost advantages from global scales of operation, there are clear strategic advantages from an international scope. Because the global competitor faces different competitive conditions in different countries, it can use its strength in some national markets to leverage its position in others. Such leveraging requires cross-subsidization: using the cash flow from countries where market position is strong to finance competition against nationally focused competitors in other markets. While the classic form of cross-subsidization, predatory pricing, is likely to contravene both GATT antidumping rules and national antitrust laws, such cross-subsidization may occur through less overt means: heavy advertising, promotion, and dealer support.[21]

Similar principles apply to retaliation against an aggressively competitive foreign MNC in one's own domestic market. The domestically focused firm is in a weak position to compete because the competitive battle is affecting its entire sales base – it has no overseas markets to rely upon for profit. Such was the position of the U.S. TV manufacturers when faced by strong Japanese competition in the 1970s. The most effective response to competition in one's home market may be to retaliate in the foreign MNC's own home market. Thus, when Kodak was attacked by Fuji in the U.S. market – an attack that was symbolized by Fuji's capture of sponsorship of the 1984 Olympic Games in Los Angeles – Kodak's response was to attack Fuji in Japan.[22] To effectively exploit such opportunities for national leveraging, some overall global coordination of competitive strategies in individual national markets is required.

MNCs are increasingly recognizing the advantages of strong market positions within the world's largest economies. During the 1980s, European and Japanese MNCs scrambled to obtain firm U.S. bases. Companies such as British Petroleum, Siemens, Thomson, Sony, ICI, and Unilever all made significant U.S. acquisitions during the 1980s, while Japanese banks and auto companies established U.S. subsidiaries. During the early 1990s, a major strategic thrust of many U.S. companies is to establish a strong footing within Europe. The head of McKinsey & Company's Tokyo office, Kenichi Ohmae, argues the case for "*Triad Power.*" His thesis is that pressures of technological change, convergence of customer preferences, scale economies, and protectionism increasingly require successful world players to become true insiders within the *three* major markets of the world: the United States, Europe, and Japan.[23]

Strategy and Organization within the Multinational Corporation

The evolution of multinational strategies and structures

The balancing of the benefits of globalization against those of adapting to national market conditions is a dominant issue not only for the strategy of multinational firms but also for their organizational structures. As we have already observed, strategy and structure are not easily changed in the short or medium term and the strategy-structure configurations adopted by today's MNCs tend to reflect the choices made by the companies at the time of their international expansion. Because of their size and international spread, MNCs are likely to find fundamental changes in their organizational structure especially difficult: once an international distribution of functions, operations, and decision-making authority has been determined, reorganization can be difficult and costly, particularly when host governments become involved. The result is that early choices with regard to strategy and structure have a lasting impact on the development of organizational capability. Bartlett and Ghoshal identify three phases in the development of MNCs, each associated with a different answer to the issue of globalization/centralization versus national differentiation/decentralization. The allocation of decision making between the parent company and overseas subsidiaries is indicated in figure 13.8.

1   *Pre-Second World War: the era of the European multinationals*   During the early decades of the twentieth century, European multinationals – companies such as Unilever, Royal Dutch/Shell, ICI, Philips, and Courtaulds – were in the forefront of international business and played a leading role in overseas industrial development. These companies have been described by Bartlett and Ghoshal as "*multinational federations*": each national subsidiary was permitted a high degree of operational independence from the parent company, undertaking its own product development, manufacture, and marketing.[24] Parent-subsidiary relations were principally oriented around the appointment of senior managers to subsidiaries, authorization of major capital expenditures, and the flow of dividends from subsidiary to parent company. Such structures were an inevitable response to an era when international transport and communication were costly and unreliable, and national markets were highly differentiated.

2   *Post-Second World War: the era of the American multinationals*   The 1950s and 1960s saw the dominance of U.S. companies across a range of manufacturing industries throughout the world. Companies such as GM, Ford, IBM, Coca-Cola, Caterpillar, and Procter & Gamble all became established as clear international leaders within their respective industries. Although the subsidiaries of U.S. companies typically operated with a high degree of autonomy in terms of product introduction, manufacturing, and marketing, a key structural feature of the U.S. multinationals was the dominant position of their domestic operations. Because the United States was the largest and most affluent market in the world, the U.S. base acted as the source of new products and process technology for the company. The primary competitive advantage of overseas national subsidiaries was their ability to utilize new products, process technology, and marketing and manufacturing know-how developed in the United States.

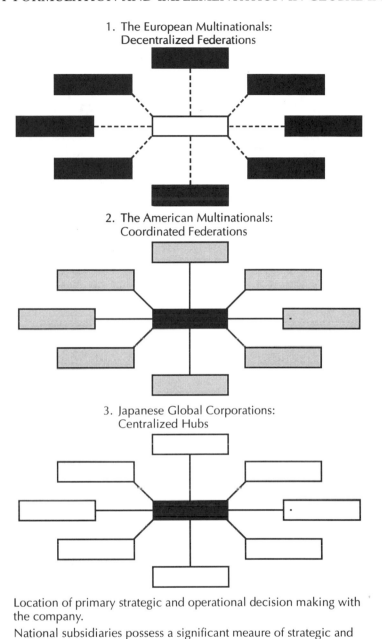

Figure 13.8
Multinational Strategies and Parent/Subsidiary Relationships

1. The European Multinationals: Decentralized Federations

2. The American Multinationals: Coordinated Federations

3. Japanese Global Corporations: Centralized Hubs

Location of primary strategic and operational decision making with the company.

National subsidiaries possess a significant meaure of strategic and operational autonomy.

National subsidiaries possess little decision-making authority.

Source: Christopher Bartlett, "Building and Managing the Transnational: The New Organizational Challenge," in *Competition in Global Industries,* ed. Michael E. Porter (Boston: Harvard Business School Press, 1986), 367–401.

3   *The 1970s and 1980s: The Japanese Challenge*   During the 1970s and 1980s, U.S. and European companies increasingly lost ground to Japanese companies across a range of manufacturing industries from steel and shipbuilding to electronics and automobiles. The key feature

of the Japanese multinationals was their pursuit of global strategies from centralized domestic bases. Companies like Honda, Toyota, Matsushita, and NEC concentrated R&D and manufacturing within Japan, while overseas subsidiaries were initially for sales, distribution, and customers. By building plants of unprecedented scale to service growing world demand, Japanese companies were able to exploit substantial scale and experience advantages.

Matching global strategies and structures to industry conditions

Although the victor's mantle in international markets has passed from the Europeans to the Americans and then to the Japanese, it is not possible to point to any particular organizational form as uniquely successful for MNCs. The strength of European multinationals was (and still is) their responsiveness to the conditions and requirements of individual national markets. The strength of the U.S. multinationals was their ability to transfer technology and proven new products from their domestic strongholds to their national subsidiaries. That of the Japanese global corporations was the efficiency advantages derived from global integration.

The relative merits of each configuration depended upon the market and competitive conditions – and hence key success factors – in different industries. In some industries, such as semiconductors, electronics, and motorcycles, the importance of scale economies and the lack of national differences in customer requirements underscore the benefits of global strategies and structures. In industries where scale economies are more modest relative to the size of national markets and where national market differences are important – such as processed foods, beer, children's clothing, and furniture – responsiveness to national customer preferences takes precedence. Figure 13.9 summarizes Bartlett and Ghoshal's arguments in relation to three industries.

Emergence of the "Transnational Corporation"

During the 1990s, the dominant trend among MNCs has been the desire to achieve simultaneously the benefits of both global integration and national adaptation. As a result of increased competitive pressure, companies across all industries have been pushed toward achieving cost-efficiency progressiveness through the global integration of manufacturing and technology development. At the same time, the resilience of national market differences and the increased turbulence of markets have forced the companies to be increasingly responsive to local circumstances. The increasing speed of technological change and the need for innovation has further exacerbated these contradictory forces. While the costs of research and new product development emphasizes the benefits of global scale, the generating of product, process, and organizational innovations is also encouraged by decentralization of innovation in order to promote and exploit creativity and participation throughout

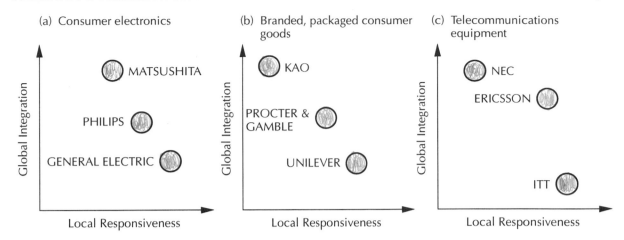

(a) Consumer electronics (b) Branded, packaged consumer goods (c) Telecommunications equipment

Figure 13.9 Strategy, Structure, and Performance in Three Industries

1   During the 1980s, Matsushita was highly globally integrated, Philips was the most multinational in terms of international spread and responsiveness of national subsidiaries to local requirements, and GE was primarily U.S.-based and oriented toward the requirements of the North American market. During the 1980s, customer preferences for consumer electronic products were highly uniform across countries, and competitive advantage was strongly determined by the ability of companies to access global economies in product development and manufacture and coordinate the global marketing of new products and new models. By the end of the 1980s, Matsushita was the clear winner, Philips was still hanging on (despite dismal profitability), and GE had exited from the industry.

2   In branded, packaged consumer goods, national differences remained strong during the 1980s. Unilever, with its locally responsive multinational spread, remained the world leader across a number of product groups, while Procter & Gamble, despite its strong U.S. base, did not achieve the same degree of international market penetration. Meanwhile, Kao, the leading Japanese soaps and personal hygiene products supplier, largely failed in its attempts to penetrate international markets.

3   In contrast to electronics and branded, packaged consumer goods, telecommunications equipment is subject to substantial global scale economies in R&D and manufacture and requires responsiveness to the specific requirements of national telecommunications operating companies. ITT, the most international of the major players, was increasingly unable to achieve the integration necessary to leverage its global position. NEC, despite its technological capabilities and dominant position in Japan, has so far failed to develop a strong position in Europe or North America. One of the most successful companies has been Ericsson, which, despite its small domestic market, has effectively combined global integration with national responsiveness.

Source: Based upon C. Bartlett and S. Ghoshal, *Managing across Borders: The Transnational Solution* (Boston: Harvard Business School Press, 1989).

the organization. Thus, there is a conflict between the decentralization that is conducive to *generating innovation* and the global centralization that is conducive to efficiency and effectiveness in *introducing innovation*. Thus, Philips, with its decentralized, nationally responsive organization structure, has been extremely successful in encouraging companywide innovation. In its TV business, its Canadian subsidiary developed its first color TV, its Australian subsidiary developed its first stereo sound TV, and its British subsidiary developed teletext TVs. However, lack of global integration has constrained its ability to successfully introduce its innovation on a global scale. Thus, despite the technical superiority of its V2000 VCR system, it was Victor Co.'s (JVC) VHS system that achieved world leadership.[25]

Developing the organizational capability to simultaneously pursue both responsiveness to national markets and global coordination requires, according to Christopher Bartlett, "a very different kind of internal management process than existed in the relatively simple multinational or global organizations they may have had previously. I term this the *"transnational organization."*[26] The distinguishing characteristic of the transnational is that it becomes an *integrated network of distributed and interdependent resources and capabilities*. Features of the transnational corporation include:

- each national unit is a source of ideas, skills, and capabilities that can be harnessed for the benefit of the total organization;
- national units achieve global scale by making them the company's world source for a particular product, component, or activity;
- the center must establish a new, highly complex managing role that coordinates relationships between units but does so in a highly flexible way. The key is to focus less on managing activities directly and more upon creating an organizational context that is conducive to the coordination and the resolution of differences. Creating the right organizational context involves "establishing clear corporate objectives, developing managers with broadly based perspectives and relationships, and fostering supportive organizational norms and values."[27] Figure 13.10 depicts this network form of organization.

Evidence of the convergence of different strategy-structure configurations around this "transnational" form is especially evident in the automobile industry. Exhibit 13.2 compares the development of Toyota and Ford.

Summary and Conclusions

Internationalization of the business environment opens a broad spectrum of opportunities and poses severe threats. The most serious implications are for companies used to the predictable and muted competitive conditions in domestic markets sheltered from the full blast of international competition. The collapse of the British motorcycle industry, the demise of RCA in consumer electronics, and the disastrous recent performance of European airlines such as Air France and Alitalia point to international competition's potential for devastation.

One of the difficulties that managers face in coming to terms with the threats and opportunities of the global business environment is the

Figure 13.10   The Transnational Corporation

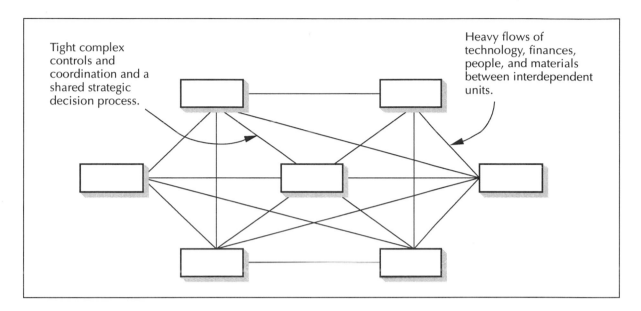

Sources: Based upon C. Bartlett and S. Ghoshal, *Managing Across Borders: The Transnational Solution* (Boston: Harvard Business School Press, 1989).

quantum leap in complexity caused by the transition from a national to an international environment. The primary contribution of this chapter is in applying fundamental concepts of strategy and extending analytical frameworks to encompass the additional complexity of international business. We have examined how the internationalization of business affects a firm's prospects for profitability both through influencing industry structure and by changing the conditions for competitive advantage. With regard to competitive advantage, a critical issue is the influence of national conditions on a firm's potential for competitive advantage. The analysis of competitive advantage is critically important to success in internationally competing industries. Because internationalization increases the intensity and diversity of competition, achieving competitive advantage is critical to success. Because internationalization greatly widens firms' opportunity sets, the potential for competitive advantage becomes the primary guideline for focusing a firm's strategy.

Internationalization means that companies become less dependent upon their own home bases for resources and customers. Across a wide range of industries, from automobiles and electronics to textiles and publishing, companies are broadening their global scope through direct investment, licensing, joint ventures, and sourcing in order to take advantage of country-specific advantages overseas. Choices over location and production and the mode of overseas market entry are critical

Exhibit 13.2 Emerging Transnationals: Ford and Toyota

In 1970, Ford was an archetypal U.S. multinational and Toyota an archetypal Japanese global corporation. Ford had established subsidiaries throughout the world during the 1920s and 1930s. The principal subsidiaries, Ford Great Britain, Ford of Germany, and Ford Australia, were more or less stand-alone subsidiaries, designing, manufacturing, and marketing their own lines of autos. For example, in Britain, Ford's most popular car was the British-made Cortina; in Germany, it was the German-built Taurus.

Toyota also had subsidiaries throughout the world, but unlike Ford, the only manufacturing that these subsidiaries undertook was to assemble some cars that were exported in broken-down form. For the most part, Toyota's overseas subsidiaries were sales and marketing organizations.

By the end of 1993, both companies had radically changed their international strategies and structures. Beginning with the integration of Ford's European subsidiaries into Ford of Europe, Ford moved toward much closer global integration. Small car design is undertaken in Europe and in collaboration with Mazda in Japan; large cars are designed in Dearborn. Ford's smallest car, the Festiva/Fiesta, is manufactured in South Korea and Spain; its Escort is manufactured in Michigan, Mexico, Britain, and Germany; and the Mercury Capri is made in Australia. Similar global specialization occurred in engines and other major subassemblies.

Although Toyota City remained the dominant core of Toyota's activities, by 1993, there was broad dispersion of production and development activities. NUMMI in California and Holden in Australia were owned jointly with GM, and Toyota plants existed in Kentucky, England, China, Indonesia, and Thailand. Toyota distributes VW and Audi cars in Japan and has its trucks and vans manufactured by VW in Germany. It has a design studio in California. Chairman Shoichiro Toyoda commented at the World Automotive Forum: "We are determined to adapt our cars to European needs and circumstances in the best spirit of the European automotive tradition. And we know the best way to do that is with an integrated local presence."

Undoubtedly, Ford is much further ahead in terms of developing a fully integrated global network that adapts to local markets while launching world cars such as the Mondeo. However, the extent to which Toyota has abandoned its monolithic, centralized, 100-percent Japanese corporate persona and moved toward increased international dispersion of activities and decisions is also significant.

Sources: Maryann Keller, *Collision: GM, Toyota, Volkswagen and the Race to Own the 21st Century* (New York: Doubleday, 1993); Ford, Annual Reports.

strategic decisions. As we have seen, these choices are highly dependent upon the resources that underlie a firm's competitive advantage, whether these resources are firm-specific or country-specific, and the transactions costs associated with their exploitation.

Organizing the multinational corporation presents some of the most complex issues in strategy implementation. The ability to reconcile the conflicting needs for efficiency, innovation, customer responsiveness, and flexibility has necessitated new and more sophisticated organizational structures and management systems. Such changes also have important implications for the skills and expertise of managers:

Intensifying international competition will make the home-grown chief executive obsolete. "Global, global, global," is how Noel Tichy, a professor of Michigan's graduate school of business, describes the wider-ranging chief executive of the future. "Travel overseas," Mr. Danforth of Westinghouse advises future chief executives. "Meet the prime minister, the ministers of trade and commerce. Meet with the king of Spain and the chancellor of West Germany. Get yourself known." With over half of Arthur Andersen's revenue generated outside the United States, the company's next chief executive "will be a person with experience outside the borders of the United States, which I have not," says Duane R. Kullberg, the head of the big accounting and consulting company. "If you go back 20 years, you could be pretty insular and still survive. Today that's not possible."[28]

Notes

1 The threat of "economic imperialism" posed by U.S. multinational corporation was especially prevalent in Western Europe. (See Jacques Servan-Schreiber, *The American Challenge* ("*Le Defi Americaine*") [New York: Athenaeum, 1968].)

2 During the 1930s, Standard Oil of New Jersey (now Exxon) and the Royal Dutch/Shell Group effectively regulated competition in the international oil industry. The world cigarette industry for much of the twentieth century was neatly divided between American Tobacco and the Imperial Tobacco Group of Britain. American Tobacco agreed not to compete within the British Empire, Imperial agreed to keep outside the Americas, while exports to other countries were handled by a jointly owned subsidiary British-American Tobacco (BAT). (M. Corina, *Trust in Tobacco* [London: Michael Joseph, 1975].)

3 A key finding was that *human capital* (knowledge and skills) was more important than *physical capital* in explaining the pattern of U.S. trade – the so-called *Leontief Paradox* (W. W. Leontief, "Domestic Production and Foreign Trade," in *Readings in International Economics*, ed. Richard Caves and H. Johnson [Homewood, IL: Irwin, 1968]).

4 M. Dertouzos, Richard Lester, Robert Solow, and the MIT Commission on Industrial Productivity, *Made in America: Regaining the Productive Edge* (Cambridge: MIT Press, 1989).

5 Paul Krugman, "Increasing Returns, Monopolistic Competition, and International Trade," *Journal of International Economics* 9 (November 1979): 469–79.

6 Michael E. Porter, *The Competitive Advantage of Nations* (New York: Free Press, 1990).

7 Porter's view differs sharply from those observers who point to the emergence of the "*stateless corporation*" (ABB's Percy Barnevik among them). Although the national market is comparatively unimportant to a number of MNCs (ABB, Nestlé, Royal Dutch/Shell Group, Philips, and Hoffman-La Roche), that is not to say that their capabilities, strategy, and management style are not influenced by their national home base ("The Stateless Corporation," *Business Week*, May 14, 1990, 98–106).

8 For a review of the Porter analysis, see Robert M. Grant, "Porter's *Competitive Advantage of Nations*: An Assessment," *Strategic Management Journal* 12 (1991): 535–48.

9 Porter's analysis has some interesting implications for national industrial policy. In particular, Porter suggests that measures intended to promote local industry by means of supporting them (e.g., by subsidies or devaluing the national currency), protecting them (by tariffs and quotas), and

increasing their dominance of their home markets through state-sponsored mergers are all likely to be counterproductive resulting in the development of companies which are not tough enough, fast enough or innovative enough to succeed against international competition.

10 *Nike: International Context,* Harvard Business School, Case 9-385-328, Boston, 1985; and *Nike in China,* Harvard Business School, Case 9-386-037, Boston, 1985.

11 "The China Bubble Bursts," *Fortune,* July 6, 1987, 86-9.

12 The role of firm-specific assets in explaining the multinational expansion is analyzed in Richard Caves, "International Corporations: The Industrial Economics of Foreign Investment," *Economica* 38 (1971): 1–27.

13 The role of transactions costs is explained in D. J. Teece, "Transactions Cost Economics and Multinational Enterprise," *Journal of Economic Behavior and Organization* 7 (1986): 21–45. See also "Creatures of Imperfection," in "Multinationals: A Survey," *Economist,* March 27, 1993, 8–10.

14 J. Peter Killing, "How to Make a Global Joint Venture Work," *Harvard Business Review,* (May–June 1982): 120-7.

15 See Robert Reich and Eric Mankin, "Joint Ventures with Japan Give Away Our Future," *Harvard Business Review* (March–April 1986).

16 "When U.S. Joint Ventures with Japan Go Sour," *Business Week,* July 24, 1989.

17 "Your Rivals Can Be Your Allies," *Fortune,* March 27, 1989, 66–76.

18 Gary Hamel, Yves Doz, C. K. Prahalad, "Collaborate with Your Competitors – and Win," *Harvard Business Review* (January–February 1989): 133–9.

19 Theodore Levitt, "The Globalization of Markets," *Harvard Business Review* (May–June 1983): 92–102.

20 "Footloose across Europe's Frontiers," *Financial Times,* March 9, 1993, 15.

21 See Gary Hamel and C. K. Prahalad, "Do You Really Have a Global Strategy?" *Harvard Business Review* (July–August 1985): 139–48.

22 R. C. Christopher, *Second to None: American Companies in Japan* (New York: Crown, 1986).

23 Kenichi Ohmae, *Triad Power: The Coming Shape of Global Competition* (New York: Free Press, 1985).

24 Christopher Bartlett and Sumantra Ghoshal, *Managing Across Borders: The Transnational Solution* (Boston: Harvard Business School Press, 1989).

25 Christopher Bartlett and Sumantra Ghoshal, "Organizing for Worldwide Effectiveness: The Transnational Solution," *California Management Review* (fall 1988): 54–74. Also, "Sony Isn't Mourning the Death of Betamax," *Business Week,* January 25, 1988, 37.

26 Christopher Bartlett, "Building and Managing the Transnational: The New Organizational Challenge," in *Competition in Global Industries,* ed. Michael E. Porter (Boston: Harvard Business School Press, 1986), 377.

27 *Ibid,* 388.

28 "Going Global: The Chief Executives in Year 2000 Will Be Experienced Abroad," *Wall Street Journal,* February 27, 1989, A1, A4.

FOURTEEN

Diversification Strategy

In diversification we have a package that is not at all what it seems. On the outside we see an array of rationalizations that make diversification seem irresistibly attractive, but we know that, on the whole, diversified companies have not done so well. When we closely examine the reasons for diversification they tend to disappear.

– Milton Lauenstein, *Sloan Management Review*

Outline
Introduction and Objectives
The Trend over Time
The Evolution of Management Thinking
Motives for Diversification
   Growth as a motive for diversification
   The alleged risk-spreading benefits of diversification
   Diversification as a means of creating value for shareholders
Competitive Advantage from Diversification
   Market power
   Economies of scope
   Economies from internalizing transactions
   The benefits of internal markets for capital and labor
   Information advantages of the diversified corporation
Diversification and Performance
   The findings of empirical research
   The meaning of relatedness in diversification
Summary and Conclusions

Introduction and Objectives

In our personal lives we face diversification decisions every day. If my car doesn't start in the morning, should I try to fix it myself or have it towed directly to the garage? There are two considerations. First, is repairing a car an attractive activity for me? If the garage charges $50 an hour but my hourly consulting rate is more than double that, then car repair is not a profitable activity for me. Second, am I any good at car repair? If I am likely to take twice as long as a skilled mechanic, then I possess no competitive advantage in car repair. Diversification decisions by firms involve these same questions:

   1 *Does the industry to be entered offer more attractive opportunities for profit than those available within the firm's existing industry?*

2 *Can the firm establish a competitive advantage over firms already established in the industry?*

These are the basic issues of strategy that were established in chapter 2 (see figure 2.2). Hence, no new analytic framework is needed for appraising diversification decisions: diversification may be justified either by the superior profit potential of the industry to be entered or by the ability of the firm to create competitive advantage in the new industry. The first issue draws upon the industry analysis developed in chapter 3; the second draws upon the analysis of competitive advantage developed in chapters 5 to 8.

The primary focus of this chapter is upon the latter question: what are the conditions under which diversification can lead to a company establishing a competitive advantage in a new industry and also strengthening its competitive position within existing industries. The key difference between single-business and multiple-business firms in sources of competitive advantage is that the multiple-business firm can exploit competitive advantages arising from the relationships between its different business activities – these are known as "synergies."

This chapter explores the trends in diversification over the last few decades, examines the objectives influencing diversification decisions, analyzes the nature and extent of synergy from diversification, and reviews some empirical evidence. Issues concerning the management of diversified corporations will be considered in the next chapter.

By the time you have completed this chapter, you will be able to:

- understand the factors that have influenced diversification decisions by large firms, including different management objectives and the impact of management ideas and fashions;
- appreciate the conditions under which diversification creates shareholder value;
- identify the potential for synergy between businesses through the sharing of resources and capabilities;
- understand the conditions under which diversification is necessary to exploit such synergies, in preference to collaborative arrangements between independent firms;
- understand the pitfalls of diversification and, in particular, why diversification has so often failed to realize its anticipated benefits.

The Trend Over Time

In chapter 12, I noted that the dominant trend of the last 100 years was for companies to broaden their product, geographical, and vertical scope. This trend is especially notable with regard to product diversification. Alfred Chandler's studies of the long-term development of large U.S. corporations observed a common pattern of development that had followed the following stages:[1]

1 Firms began as single product businesses supplying a local market.
2 The availability of improved methods of transport and communication permitted firms to serve wider regional and even national markets.
3 Firms grew by vertical integration – in particular, firms seeking national marketing integrate forward into marketing and distribution systems.
4 Excess capacity in marketing and distribution systems causes firms to diversify their product ranges.

Empirical evidence for the U.S. shows that during the postwar period the trend toward diversification has been persistent and strong. Wrigley and Rumelt classified corporations into strategic types based upon the pattern of their diversity.[2] Over time, the number of single business companies among the ranks of the Fortune 500 has fallen steadily, while the most diversified companies, whether related business or unrelated business (i.e., conglomerates) have increased in number (see table 14.1). Similar trends are apparent among large companies in other industrialized nations (see tables 14.2 and 14.3).

During the 1980s and 1990s, there has been a clear reversal of the diversification trend. In Britain, companies that had diversified most extensively during previous years became less diversified during the late 1970s and early 1980s.[3] Among U.S. companies, unprofitable diversified businesses were increasingly being divested during the later 1980s, while a number of diversified companies fell prey to LBOs. Despite the fact that acquisition activity was extremely heavy during the 1980s – some $1.3 trillion in assets were acquired and 23 percent of the *Fortune 500* were acquired between 1980 and 1989 – only 4.5 percent of acquisitions during the 1980s represented unrelated diversification.[4] Moreover,

	1949 (%)	1954 (%)	1959 (%)	1964 (%)	1969 (%)	1974 (%)
Single-business companies	42.0	34.1	22.8	21.5	14.8	14.4
Vertically integrated companies	12.8	12.2	12.5	14.0	12.3	12.4
Dominant-business companies	15.4	17.4	18.4	18.4	12.8	10.2
Related-business companies	25.7	31.6	38.6	37.3	44.4	42.3
Unrelated-business companies	4.1	4.7	7.3	8.7	18.7	20.7

Table 14.1 Changes in the Diversity of the Fortune 500, 1949-74

Note: Single-business companies have more than 95 percent of their sales within their main business.
Vertically integrated companies have more than 70 percent of their sales in vertically related businesses.
Dominant-business companies have between 70 percent and 95 percent of their sales within their main business.
Related-business companies have more than 70 percent of their sales in businesses that are related to one another.
Unrelated-business companies have less than 70 percent of their sales in related businesses.
Source: Richard Rumelt, "Diversification Strategy and Profitability," *Strategic Management Journal* 3 (1982): 359–70.

Table 14.2 Changes in
the Diversity of 305
Large British
Manufacturing
Companies, 1960-80

	1960 (%)	1970 (%)	1975 (%)	1980 (%)
Single-business companies	34.2	14.5	12.5	9.5
Vertically integrated companies	2.0	3.3	3.4	3.0
Dominant-business companies	23.5	26.0	21.6	24.7
Related-business companies	32.0	44.4	49.0	49.7
Unrelated-business companies	7.4	11.8	13.5	13.2

Source: Azar P. Jammine, *Product Diversification, International Expansion and Performance: A Study of Strategic Risk Management in U.K. Manufacturing,* Ph.D. diss., London Business School, 1984, 215.

Table 14.3
Diversification among
118 Large Japanese
Industrial Corporations,
1958-1973

	1958 (%)	1963 (%)	1968 (%)	1973 (%)
Single-business companies	26.3	24.6	19.5	16.9
Vertically integrated companies	13.2	15.3	18.6	18.6
Dominant-business companies	21.0	16.9	18.7	17.8
Related-business companies	30.7	35.6	36.4	39.8
Unrelated-business companies	8.8	7.6	6.8	6.8

Source: Based upon information in H. Itami, T. Kagono, H. Yoshihara, and A. Sakuma, "Diversification Strategies and Economic Performance," *Japanese Economic Studies* 11, no. 1 (1982): 78-110.

acquisitions by the *Fortune* 500 were outnumbered by dispositions. One study of acquisitions and divestitures by large diversified, U.S. corporations found that the dominant trend was the divestment of unrelated businesses and a restructuring around fewer, more closely related businesses.[5]

The "back to basics" trend is certainly strong in North America and Western Europe but is less evident elsewhere in the world. In East Asia, there is no apparent divestment trend among large diversified corporations. A handful of *chaebols* – Samsung, Daewoo, Hyundai, and Gold Star – continue to dominate the South Korean business sector, while in Southeast Asia sprawling conglomerates such as Charoen Pokphand of Thailand, Lippo of Indonesia, and Keppel Group of Singapore have increased their prominence.[6]

The Evolution of Management Thinking

In chapter 12, I noted that the long-term trend toward a widening of firm boundaries was reversed during the mid-1970s, and the last 20 years have seen a narrowing of firm scope. These trends can be explained in terms of transactions costs. In relation to the pattern of diversification over time, management developments such as techniques of financial management, strategic planning systems, and organizational innovations such as the multidivisional structure and strategic business units facilitated the management of multibusiness corporations. During the last two decades, increased market turbulence has reduced the efficiency and exposed the sluggishness of these sophisticated management systems. As a result, the performance of diversified corporations appears to have deteriorated relative to that of more specialized companies.

But there are also other forces at work. Two factors have been especially influential: first, changes in prevailing thinking about corporate strategy, and, second, a reordering of corporate objectives. Let me begin with a brief review of the evolution of "conventional wisdom" concerning diversification; in the next section, I will then address corporate objectives.

Michael Goold and Kathleen Luchs identify a number of concepts and techniques that have exercised a profound influence over prevailing thought about corporate strategy (see figure 14.1).[7] The principal developments over time have been as follows:

1 During the 1950s and 1960s, the rapid advancement of the "science of management" propagated the view that the essence of management

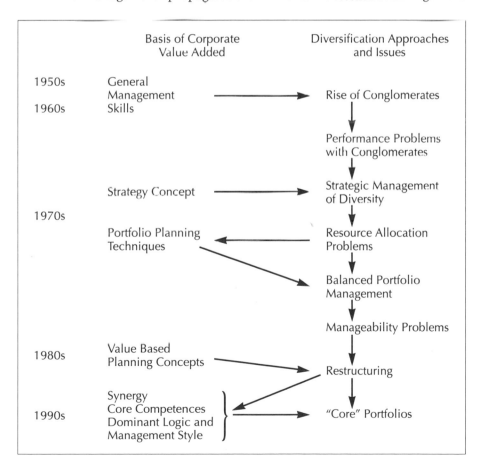

Figure 14.1 Evolution of thinking on corporate strategy and diversification

Source: Michael Goold and Kathleen Luchs, "Why diversify? Four decades of management thinking," *Academy of Management Executive,* Vol. 8, No. 3, August 1993.

was not the deployment of industry-specific, experiential knowledge but the application of the tools and principles of general management. The universality of the principles of management implied that professional managers could run widely diversified corporations through the application of a common set of financial controls, capital appraisal systems, human resource management policies, and decision rules.

2   With the emergence of corporate strategy as the primary responsibility of top management during the 1970s, a more restrained view of the ability of individual corporations to diversify across multiple, unrelated sectors emerged. The simple logic that had driven opportunistic growth of conglomerates was refined into a more sophisticated evaluation of basic strategic decisions such as the choice of industries within which to locate and competitive positioning within those industries. The primary tools of corporate strategy were portfolio planning techniques, which provided top management with a common framework in which to view their different businesses and what Goold and Luchs call a "helicopter view" of the company. I will discuss these portfolio techniques in the next chapter. The result was a standardized basis on which to make diversification and divestment decisions, allocate resources between different businesses, and establish strategies for individual businesses.

3   In response to the poor financial and stock market performance of many highly diversified companies and the disappointing results of many diversifying mergers, the dominant theme of the 1980s was shareholder value maximization. Not only was each business unit within the diversified corporation scrutinized to determine whether it created or destroyed shareholder value, but corporate headquarters were also viewed as overhead with potential for pruning. Value-based planning tools illuminated the link between share price and competitive strategy. The rigorous application of these tools resulted in the divestment of businesses that were failing to create "economic value added." These tended to be diversified businesses rather than core businesses, thus reinforcing the "back to basics" trend.

4   The 1990s have seen the reemergence of the logic that drove the conglomerate diversification of the 1960s – synergy. But while synergy in the 1960s was seen as financial in nature, the synergies that have captured management attention in the 1990s relate much more to establishing a core of businesses that create value by sharing a common, integrated set of resources and capabilities. The commonality of resources and capabilities provides a rationale for the company's spread of activities, which has been referred to as *"dominant logic."*[8]

Motives for Diversification

A second factor explaining the reversal of the postwar diversification trend is a reordering of top management objectives over the period. To the extent that managers pursue their own individual interests and are motivated by financial gain, status, security, and power, there are good reasons to expect that they will pursue *growth maximization* rather than *profit maximization*. However, top management's ability to pursue objectives other than profitability is constrained by several factors. First, over the long term a firm must earn a return on capital greater than its cost of capital or it does not survive. Second, if management sacrifices profitability for other objectives, managers run the risks of losing their jobs either from a shareholders' revolt or from acquisition. During the 1980s, these latter threats exerted a stronger discipline on management: shareholders (pension funds in particular) became more active in unseating incumbent management, and the LBO of RJR Nabisco in 1989 indicated that even the largest U.S. corporations were not safe from acquisition. The increasing insecurity of top management positions is indicated by the ousting of a number of CEOs during the early 1990s. These included Robert Stempel at General Motors, James Robinson at American Express, Ken Olsen at Digital Equipment, and John Akers at IBM.[9] Let us examine three motives that can explain the diversification behavior of firms: growth maximization, risk spreading, and the quest for market power.

Growth as a motive for diversification

Growth is a powerful motivation for senior managers and for employees in general. Growth of the firm creates opportunities for promotion, and it is especially beneficial to top management whose salaries tend to be determined more by the size of the enterprise than by its profitability and whose power and status grow with organizational size. For firms in declining industries, the desire to avoid decline may provide particularly pressing motives for diversification. The conflict between growth and profitability is particularly apparent in the tobacco and oil industries:

- the decline in cigarette consumption that followed the Surgeon General's report on the health risks of smoking in 1963 was followed by a rash of diversification by the major tobacco companies, despite the fact that the businesses that they entered were all substantially less profitable than the tobacco industry. RJR Nabisco under the leadership of Russ Johnson is a classic case of a company run in the interests of management rather than shareholders. A strategy of diversification achieved growth without profitability, ultimately resulting in Kohlberg Kravis Roberts & Company's $25 billion LBO aimed at creating value through divestment.[10] BAT Industries was also threatened by acquisition, and it too resorted to divesting several previous acquisitions. In the meantime, Philip Morris was embroiled in the decision on whether to split into separate tobacco and food companies;
- declining demand for oil during the late 1970s and early 1980s also translated into the drive to diversify in order to sustain growth. Almost all the companies diversified into minerals, coal, and alternative energy sources. While Exxon established a large computer and office automation subsidiary, Mobil acquired retailer Montgomery Ward, and Brit-

ish Petroleum built a large animal feeds subsidiary. By 1992, pressure on profitability and increased attentiveness to shareholder value resulted in the divestment of almost all of the diversification of the previous decade.[11]

This view of diversification being motivated by managers' growth objectives is formalized in Marris's theory of managerial capitalism.[12] The desire for growth results in firms investing at a greater rate than that consistent with profit maximization. Firms continue to trade profits for growth to the point that the valuation ratio of the firm (the ratio between the firm's stock market value and its book value) declines to levels where the firm becomes vulnerable to acquisition. Evidence supporting the Marris model is provided by the propensity of managers to divest diversified businesses when their control of the firm is threatened directly by a takeover bid or indirectly by a fall in profitability that reduces share prices and hence attracts potential predators.[13] Further support is provided by the finding that most mergers, diversifying mergers in particular, fail to increase the profitability of the merged companies.[14]

The alleged risk-spreading benefits of diversification

A second motive for diversification is the desire to spread risks. To consider the alleged benefits of risk-spreading through diversification we need to consider "pure diversification," otherwise referred to as "conglomerate" diversification. This is where diversification simply extends corporate ownership over several independent businesses, and the change of ownership has no impact on the independent profit streams of the separate businesses. By combining businesses with profit streams that are imperfectly correlated, diversification can achieve a reduction in the variability of the firm's overall profits. Because most individuals are risk-averse, risk reduction can be viewed as consistent with shareholder interests. However, this ignores a critical factor: to achieve a diversification of risk, shareholders can hold diversified portfolios or invest through mutual funds. Not only does this achieve wider diversification than even the most diversified corporations can attain, it can also be achieved at lower cost. The transactions costs to shareholders of diversification are far less than the transactions costs to firms of diversifying through acquisition. Not only do acquiring firms incur heavy costs of using investment banks and legal advisers, they must also pay an acquisition premium in order to gain control of an independent company.

The *capital asset pricing model* formalizes this argument. Assuming efficient securities markets, the theory postulates that the risk that is relevant to determining the price of a security is not the overall variance of the security's return but *systematic risk*: that part of the variance of the return that is correlated with overall market risk. Systematic risk is measured by the security's "*beta coefficient.*" Corporate diversification does not reduce systematic risk: other things being equal, the beta coefficient of the conglomerate company is simply the weighted average of the beta coefficients of the constituent companies of the conglomerate. Hence, on its own, corporate diversification does not create value for shareholders.[15]

Empirical studies are generally supportive of the absence of shareholder benefit from diversification that simply combines independent businesses. Studies of conglomerates in the United States have shown that their risk-adjusted returns to shareholders are typically no better than those offered by mutual funds or by matched portfolios of specialized companies.[16] A recent study also points to the failure of unrelated diversification to lower either systematic or unsystematic risk, though it does find lower levels of both for firms pursuing moderate, closely related diversification.[17]

For pure diversification to yield shareholder benefits, market imperfections must be present in the form of transactions costs in securities dealing or restrictions on the investment opportunities available to shareholders. For example, if individuals are unable to purchase the securities of overseas companies, there may be risk-spreading benefits from multinational diversification by domestic firms.

All this has been discussed from the viewpoint of the owners of the firms. Let us consider the benefits of risk-spreading available to other stakeholders in the firm. If cyclicality in the firm's profits are accompanied by cyclicality in employment, then, so long as employees are transferable between the separate businesses of the firm, there may be benefits to employees from diversification's ability to smooth output fluctuations. Managers appear to be especially enthusiastic about the risk-spreading benefits of diversification. Managers' risk-aversity is probably motivated by their desire to protect their independence and their jobs. Downturns in profit, even if only temporary, can stimulate concern among shareholders and stock analysts, may make the company temporarily dependent upon financial markets for borrowing and may encourage takeover bids.

Special issues arise once we consider the risk of bankruptcy. For a marginally profitable firm, diversification can help avoid cyclical fluctuations of profits that can push it into temporary insolvency. It has been shown, however, that diversification that reduces the risk of bankruptcy is beneficial to the holders of corporate debt rather than to equity holders. The reduction in risk that bondholders derive from a diversifying merger is termed the *coinsurance effect*.[18] In addition, managers and other employees are likely to have strong interests in any strategy that reduces the risk of bankruptcy.

Diversification as a means of creating value for shareholders

If we return to the assumption that corporate strategy should be directed toward the interests of shareholders, what are the implications for diversification strategy? Michael Porter proposes three "essential tests" to be applied in deciding whether diversification will truly create shareholder value:

1   *The attractiveness test*   The industries chosen for diversification must be structurally attractive or capable of being made attractive.
2   *The cost-of-entry test*   The cost of entry must not capitalize all the future profits.
3   *The better-off test*   Either the new unit must gain competitive advantage from its link with the corporation, or vice versa.[19]

The attractiveness and cost of entry tests   The assessment of industry attractiveness was outlined in chapter 2: industry analysis is especially relevant to diversification decisions because diversification is a means by which the firm can access more attractive investment opportunities than are available in its own industry. However, the second test, "cost of entry," explicitly recognizes that the attractiveness of an industry to a firm already established in an industry may be different from its attractiveness to a firm seeking to enter the industry. More specifically, industries such as pharmaceuticals, defense equipment, and cigarettes may be profitable precisely because they are surrounded by high entry barriers. For firms seeking to enter these industries, the costs of surmounting these barriers may well outweigh the benefits of being in the industry.

Consider the two alternative means of diversification, new ventures and acquisitions. New corporate ventures must directly confront the barriers to entering a new industry. This involves high risk and low returns over a long period. A study of 68 diversifying ventures by established companies found that, on average, breakeven was not attained until the seventh and eighth years of operation. If diversification is by acquisition, barriers to entry are avoided, but the market price of the target company's shares will accurately reflect its future profit prospects. Because the acquirer must offer a premium of between 20 and 35 percent over the market price to gain control, it is likely that any superior profit prospects in the industry will be fully capitalized into the cost of entry. Although movie and TV production appeared to be an attractive industry during the late 1980s and early 1990s, the extremely high acquisition prices paid by Sony for Columbia Pictures, Matsushita for MCA, and Viacom for Paramount Communications suggest that diversification simply aimed at becoming established within an attractive industry is likely to destroy rather than create shareholder value.

The better-off test   Porter's third criterion for successful diversification – the "better-off" test – addresses the following issue: if two companies producing different products are brought together under the ownership and control of a single enterprise, is there any reason why they should become any more profitable? Diversification has the potential to enhance the competitive advantage of the diversified business, the original core business, or both businesses. Thus, in the case of the above mentioned acquisitions of Hollywood studios, Sony, Matsushita, and Viacom believed that there were opportunities to create value by matching their existing businesses in consumer electronics and communication with movie and TV production. The potential for enhancing competitive advantage by bringing together separate businesses under common ownership is complex. The opportunities for value creation are many, but the practical difficulties of exploiting such opportunities have made diversification a mine field for many companies. Let us examine the issues systematically.

Competitive Advantage from Diversification

Market power

One of the issues that has occupied antitrust authorities in the United States and Europe is whether diversification can enhance profitability not by increasing efficiency but by creating market power. During the "conglomerate era" of the late 1960s and early 1970s, it was claimed that large diversified companies could exercise market power through three mechanisms:

1 *Predatory pricing*   Just as global corporations derive strength from their ability to finance competitive battles in individual markets through cross-subsidization, so conglomerates can similarly use size and diversity to discipline or even drive out specialized competitors in individual product markets. The key competitive weapon is predatory pricing, the ability to cut prices below the level of rivals' costs and sustain losses over the period needed to cause the competitor to exit or sell out.

2 *Reciprocal buying*   A conglomerate can leverage its market share and profitability by reciprocal buying arrangements with customers. This means giving preference in purchasing to firms that are good customers for the conglomerate's own products. For instance, General Dynamics's acquisition of Liquid Carbonic Corporation in 1957 was based on the belief that General Dynamics's subcontractors were likely to shift their purchases of industrial gases to Liquid Carbonic.[21]

3 *Mutual forbearance*   Corwin Edwards has argued that:

When one large conglomerate enterprise competes with another, the two are likely to encounter each other in a considerable number of markets. The multiplicity of their contacts may blunt the edge of their competition. A prospect of advantage in one market from vigorous competition may be weighed against the danger of retaliatory forays by the competitor in other markets. Each conglomerate may adopt a live-and-let-live policy designed to stabilize the whole structure of the competitive relationship.[22]

Despite the plausibility of these arguments, evidence on anticompetitive practices of these types is sparse. Certainly common patterns of diversification among competing firms in the same industries occur that point to an awareness of the need to build countervailing strategic positions, but overt abuse of conglomerate power is rare judging by the few actions that the antitrust authorities have initiated against conglomerates.[23]

Economies of scope

The most general argument concerning the benefits of diversifications focuses upon the presence of *economies of scope* in common resources. If a certain input is used in the production of two products and this input is available only in units of a certain minimum size, then a single firm producing both products will be able to spread the cost of the input over a larger volume of output and so reduce the unit costs of both products.[24] Thus, economies of scope exist for similar reasons as economies of scale. The principal difference is that the cost reduction we gain from economies of scope arises from the increase in production volume that is achieved through producing multiple products.

Economies of scope can be examined in relation to three categories of resource: tangible resources that are used in joint production, intangible resources, and management capabilities.

Tangible resources   Economies of scope in tangible resources arise from the ability to eliminate the duplication of certain activities across several products or services. Consider the following examples:

- distribution and service networks tend not to be highly specialized by product. Because there tends to be a minimum fixed cost of supplying and servicing a single outlet, there are economies in spreading distribution and sales costs over a range of products. The recent entries by cable TV companies into telephone services and telephone companies into cable TV reflect the desire of the companies to spread the costs of their wire networks over as wide a volume of business as possible;
- similar considerations apply to service activities. For IBM and Xerox, economies of scope in the companies' service networks provided an incentive for the companies to supply a range of office equipment;
- in technology-intensive industries, economies of scope in R&D facilities have provided a similar incentive for diversification. Companies typically have a single corporate research facility that supports a number of product divisions. An advantage that Sony, Matsushita, and Philips have over specialized consumer electronics companies like Zenith or Bang & Olufsen is the ability of the former to spread R&D costs over a broader product base. In aerospace, the ability of leading U.S. suppliers to spread research expenditures over both defense and civilian products has given these companies an advantage over overseas competitors without access to large military contracts. More generally,

studies of interindustry patterns of diversification show research intensity to be strongly associated with the extent of diversity.[25]

Intangible resources   Intangible resources that can be utilized across several businesses also provide important opportunities for exploiting economies of scope. Assets such as brand names, corporate reputation, and technology can be transferred from one business area to another without necessitating any physical integration of operations.[26] Many of these assets have the characteristics of "public goods" – they can be utilized in additional employment at negligible marginal cost. Thus, when American Express diversified its range of financial services with the acquisitions of Shearson Lehman Brothers, IDS Financial Services, and Trade Development Bank, the new subsidiaries all clearly identified their new affiliations by prominent display of the American Express blue-and-white corporate logo and the addition of the suffix "An American Express Company" to their company names. The strategy was outlined as follows:

we are creating a new kind of enterprise – one with multiple distribution channels that target select market segments with strong brand-name products and services. One expression of our multiple marketing strategy is the new logos and names for the American Express family. Our marketing strategy for the decade ahead is to sharpen our focus on the individual brand names as well as on the multiple distribution channels and carefully targeted market segments these brand names represent. At the same time, each business will continue to draw upon the marketing power and identification of the American Express name.[27]

Functional capabilities   For most diversified companies, the major source of economies of scope are organizational capabilities. Exploiting economies of scale in capabilities such as marketing, product development, and customer responsiveness does not usually require the pooling of activities to share the common capability but requires instead the ability to *transfer* the capability to different businesses. Examples of the exploitation of economies of scope through the transfer of capabilities across businesses include the following:

- Philip Morris's success in increasing both the profitability and the market share of Miller Brewing Company was primarily due to the application of the marketing skills developed in the cigarette market. Philip Morris's success in leveraging the market position of its Marlboro brand can be attributed to its expertise in brand repositioning, market segmentation, proliferation of subbrands (Marlboro Light, Marlboro 100s), and advertising. Thus, many of the marketing techniques applied in the beer market – the repositioning of Miller toward the mass-market, the promotion of Miller Lite, and the introduction of other Miller beers – were similar to those used in cigarettes;

- Motorola's remarkable long-term success in semiconductors, wireless telecommunication products, and, most recently, wireless communication services has been built upon the development of a set of core technological capabilities that are transferred and integrated across a number of different business areas. These technological capabilities relate to the development of microelectronic and communications technology; the embodiment of new technology into innovative, well-designed new products; and expertise in their manufacturing.

General management capabilities   Marketing and technological capabilities generally imply diversification across businesses which are closely related in terms of demand or technological characteristics. However, other capabilities can be deployed over a broader range of businesses. Consider the following examples:

- Motorola's organizational capabilities have been viewed as technology-based. However, Motorola's capabilities also relate to its expertise in total quality management, in developing management systems that combine decentralized decision making with extensive integration, and human resource management – especially employee training and management development. The fact that Motorola offers management training seminars to executives from other companies suggests that these capabilities are applicable over a broad range of products and markets;[28]
- the same may be true of financial management capabilities. Although technology-based industries may call for different approaches to budgeting, appraisal, and control than mature, low-tech industries, financial management capabilities are fundamentally of potentially broad application;
- General Electric's remarkable record over the last half century as one of America's most diversified and consistently profitable corporations owes much to its strategic management capabilities. The effectiveness of GE's strategic management systems in guiding acquisitions and divestitures, and its reconciling rigorous cost efficiency with innovation and global expansion is indicated by its repositioning of its business portfolio and its gaining world leadership in jet engines, turbine generators, and medical diagnostic equipment;[29]
- among Hanson's businesses, there is little apparent relatedness between Peabody coal mines, Imperial Tobacco, and Jacuzzi whirlpools. The successful performance of Hanson's businesses lies in common management capabilities that relate to its identification of takeover targets, its sophisticated postacquisition restructuring skills, and its systems of financial control, which have enabled Hanson to secure drastic cost reductions and attractive margins in mature, often unglamorous businesses.[30]

Economies from internalizing transactions

While economies of scope provide cost savings from using the same resource in the production of several products, a critical issue is whether exploiting these economies requires that different businesses are brought under common ownership.[31] Why cannot economies of scope be exploited by selling the use of the common resource to independent firms? In practice, economies of scope frequently are exploited by market transactions. In chapter 10, we observed that a firm can exploit proprietary technology by licensing it to other firms. In chapter 13, we noted how technology and trademarks are licensed across national frontiers as an alternative to direct investment. There are many examples of firms exploiting economies of scope by selling the use of the resource to firms in other industries. In the case of trademarks, the owners of well-established brand names including Gucci, Yves St Laurent, Harrods, Guinness, and Harley-Davidson license the use of their names to other firms for use with designated products. For Walt Disney, the licensing of its characters to publishers, toy manufacturers, and food and drink processors earns over $500 million each year. In some industries, selling the use of physical plant and facilities to independent companies is well established. Thus, in airports and railroad stations there are economies of scope from using the physical plant for multiple uses. But typically the owners of airports do not supply food, drink, and car rental services – specialized firms lease space for these activities. A similar trend is evident in department stores where the stores lease floor space to specialty retailers ("shops-within-shops").

Hence, economies of scope are not a sufficient condition for diversification. For diversification to yield competitive advantage requires not only the existence of economies of scope in common resources but also the presence of *transactions costs* that discourage the firm from selling or renting the use of the resource to other firms. Transactions costs include the costs involved in drafting, negotiating, monitoring, and enforcing a contract. Transactions costs can be substantial when transferring intangible resources such as brand names and technology, thus providing an important motive for diversification.[32] For example:

- during the early 1980s, Texaco developed a process for converting coal into gas that could then be used for electricity generation. Rather than license the process and face the problems of adequately safeguarding its technology, Texaco chose to utilize its coal gasification process directly by building a number of cogeneration plants;
- TRW has used its "service competency" in the development and management of database services for credit checking as a springboard for expanding into several related areas. These include the development of software for field information updating and artificial intelligence-based testing procedures and the maintenance and support services for users of large complete systems;[33]
- licensing of the use of a brand name by other firms runs the risk that the licensee may adversely affect the reputation of the brand through poor quality products. The exclusivity value of the brand names of some European fashion houses (Yves St Laurent in particular) have

been adversely affected by excessive licensing with inadequate control over the quality of the licensed products.

In the case of organizational capabilities, it is especially difficult to envisage the types of contractual arrangements under which these can be sold to independent companies. Thus, 3M Company's unrivaled technical capabilities in adhesives, bonding, and thin film cannot easily be exploited by directly selling these capabilities to other firms. The technical capabilities of 3M are embodied within a broadly diversified and constantly growing range of products that include various adhesive tapes, magnetic tape, computer disks, fasteners for surgical use, and water-resistant suntan lotion.[34] The more deeply embedded are a firm's capabilities within the management systems and the culture of the organization, the greater the likelihood that these capabilities can only be deployed internally within the firm.

The benefits of internal markets for capital and labor

The presence of transactions cost in any type of common resource can encourage diversification – even where economies of scope are not present. For example, the costs incurred by firms in using financial markets (in terms of the margin between borrowing and lending rates and the underwriting costs from new issues of securities) encourage large companies to develop internal capital markets. By transferring cash between its businesses, the diversified company can achieve greater independence from financial markets. One of the objectives of portfolio analysis (see chapter 15) is to achieve a balance between cash-generating and cash-using businesses such that the corporation is largely independent of the external capital market.

An important development among a number of large, diversified corporations has been the establishment of internal banks to offer banking facilities to internal business units. For example, in 1985 British Petroleum set up British Petroleum Finance International to arrange the financing of BP's 70 operating companies, undertake standard treasury functions, trade in foreign exchange, manage leasing, and offer 24-hour trading capability in short-term instruments. By 1986, BP Finance International had over 100 employees; maintained offices in London, New York and Melbourne; and made over $50 million in profit.[35] A key advantage of internal corporate banks is that they are not subject to the myriad of regulations that raise the costs of using external financial institutions.[36]

Cost savings can also arise from the internal transfer of employees, particularly managers and technical experts, between the divisions of a diversified company as compared with hiring and firing to and from the labor market. As companies develop and encounter new circumstances, so different management skills are required. The costs associated with hiring include advertising, the time spent in interviewing and selection, and the costs of "head-hunting" agencies. The costs of dismissing employees can be elevated sharply through severance payments. A diversified corporation has a pool of employees and can respond to the specific needs of any one business through a transfer from elsewhere within the corporation. Not only are such internal transfers less costly than external transfers, they are also much less risky because of the superior information that the firm possesses on internal job candidates (see the next section). The broader set of opportunities available in the diversified corporation as a result of internal transfer may also attract a higher caliber of employee. Graduating students compete strongly for entry-level positions with diversified corporations such as Matsushita, General Electric, Unilever, and Nestlé.

Information advantages of the diversified corporation

An important benefit of internal capital and labor markets within the diversified corporation is that the corporate head office of the diversified corporation has better access to information than that available to external capital and labor markets. As a result, the diversified corporation may be more efficient in reallocating labor and capital between its divisions than external capital and labor markets are in allocating labor and capital between independent businesses. In the case of capital, these information advantages may be especially great with respect to new ventures. Despite a well-developed market for venture capital in the United States and Europe, the risks associated with such ventures are compounded by limited information available to potential lenders and investors. A diversified company such as 3M or Hewlett-Packard has full access to the information on performance and prospects for each of its business units.

These information advantages may be even greater in the case of labor. A key problem of hiring from the external labor market is not just cost but limited information. A resume, references, and a day of interviews are an uncertain indicator of how an otherwise unknown person will perform in a specific job. The diversified firm that is engaged in transferring employees between business units and divisions has access to much more detailed information on the abilities, characteristics, and past performance of each of its employees. This informational advantage exists not only for individual employees but also for groups of individuals working together as teams. As a result, in diversifying into a new activity, the established firm is at an advantage over the new firm that must assemble a team from scratch with poor information on individual capabilities and almost no information on how effective the group will be in working together. Hence, in an economy where new industries are constantly arising, there are reasons to expect that diversification by established firms offers some advantages over exploiting new opportunities than do entirely new ventures.[37]

Diversification and Performance

The findings of empirical research

The implications of these arguments for the impact of diversification on firm performance are as follows. First, if the diversified corporation can carry out the tasks of resource allocation and the monitoring and control of operational managers more effectively than the market system, then we would expect that, over the long term, diversified firms would show higher profitability and more rapid growth than specialized firms. Second, because of the importance of economies of scope in shared resources, diversification into *related* industries will be more profitable than diversification into *unrelated* industries.

Initially, empirical research into the impact of diversification on firm performance produced clear and consistent findings on the second hypothesis. A study by Richard Rumelt found that, while diversification per se showed no clear relationship with profitability, sharp differences emerged between different diversification strategies. In particular, firms that diversified into businesses that were closely related to their existing activities were significantly more profitable than those that pursued unrelated diversification. Subsequent research confirmed Rumelt's findings both for the United States and for other countries (notably Canada, West Germany, and Japan). At the same time, the problems associated with wide-ranging unrelated diversification were highlighted by the poor performance of conglomerates such as LTV, ITT, and Allegheny International. The apparent consistency of the evidence was such that, in 1982, Tom Peters and Robert Waterman were able to conclude: "virtually every academic study has concluded that unchannelled diversification is a losing proposition."[38]

On the basis of both academic research and their own observations, they coined one of their "golden rules" of excellence – "*Stick to the Knitting*":

Our principal finding is clear and simple. Organizations that do branch out but stick very close to their knitting outperform the others. The most successful are those diversified around a single skill, the coating and bonding technology at 3M for example. The second group in descending order, comprise those companies that branch out into related fields, the leap from electric power generation turbines to jet engines from GE for example. Least successful, as a general rule, are those companies that diversify into a wide variety of fields. Acquisitions especially among this group tend to wither on the vine.[39]

However, recent studies undermined the apparent consistency of these findings. Some studies have shown that the apparent superior performance of related diversifiers was, in fact, due to industry factors rather than to the type of diversification strategy, while other studies have found unrelated diversification to be more profitable than related diversification.[40]

It seems likely that there are limits to the degree of diversity that can be profitably managed. Thus, very high levels of diversification appear to give rise to problems of managing complexity. One recent study found that diversified British companies were more profitable than specialized companies up to a point, after which further increases in diversity were associated with declining profitability (see figure 14.2). However, in all the studies of diversification and profitability *association* does not imply *causation*. To the extent that increased diversification is associated with increased profitability, is this because increased diversification increases firm profitability, or is it because profitable firms use their cash flows to finance diversification? Observation of high-profit, low-growth companies such as the tobacco and oil companies during the early 1980s suggests a preference by top management to channel profit earnings into diversification rather than distributing them to shareholders.

It appears that the relationship between diversification and profitability has shifted over time – with diversification becoming a less profitable activity during the 1980s and 1990s than during the 1960s and 1970s. Such a change in the relationship is consistent with the arguments that have already been made about the impact of environmental turbulence on the costs of managing large complex enterprises. The stock market's verdict on diversification is unambiguous. The high price/earnings ratios attached to conglomerates during the 1960s have been replaced by a "conglomerate discount." The result is that diversified companies have

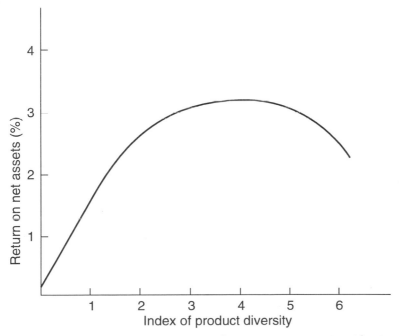

Figure 14.2 The Relationship between Diversity and Profitability among 304 British Manufacturing Companies, 1972-84

Source: Robert M. Grant, A. P. Jammine, H. Thomas, "Diversity, Diversification and Profitability among British Manufacturing Companies," *Academy of Management Journal* 31 (December 1988).

come under attack from LBO specialists seeking to add value by dismembering these companies. Costas Markides has found refocusing announcements by diversified companies have been accompanied by abnormal stock market returns.[41] Conversely, the tendency for acquisition announcements to generate abnormal stock market returns to the acquiring companies during the 1960s and 1970s was reversed by the 1980s.[42]

The studies that have found either that unrelated diversification is more profitable than related diversification or that relatedness has no significant impact on the profitability of diversification are something of a puzzle. Because the principal benefits of diversification are exploiting economies of scope in common resources and capabilities, what factors might explain the failure of empirical research to find the consistent superiority of related over unrelated diversification? Two factors may be important. First, related diversification may offer greater potential benefits but may also pose more difficult management problems for companies. Second, it is not entirely clear what "related" and "unrelated" diversification really are.

The first of these factors, the problems of managing related diversification, is a large and complex issue. It goes right to the heart of the issues surrounding the implementation of diversification strategies and the management of diversified corporations. For this reason, I shall defer its discussion to the next chapter. Suffice it to say here that if there are potential economies from exploiting the linkages between businesses within the diversified company, then these linkages must be managed. As with any management activity, it is not costless.

The meaning of relatedness in diversification

Our discussion of economies of scope identified two major types of relatedness offering synergistic benefits from diversification: the use of common physical resources between businesses such as a common distribution system or R&D department and the transfer of skills and reputation between businesses. Distinguishing the potential for exploiting economies of scope between businesses is no easy matter, and researchers have used simple criteria for determining whether or not businesses are related. Typical criteria are similar technologies and similar markets. Under the first criterion, missile guidance systems and personal computers are related by their common utilization of electronic technology. Under the second criterion, canned vegetables and frozen desserts are related because they are sold to the same customers through the same retail outlets.

However, similarities in technology and markets refer primarily to relatedness at the *operational* level – in activities such as product development, manufacturing, and marketing. Relatedness may also exist at the *strategic* level through the application of common management skills to different businesses. Hence, in determining whether an acquisition or a new venture will "fit" with a company's existing range of activities, the most important factors are likely to be the ability of corporate management to apply strategies, resource allocation procedures, and control systems similar to those applied to the company's present businesses. Table 14.4 lists some of the strategic factors that determine whether there are similarities between businesses in relation to corporate management activities.[43]

Unlike operational relatedness, where the benefits of exploiting economies of scope in joint inputs are comparatively easy to forecast and even to quantify, relatedness at the strategic level may be much more difficult to appraise. There are numerous examples of companies that identified potential synergies between businesses that in practice proved either elusive or nonexistent. A classic example is the creation and rapid demise of the Allegis Corporation as in the case of exhibit 14.1.

Actual relatedness between businesses is not the same as perceived relatedness. There has been a good deal of recent interest in business relatedness as a cognitive concept. Prahalad and Bettis refer to this as *dominant logic*.[44] Certainly a dominant logic in the form of a common view as to a company's identity and rationale is a critical precondition for effective integration (this issue will be discussed further in the next chapter). There is a danger, however, that dominant logic may not be underpinned by any objective linkages. In the same way that Allegis Corporation attempted to diversify around serving the needs of the traveler, so General Mills diversified into toys, fashion clothing, specialty retailing, and restaurants on the basis of "understanding the needs and wants of the homemaker."

Corporate Management Tasks	Determinants of Strategic Similarity
Resource Allocation	Similar sizes of capital investment projects. Similar time spans of investment projects. Similar sources of risk. Similar general management skills required for business unit managers.
Strategy Formulation	Similar key success factors. Similar stages of the industry life cycle. Similar competitive positions occupied by each business within its industry.
Monitoring and Control of Business Unit	Goals defined in terms of similar performance variables.
Performance	Similar time horizons for performance targets.

Table 14.4 The Determinants of Strategic Relatedness between Businesses

Source: Robert M. Grant, "On Dominant Logic, Relatedness, and the Link between Diversity and Performance," *Strategic Management Journal* 9 (1988): 641.

Exhibit 14.1   The Rise and Fall of Allegis

On May 1, 1987, Richard J. Ferris, Chief Executive of United Airlines Inc. (UAL), inaugurated a new era in the company's history under the new name of "Allegis Corporation." The name change symbolized the metamorphosis of UAL from an airline into a diversified travel company. Ferris explained the company's mission as follows:

"Allegis is United, the airline industry leader. It is Hertz, the top car-rental company. It is Westin, a luxury hotel group. Allegis is Covia, whose Apollo product is a multinational computer reservations network. It is MPI, a full-service direct marketing agency. It is United Vacations, a wholesale travel tour operator. And Allegis will soon be Hilton International, when we complete our purchase of that leading company with 88 luxury hotels in 42 countries. . . .

Allegis Corporation . . . caring for travelers worldwide . . . a distinctive partnership of companies . . . where people are pledged to service and quality. . . .

Allegis will be the world's premier travel-related corporation – recognized by customers, employees, and investors as the source of superior quality and value.

Allegis customers will prefer the services of its worldwide operating partnership because they represent the best in dependability, comfort and convenience . . . and because they are delivered by people whose attention to detail enhances every aspect of the travel experience. . . .

Allegis will also be unwavering in its dedication to bring quality and care back into the total travel experience. So we pledge to you, our customers, value, convenience, dependability, security, comfort – in sum, ease of travel that no other single corporation can match."

On June 9, only six weeks after formally adopting the Allegis name, Dick Ferris was ousted by the board. The car rental and hotel subsidiaries were sold, and the company reverted to its name of United Airlines Inc.

What had gone wrong? Allegis broke two out of three of Porter's "essential tests" of a diversification strategy. First, its cost of entry, in terms of the prices it paid for companies during its two-year, $2.3 billion acquisition binge, was too high. Second, in terms of the "better-off" test, it appeared that Ferris had greatly overestimated the synergies to be exploited in bringing together airlines, hotels and car rental under a common ownership. Indeed, it was not apparent that the chief benefit, providing one-stop shopping for the business traveler through an integrated reservations system, could not be achieved equally well by collaboration among independent companies.

While market-relatedness provided the principal benefits, the key stumbling blocks for the company were the strategic dissimilarities between the different businesses. While Allegis's up-market hotel chains competed on the basis of service and reputation, the principal requirement for success in the deregulated airline industry was rigorous cost cutting and the maintenance of high load factors through quick-footed operational management. Allegis's focus on servicing the needs of the business traveler deflected its attention from its critical need: reducing costs and increasing efficiency at United Airlines.

Sources: Richard J. Ferris, "From Now On," *Vis-à-Vis*, March 1987, 13; "Allegis: Is a Name Change Enough for UAL?" *Business Week*, March 2, 1987, 54–8; "The Unravelling of an Idea," *Business Week*, June 22, 1987, 42–3.

Summary and Conclusions

Diversification is a corporate mine field. In no other area of corporate strategy have so many companies made such disastrous investments. Ever since the 1960s, academics and business commentators have pointed to the dismal record of diversification by large companies – particularly those that have diversified by acquisition. Yet, despite the trend toward specialization and divestment, diversification continues to exert an irresistible attraction for many companies. The move by Ford, General Motors, General Electric, and several other industrial corporations into financial services; the moves during 1994 toward merger between telephone and cable TV companies; and the convergence between computing and communication symbolized by AT&T's acquiring of NCR show that diversification is far from being a dead duck in the business world of the 1990s. Consistent with the overall track record, few of these diversifications have so far been successful. Indeed, few of the proposed mergers between cable and telephone companies were actually consummated.

The inconsistency of the empirical evidence on diversification points to the impossibility of generalizing about the performance outcomes of diversification. However, the above discussion does point to a few conclusions and guidelines for the management of diversification.

First, in a changing world, diversification is inevitable. Changing demand and technology is constantly redrawing industry boundaries. The result is that what may, in terms of conventional definitions of industry boundaries, appear to be diversification, may in fact be a natural extension of existing resources and competences. While telecommunications were analog-based, computers and telephones were separate markets. In a digital era, this is no longer the case. Products like the Apple Newton span both markets.

Second, the performance outcomes of diversification are likely to be highly dependent on motives. Behind many of the most ambitious and spectacular diversification initiatives is the worry that these investments may be motivated more by managerial than stockholder interests. The empirical evidence points to the fact that while diversification through acquisition fails to offer gains in profitability or increasing returns to stockholders, it is highly effective in the creation of large corporate empires. There is also the possibility that diversification may be a form of escapism resulting from the unwillingness of top management to come to terms with difficult competitive circumstances in its core markets. Diversification may then be a diversion.

Hence, any diversification proposal must be subject to candid questioning of the motives that underlie it. Careful and systematic evaluation of the rationale for a merger combined with estimation of its costs and benefits can also help to avoid one of the most common errors of diversifying companies: paying over the odds for an acquisition.

Third, such evaluation must focus upon the analysis of competitive advantage. The key issue for diversification strategy is whether a multimarket presence created value for stockholders. This depends upon two critical factors:

- does diversification permit the exploiting of economies of scope in resources and capabilities?
- is diversification really necessary to exploit these opportunities – or could other types of licensing arrangements of strategic alliances suffice?

The first issue requires the analysis of the commonality of resources and capabilities between different businesses and the cost and differentiation advantages associated with exploiting these commonalities. The second necessitates an assessment of the transactions cost issues.

In analyzing the potential for exploiting economies of scope, it is important to recognize that the linkages between businesses occur not only at the operating level but also at the strategic level. Because there are technological or market links between products or services, this does not imply that diversification can profitably exploit the commonalities in resources and capabilities.

Finally, for diversification to build competitive advantage it is also necessary that the costs of managing the diversified corporation do not outweigh the benefits that diversification offers through the sharing of resources and capabilities. To explore this issue further we need to consider the corporate management of the diversified enterprise.

Notes

1   Alfred Chandler Jr., *Strategy and Structure: Chapters in the History of the Industrial Enterprise* (Cambridge: MIT Press, 1962); and *The Visible Hand: The Managerial Revolution in American Business* (Cambridge: Harvard University Press, 1977).

2   Leonard Wrigley, *Divisional Autonomy and Diversification,* Doctoral diss., Harvard Business School, 1970; Richard P. Rumelt, *Strategy, Structure and Economic Performance* (Cambridge: Harvard University Press, 1974); Richard P. Rumelt, "Diversification Strategy and Profitability," *Strategic Management Journal* 3 (1972): 359–70.

3   Azar P. Jammine, *Product Diversification, International Expansion and Performance: A Study of Strategic Risk Management in U.K. Manufacturing,* Ph.D. diss., London Business School, 1984.

4   A. Shleifer and R. W. Vishny, "The Takeover Wave of the 1980s," *Science* 248 (July–September 1990): 747–9.

5   J. R. Williams, B. L. Paez, L. Sanders, "Conglomerates Revisited," *Strategic Management Journal* 9 (1988): 403–14.

6   "South-East Asia's Octopuses," *Economist,* July 17, 1993, 61.

7   Michael Goold and Kathleen Luchs, "Why Diversify? Four Decades of Management Thinking," *Academy of Management Executive* 7, no. 3 (August 1993): 7–25.

8   C. K. Prahalad and R. Bettis, "The Dominant Logic: A New Linkage between Diversity and Performance," *Strategic Management Journal* 7 (1986): 495–511.

9   "The King Is Dead," *Fortune,* January 11, 1993, 34–46.

10 B. Burrough, *Barbarians at the Gate: The Fall of RJR Nabisco* (New York: Harper & Row, 1990).

11 Robert M. Grant, *Restructuring and Strategic Change in the Oil Industry* (Milan: Franco Angeli, 1993).

12 Robin Marris, *The Economic Theory of Managerial Capitalism* (London: Macmillan, 1964).

13 David A. Ravenscraft and F. M. Scherer, "Divisional Selloff: A Hazard Analysis," in *Mergers, Selloffs and Economic Efficiency* (Washington, D.C.: Brookings Institute, 1987); and Michael E. Porter, "From Competitive Advantage to Corporate Strategy," *Harvard Business Review* (May–June 1987): 43–59.

14 For the United Kingdom, see G. Meeks, *Disappointing Marriage* (Cambridge: Cambridge University Press, 1976); for the United States, see David A. Ravenscraft and F. M. Scherer, *Mergers and Managerial Performance* (Washington, D.C.: Brookings Institute, 1987).

15 See, for example, Stephen A. Ross and Randolph W. Westerfield, *Corporate Finance* (Homewood, IL: Irwin, 1988).

16 See, for example, H. Levy and M. Sarnat, "Diversification, Portfolio Analysis and the Uneasy Case for Conglomerate Mergers," *Journal of Finance* 25 (1970): 795–802; R. H. Mason and M. B. Goudzwaard, "Performance of Conglomerate Firms: A Portfolio Approach," *Journal of Finance* 31 (1976): 39–48; F. W. Melicher and D. F. Rush, "The Performance of Conglomerate Firms: Recent Risk and Return experience," *Journal of Finance* 28 (1973): 381–8; J. F. Weston, K. V. Smith, and R. E. Shrieves, "Conglomerate Performance Using the Capital Asset Pricing Model," *Review of Economics and Statistics* 54 (1972): 357–63

17 M. Lubatkin and S. Chetterjee, "Extending Modern Portfolio Theory into the Domain of Corporate Strategy: Does It Apply?" *Academy of Management Journal* 37 (1994): 109–36.

18 Stephen A. Ross and Randolph W. Westerfield, *Corporate Finance* (St Louis: Times-Mirror/Mosby College, 1988), 681.

19 Michael E. Porter, "From Competitive Advantage to Corporate Strategy," *Harvard Business Review* (May–June 1987): 46.

20 Ralph Biggadike, "The Risky Business of Diversification," *Harvard Business Review* (May–June, 1979).

21 Erwin Blackstone, "Monopsony Power, Reciprocal Buying and Government Contracts: The General Dynamics Case," *Antitrust Bulletin* 17 (summer 1972): 445–62.

22 U.S. Senate, Subcommittee on Antitrust and Monopoly Hearings, *Economic Concentration*, Part 1, Congress, 1st session, 1965, 45.

23 The strongest recent evidence of multimarket competition causing mutual forbearance is in the airline industry. See J. Gimeno, *Multipoint Competition, Market Rivalry, and Firm Performance: A Test of Mutual Forbearance in the U.S. Airline Industry*, Ph.D. diss., Purdue University, 1994.

24 The formal definition of economies of scope is in terms of "sub-additivity." Economies of scope exist in the production of goods $x_1, x_2, \ldots . x_n$, if:

$$C(X) < \Sigma_i C(x_i)$$

Where $X = \Sigma_i x_i$, $C(X)$ is the cost of producing all n goods within a single firm, and $\Sigma_i C(x_i)$ is the cost of producing the goods in n specialized firms. See W. J. Baumol, John C. Panzar, Robert D. Willig, *Contestable Markets and the Theory of Industry Structure* (New York: Harcourt Brace Jovanovich, 1982), 71–2.

25 For the United States, see C. H. Berry, *Corporate Growth and Diversification* (Princeton, NJ: Princeton University Press, 1975); for the United

Kingdom, see Robert M. Grant, "Determinants of the Inter-Industry Pattern of Diversification by U.K. Manufacturing Companies," *Bulletin of Economic Research* 29 (1977): 84–95.

26 Among service companies, the ability to transfer corporate reputation across different service markets was found to be an important influence on the profitability of diversification (P. R. Nayyar, "Performance Effects of Information Asymmetry and Economies of Scope in Diversified Service Firms," *Academy of Management Journal* 36 [1993]: 28–57).

27 *American Express Company 1984 Annual Report,* 3.

28 "Keeping Motorola on a Roll," *Fortune,* April 18, 1994, 67–78.

29 "Can Jack Welch Reinvent GE?" *Business Week,* June 39, 1988, 40–5.

30 For a description of Hanson's diversification strategy, see Michael Goold and Andrew Campbell, *Strategies and Style* (Oxford: Basil Blackwell, 1987).

31 This section draws heavily upon Robert M. Grant, "Diversification and Firm Performance in a Changing Economic Environment," in *Firm-Environment Interaction in a Changing Productive System,* ed. H. Ergas et al. (Milan: Franco Angeli, 1988).

32 This argument is stated more fully by David Teece, "Towards an Economic Theory of the Multiproduct Firm," *Journal of Economic Behavior and Organization* 3 (1982): 39–63.

33 James Brian Quinn, *Intelligent Enterprise* (New York: Free Press, 1992), 81.

34 "3M's Stumbling Steps into the Limelight," *Financial Times,* June 1, 1987, 14.

35 "Inside the New In-House Banks," *Euromoney,* February 1986, 24–34.

36 Robert K. Ankrom, "The Corporate Bank," *Sloan Management Review* (winter 1994): 63–72.

37 Armen A. Alchian and Harold Demsetz ("Production, Information Costs and Economic Organization," *American Economic Review* 62 [1972]: 777–95) argue that the collection and processing of information is the basic role of management and provides the primary rationale for the existence of the firm.

38 Tom Peters and Robert Waterman, *In Search of Excellence* (New York: Harper & Row, 1982), 294.

39 *Ibid,* 294.

40 H. K. Christensen and C. A. Montgomery, "Corporate Economic Performance: Diversification Strategy versus Market Structure," *Strategic Management Journal* 2 (1981): 327–43; R. A. Bettis, "Performance Differences in Related and Unrelated Diversified Firms," *Strategic Management Journal* 2 (1981): 379–83. Studies finding unrelated diversification to be more profitable than related diversification include A. Michel and I. Shaked, "Does Business Diversification Affect Performance?" *Financial Management* 13, no. 4 (1984): 18–24; and G. A. Uffman and R. Reed, *The Strategy and Performance of British Industry,* 1970–80 (London: Macmillan, 1984).

41 C. Markides, "Consequences of Corporate Refocusing: Ex Ante Evidence," *Academy of Management Journal* 35 (1992), 398–412.

42 G. A. Jarrell, J. A. Brickly, and J. M. Netter, "The Market for Corporate

Control: Empirical Evidence since 1980," *Journal of Economic Perspectives* 2, no. 1 (winter 1988): 49–68.

43   For a discussion of the role of strategic linkages between businesses in affecting the success of diversification, see C. K. Prahalad and R. Bettis, "On Dominant Logic: A New Linkage between Diversification and Performance," *Strategic Management Journal* 7 (1986): 485–501; and Robert M. Grant, "On Dominant Logic, Relatedness, and the Link between Diversity and Performance," *Strategic Management Journal* 9 (1988): 639–42.

44   C. K. Prahalad and R. A. Bettis, "The Dominant Logic: A New Linkage between Diversity and Performance," *Strategic Management Journal* 7 (1986): 485–502.

FIFTEEN

Managing the Multibusiness Corporation

Some have argued that single-product businesses have a focus that gives them an advantage over multibusiness companies like our own – and perhaps they would have but only if we neglect our own overriding advantage: the ability to share the ideas that are the result of wide and rich input from a multitude of global sources.

GE businesses share technology, design, compensation and personnel evaluation systems, manufacturing practices, and customer and country knowledge. Gas Turbines shares manufacturing technology with Aircraft Engines; Motors and Transportation Systems work together on new propulsion systems; Lighting and Medical Systems collaborate to improve x-ray tube processes; and GE Capital provides innovative financing packages that help all our businesses around the globe. Supporting all this is a management system that fosters and rewards this sharing and teamwork, and, increasingly, a culture that makes it reflexive and natural at every level and corner of our Company.

> – Jack Welch, letter to share owners,
> *General Electric Company 1993 Annual Report*

Outline

Introduction and Objectives

Chapter 14 was concerned with diversification decisions. We observed that the generally disappointing performance outcomes from diversification were often consequences of the difficulties that companies experienced in managing their diverse businesses. The wide disparities in the performance of different diversified companies may reflect the same factors. The inconsistent findings of the empirical research into the differential performance of alternative diversification strategies (e.g., related diversification versus unrelated) suggests that the critical determinant of the performance of diversified companies is the structure, systems, and style through which the strategy is implemented. This chapter is concerned with strategic management in the multibusiness company. As we will see, corporate strategy is not simply a matter of answering the question "What businesses should we be in?" Some of the most difficult issues of corporate strategy are concerned with the role and activities of managers at the corporate head office and the relationships between the businesses and the corporate headquarters. We will be concerned with five main areas of corporate-level strategic management:

- The composition of the company's portfolio of businesses (decisions over diversification, acquisition, and divestment);
- Resource allocation between the company's different businesses;
- The role of the head office in the formulation of business-unit strategies;
- Controlling business-unit performance;
- Coordinating business units and creating overall cohesiveness and direction for the company.

By the time you have completed this chapter, you will:

- Be familiar with the central issues of formulating and implementing corporate strategy;
- Be equipped with the concepts and techniques necessary for making judgments about these issues;

- Understand the underlying relationships between the resources and capabilities of the firm, its corporate strategy, and the implementation of the strategy through an appropriate organization structure, management systems, and leadership style.

The Structure of the Diversified Company

The evolution of the structure and management of large enterprises

To understand the issues that face the top management of multibusiness corporations, even basic ones such as the distinctions between corporate and business strategy, we need to be familiar with the basic characteristics of the structure of these companies.

The growth over time in the size and diversity of companies has transformed the structure and the work of top management. Some of the most interesting features of Alfred Chandler's studies of the evolution of large U.S. corporations are the fascinating insights they offer into the strategic and administrative roles of top management.[1] As we observed in the last chapter, the driving force for corporate evolution was technological change and economic expansion that encouraged first horizontal, then vertical, then diversifying expansion. Each of these phases of growth placed increasing strains upon management. Growth in geographic scope and company size created the need for new management techniques; new systems of information, communication and control; and organizational structures that facilitated the increased specialization and coordination required by higher levels of complexity.

Chandler identified two critical transformations in the organization of the modern corporation. The first, during the latter part of the nineteenth century was the development of the large multifunctional enterprise. The railroad companies (as a result of their rapid geographical expansion) were the first to establish hierarchical organizational structures with management responsibilities specialized by function:

safe, regular reliable movement of goods and passengers, as well as the continuing maintenance and repair of locomotives, rolling stock, . . . and other equipment, required the creation of a sizable administrative organization. It meant the employment of a set of managers to supervise these functional activities over an extensive geographical area; and the appointment of an administrative command of middle and top executives to monitor, evaluate, and coordinate the work of managers responsible for the day-to-day operations. It meant, too, the formulation of brand new types of internal administrative procedures and accounting and statistical controls. Hence, the operational requirements of the railroads demanded the creation of the first administrative hierarchies in American business.[2]

The second development was the emergence during the 1920s of the divisionalized corporation, that, over time, was to replace both the centralized, functional structures that characterized most industrial corporations and the loosely knit, holding company structure that was a feature of firms that had grown by merger. The pioneers were Du Pont, which adopted a product divisions to replace its functional structure in 1920, and General Motors, which arrived at a similar structure but from a quite different starting point:

- At Du Pont, it was the strains of increasing size and a widening product range that stimulated the adoption of a divisionalized structure. Under its centralized, functional structure, coordination between the various functional departments for each product area became increasingly difficult, and top management became overloaded. As Chandler observed: "the operations of the enterprise became too complex and the problems of coordination, appraisal and policy formulation too intricate for a small number of top officers to handle both long-run, entrepreneurial and short-run, operational administrative activities."[3] The solution devised by Pierre Du Pont was to decentralize, to create product divisions where the bulk of operational decisions would be made, leaving the corporate head office the task of coordination and overall leadership.
- At General Motors, reorganization from a holding company to a more coordinated, divisionalized structure was a response to the acute financial and organizational difficulties that the company faced in 1920. A slump in demand exacerbated the problems of lack of inventory control, absence of a standardized accounting system, lack of information, and a confused product line. The new structure was based upon two principles: the chief executive of each division was fully responsible for the operation and performance of that division, while the general office, headed by the president, was responsible for the development and control of the corporation as a whole including:
  - the monitoring of divisional return on invested capital,
  - coordinating the divisions (including establishing terms for interdivisional transactions),
  - establishing a product policy.[4]

The primary feature of the divisionalized corporation was the separation of operating responsibilities that were vested in general managers at divisional level, from strategic responsibilities that were located at the head office. The divisionalized corporation represented a reconciliation of the efficiencies associated with decentralization with those resulting from centralized coordination. Table 15.1 summarizes some major features of the evolutionary pattern observed by Chandler.

The theory of the M-form corporation[5]

Chandler's observation of the tendency for diversification to be proceeded by the adoption of divisionalized organizational structures has been developed by Oliver Williamson into a more general theoretical analysis of the merits of the multidivisional corporation – or, in William-

DATE	ENVIRONMENTAL INFLUENCES	STRATEGIC CHANGES	ORGANIZATIONAL CONSEQUENCES	Table 15.1 The Evolution of the Modern Industrial Corporation
Early 19th century	Local markets. Transport and communication slow. Labor-intensive production.	Firms specialized and focused upon local market.	No complex administrative or accounting systems. No middle management.	
Late 19th and early 20th century	Railroads, telegraph, and mechanization permit large-scale production and distribution.	Geographical expansion: national distribution, large-scale production. Broadening of product lines. Forward integration.	Emergence of functional organization structures. Top management responsible for integrating the separate functions. Development of accounting systems, MIS and line and staff distinction.	
1920s onward	Excess capacity in distribution systems, increased availability of finance. Desire for growth.	Product diversification.	Increased difficulties of coordination at functional level; top management overload. Functional structure replaced by product divisions. Separation of operational and strategic functions of management. Establishment of general office for strategic management and the provision of corporate services.	

Sources: Based upon A.D. Chandler, *The Visible Hand,* Belknap, Cambridge, 1977.

son's terminology, the "*M-form*" firm. The efficiency advantages of the divisionalized firm rest on four propositions concerning management and organization:

1 "*Bounded rationality*" Managers are limited in their cognitive, information processing, and decision-making capabilities. Hence, the top management team cannot be responsible for all coordination and decision-making within a complex organization – management responsibilities must be decentralized.

2 The division of decision-making responsibilities within the firm should be based upon *the frequency with which different types of decisions are made*. Thus, decisions that are made with high frequency – operating

decisions – need to be separated from decisions that are made infrequently – strategic decisions.

3 *Minimizing the need for communication and coordination* In the functional organization, decisions concerning a particular product or business area must pass up to the top of the company before all the relevant information and expertise can be brought to bear. In the divisionalized firm, so long as close coordination between different business areas is not necessary, most decisions concerning a particular business can be made at the divisional level. This eases the information and decision-making burden on top management.

4 *Global rather than local optimization* Functional organizations are likely to give rise to managers, even at a senior level, emphasizing functional interests over the objectives of the organization as a whole. In the multidivisional firm, the locating of strategic decision-making in a general head office means that companywide interests are given primacy. Also, at the divisional level, the interests of the business and of products are emphasized over functional interests.

The separation between head office and operating divisions, that is the major characteristic of the multidivisional company, offers two further advantages over other organizational forms: efficiency in resource allocation and resolution of agency problems.

Allocation of resources The divisionalized company can operate a competitive internal capital market. While in the functionally structured company, resource allocation decisions are subject to internal political considerations, in divisionalized companies (such as General Electric, Hanson, and ITT) each business competes for corporate funds on the basis of its past financial performance and the attractiveness of its project proposals. As was argued in the last chapter (see "The information advantages of the diversified corporation"), the head office of a diversified, divisionalized company has better access to information on the performance and prospects of its divisions than the capital market does on the performance and prospects of independent companies. As a result, an internal capital market can allocate resources more effectively than the external capital market.

Resolution of the agency problem A second potential advantage of the multidivisional structure is its ability to deal with the central flaw of the large, manager-controlled corporation – the *agency problem*. In the last chapter, I noted that managers' objectives do not necessarily coincide with those of owners. How can owners (the shareholders) ensure that their salaried managers will run the company in the interests of shareholders when the incentive and the power of shareholders to discipline and replace managers is so limited? Shareholders do not exercise direct control; their representatives, the board of directors, control the company. But the board may either be lax in its direction of salaried managers, or it may even be dominated by top managers. Thus, the primary constraint upon managers' pursuit of self-interest is the stock market – as market valuation falls, so the firm becomes vulnerable to hostile takeover. The takeover threat is, at best, a haphazard discipline on self-serving, lazy, or incompetent managers.

In these circumstances, an advantage of the divisionalized firm, claims Williamson, is that corporate management acts as an interface between the stockholders and the divisional managers and can ensure adherence to profit goals. Because divisions and business units are typically profit centers, financial performance can readily be monitored by the head office and divisional managers held responsible for performance failures. What the multidivisional corporation is doing is to create the disciplines of the capital market *within* the diversified corporation. So long as the corporate management is focused upon shareholder goals, the superior access of corporate management to information on the performance of each division can be used much more effectively to allocate funds, to threaten divestiture, or to fire divisional managers. This ability of the head office to replace the managers of underperforming divisions and reward good performance provides powerful incentives for divisional profit maximization. General Electric under Jack Welch, ITT under Harold Geneen, and Hanson under Lord Hanson, are all companies where the multidivisional structure proved to be highly effective in imposing a strong profit motivation among divisional managers. Oliver Williamson explains the merits of the multidivisional corporation ("*M-form*") in economizing on transactions costs and overcoming agency problems as follows:

the M-form conglomerate can be thought of as substituting an administrative interface between an operating division and the stockholders where a market interface had existed previously. Subject to the condition that the conglomerate does not diversify to excess, in the sense that it cannot competently evaluate and allocate funds among the diverse activities in which it is engaged, the substitution of internal organization can have beneficial effects in goal pursuit, monitoring, staffing and resource allocation respects. The goal-pursuit advantage is that which accrues to M-form organizations in general: because the general management of an M-form conglomerate is disengaged from operating matters, a presumption that the general office favors profits over functional goals is warranted. Relatedly, the general office can be regarded as an agent of the stockholders whose purpose is to monitor the operations of the constituent parts. Monitoring benefits are realized in the degree to which internal monitors enjoy advantages over external monitors in access to information – which they arguably do. The differential ease with which the general office can change managers and reassign duties where performance failures or distortions are detected is responsible for the staffing advantage. Resource allocation benefits are realized because cash flows no longer return automatically to their origins but instead revert to the center, thereafter to be allocated among competing uses in accordance with prospective yields.[6]

The assumption behind this argument is that corporate managers are somehow different from other managers, in that, while managers generally pursue their own financial and status goals, corporate managers act as faithful stewards of shareholder interests. One justification is that the top executives of diversified companies are less emotionally committed to particular businesses and are therefore less likely to engage in the destruction of shareholder value through personal ambitions, such as Howard Hughes's desire to build the world's largest aircraft (the Spruce Goose) or the Saatchi brothers' drive to create the world's largest advertising agency. However, the performance of top managers at some diversified, multidivisional corporations suggests that the introduction of a layer of corporate management between operating managers and the firm's shareholders can just as easily compound the agency problem as resolve it.

The proposition that the M-form structure is more efficient for the management of diversified firms has been tested in a number of studies. Most studies have found that among diversified firms, those with multidivisional structures have outperformed the others.[7]

The divisionalized firm in practice

Despite the theoretical arguments in favor of the divisionalized corporation and empirical evidence of its efficacy, close observation reveals that its reconciliation of the benefits of decentralization with those of coordination is far from perfect. Henry Mintzberg points to two important rigidities imposed by divisional structures:[8]

1   *Constraints upon decentralization*   While operational authority in the M-form firm is dispersed to divisional level, the divisions often feature highly decentralized power that is partly a reflection of the divisional CEOs' personal accountability to the head office. In addition, the operational freedom of the divisional management exists only so long as the corporate head office is satisfied with divisional performance. Corporate control is usually so tight that shortfalls in divisional performance precipitate speedy corporate intervention into divisional affairs.

2   *Standardization of divisional management*   An advantage of the divisionalized form is that, in principle, divisions can be differentiated according to the requirements of their particular business needs. In practice, there are powerful forces for standardization across divisions. The corporate head office is likely to play an important training function and tends to orient divisional mangers toward overall corporate goals and values. More importantly, the maintenance of control by the corporate head office requires the establishment of clearly defined performance standards, which tend, inevitably, to be quantitative. The need for a common system of divisional appraisal encourages the divisions to seek similar goals and to adopt bureaucratic patterns of organization and management consistent with hierarchically imposed

quantitative goals. Many of Exxon's problems in managing its high-tech ventures, such as Exxon Office Systems stemmed from a set of corporate systems that were appropriate for the oil business but not for fast-moving entrepreneurial businesses.

Finally, the multidivisional corporation's separation of business from corporate decisions is most clearly defined when each division is operationally separate from each other. Then, cross-functional coordination can take place within each division and the corporate headquarters can devote itself to resource allocation, control, and influencing divisional strategies. Once there are relationships between divisions that need managing, strategic tasks of top management become much more complex.

The Functions of Corporate Management

We have looked at the structure of the diversified, divisionalized corporation and at the separation that it achieved between strategic and operational management. However, we have yet to discuss what the role and functions of corporate management are. As a starting point, let us return to the discussion of corporate strategy in chapter 2. Corporate strategy was defined by the answer to the question "*What business are we in?*" – it is concerned with issues of diversification, acquisition, divestment, and the allocation of resources between different business areas. These activities form a major part of corporate strategy decisions, but the role and responsibilities of corporate management extend much further. Strategic management at corporate level is partly concerned with shaping the corporate portfolio. Equally important, however, are the administrative and the leadership roles of corporate management in terms of implementing corporate strategy, participating in strategy formulation at divisional level, providing the coordination between the various departments and divisions of the company, and providing a sense of cohesion, identity, and direction to the company as a whole. These are essential ingredients for the success of any organization.

The functions and responsibilities of corporate management in the diversified company can be grouped into four areas: managing the corporate portfolio in terms of the businesses included and resource allocation between them, formulating business-level strategies, providing coordination between the different businesses, and controlling performance. We will discuss each in turn.

Managing the corporate portfolio: diversification, divestment, resource allocation

The formulation of corporate strategy is primarily reflected in decisions concerning the composition and balance of the corporate portfolio.

These include extensions of the portfolio through diversification, deletions from the portfolio through divestment, and changes in the balance of the corporate portfolio through the allocation of investment between the different businesses. While additions to and deletions from the corporate portfolio represent major but infrequent corporate strategy decisions, the allocation of resources between businesses is the primary, ongoing strategic responsibility of corporate management. While resource allocation is primarily thought of in terms of investment funds, the assignment and transfer of senior divisional managers is also a vital corporate management activity. In the next three sections we will examine some of the techniques used by diversified companies for assisting their resource allocation decisions.

The role of corporate management in the allocation of resources distinguishes the divisionalized company from the holding company. The individual subsidiaries of a holding company determine their own financial policies: they retain profits required for reinvestment and pay the remainder in dividends to the parent company. Within the divisionalized company, financial strategy is the preserve of the head office: profits are returned to the corporate headquarters, which is also responsible for their allocation and for all external borrowing.

Business strategy formulation

While corporate strategy is formulated and implemented by top management, business strategies are formulated jointly by corporate and divisional managers. In most diversified, divisionalized companies initiation of strategy proposals is the responsibility of divisional managers and the role of corporate managers is to probe, appraise, amend, and approve divisional strategy proposals. The extent of the influence of corporate headquarters on divisional strategies depends upon two main factors: divisional performance and divisional relatedness.

Divisional performance   Satisfactory divisional performance encourages a high level of autonomy. Conversely, if a division is performing poorly, corporate management is likely to intervene more intensively. General Electric's hands-off management of its investment banking subsidiary Kidder Peabody lasted until the Wall Street firm was rocked by a collapse of profits and an insider-trading scandal. GE installed a new top management team, reformulated Kidder Peabody's strategy, and imposed a new framework of controls.[9] The emergence of a new scandal at Kidder Peabody involving phantom trading in mortgage-backed securities resulted in GE dismissing Kidder's CEO, reimposing direct corporate control and, finally, disposing of Kidder.[10]

Divisional relatedness and strategic similarity   The closer are the interrelationships between divisions, the greater is head office involvement in divisional affairs because of the need for coordination.

Even in companies where primary responsibility for formulating business strategies is at the divisional level, the input of corporate headquarters is likely to be critical. If corporate management is to add value to the diversified corporation, then it can only come through corporate management's contribution to divisional performance. At the same time, if the input of headquarters into business strategy formulation is to be valuable, then it is important that corporate management must understand the business. For this reason it has been argued that, even in the most diversified companies, there must be some underlying similarities that link the different businesses. The mindset and underlying rationale that gives cohesiveness to the diversified company has been defined by C. K. Prahalad and Richard Bettis as the *dominant logic* of the enterprise.[11] They define *dominant logic* as "the way in which managers conceptualize the business and make critical resource allocation decisions"[12] For a diversified business to be successful, argue Prahalad and Bettis, there must be sufficient strategic similarity between the different businesses so that top management can administer the corporation with a single dominant logic. For example:

- *Emerson Electric* comprises a number of different businesses (electric motors, air conditioning, electrical appliances, control instruments), but the common goal of being a low-cost producer in each of its businesses provides a unifying thread.[13]
- The British conglomerate *Trafalgar House* comprises a range of businesses including Cunard, Ritz Hotel, Express Newspapers, and Cementation Construction and Engineering. These diverse businesses share several strategic similarities: all are mature, capital-intensive businesses, many of them with high-profile images.
- Jack Welch's restructuring of GE's business portfolio was preceded by his conceptualizing of GE as three intersecting circles each comprising 15 businesses. One circle was GE's core businesses (such as lighting, appliances, and turbines), the second was high-technology businesses (such as aerospace, medical equipment, and electronics), the third was service businesses (such as financial and information services).[14]

Such strategic similarities can promote learning within the company as strategies that proved successful in one business can be applied in others. At the same time, the tendency for headquarters to encourage uniformity in the strategies applied in different businesses can cause a failure to fit strategy to the circumstances of the individual business. Although Philip Morris successfully transferred its marketing capabilities from its cigarette business to Miller Brewing, the deployment of these same capabilities and approaches at its Seven-Up soft drink subsidiary was a costly failure.[15]

Coordination

We have observed that in the conglomerate, the independence of each business limits the need for coordination. The principal coordinating role of a conglomerate's head office is likely to be the budgetary process through which divisional operating plans and strategic plans are integrated to ensure that overall investment spending is within the company's financial capacity. A second coordinating role is in establishing "framework conditions" for divisional planning in the form of medium-term forecasts of economic trends and/or scenarios for the general business environment. There may also be company-wide issues that the different divisions have to face at similar times. Thus, corporate management may intervene to stress the need for cost reduction, for innovation, or for quicker responsiveness to changing customer preferences.

In more closely related companies such as the highly vertically integrated oil companies or companies with close market or technological links (such as IBM, Procter & Gamble, American Express, and Alcoa), corporate management is likely to play a much greater coordinating role. This is likely to involve not only coordination of strategies but also operational coordination in order to exploit the economies of scope and transferable skills that were discussed in the previous chapter. One indicator of the impact of divisional interrelationships upon the coordinating role of corporate management is the size of the corporate headquarters in different types of companies. Hanson, a conglomerate with few linkages between divisions, operates with a "hands-off" corporate management style and has fewer than 200 employees in its London and New York head offices. Hewlett-Packard, with about the same sales but with much closer linkages between its divisions, employs about 3,000 people at its Palo Alto head office. The essential difference is that Hanson's corporate headquarters are concerned only with monitoring subsidiaries' performance and planning acquisitions, group financial strategy, external relations, and a few other functions. Hewlett-Packard's narrower range of activities and close technological linkages makes it desirable to centralize more activities at headquarters.

The need to marry decentralized decision making with multiple dimensions of coordination gives rise to complex issues of organizational design. Among the organizational devices that have been developed to facilitate coordination in the diversified firm are the following:

- *Matrix organization* attempts to resolve the conflicting objectives of decentralization and coordination by superimposing a functional structure onto the basic product-division structure. For example, Hewlett-Packard is organized into product-based divisions. At the same time, the Director of Corporate Manufacturing provides a link between manufacturing managers in each division, which permits coordination of manufacturing policies and diffusion of technological development.
- *Task forces* represent a more flexible and less comprehensive mechanism for achieving cross-divisional cooperation on specific issues and areas. For example, Hewlett-Packard introduced "Total Quality Control" task forces as means of implementing its companywide quality

enhancement program. At 3M, task forces are used as vehicles for developing and introducing new products.

- Corporate head office's identification of *companywide issues* can also play a role in encouraging divisional managers to respond to threats and opportunities that affect the whole company. General Electric issued annual "challenges" to its divisional and business-unit managers to encourage a particular issue, such as cost reduction, or innovation, or quality, to be incorporated within the annual planning cycle.

Coordination also involves promoting the overall cohesiveness of the diversified company. Coordination is not simply about reconciling interdivisional conflicts and exploiting synergies between businesses. Similarly, the corporate strategy of a diversified company is not completely described by the portfolio of businesses that the company holds. Unlike the portfolio of securities held by an individual investor or a mutual fund, the diversified firm is involved in managing each of its businesses. Hence, just as the single-business company needs clarity of purpose to provide its strategy with direction and its employees with commitment, so the diversified firm typically needs an identity and a rationale that gives meaning to its strategy beyond the composition of its portfolio. Hence, key roles of corporate management in coordinating the diversified company are providing *leadership,* defining *mission,* and establishing a set of values and beliefs that create a unifying *corporate culture.*

Unity within the diversified company may be achieved partly through strategic similarities (or "dominant logic") between the different businesses. But companies also need a stronger integrating force if they are to develop the loyalty and commitment necessary to mobilize the efforts and talents of their employees. Because of its very diversity, the multibusiness corporation may find it difficult to establish a common culture that bonds the various businesses and the scattered employees to one another. LVMH, the French producer of Moet champagne, Hennessey cognac, Dior and Givenchy perfumes, and Louis Vuitton luggage is a company that has made great efforts to establish a unifying set of values and traditions: "the common cultural trunk is based upon the permanent search for quality of the products and the management, human relations based upon responsibility and initiative, and rewarding competences and services."[16] A major theme in American Express's "one enterprise" program, aimed at integrating its various financial service companies has been the development of a common set of values oriented around quality, outstanding customer service, and marketing excellence.

Monitoring and controlling performance

The corporate head office is responsible for setting, monitoring, and enforcing performance targets for the individual divisions. Performance targets may be financial (return on invested capital, gross margin, growth of sales revenue), strategic (market share, rate of new product introduction, market penetration, quality), or both. Performance targets may be short term (monthly, quarterly), medium term (annual), or long term (five year). The primary function of the management information system in a diversified corporation is to enable the head office to monitor divisional performance and identify deviations from targets.

Incentives for achieving target performance include financial returns (salary, bonuses, stock options), organizational status (through praise and recognition), and promotion. Sanctions include blame and loss of reputation, demotion, and, ultimately, dismissal. Some diversified companies have proved to be highly effective in using performance monitoring and a combination of incentives and sanctions to create an intensely motivating environment for divisional managers. At ITT, Geneen's obsession with highly detailed performance monitoring, ruthless interrogation of divisional executives, and generous rewards for success, developed a highly motivated, strongly capable group of young, senior executives who were willing to work unremittingly for long hours and who demanded as high a standard of performance from their subordinates as Geneen did of them.[17] The existence of precise, quantitative performance targets that can be monitored on a short-term (e.g., month-to-month) basis can provide an intensely competitive internal environment that is highly effective in motivating business unit and divisional managers. Hanson's "high-wire" profit targets provide a relentless pressure for cost cutting within its diverse businesses, while PepsiCo's obsession with monthly market share results nourishes an intense and aggressive, marketing-oriented culture. As one PepsiCo executive explained: "The place is full of guys with sparks coming out of their asses."[18]

For companies in rapidly developing and technology-based industries, formulating and implementing appropriate controls is a difficult task. Despite the clarity and measurability of financial and sales targets, such targets may stunt innovation. One approach to reconciling the unpredictability and long-time horizons in technology-based industries with corporate control is for headquarters and business divisions to agree on a series of *milestones* that establish dates for the achievement of particular stages in the development of a new product or a new business. Such milestones might relate to the filing of patent applications, the production of a product prototype, the market launch of a new product, or the achievement of particular levels of market penetration and productivity gains. The merit of this approach is that it can marry the motivation and control of short- to medium-term targets with the corporate need for a longer term development strategy.

The Development of Strategic Planning Techniques: General Electric in the 1970s

The difficulties associated with the management of large diversified corporations have stimulated the development of a variety of ideas, structural innovations, and analytic techniques designed to facilitate the process of corporate management. A large number have been pioneered by a single company: General Electric. GE has been featured regularly among the leading group of *Fortune* magazine's "America's Most Admired Corporations" since its listings began. The key feature of GE's success is its highly effective and constantly evolving system of corporate management. As one executive remarked : "When Japanese managers come to visit us, they don't ask to see our research centers or manufacturing facilities. All they want to know is about our management system."[19]

During the 1970s, GE developed a number of techniques of corporate-level strategic planning that were widely adopted by other companies. These techniques were responses to difficulties that it experienced in managing its diverse corporate empire. At the beginning of the 1970s GE competed in 23 out of a total of 26 two-digit SIC industries and was organized into 46 divisions and over 190 departments. In 1969, GE launched a series of initiatives aimed at developing a more effective system of corporate planning backed by better analytical techniques. Working with the Boston Consulting Group, McKinsey & Company, Arthur D. Little, and Harvard Business School, GE spawned three innovations that were to transform the formulation and implementation of corporate strategy.

1 *The strategic business unit* A key feature of McKinsey's recommendations was the creation of a new unit for strategic planning purposes. The Strategic Business Unit (SBU) is a business for which it is meaningful to formulate a separate strategy. Typically, an SBU is a business that comprises a number of closely related products and for which most costs are not shared with other businesses.

2 *Portfolio planning models* All three consulting companies developed simple, matrix-based frameworks to be used in evaluating business-unit performance, formulating business-unit strategies, and assessing the overall balance of the corporate portfolio. We will consider these in greater detail in the next section.

3 *The PIMS database* To informational and analytical inputs into the corporate planning system, GE developed a database that comprised strategic, market, and performance data on each of GE's businesses and was later supplemented with data from other companies. The primary purpose of the database, as we saw in chapter 3, was investigation into the impact of market structure and strategy variables upon profitability.

While GE is known for its techniques and systems of corporate planning, a key feature of GE's strategic planning has been the balance that it achieves between the discipline of formal systems and the flexibility and opportunism of its top management. Balancing the bottom-up system of strategy formulation is a strong leadership style that has restructured GE's business portfolio. This restructuring included the acquisition of financial service companies (Kidder Peabody, Employers Reinsurance Corporation, Navistar Financial, and Montgomery Ward Credit) and the sale of Utah International Mining, GE Consumer Electronics, and its semiconductor business. Other critical strategic shifts have been its drive toward global market leadership and its aggressive efforts toward cost reduction.[20]

Portfolio Planning Models

Portfolio analysis is probably the best-known and most widely applied technique of strategy analysis ever to be developed. The basic idea is to represent the businesses of the diversified company within a simple graphic framework that can assist in four areas of strategy formulation:

1 *Allocating resources* Portfolio analysis examines the position of a business unit in relation to the two primary sources of profitability: industry attractiveness and competitive position, thus enabling its investment attractiveness to be compared with that of other business units.

2 *Formulating business-unit strategy* On the basis of a business unit's location in relation to the same basic variables – industry attractiveness and competitive position – portfolio analysis yields simple and straightforward strategy recommendations. For example, the McKinsey matrix offers three recommendations: grow, hold, or harvest. Further analysis may generate more sophisticated recommendations, for instance, suggesting how a poorly positioned business may be developed into a more attractively positioned business.

3 *Setting performance targets* To help establish performance targets for individual businesses, standardized procedures based upon a limited number of key environmental and strategic variables can be used to estimate what kind of profit performance can reasonably be expected for such a business.

4 *Analyzing portfolio balance* A single diagrammatic representation of the positions of the different businesses within the company is a valuable means of representing the overall balance, cohesiveness, and performance potential. Portfolio analysis can assist in examining several dimensions of portfolio balance:
   • *Cash flow* Diversified companies often seek independence from the external capital market by achieving a balanced cash flow within the company. This requires that businesses that generate a surplus cash flow finance businesses that are in their growth phases and that are net absorbers of cash.
   • *Continuity* To maintain the company over the long term, companies frequently seek a portfolio that is composed of businesses in different stages of their life cycle. As older businesses decline and die, they are replaced by younger, growing businesses.

- *Risk* Managing risk may involve risk reduction by spreading the firm's activities over businesses whose returns are imperfectly correlated.

The GE/McKinsey matrix

One of the fruits of GE's collaboration with McKinsey & Company was the portfolio analysis matrix shown in figure 15.1.

The two axes of the matrix are familiar: they are the two basic sources of superior profitability for a firm – industry attractiveness and competitive advantage. In the case of the McKinsey matrix the axes are

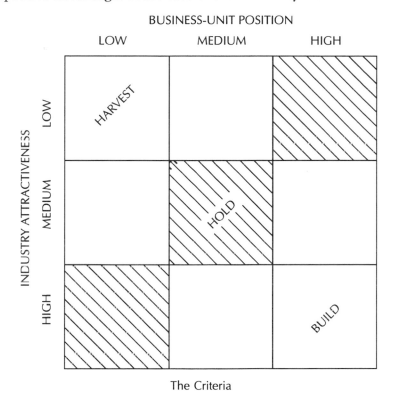

Figure 15.1 The McKinsey-General Electric Portfolio Analysis Matrix

The Criteria

Industry attractiveness
1 Market size
2 Market growth (real growth rate over 10 years)
3 Industry profitability (3-year average ROS of the business and its competitors)
4 Cyclicality (average annual percentage trend deviation in sales)
5 Inflation recovery (ability to cover cost increases by higher productivity and increased prices)
6 Importance of overseas markets (ratio of international to U.S. markets)

Business-unit position
1 Market position (average U.S. market share; average international market share; market share relative to 3 major competitors)
2 Competitive position (superior, equal, or inferior to competitors with regard to: quality, technology, manufacturing & cost leadership, distribution & marketing leadership)
3 Relative profitability (SBU's ROS less average for three main competitors)

Source: Adapted from *General Electric: Strategic Position* – 1981, Harvard Business School, case 9381-174, Boston, 1981

composite variables. Figure 15.1 also shows the individual variables that together determine the levels of industry attractiveness and competitive position for a business unit. The strategy recommendations derived from the matrix are quite simple:

- business units that rank high on both dimensions have excellent profit potential and should be "*grown*"
- those that rank low on both dimensions have poor prospects and should be "*harvested*"
- in-between businesses are candidates for a "*hold*" strategy.

The value of this technique is its simplicity: even for a highly complex and diverse company such as General Electric, which in 1980 comprised 43 SBUs, the positions of all the firm's SBUs can be combined into a single display. Thus, while the matrix may be simplistic, its power lies in its ability to display the businesses of the whole company and to compress a large amount of data into two dimensions.

Boston Consulting Group's growth-share matrix

The BCG matrix follows a similar approach: it combines market attractiveness and competitive position to compare the situation of different SBUs and to draw strategy prescriptions. It differs from the McKinsey matrix in that the two axes measure single variables: *market growth rate* and *relative market share* (i.e., the business unit's market share relative to that of the largest competitor). This choice of variables reflected BCG's view, first, that growth is the primary determinant of industry attractiveness, and, second, that competitive position is primarily determined by market share (because of its link, through the experience curve, with relative cost position).

The BCG matrix provides clear predictions as to the pattern of profit earnings and cash flow associated with the different quadrants. It also provides recommendations as to appropriate strategies: milk the cows, invest in the stars, divest the dogs, and analyze the question marks to determine whether they can be grown into stars or will degenerate into dogs (see figure 15.2).

The BCG's growth-share matrix is even more elementary than the McKinsey matrix and at best it can provide only a rough, first-cut analysis. Nevertheless, the BCG matrix has been widely used and has been found useful even by some of the most sophisticatedly managed companies in America and Europe. It is the very simplicity of the analysis that is its strength:

- As with other portfolio analyses, all the business units of the firm can be displayed within a single diagram;
- Because information on only two variables is required, the analysis can be prepared easily and quickly;

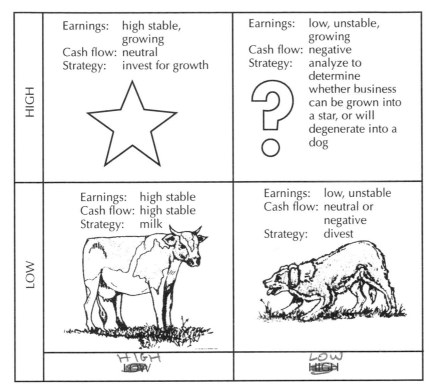

Figure 15.2 The Boston Consulting Group's Growth-Share Matrix

Annual real rate of market growth (%)

Relative market share

Notes

1 Relative market share measures the market share of the business relative to the market share of the largest competitor. For example, if a business has a market share of 10 percent, while the largest competitor has 20 percent, relative market share is 0.5.

2 Various items of additional information can be added. In this exhibit, the areas of the circles are proportional to each business's total revenue.

Source: Adapted from *Using PIMS and Portfolio Analyses in Strategic Market Planning: A Comparative Analysis*, Harvard Business School, Boston, 1977.

- It assists senior managers in cutting through vast quantities of detailed information to reveal key differences between the positioning of individual business units;
- The analysis is versatile – in addition to comparing the position of different business units, the framework can be used to examine the performance potential of different products, different brands, different regions, different distribution channels, and different customers;
- It provides a useful point of departure for more detailed analysis and discussion of the competitive positions and strategies of individual business units.

The ability to combine several elements of strategically useful information in a single graphical display is indicated by the application of the matrix to a diversified food processing company. Not only can the display show the positioning of the business units with regard to market growth and relative market share, it can also indicate the relative sales revenues of the units, their patterns of distribution, and movements in strategic position over time (see figure 15.3).

Despite the widespread use of the BCG growth-share matrix, it suffers from critical weaknesses. These include:

- It focuses upon just two determinants of business-unit performance. As we know, market attractiveness depends upon many variables of which growth rate is just one. Similarly, market share is an imperfect indicator of competitive advantage – while market share is important in industries with substantial scale economies, in fragmented industries scale may be unimportant.[21]
- The positioning of businesses within the matrix depends upon how market growth and market share are measured. Critical here is market definition. Is BMW's North American auto business a "dog" because it holds less than 1 percent of a low-growth market or a cash cow because it is market leader in the luxury car segment?
- All portfolio approaches assume that each business is entirely independent. Where relationships exist between business units, strategies can-

Figure 15.3
Application of the BCG Matrix to the BM Foods Inc.

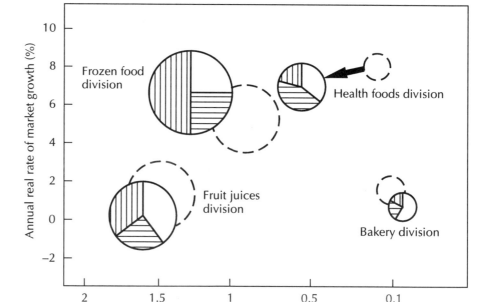

Notes:
1 The continuous circles show the position of each division in 1987; the broken circles show the position in 1984.
2 The sizes of the circles are proportional to sales revenue *at 1987 prices*.
3 The vertically shaded segments show sales to supermarket chains, the horizontally shaded segments show sales to other retailers, and the unshaded segments show sales to wholesalers and caterers.
4 The figures outside the circles show pretax operating income as a percentage of invested capital.
Source:

not be decided exclusively on the basis of the strategic positioning of the individual businesses. Resource-based approaches to strategy suggest that resources and capabilities rather than individual products or businesses should be regarded as the fundamental units of strategy analysis.

The Application of PIMS Analysis to Corporate Strategy

The development of PIMS

The PIMS Program, as noted, has its origins in the internal database constructed by General Electric as a means of testing the reasonableness of the strategic and budgetary plans submitted by operating units. Since 1975, the database has been owned and operated by the Strategic Planning Institute, which conducts research and provides advisory services to the member companies. By the end of the 1980s, PIMS incorporated data on almost 3,000 businesses, mostly in North America but with a rapidly growing number of businesses from Europe and elsewhere. Annual data on three sets of variables are included:

- Profitability: pretax operating profit as a percentage of sales (ROS) and invested capital (ROI);
- Strategy variables (e.g., market share, product quality, new product introduction, marketing and R&D expenses);
- Industry variables (e.g., market growth, life cycle stage, unionization, customer concentration).

PIMS then uses multiple regression analysis to relate performance to industry and strategy factors. Table 15.2 shows an estimated PIMS equation.

Applying PIMS to strategic decisions

1 *Setting performance targets for business units* One of the main problems that corporate managers face in appraising the performance of their business units is determining what level of performance is appropriate for different types of business. Top management can, of course, set out companywide performance targets ("Businesses must earn a pretax ROI of 20 percent or more."), but, while some businesses can easily achieve such a target (e.g., a pharmaceuticals producer), a business located within a depressed industry (TV manufacture, farm equipment) might find the general target impossible.

PIMS analysis shows how a business's profitability is determined by some 30 strategy and industry variables. Hence, by plugging in the actual levels of a business's strategy and industry variables into the PIMS regression estimates, it is possible to calculate that business's *Par ROI*. Par ROI is the normal level of ROI for a business given its profile

Table 15.2 The PIMS
Multiple Regression
Equations: The Impact
of Industry and Strategy
Variables on
Profitability

Profit influences	Impact on:	
	ROI	ROS
Real market growth rate	0.18	0.04
Rate of price inflation	0.22	0.08
Purchase concentration	0.02	N.S.
Unionization (%)	−0.07	−0.03
Low purchase amount:		
low importance	6.06	1.63
high importance	5.42	2.10
High purchase amount:		
low importance	−6.96	−2.58
high importance	−3.84	−1.11
Exports-Imports (%)	0.06	0.05
Customized products	−2.44	−1.77
Market share	0.34	0.14
Relative quality	0.11	0.05
New products (%)	−0.12	−0.15
Marketing, percentage of sales	−0.52	−0.32
R&D, percentage of sales	−0.36	−0.22
Inventory, percentage of sales	−0.49	−0.09
Fixed capital intensity	−0.55	−0.10
Plant newness	0.07	0.05
Capacity utilization	0.31	0.10
Employee productivity	0.13	0.06
Vertical integration	0.26	0.18
FIFO inventory valuation	1.30	0.62
R^2	0.39	0.31
F	58.3	45.1
Number of cases	2,314	2,314

Note: For example, if the Real Market Growth Rate of a business was to increase by one percentage point, the equation predicts that its ROI would rise by 0.18 percent.
Source: Robert D. Buzzell and Bradley T. Gale, *The PIMS Principles: Linking Strategy to Performance* (New York: Free Press, 1987), 274.

of strategic and industry characteristics. Hence, *Par ROI* is a benchmark for the business; it is the ROI that would be expected for a business of this type as indicated by all the PIMS databases as a whole. *Par ROI* can be used to set a target level of profitability for a business, and it can be used as the standard against which the actual profitability of a business is judged. For example, in figure 15.4, Business A earned a higher ROI than Business B, but because Business A is a textile business with a small market share and unionized employees and Business A had a large market share of the fast-growing medical equipment industry, Business A achieved an ROI well above its par level, while Business B underperformed its par.

2 *Formulating business-unit strategy* Because the PIMS regression equations estimate the impact of different strategy variables on ROI,

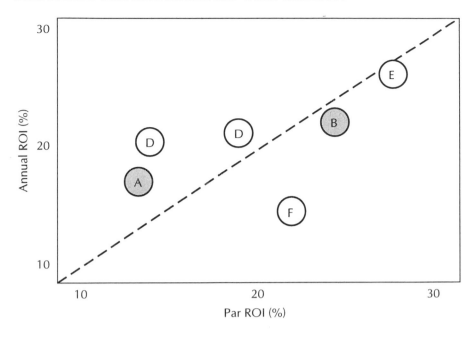

Figure 15.4 Using the PIMS *Par ROI* to Evaluate Business-Unit Performance

these estimates can indicate how a business can adjust its strategy in order to increase its profit performance. The Strategic Planning Institute offers several analyses that indicate the potential for changes in strategy to increase profit performance:

- The PIMS Strategy Report simulates the short- and long-term consequences of changes in the values of different strategy variables for a specific business. It identifies an "optimum strategy" that nominates a combination of market share, investment intensity, vertical integration, and other strategic moves that promises to optimize a given performance measure.
- The ability to predict the consequences of different strategy moves is further assisted by the *PIMS Analysis of Lookalikes*. This analysis scans the database for businesses with similar characteristics to that of the business under review. It focuses on the differences between similar businesses that have been successful in achieving a specific objective and those that have not. It highlights opportunities for improving the performance of a business and indicates ways of achieving above-average performance.

3 *Allocating investment funds between businesses* One of the most difficult areas of corporate strategy is the allocation of investment funds between the different business units. Past profitability is a poor basis for allocation because the correlation between a business's recent level of ROI and the ROI earned on *new investment* is extremely low. Discounted cash flow analysis is excellent for appraising individual projects but is less useful in allocating funds between whole businesses. A useful PIMS tool is its *Strategic Attractiveness Scan*. A business unit's investment attractiveness is assessed in relation to:

1 Estimated future real rate of growth of its market, and
2 Its *Par ROI*.

The analysis offers predictions as to the "strategic attractiveness" of investment in the business and the cash flow that can be expected from the business. The underlying rationale for this analysis is that the best predictors of the future returns on new investment in an industry are industry characteristics, the strategic position of the business within the industry, and the expected growth rate of the industry. Figure 15.5 shows the framework.

Valuing Businesses and Analyzing Restructuring Opportunities

The McKinsey "pentagon framework"

Portfolio analysis such as PIMS techniques is primarily useful for assisting resource allocation within the multibusiness corporation. These "strategic" approaches to resource all allocation decisions are justified by the fact that the rate of return that will be earned on new investment in a business is likely to bear a closer relationship to the underlying determinants of industry attractiveness and competitive position than to the rate of return currently being earned on past investments in the business. However, portfolio techniques are less useful as a guide to

Figure 15.5 Using PIMS in Allocating Resources between Business Units: The Profitable Opportunities Screen

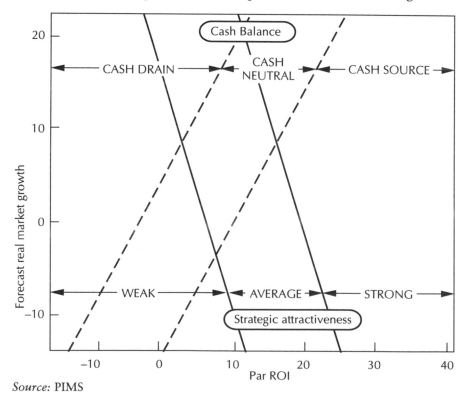

Source: PIMS

divestment and restructuring decisions. Just as the fundamental criterion for evaluating diversification decisions is whether or not the diversification will add value to the corporate whole, so the fundamental criterion for determining whether or not a particular business should be retained within the corporate fold is the value that the business adds to the corporation as a whole. Valuation of a business also permits the appraisal of alternative strategic options. To the extent that it is possible to predict the implications of alternative strategies for expected returns and risk, it is possible to evaluate them in terms of their impact on the value of the business.

McKinsey & Company propose five stages in valuing a company and assessing the opportunities for restructuring.[22] They organize their analysis around a "Pentagon framework" (see figure 15.6). The five stages of the analysis are:

- the current market value of the company;
- the value of the company as is;
- the potential value of the company with internal improvements;
- the potential value of the company with external improvements;
- the optimal restructured value of the company.

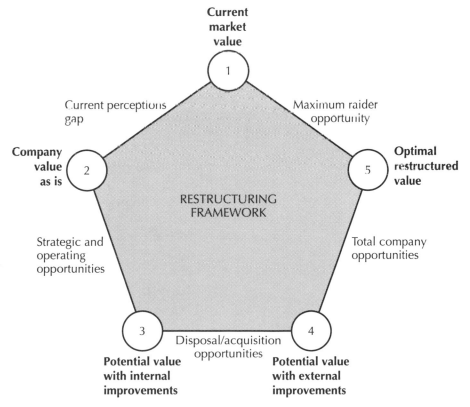

Figure 15.6 The McKinsey Pentagon for Analyzing Restructuring

Source: Tom Copeland, Tim Koller, and Jack Murrin, *Valuation: Measuring and Managing the Value of Companies* (New York: John Wiley, 1990), 249.

The current market value of the company   The starting point is the market value of the company, which comprises the market value of the company's equity (number of shares outstanding multiplied by the price of the shares) and the market value of the debt (nominal amount of debt multiplied by its market price).

The value of the company as is   The market value of the company will represent the stock market's estimate of the discounted cash flow of the company. To the extent that this is below management's estimate of the discounted cash flow valuation of the company, management must seek to close this "perceptions gap" through more effective communication with the market. As General Electric chairman Jack Welch replied when asked about his company's 1989 share repurchase program: "They're the best investment we can find." I shall defer explaining the principles of company valuation until a little later.

The potential value of the company with internal improvements   Within the present portfolio of the company's businesses it may be possible to increase the company's value through operating improvements that cut costs and increase efficiency and strategic initiatives that enhance cash flows.

The potential value of the company with external improvements   The company may also be able to increase its value through changes in its business portfolio. Poorly performing businesses may have a higher sale price than their contribution to the present value of the company. Businesses whose rate of return is below their cost of capital are likely to be reducing the overall value of the company. Such businesses should be liquidated if they cannot be either sold or turned around.

The optimal restructured value of the company   The potential for value-enhancing internal adjustments together with changes to the company's business portfolio determine the company's maximum possible present value. The difference between this "optimal restructured value" and the current market value shows the profit potential available to a raider from acquiring the company.

Valuing the company

To determine the value of a company "as is" and to estimate the impact on value of restructuring measures a DCF (discounted cash flow) analysis of the constituent parts of the company is necessary. The valuation of each business unit follows the principles for company valuation outlined in chapter 1 (and in the appendix to chapter 1 in particular). For the external analyst, a major problem is the paucity of data in corporate financial statements on divisional operations. However, typically, operating income and capital expenditures is disaggregated by division, which may make it easier to estimate divisional cash flows than divisional accounting returns on assets.

In discounting divisional cash flows it is important to use a cost of capital for the division rather than for the corporation as a whole. Because different divisions typically have different levels of operating risk, their costs of capital will differ. But the cost of capital to a division is not directly observable. Hence, the appropriate approach to measuring cost of capital is to estimate the risk premium for publicly traded competitors whose risk characteristics can be assumed to be the same. In the appendix to chapter 1, cost of equity (k_E) capital was shown to comprise a risk-free rate of interest (i) plus a risk premium:

$$k_E = i + \beta(R_m - i)$$

Where β is the *beta coefficient* or *coefficient of systematic risk* for the company, and R_m is the expected return on the stock market as a whole. The beta coefficient for the shares of similar companies can be used as indicators of the beta for the division of a diversified company. However, some adjustment must be made to take account of any differences in leverage ratios between the competitor companies and the diversified corporation. For example, if competitors have higher debt/equity ratios than those of the diversified corporation, competitors' greater financial risk will be reflected in a higher beta coefficient than that appropriate for the division of the diversified company.[23]

The McKinsey authors advocate treating corporate headquarters as a separate division. While corporate headquarters is conventionally viewed as a cost rather than a profit center, it is, in principle, possible to measure the value added by the corporate services, the transfer of managerial and technological expertise between divisions, and the offering of tax shelter benefits. However, because most of these synergistic benefits are included in the cash flows of the individual business units, separating them is likely to prove a near impossible task.

Valuation analysis in corporate strategy formulation

Until recently, valuation analysis has been undertaken more by corporate raiders than by corporate managers. The acquisition of RJR Nabisco by Kolberg, Kravis, Roberts & Company, and the attempted takeover of BAT by Coniston Group and ICI by Hanson were attempts by outsiders to release the value potential from dismantling and financially restructuring poorly performing diversified companies. Indeed, it has been the failure of corporate management to effectively utilize the tools of value management that has made so many diversified companies attractive targets for acquisition and restructuring.

Michael Jensen[24] argues that the wave of hostile takeovers during the 1980s led by takeover specialists such as Carl Icahn, James Goldsmith, Saul Steinberg, and T. Boone Pickens, rather than reflecting myopia on the part of the stock market, was primarily a product of myopia on the part of the corporate managers of the target companies. The propensity for managers to invest the free cash flow from their profitable core businesses in diversification rather than distribute it to shareholders resulted in companies sacrificing shareholder wealth for growth with consequent reduction in valuation ratios.

By evaluating the effects of acquisitions, divestments, and changes in financial structure upon overall corporate value, managers have the ability to improve upon the dismal performance that has characterized many large diversified corporations in America, Europe and Japan during the 1980s.

Corporate Management Systems and the Role of Headquarters

I have discussed several areas of strategic management in the multibusiness company: determining the composition of the corporate portfolio, allocating resources between businesses, formulating business strategies, and controlling performance. While all diversified companies address these issues, companies face a range of options concerning how responsibilities for these various tasks are allocated between the head office and operating units as well as the nature of the interaction between the head office and operating units. A company's choices with regard to these two sets of issues determine the role of corporate management in a diversified company.[25]

The appropriate role for corporate management depends critically upon the way in which corporate management adds value to the individual businesses of the diversified corporation, which takes us to the basic rationale or the "dominant logic" of the corporation. Michael Porter has identified four concepts of corporate strategy that are defined in terms of the basis upon which corporate management creates profit within the diversified company.[26]

Porter's "concepts of corporate strategy"

1 *Portfolio Management* The essence of a portfolio management strategy is the acquisition of attractive, soundly managed companies and linking these companies with an efficient internal capital market. The acquired companies are operated autonomously, they formulate their own business strategies, and corporate control is exercised primarily through the allocation of investment funds.

The role of corporate management in pursuing a portfolio management approach is limited to four main activities:

- Identifying acquisition candidates and purchasing them at a favorable price. (Because there are few operating synergies to be exploited, it is vital that the takeover price does not exceed the value of the assets acquired.)

- Reducing the costs of the acquired companies because of the lower cost of capital of the large, diversified company.
- Increasing the efficiency with which investment funds are allocated by using corporate management's expertise and access to information to rigorously review business strategies and project proposals and accurately assess the relative merits of alternative investments.
- Establishing close monitoring of business-unit financial performance, demanding targets of divisional and business-unit managers, and creating an environment of fierce internal competition for investment funds that is conducive to intense and sustained effort by operating managers.

2 *Restructuring* Like the portfolio management companies, the key strategic role of top management in companies that pursue a restructuring strategy is acquisition. However, in addition to the postacquisition roles of banker, reviewer, and monitor that corporate managers in the portfolio management companies occupy, a restructuring strategy requires much more interventionist postacquisition management by corporate management. Intervention takes the form of changing the management of acquired companies, increasing efficiency, and disposing of underutilized assets. For a restructuring strategy to be successful requires, first, that inefficient firms with undervalued assets be available for acquisition, and, second, that after successful restructuring, the company realizes the return from its efforts by selling off its restructured subsidiaries.

3 *Transferring Skills* Corporate management can add value to its business units by transferring capabilities between them and thereby creating or enhancing competitive advantage. Examples are Philip Morris's acquisition of General Foods and Kraft with a view to transferring marketing and distribution capabilities; General Motors's acquisition of EDS with a view to transferring its information technology capabilities to GM; and AT&T's acquisition of NCR.

For the transfer of capabilities to be effective, the following conditions must be met:

- There must be commonalities between the businesses in terms of similar skills being applicable across the businesses and the importance of these skills in establishing competitive advantage.
- Corporate management must take an active role in the transfer of skills through the transfer of key personnel and the creation of interdivisional working parties.

4 *Sharing Activities* An important source of cost efficiency for the diversified company is economies of scope in common resources and activities. Examples of the exploitation of economies of scope through

diversification were discussed in the previous chapter. For these economies to be realized, corporate management must play a key coordinating
role. This requires involvement in the formulation of business-unit strategies and intervention in operational matters to ensure that opportunities
for sharing R&D activities, advertising campaigns, distribution systems,
and service networks are fully exploited. Porter suggests several mechanisms that can assist collaboration in the sharing of activities:

- a strong sense of corporate identity
- a clear corporate mission statement that emphasizes the importance
  of integrating business-unit strategies
- an incentive system that rewards cooperation between businesses
- interbusiness task forces and other vehicles for cooperation.

Alternative roles for corporate headquarters in the diversified corporation

Porter argues that the potential for management to create value for
shareholders increases as a company moves from the loose, portfolio-
management strategy toward the more integrated shared-activities strategy. However, the evidence on this point is mixed. A study by Lorsch
and Allen compared corporate management practices and corporate-
divisional relationships in three conglomerates (which adopted "portfolio management" and "restructuring" approaches) with those of three
vertically integrated paper companies (which pursued "transfer of skills"
and "sharing of activities" approaches).[27] The need to manage divisional
linkages and coordinate operations resulted in the paper companies
showing:

- greater involvement of head office staff in divisional operations,
- larger head office staffs,
- more complex planning and control devices,
- lower responsiveness to change in the external environment.

The administrative burden of coordination imposed by close relationships between the divisions of the paper companies was such that: "the
conglomerate firms we had studied seemed to be achieving appreciable
degrees of financial and managerial synergy but little or no operating
synergy. Some of the firms saw little immediate payoff in this operating
synergy; others had met with little success in attempting to achieve it."[28]

A study by Goold and Campbell investigated the nature and effectiveness of different *"strategic management styles"* among a sample of
large, diversified British companies.[29] They found that no single style
of corporate management was generally superior. Different styles are
appropriate to different types of business and different types of corporate
management. They focused upon two key corporate management functions: involvement of corporate head office in business strategy formulation and the type of performance control imposed by the head office.

On the basis of these two functions, they identified three corporate management styles – *financial control, strategic control,* and *strategic planning* – plus two additional categories – *centralized* and *holding company* – which they believed to be largely defunct among contemporary diversified companies. Figure 15.7 shows these categories.

The principal contrast is between companies where the corporate head office plays an important role in formulating and coordinating business-unit and divisional strategies (the *strategic planning style*) and those where the corporate head office concentrates on financial management (the *financial control style*). A third style, *strategic control*, identified with ICI, Courtaulds, Plessey, and Vickers, is a hybrid of the other two. It aims to balance a high degree of divisional autonomy with the benefits of head office coordination. The main features of the two principal styles are described in the next two sections.

Strategic Planning   A strategic planning style of corporate management was found in British Petroleum, Cadbury-Schweppes, Lex, and STC. In these companies, there was substantial involvement by corporate headquarters in business-unit planning. This included intensive discussion between business-unit managers and corporate staff as to the content and goals of strategy and a large corporate role in integrating and coordinating business-unit strategies. Because of the involvement of the

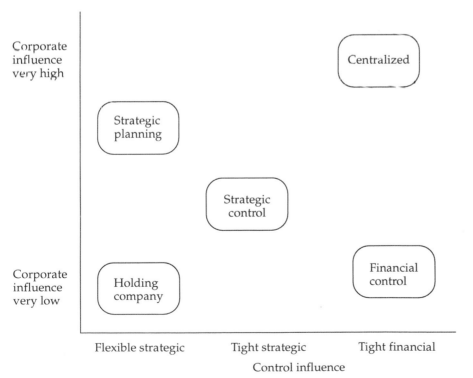

Figure 15.7 Corporate Management Styles

Source: Michael Goold and Andrew Campbell, Ashridge Strategic Mangement Center, London.

corporate level and the ability to call upon corporate support, the strategy formulation process was conducive to the adoption of ambitious strategies aimed at establishing long-term competitive advantage. This was typically reflected in performance goals that emphasized strategic objectives (market share, innovation, quality leadership, overseas penetration) over financial objectives and emphasized the long term over the short term.

Key drawbacks of the strategic planning style are:

- the lack of autonomy that business-unit managers possess can be demoralizing for them
- the strategy-making process can become slow and cumbersome with resulting loss of flexibility and speed in adjusting to new circumstances and opportunities
- headquarters may impose a single, unitary view on the whole company
- mistakes can be slow being reversed.

A strategic planning style is appropriate for companies whose businesses are small in number, do not span too wide a range of products and industries, and where links are strong between them (particularly through shared skills and resources). The style is more appropriate to companies that were competing in international markets and where innovation was important – hence, longer-term, strategic goals were more appropriate than short-term profits.

Financial control   The financial control style of several leading British conglomerates including Hanson, BTR, General Electric, and Ferranti, combined Porter's "portfolio management" and "restructuring" approaches to corporate management, in contrast to the strategic planning style that was oriented toward the "sharing skills" and "shared activities" approaches.

Corporate headquarters had limited involvement in business strategy formulation – this was the responsibility of divisional and business-unit managers. The primary influence of headquarters was through short-term budgetary control, the objective being for the divisions and business units to accept and pursue ambitious profit targets. Because targets were short term, quantitative, and easily measured, they provided strong motivation to managers to increase efficiency and expand business into profitable areas. Careful monitoring of performance by headquarters, with rigorous questioning of managers responsible for deviations from target, maintained constant pressure on divisional management and created a challenging working environment.

Apart from being highly conducive to profitability, the financial control style has three important benefits:

- because of the autonomy it gives to business units, it provides an excellent environment for developing executives

- by placing strong pressure on business-unit managers for profitability, it encourages these managers to break away from ineffective strategies at an early stage.
- because the major operating and strategic decisions are taken at business-unit level, headquarters staff does not need to have an intimate knowledge of the business units.

While financial control has been identified with "managing by the numbers" and relying very heavily upon monetary incentives, research by John Roberts indicates that a feature of the management environment in conglomerates such as Hanson is the motivation and commitment of divisional managers as a result of their high level of decision-making autonomy and their feeling of "ownership" in the business.[30]

The principal weaknesses of the financial control style are:

- Emphasis on short-term profitability targets results in a bias against projects and strategies with long lead times and payback periods and can make businesses vulnerable to competition from rivals adopting a longer-term strategic approach (in consumer electronics, when GE and RCA were attacked by Far Eastern competitors, they yielded segment after segment because profitability was depressed until both ultimately withdrew from the industry).
- Its difficulty in exploiting synergies between each business – each business is treated as a single entity and corporate headquarters lacks a mechanism for coordination and cooperation between businesses.

The financial control style is suited to companies that feature:

- wide diversity with many business units
- investment projects that are mainly short and medium term in fruition, and in which innovation is relatively low
- mature industries with low levels of international competition.

Table 15.3 summarizes key features of the two styles.

Subsequent work by Ashridge Strategic Management Center has extended Goold and Campbell's work on the strategic management styles of diversified companies combining different strategic management styles with different degrees of divisional linkage creates a classification of "*corporate parenting roles*." In order of increasing corporate involvement in business-unit affairs, three "corporate parenting roles" are identified: *controller, coach,* and *orchestrator* (figure 15.8).[31]

Recent Trends in the Management of Multibusiness Corporations

Defining corporate management styles in terms of "parenting roles" as compared with "systems of corporate control" represents a shift in

	STRATEGIC PLANNING	FINANCIAL CONTROL
Business Strategy Formulation	Business units and corporate center coordinate in strategy formulation. Center responsible for coordination of strategies between business units.	Strategy formulated at business-unit level. Corporate headquarters largely reactive, offering little coordination.
Controlling Performance	Primarily strategic goals with medium- to long-term horizon.	Financial budgets that set out annual (and shorter-term) targets for ROI and other financial variables.
Advantages	Can exploit linkages between businesses. Can give appropriate weight to innovation and longer-term competitive positioning.	Business units given autonomy and initiative. Business units can respond quickly to change. Encourages development of business-unit managers. Highly motivating.
Disadvantages	Loss of divisional autonomy and initiative. Conducive to unitary view. Resistance to abandoning failed strategy.	Short-term focus discourages innovation and building longer-term competitive position. Businesses may be willing to give ground to determined competitors. Little scope for exploiting shared resources and skills and skills between businesses.
Style suited to: Portfolio Structure	Small number of businesses across narrow range of sectors with close inter-relations.	Many businesses across wide range of industries. Linkages ideally few.
Type of Investments	Large projects with long-term paybacks.	Small capital investments with short payback periods.
Environmental Features	Industries with strong technological and global competition	Mature industries (technical change modest or slow). Stable industry environment without strong international competition.
U.K. Examples	BP, BOC, Cadbury-Schweppes, Lex Group, STC., United Biscuits.	Hanson Trust, BTR, General Electric Company (U.K.), Ferranti, Tarmac.

emphasis that is symbolic of a wider transition in thinking about the role of corporate in the multibusiness corporation. Key features of this transition are:

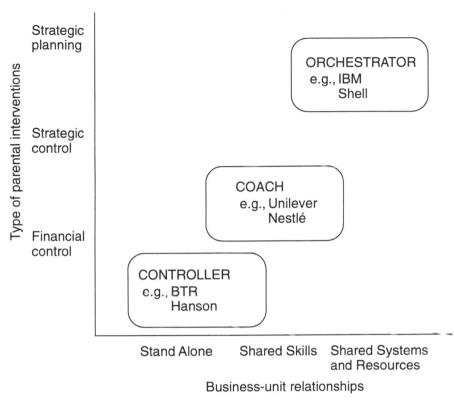

Figure 15.8 Corporate Parenting Roles

Notes:
1 In the *Controller* role, head office has little involvement in the individual businesses except to set targets and monitor their achievement.
2 In the *Coach* role, operating businesses are separate but gain from sharing knowledge and skills. The corporate role is to encourage each business to develop its full potential through drawing upon capabilities within the group.
3 In playing an *Orchestrator* role, the corporate head office is indispensable in coordinating businesses and ensuring that resources, activities, and systems are shared between businesses.

Source: Andrew Campbell and Michael Goold, Ashridge Strategic Management Center, London.

- A view of corporate headquarters less as the apex of a hierarchy and more as a support service for the businesses.
- Less emphasis on formal systems and techniques and more on relationships and informal interaction.
- Decentralization of both operational and strategic decisions from corporate to divisional levels.
- Emphasis on the role of headquarters, and the CEO in particular, as a catalyst and driver of organizational change.

In the same way that General Electric was the pioneer in the development of formalized approaches to corporate strategy and control, so it has also been a prime mover in the dismantling of formal controls in favor of a more flexible, informal, and dynamic approach to corporate strategy. The "reinventing" of GE has been closely associated with the role of CEO Jack Welch.

Reinventing General Electric

The early part of Jack Welch's tenure was associated with a restructuring of GE's business portfolio – moving out of mining, consumer electronics, and housewares and into financial services, plastics, and factory automation. Simultaneously, GE's corporate management pressed two major themes: cost reduction and global expansion. These initiatives were enshrined in Welch's slogan that GE would only compete in those businesses where it was or could be *number one or number two in their global industry.*

Toward the mid-1980s, Welch's attention shifted from the business portfolio to the structure, systems and style of GE. The major changes initiated by Welch are discussed in the following section:

Delayering   Welch's fundamental criticism of GE's management was that it was slow and unresponsiveness. A precondition for a more nimble enterprise was fewer levels of management. Welch eliminated GE's *sector* level of organization (which combined a number of businesses) and within each business pressed for the flattening of management pyramids by reducing the layers of hierarchy from nine or ten to four or five: "We used to have things like department managers, subsection managers, unit managers, supervisors. We're driving those titles out . . . We used to go from the CEO to sectors, to groups, to businesses. We now go from the CEO to businesses. Nothing else."[32]

Changing the strategic planning system   During the 1970s, GE had developed a systematic and formalized approach to strategy formulation and appraisal. Welch believed the system to be slow, inefficient in its use of management time, and stifling of innovation and opportunism. A Harvard case study outlines the changes:

Nowhere was the change more striking than in the area of strategic planning and operational reviews. Although the basic processes were retained, the old staff-led, document-driven process of the 1970s was largely replaced by more personal, less formal but very-intensive face-to-face discussions and small meetings. To cut through the bureaucracy Welch asked each of his 13 business heads to reduce the complex, multivolume planning documents to a slim "playbook" that summarized key strategic issues and actions. On each page, they provided concise answers to questions about their global market dynamics, key competitive activity, major competitive risks, and proposed GE business responses. These documents became the basis for a half day shirtsleeve review in mid-summer. Business heads and their key people (usually from three to ten in total) met with the Office of the CEO members and their key staff in an open dialogue on core plans and strategies.[33]

Redefining the role of headquarters The changes in the strategic planning systems are indicative of a broader set of changes in the role of the corporate headquarters. Welch viewed headquarters as interfering too much in the businesses, generating too much unnecessary paper, and failing to add value. His objective was to "turn their role 180 degrees from checker, inquisitor, and authority figure to facilitator, helper and supporter of the 13 businesses. Ideas, initiatives and decisions could now move quickly."[34] Welch explained his view of corporate HQ as follows: "What we do here at headquarters . . . is to multiply the resources we have, the human resources, the financial resources, and the best practices . . . Our job is to help, it's to assist, it's to make these businesses stronger, to help them grow and be more powerful.[35]

The coordinating role of corporate Placing increased emphasis on informal aspects of corporate-business relations increased the role of corporate in facilitating coordination across GE's businesses. The Corporate Executive Council was reconstituted to include the leaders of GE's 13 businesses and several key corporate executives. It met two days each quarter to discuss common problems and issues. The Council became an important vehicle for identifying and exploiting synergies.

By 1990, Welch had formulated his notions of coordination and integration within his view of the "boundaryless company." A key element of this concept was a blurring of internal divisions so that people could work together across functional and business boundaries. Welch aimed at "integrated diversity" – the ability to transfer the best ideas, most developed knowledge, and most valuable people freely and easily between businesses.

Boundaryless behavior is the soul of today's GE . . . Simply put, people seem compelled to build layers and walls between themselves and others, and that human tendency tends to be magnified in large, old institutions like ours. These walls cramp people, inhibit creativity, waste time, restrict vision, smother dreams and, above all, slow things down. . . . Boundaryless behavior shows up in the actions of a woman from our Appliances business in Hong Kong helping NBC with contacts needed to develop satellite television service in Asia. . . . And finally, boundaryless behavior means exploiting one of the unmatchable advantages a multibusiness like GE has over almost any other company in the world. Boundaryless behavior combines 12 huge global businesses – each number one or number two in its markets – into a vast laboratory whose principal product is new ideas, coupled with a common commitment to spread them throughout the Company.[36]

Corporate as the driver of organizational change and development Devolution of decision-making authority from corporate to business level did not imply a passive role for the corporate headquarters. In many respects, corporate became more interventionist in attempting to influence business operations. A critical role for corporate was attempting to drive large-scale organizational change. An example of this was GE's "workout" initiative, which encourages the businesses to establish forums where employees could speak their minds about management and to propose changes in business and operating practices. Workout was a vehicle for cultural change in which the relationship between boss and subordinate was redefining and the creativity of employees was unleashed.

Redefining the corporate role at other companies

Although General Electric is one of the best known of the companies that have radically altered their corporate strategies and the structures, systems, and styles through which those strategies are implemented, the changes at GE have reflected factors that have affected most multibusiness corporations. These include: the overriding need to establish competitive advantage within each of the business areas within which the firm competes, the need for responsiveness to external change, the need to foster innovation, and the need for cost efficiency. The problem for large diversified corporations is that these challenges require conflicting adjustments. For example:

- Rigorous financial controls are conducive to cost efficiency; autonomy and flexible controls are conducive to responsiveness and innovation.
- Multibusiness companies have typically been based upon the advantages of exploiting existing resources and capabilities across different markets, yet competitive advantage in the future is dependent upon the creation of new resources and capabilities.
- Active portfolio management based upon the maximization of shareholder value is best achieved with independent businesses; the creation of competitive advantage increasingly requires the management of business interdependencies.

The central dilemma is one that has preoccupied GE: how to exploit the resource advantages of the large company, while achieving the responsiveness and creativity associated with small companies.

The implication is that the management systems of multibusiness companies must also become more sophisticated and flexible. In chapter 13, we noted how conflicting pressures for globalization and local adaptability were resolved by multinationals moving toward a "transnational" structure. Similar tendencies are observable in managing the tensions within diversified corporations. At IBM, it is interesting to observe that CEO Lou Gerstner resisted stock market pressures for a breakup of the company in favor of limited and selective divestment. The internal changes occurring at IBM under the leadership of Gerstner parallel many of the changes introduced by GE:

- Aggressive cost cutting and employee reduction.

- Encouraging responsiveness and flexibility through greater autonomy, while more effectively exploiting internal resources and capabilities through internal coordination.
- A breaking down of corporate boundaries and an increased willingness to learn from other companies and to collaborate with other companies in strategic alliances.

ABB as a new form of multibusiness corporation

We introduced Asea Brown Boveri (ABB) as a multinational corporation in chapter 13. ABB is also a highly diversified corporation. Because ABB is a relatively new company (created in 1987 from the merger of Asea and Brown Boveri); because its structure and systems are very different from those associated with traditional industrial giants such as GE, ICI, or Hitachi; and because its organizational characteristics are being increasingly adopted by other companies, Bartlett and Ghoshal use ABB to illustrate what they regard as the emerging model of the multibusiness corporation.[37] The main characteristics of ABB that they identify as emerging themes in complex organizations are the following:

1 *Matrix organization*   The M-form model is one of a number of product divisions reporting to a corporate headquarters. Most large industrial organizations are matrices where a business-unit/subsidiary general manager reports both to a sector manager and a country or regional manager.

2 *Radical decentralization*   The fundamental units of organization in ABB are not product divisions as assumed in the traditional M-form model but individual businesses within each country. ABB possesses 1,300 such businesses. These are freestanding legal entities with average employment of 200. These businesses are where strategic and operating decisions are made. Between them and the corporate headquarters is a single management layer formed by worldwide business area managers and country managers. However, the intermediate layer is exceptionally lean, and corporate headquarters employs less than 100 people.

3 *Bottom-up management*   The M-form presupposes that decision-making power has been devolved from corporate down to the divisions. In ABB, authority lies with the individual businesses. Each has its own balance sheet and is able to retain one-third of its net income. Frontline managers are entrepreneurs – not implementors of corporate and divisional decisions.

4 *Informal collaboration and integration*   The traditional view of economies of scope in the diversified corporation views corporate headquarters as exploiting economies in joint resources (corporate research labs, corporate provision of MIS and administrative services). In ABB corporate headquarters is horizontal linkages between the frontline business units facilitated by country and business area managers through which capabilities are transferred and common resources are shared.

Bartlett and Ghoshal identify three central management processes occurring in the multibusiness corporation: *the entrepreneurial process* (decisions about the opportunities to exploit and the allocation of resources), the *integration process* (how organizational capabilities are built and deployed), and the *renewal process* (the shaping of organizational purpose and the initiation of change). In traditional approaches to the multibusiness corporation, all three processes have been centered within the corporate headquarters, the key feature of ABB, and the Bartlett-Ghoshal "managerial theory of the firm" is the distribution of these functions between three levels of the firm: corporate ("top management"), the business and geographical sector coordinators ("middle management"), and the business units ("frontline management"). The critical feature of the relationships between these management levels and between the individual organizational members is that they form a social structure based upon cooperation and learning. Figure 15.9 illustrates their framework.

Summary and Conclusions

The formulation and implementation of corporate strategy presents top management with a tangle of issues of almost impenetrable complexity. The tendency for multibusiness corporations to also expand multinationally represents a further quantum leap in complexity. The difficulty of establishing ground rules for corporate strategy reflects several factors: first, the variety of objectives and rationales for diversification; second, the size and administrative complexity of multibusiness corporations involved; third, the long period of development of many multibusiness corporations, which results in inertia and an institutionalized culture; and, fourth, the inability of empirical research to offer clear guidance as to the correlates of superior performance in multibusiness corporations.

These correlates include the following:

- diversified companies may be more or less successful than specialized companies;
- closely linked diversified businesses may be more or less successful than conglomerates;
- exploiting shared resources and skills can lead to cost efficiencies and the transfer of competitive advantages; it can also lead to high administrative cost, management inertia, and inflexibility;
- for some diversified companies, rigorous financial controls are conducive to high performance; in others longer-term strategic goals are more effective.

Designing the appropriate organizational structure, management systems, and leadership style for a multibusiness corporation depends criti-

Managing the tension between short-term ambition	**RENEWAL PROCESS** Creating and Maintaining organizational trust	Shaping and embedding corporate purpose
Managing operational interdependencies and personal networks	**INTEGRATION PROCESS** Linking skills, knowledge, and resources	Developing and nurturing organizational values
Creating and pursuing opportunities	**ENTREPRENEURIAL PROCESS** Reviewing, developing, and supporting initiatives	Establishing strategic mission and performance standards
Front-line Management	Middle Management	Top Management

Source C. A. Bartlett and S. Ghoshal, "Beyond the M-form: Toward a Managerial Theory of the Firm," *Strategic Management Journal,* special issue, 14 (winter 1993): 23–46.

cally upon *fit* with the corporate strategy of the company. Fundamental to this fit is the *rationale* for the firm. As we noted in the previous chapter, diversification may create value in different ways. Each source of gain from diversification is likely to imply a quite different approach to managing the firm. For a conglomerate firm, value can be created through the strategic judgment of the CEO with regard to business prospects and company valuation and the ability to operate a highly efficient internal capital market. Hence, organization and management systems should be oriented toward a clear separation of business level on corporate decisions and a highly effective system for budgetary control and project evaluation. For a technology-based diversified corporation, value is created through the transfer and integration of knowledge, ideas, and expertise. The company must be organized in order to facilitate the transfer and application of knowledge; corporate headquarters is likely to play a critical role in technological guidance and in divisional integration.

At a more detailed level, the design of structure and systems, and the allocation of decision-making responsibilities depends upon specific issues such as:

- The characteristics of the resources and capabilities that are being exploited within the multibusiness corporation. If capital is the primary common resource, then the corporate system must be established to ensure its efficient allocation. If common corporate services such as information technology and administrative services are the primary sources of economies of scope, then these activities need to be grouped together at the corporate level. If the brand marketing capability is the key common resource, then systems need to be established that facilitate the transfer of marketing capabilities between businesses.

- The characteristics of the businesses. If the businesses are highly diverse in terms of their industry characteristics and competitive positions, then a high degree of divisional autonomy is required and the establishment of corporate systems that are sufficiently flexible to accommodate that flexibility. If the businesses are more similar (e.g., P&G's diversification across branded, packaged consumer goods) then a greater uniformity of systems and style is desirable.

Ultimately, finding the appropriate structure, systems, and style with which to manage a multibusiness corporation is dependent upon establishing an identity for the company. The failure of most of the conglomerates of the 1960s and early 1970s was either that they failed to establish a clear identity or that their identity was so closely linked with a single person (e.g., Geneen at ITT) that the companies had difficulty surviving the demise of that person. In other cases, the rationale upon which the identity was based was found to be flawed (e.g., Allegis Corporation).

Hence, the starting point for the formulation and implementation of corporate strategy is the possession of *vision*. This provides the basic cohesiveness to the corporation and an inspiration. Vision typically embodies two elements – a statement of values, and a delineation of the scope of the company. These permit an answer to the question, *"What kind of company are we seeking to become?"* The contribution of Jack Welch to GE is in reformulating GE's vision to be consistent with the new economic circumstances of the 1990s. By the early 1990s, GE's strategy and structure had been built around a broad-based consensus concerning the sources of GE's value creation. The uncertainty at Philip Morris during mid-1994 reflected the absence of such a consensus. Although Philip Morris was achieving impressive performance in both its tobacco, food, and drink businesses, the dominant logic of the corporation remained unclear.

Notes

1. Alfred D. Chandler, *Strategy and Structure* (Cambridge: MIT Press, 1962); A.D. Chandler, *The Visible Hand: The Managerial Revolution in American Business* (Cambridge: Harvard University Press and Belknap Press, 1977).
2. Alfred D. Chandler, *The Visible Hand: The Managerial Revolution in American Business* (Cambridge, MA: Belknap Press, 1977), 87.
3. Chandler, (1966), 382–3.

4. Alfred P. Sloan Jr., *My Years at General Motors* (London: Sidgewick & Jackson, 1963), 42–56.

5. This section draws heavily upon Oliver E. Williamson, *Markets and Hierarchies: Analysis and Antitrust Implications* (New York: Free Press, 1975); and Oliver E. Williamson, "The Modern Corporation: Origins, Evolution, Attributes," *Journal of Economic Literature* 19 (1981): 1537–68.

6. O. E. Williamson, "The Modern Corporation: Origins, Evolution, Attributes," *Journal of Economic Literature* 19 (December 1981): 1558–89.

7. See, for example, Peter Steer and John Cable, "Internal Organization and Profit: An Empirical Analysis of Large UK Companies," *Journal of Industrial Economics* 21 (September 1978): 13–30; Henry Armour and David Teece, "Organizational Structure and Economic Performance: A Test of the Multidivisional Hypothesis," *Bell Journal of Economics* 9 (1978): 106–22; and David Teece, "Internal Organization and Economic Performance," *Journal of Industrial Economics* 30 (1981): 173–199.

8. Henry Mintzberg, *Structure in Fives: Designing Effective Organizations* (Englewood Cliffs, NJ: Prentice-Hall, 1983), chapter 11.

9. "GE's Costly Lesson on Wall Street," *Fortune*, May 9, 1988, 72–80.

10. "General Electric's Wall Street Shock," *Economist*, May 28, 1994, 71–2.

11. C. K. Prahalad and R. Bettis, "The Dominant Logic: A New Linkage between Diversity and Performance," *Strategic Management Journal* 7 (1986): 485–502.

12. *Ibid*, 490.

13. "Shades of Geneen at Emerson Electric," *Fortune*, May 22, 1989, 39.

14. "General Electric – Going with the Winners," *Fortune*, March 26, 1984, 106.

15. *The Seven-Up Division of Philip Morris Inc.*, Harvard Business School, 1989.

16. Roland Calori, "How Successful Companies Manage Diverse Businesses," *Long Range Planning* 21 (June 1988): 85; "LVMH Tries to Adjust after a Life of Luxury," *Financial Times*, June 11, 1993, 26.

17. Geneen's style of management is discussed in chapter 3 of Richard T. Pascale and Anthony G. Athos, *The Art of Japanese Management* (New York: Warner Books, 1982).

18. "Those Highflying PepsiCo Managers," *Fortune*, April 10, 1989, 79.

19. *General Electric: Strategic Position – 1981*, Harvard Business School, Case 381-174, 1981, p. 1.

20. "Inside the Mind of Jack Welch," *Fortune*, March 27, 1989, 39–50; *General Electric: Reg Jones and Jack Welch,* Harvard Business School, Case 9-391-144, 1991.

21. As we noted in chapter 7, the relationship between market share and profitability is contentious.

22. T. Copeland, T. Koller and J. Murrin, *Valuation: Measuring and Managing the Value of Companies* (New York: Wiley, 1990) Chapter 9.

23. *Ibid*, 262–9.

24. M. Jensen, "Takeovers: Their Causes and Consequences," *Journal of Economic Perspectives* 2(Winter 1988): 21–48.

25. In a recent study (*Strategies and Style* [Oxford: Basil Blackwell, 1987])

Michael Goold and Andrew Campbell refer to the corporate management's role as its "strategic management style."

26. M. E. Porter, "From Competitive Advantage to Corporate Strategy," *Harvard Business Review* (May-June 1987): 43–59.

27. Jay W. Lorsch and Stephen A. Allen III, *Management Diversity and Interdependence: An Organizational Study of Multidivisional Firms* (Boston: Harvard Business School Press, 1973).

28. *Ibid,* 168.

29. Michael Goold and Andrew Campbell, *Strategies and Styles* (Oxford: Basil Blackwell, 1987). For a summary, see Michael Goold and Andrew Campbell, "Many Best Ways to Make Strategy," *Harvard Business Review* (November–December 1987): 70–6.

30. John Roberts, "Strategy and Accounting in a U.K. Conglomerate," *Accounting, Organizations and Society* 15, 1/2(1990): 107–26.

31. Recent research by Ashridge Strategic Management Center on corporate strategy is described in M. Goold, A. Campbell and M. Alexander *Corporate-Level Strategy: Creating Value in the Multibusiness Company* (New York: Wiley, 1994).

32. "GE Chief Hopes to Shape Agile Giant," *Los Angeles Times,* June 1, 1988, D1.

33. *General Electric: Jack Welch's Second Wave (A),* Harvard Business School, Case 9-391-248, 1991.

34. *Ibid,* 5.

35. Jack Welch, "GE Growth Engine," speech to employees, 1988.

36. "Letter to Share Owners," *General Electric Company* 1993 *Annual Report* (Fairfield, CT: General Electric, 1994), 2.

37. Christopher A. Bartlett and S. Ghoshal, "Beyond the M-Form: Toward a Managerial Theory of the Firm," *Strategic Management Journal,* special issue, 14 (winter 1993): 23–46.

Index